A Commentary Upon the Prophet Ezekiel

A
COMMENTARY
Upon the
Prophet *EZEKIEL*.

By WILLIAM LOWTH, *B.D.*
Prebendary of *WINCHESTER*.

LONDON:
Printed for W. MEARS at the *Lamb* without
Temple-Bar. MDCCXXIII.

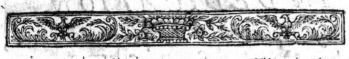

TO THE
Moſt Reverend Father in GOD,
WILLIAM,
By Divine Providence
LORD-ARCHBISHOP
OF
CANTERBURY,
Primate of All ENGLAND, and Metropolitan; and One of his MAJESTY's moſt Honourable Privy Council.

May it pleaſe your GRACE,

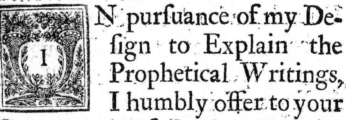

N purſuance of my De-ſign to Explain the Prophetical Writings, I humbly offer to your GRACE the following *Commen-*

A 2   *tary*

tary upon the Prophet *Ezekiel*; the Depth of whose Thoughts and Expreſſions might juſtly deter me from undertaking a Work of ſo much Difficulty: But begging your GRACE's and my Reader's Pardon if I have been guilty of leſſer Miſtakes, I hope at leaſt that I have avoided committing any dangerous Errors, by carefully following thoſe Directions, which the Text itſelf, and the Labours of ſeveral judicious Commentators upon it, have ſuggeſted to me; having had likewiſe the Aſſiſtance of ſome very Learned Friends, who have been pleaſed to communicate their Thoughts to me upon the moſt difficult Paſſages of it.

The

The moſt remarkable Difficulties of this Prophecy relate to the Deſcription of the *Temple*, repreſented to the Prophet in an Heavenly Viſion. By the general Conſent of Interpreters, this Viſion in its Myſtical Senſe, ſets forth a Model or Pattern of the *Catholick Church of Chriſt*, viewed in its State of Perfection ; of its Largeneſs and Extent, its Strength and Compactneſs, its Beauty and Order, and all thoſe other Qualifications which are proper to Edify and Adorn this Spiritual *Houſe of the Living God, the Pillar and Baſis of Truth.*

Our Church, in Conformity with that of the Firſt and Pureſt Ages,

Ages, hath always been careful to maintain thofe Principles of *Catholick Unity and Charity*, which, if they were generally embraced and received, would render the Chriftian Church like that *Jerufalem* which was a Figure of it, *a City at Unity in itfelf.* And fince it hath pleafed the Divine Providence to appoint your GRACE as a *wife Mafter-Builder* to prefide over it, we may hope that under his MAJESTY's moft Gracious Protection, and your GRACE's Aufpicious Conduct, it may receive New Acceffions of Strength and Edification, and according to the obliging Words of the late ROYAL *Promife*, *be not only in a Safe, but* likewife *in a Flourifhing Condition.*

That

That becoming Zeal which your GRACE expreſſed againſt thoſe *dangerous Opinions* which every where ſpread and abound, in your excellent *Speech* at the *Opening* of the *Convocation*, as it gave great Satisfaction to all thoſe who had the Honour to hear it; ſo it may juſtly be looked upon as a certain Indication of your continual Care and Concern for the Advancement of true Piety and Religion among us.

That GOD who hath advanced your GRACE to this high Station, may long continue you in it, and may proſper all your pious Deſigns for the promoting his *Glory,* and the *Good of his Church,*

as

as it is the united Prayer of that GREAT BODY of the CLERGY placed under your GRACE's Jurisdiction, so it is of none more earnestly than of Him who begs Leave to subscribe himself,

My L O R D,

Your GRACE's

Most Dutiful and

Obedient Servant,

William Lowth.

THE

THE

PREFACE.

ZEKIEL *was a Prophet of the Priestly Order, carried away into* Babylon *with several other* Jews *in* Jehoiachin's *Captivity, and therefore dates his Prophecies by the Years of that Captivity.* Clemens Alexandrinus *tells us, some thought him contemporary with* Pythagoras, *and that they had conversed together in* Babylon, Strom. lib. 1. n. 15. *This Opinion he rejects as inconsistent with the Age of* Pythagoras, *whom he supposes to have flourished about the* 62d *Olympiad, ibid. n.* 21. *which was near* 60 *Years after* Ezekiel *was carried into* Babylon. *The late learned Bishop of* Worcester, *in his Chronological Ac-*

a   count

count of *Pythagoras's* Life, *suppoſes him born a-
bout nine Years after* Ezekiel's *coming to* Babylon,
and that Pythagoras *himſelf came to* Babylon *at
eighteen Years of Age ; but there is no Proof that
ever he converſed with* Ezekiel. *Though it appears by the Teſtimony of* Hermippus, *in* Joſephus,
lib. 1. cont. Appion. *n.* 22. *that he had Conver-
ſation with ſome* Jews *; and learned Men have obſerved, that there is great Reſemblance between
ſeveral of his* Symbols, *and ſome of the Precepts
of the* Jewiſh Law.

But whatever became of Pythagoras, *the Accounts of whoſe Life are very uncertain : It is
certain that* Ezekiel, *being at* Babylon, *directed
many of his Prophecies to his Fellow Exiles there,
who, as St.* Jerom *obſerves in his* Preface *to* Ezekiel, *repined at their Ill-Fortune, and thought
their Countrymen, who remained in* Judea, *in a
much better Condition than themſelves. The Prophet with Regard to thoſe Circumſtances ſets before their Eyes that terrible Scene of Calamities
which God would bring upon* Judea *and* Jeruſalem, *which ſhould end in the utter Deſtruction of
the* City *and* Temple. *He recounts the heinous Provocations of the* Jews, *which brought down theſe
heavy Judgments upon them, in ſtrong and lively Colours ; his Stile exactly anſwering the Character*

racter the Greek Rhetoricians *give of that Part of Oratory they call* Δείνωσις, *which* Quintilian *defines to be* Oratio quæ rebus asperis, indignis & invidiosis vim addit, lib. vi. cap. 3. *its Property being to aggravate Things in themselves monstrous and odious, and represent them with great Force and Efficacy of Expression. For the same Reason* Rapin, *in his Treatise of* Eloquence, *calls* Ezekiel's *Style* le Terrible, *as having something in it that strikes the Reader with an Holy Dread and Astonishment.*

Josephus lib. x. Antiq. cap. 6. *divides this Prophecy into two Books ; but it is generally supposed, that he took that Part of the Prophecy which contains a Description of the Temple, beginning at the XLth Chapter, for a distinct Book from the rest, as treating altogether of a different Subject.*

St. Jerom *hath more than once observed,* (a) *that the Beginning and latter Part of this Prophecy is more than ordinary difficult and obscure, and may justly be reckoned among the* Δυσνοητὰ, *or Things in Scripture which are* Hard to be understood. *To contribute what I could to the clear-*

(a) Præfat. in Ezek. & in Prolog. Galeato.

ing

ing of these Difficulties, I have took the Liberty of transferring into the following COMMENTARY *whatever I thought useful for that Purpose in the elaborate Work of* Villalpandus, *a Book which is in very few Hands*; *and in the later Observations of* Bernardus L'Amy, *in his learned Book* de Tabernaculo Fœderis.

    But I must not conceal the kind Assistance I have received upon this and former Occasions, from that Great Master of Divine and Human Learning, the Right Reverend Father in GOD, *E DWARD,* Lord Bishop of COVENTRY and LICHFIELD; *and I gladly embrace the Opportunity of making my grateful Acknowledgments to his* LORDSHIP *in this Publick Manner, for his many and constant Favours.*

A COM-

A

COMMENTARY

ON THE

Prophecy of *EZEKIEL*.

CHAP. I.

The first Chapter contains a Description of God's Appearing in a Glorious manner to Ezekiel, in order to the giving him a Commission to execute the Prophetical Office.

Ver. 1. **N**OW *it came to pass*] The He-brew Text reads, *And it came to pass,* but it is usual in that Language to begin a Discourse or Book with the Particle *Vau* or *and*; See *Jonah*

B

i. 1. and the beginning of moſt of the Hiſtorical Books of the Old Teſtament; which Particle is very properly tranſlated in thoſe places, *Now it came to paſs*: So that there is no ground for the Fancy of *Spinoza*, who would conclude from hence that this Book of *Ezekiel* is but a Fragment of a larger Book, and contained ſeveral Prophecies, now loſt, which were in order of time before thoſe ſet down in theſe and the following Chapters.

Ibid. *In the Thirtieth Year*] It is a great Queſtion from whence this Computation of Time commences The moſt probable Anſwers are; firſt that of *Scaliger*, who ſuppoſes this Thirtieth Year to be meant of the Years of *Nabupolaſſar*'s Reign: who, as he tells us from *Beroſus*, quoted by *Joſephus*, l. 1. *Contr. App.* reigned 29 Years compleat: So the Thirtieth Year, here mentioned, was the laſt Year of his Reign and Life: And is likewiſe the 13th Year current of his Son *Nabuchadnezzar*'s Reign, who reigned ſo many Years together with his Father. See *Scaliger*'s *Canon Iſagog.* p. 281. 294. his *Prolegom. ad Lib. de emend. Temporum*; and his Notes on the *Greek Fragments*, at the end of thoſe Books.

But there is one conſiderable Objection againſt this Opinion of *Scaliger*, that according to *Beroſus*'s Account, as his words are quoted in another place of *Joſephus*, *Antiq.* l. x. c. ii. *Nabupolaſſar* reigned only 21 Years, the Greek Text reading by a little Variation, εἴκοσι ἓν for εἴκοσι ἐννέα. Which is the ſame number of Years aſſigned to *Nabupolaſſar* in the *Æra Nabonaſſari*, and agrees better with *Beroſus*'s own ſtory, *viz.* that when he had committed the command of the Army to his Son, and ſent him on

an

an Expedition to *Syria* and *Phœnicia*, he died in a
short time after.

Villalpandus in like manner makes this Computation to commence from the beginning of *Nabupolaffar*'s Reign: See his Commentary upon *Ezek.* xl.
1. He allows 19 Years for his Reign diftinct from
that of his Son, and fuppofes *Nebuchadnezzar* to
reign two Years with his Father; which indeed a-
grees with the Scripture Computation. See the
Note on *Jer.* xxv. 1. But according to that very
Account, the 5th Year of *Jehoiakin*'s Captivity will
be coincident with the 13th Year of *Nebuchadnezzar*'s Reign. For the 19th Year of the fame Reign
is affigned for the Deftruction of *Jerufalem*, *Jer.*
lii. 12. which was about fix Years afterwards. So
this Computation will make *Jehoiakim*'s Captivity
to have happened not in the 30th, but in the 32d.
Year, reckoning from the beginning of *Nabupolaffar*'s Reign.

A more probable Anfwer to this difficulty is
that which the *Chaldee Paraphraft*, Arch-Bifhop
Ufher A. M. 3409. Dr. *Prideaux* ad an. A. C. 594.
and other Learned Men follow, *viz.* that thefe
Thirty Years are to be reckoned from the time
when *Jofiah* and all the People of *Judah* entred
into that folemn Covenant mentioned 2 *Kings* xxii.
3. which was in the 18th Year of *Jofiah*, Ibid.
from which time the fame Learned Writers compute the 40 Years of *Judah*'s Tranfgreffion, mentioned Chap. iv. 6.

Ibid. *As I was among the Captives by the River
Chebar*] Thofe which were carried away with *Jehoiakin*, King of *Judah*; fee the next Verfe. Thefe
were placed in Towns or Villages that lay upon
the River *Chebar* in *Mefopotamia*, called by *Ptolemy*

     and

Chapter
I.

Verſe 2.

Verſe 3.

Verſe 4.

and *Strabo, Chaboras* or *Aboras* ; and by *Pliny* Lib. I. c. xxvi. *Cobaris.*

Ver. 2. *Which was in the Fifth Year of Jehoiakin's Captivity*] This was coincident with the Thirteenth Year of *Nebuchadnezzar's* Reign : For *Jehoiakin* was carried Captive in the Eighth Year of his Reign ; ſee 2 *Kings* xxiv. 12. the Hebrew Writers uſe ſeveral Computations of the beginning of the *Babyloniſh* Captivity : ſee the Note upon *Jerem.* xxv. 11. That under *Jehoiakin,* wherein *Ezekiel* was made a Captive, is the Computation he always follows in the ſucceeding parts of his Prophecy ; ſee *Chap.* viii. 1. xx. 1. xxix 1, 17. xxxi. 1. xxxiii. 1. xl. 1.

Ver. 3. *The word of the* L O R D *came expreſly &c.*] The word of the L O R D ſignifies any ſort of Revelation, whether by Viſion, ſuch as is related in the following Verſes, or by a Voice, as *Chap.* ii. 3.

Ibid. *And the hand of the* L O R D *was there upon him*] He felt ſenſible Impreſſions of God's power and Spirit. Compare *Chap.* iii. 14, 22. viii. 1. xxviii. 1. xl. 1. 1 *Kings* xviii. 46. 2 *Kings* iii. 15.

Ver. 4. *And I looked, and behold a Whirlwind came out of the North*] God's Anger and Judgments are often compared to a Whirlwind ; ſee *Iſa.* xxi. 1. *Jerem.* xxiii. 19. xxv. 32. *Pſal.* lviii. 9. it is deſcribed here as coming out of the North, becauſe of the Northerly Situation of *Babylon* with reſpect to *Judea.* Compare *Jer.* i. 13. iv. 6. vi. 1. and *Chap.* xliii. 3. of this Prophecy.

Ibid. *A great Cloud, and a Fire infolding it ſelf, and a brightneſs was about it*] The divine Preſence is uſually deſcribed in Scripture, as a bright Light or flaming Fire breaking out of a thick Cloud ; ſee *Pſal.*

Pfal. xviii. 2. l. 3. xcviii. 2, 3. God alfo is defcribed Chapter as a *confuming Fire*, when he comes to execute his judgment upon Sinners, *Deut.* iv. 24. Compare *ver.* 13. of this *Chap.* Fire infolding it felf, is the fame as appearing in folds, like one wreath within another.

Ibid. *And out of the midft thereof as the colour of Amber*] Compare *Chap.* viii. 2. Fire refembles the colour of Amber, efpecially the lower Parts of it: So in that Vifion of Chrift, defcribed *Rev.* i. 13. *&c.* 'tis faid *ver.* 15. that *his Feet*, or lower parts, *were like unto fine Brafs*, or rather unto *Amber*, as Dr. *Hammond* rightly explains the Word χαλκολίβαγ⊙·

Ver. 5. *Alfo out of the midft thereof came the like-* Verfe 5. *nefs of four living creatures*] Compare Rev. iv. 6. where our Englifh Tranflation improperly renders the word Ζῶα *Beafts*, whereas it fhould be rendred *living Creatures*, the better to diftinguifh them from the *Antichriftian Beaft* always expreffed in that Book by Θηρίον. Thefe living Creatures were four Cherubims that carried or fupported God's Throne in the following Vifion : It may be in allufion to the Triumphal Chariots of the Eaftern Kings, which were drawn by feveral forts of Beafts ; the Cherubims as they were placed in the Temple being called God's *Chariot*, 1 *Chron.* xxviii. 18.

Ibid. *They had the likenefs of a Man*] Their fhape was erect like the form of a Man.

Ver. 6. *And every one had four Faces*] Of a Man, Verfe 6. of a Lion, of an Oxe, and of an Eagle, *ver.* 10. each of them refembled the Cherubims, which overfhadowed the mercy feat in the Temple ; fee *Chap.* x. 20. The Jewifh Tabernacle was a *pattern of Heavenly*

venly things, Heb. viii. 5. *Wisd.* ix. 8. and the In-
campment of the 12 Tribes about the Tabernacle
in the Wilderness, was a representation of the Angelical Ministry about the Throne of God in Heaven. So there is an Analogy between the Cherubims, as they attended the Divine Presence in the
Holiest of all, and as here described, in a Figure of
their Heavenly Ministry, and the body of the
Jewish Nation placed round about the Tabernacle, and divided into four Standards, and a several Ensign allotted to each Standard, as you may
read *Num.* xi. 2, 3, 10. 18. 25. What those Ensigns
were, that Text does not express; but the Jewish
Writers unanimously maintain that they were a
Lion for the Tribe of *Judah*, An Oxe for the Tribe
of *Ephraim* ; a Man for the Tribe of *Reuben,* and
an Eagle for the Tribe of *Dan,* under which variety
each of these four Cherubims is here represented.
Compare Rev. iv. 7. Here likewise may be an Allusion to the four Cherubims in *Solomon's* Temple :
For he placed two others of larger Dimensions ;
one on each side of the Ark and of the two Cherubims, which *Moses* had placed in the Tabernacle. Compare 1 *Kings* vi. 24. with *Exod.* xxv. 17,
20.

ibid. *And every one had four Wings*] See *ver.* 11.

Ver. 7. *And their Feet were streight Feet*] Like
a Man's, without such a middle joint as Beasts
have, the use of which is to secure them against
weariness; to denote their steadiness and resoluti-
on in executing all God's Commands.

ibid. *The sole of their Feet was like the Sole of
a Calf's Foot*] A Creature remarkable for its tread-
firm and sure. These living Creatures are a
sort

Verse 7.

sort of Hieroglyphicks made up of several shapes, but yet they resembled most that of an Oxe or a Calf; and therefore were called *Cherubims*, that word signifying an Oxe; in which sense it is taken, *Chap.* x. 14. of this Prophecy, where the *Face of a Cherub* is equivalent to the *Face of an Oxe*; at the 10. *ver.* of this Chapter.

Ibid. *And they sparkled like the colour of burnished Brass*] Compare *Dan.* x. 6. *Revel.* i. 15. The appearance of their Feet was bright and flaming; see *ver.* 13. and *Psal.* civ: 4. The *Seraphims* have that name from their bright and flaming Colour.

Ver. 8. *And they had the hands of a Man under their Wings*] Compare *Chap.* x. 8. *Isa.* vi. 6. This denotes the prudence and dexterity of their management: The Hand being peculiar to Mankind among all living Creatures, and the chief Instrument of all Artificial Operations.

Ibid. *They four had their Faces and their Wings*] They had all the same Appearances and Proportions: or, had Wings equal to their Faces.

Ibid. *Their Wings were joyned one to another*] See *ver.* 11.

Ibid. *They turned not when they went*] They needed not to turn their Bodies, that their Faces might stand the way they were to go; for go which way they would, they had a Face that looked that way. This signifies that nothing ever diverted them from fulfilling God's Commands; see the Note on *Chap.* x. 11. where these living Creatures are represented as coming near to a square Figure, which is equal on all sides, the Emblem of Firmness and Constancy.

Ver. 10.

Chapter
I.
Verſe 10.

Ver. 10. *They four had the Face of a Man, and of a Lion on the right ſide, &c.*] See the Note on ver. 6. *Grotius* and *Villalpandus* by the word Face underſtand the ſhape or appearance, and explain the words to this ſenſe : That theſe living Creatures were like a Man with reſpect to their viſage, or their upper parts ; they reſembled a Lion with re-ſpect to their back parts ; their Wings were like the Wings of an Eagle, and their Feet like thoſe of an Ox. But this Expoſition does not well agree with what is ſaid here, that the Face of the Lion was on the right ſide, and that of the Ox on the left : Or as *Caſtellio* tranſlates it, and I think to a better and clearer ſenſe, *that the face of the Man and the Lion were on the right ſide, and the Face of the Ox and Eagle on the left.* And by comparing the ſeveral parts of this Deſcription, their Figure may be rather concluded to be Quadruple ; and as the Wheels were made to turn every way, ſo the living Creatures could move toward any point without turning about. To ſignifie, as I obſerved before, the ſteadfaſtneſs of their motions and pur-poſes. Compare *ver.* 15, 19, 20, of this Chapter, with *Chap.* x. 11, &c.

Verſe 11.

Ver. 11. *Their Wings were ſtretched upwards*] In a poſture of flying, to ſhow their readineſs to exe-cute God's Commands. Compare *ver.* 24. with *Chap.* x. 16. or they were ſtretched to cover their Faces, as the *Seraphims* are repreſented, *Iſa.* vi. 2. Com-pare *ver.* 23, of this Chapter. Some tranſlate the former part of the Verſe thus : *Their Faces and their Wings were ſtretched upward,* to denote a poſ-ture of attention, and as if *they were hearkning to the voice of God's Word,* as the Angels are repre-ſented, *Pſal.* ciii. 20.   Ibid.

Ibid. *Two Wings of every one were joyned one to* Chapter
another] Being thus stretched out, they touched I.
one another, or the Wings of one living Creature
touched those of another, as the Wings of the
Cherubims did over the Mercy-Seat; see 1 Kings
vi. 27.

Ibid. *And two covered their Bodies*] See *Isa.* vi.
2. *Grotius* upon *ver.* 6. of this Chapter, assigns a
Reason why in that Text of *Isa.* and *Rev.* iv. 6.
each Seraphim hath six Wings assigned him, whereas the living Creatures here have but Four, *viz.*
The Seraphims in these Texts make use of two of
their Wings to cover their Faces out of Reverence
to the Divine Presence, before which they stand ;
whereas here the living-Creatures are supposed to
stand under the Throne, as supporting it; compare
Chap. x. 19.

Ver. 12. *And they went every one straight for-*
ward] see *ver.* 9.

Ibid. *Whither the Spirit was to go, there they*
went.] that is, that Spiritual or Angelical Power,
which was the principle of all their Motions ; see
ver. 20.

Ibid. *And they turned not as they went*] see *ver.* 17.

Ver. 13. *Their Appearance was like Burning* Verse 13.
Coals of Fire, &c.] The Angels are always described of a bright and flaming Colour ; see *ver.* 4, 7.
But here the Coals of Fire and the Lightning breaking forth out of the Fire, denote God's Vengeance
coming in Flaming Fire to destroy the City and
Temple of *Jerusalem*; compare *Chap.* x. 2. *Psal.*
xviii. *Revel.* iv. 12. 5.

Ver. 14. *And the living Creatures ran and re-* Verse 14.
turned, as the Appearance of Lightning] The swift-
C   ness

Chapter
I.
Verſe 15.

Ver. 15. *And behold one Wheel* [or the ſame ſort
of Wheel] *upon the Earth by the living Creatures,
with his four faces*] or *on his four ſides,* that is, on
the four ſides or Faces of the ſquare Body as it ſtood:
So that a Wheel was before every one of the living
Creatures on the outſide of the Square. So Dr.
Lightfoot expounds the Words, in his *Deſcription
of the Temple, Chap.* xxxviii. The Sentence may
be tranſlated thus: *Behold one Wheel upon Earth
by the living Creatures to each* of the Creatures *with
the four Faces*; ſo the word *Learbang* is uſed *ver.*
10. The word *Wheel* is certainly uſed Collectively
for each Wheel: As the *Cherub* ſtands for Cherubims, *Chap.* ix. 3. x. 4. and *Living Creature* ſignifies the four living Creatures, *ibid. ver.* 15, 19.
That there were four Wheels, according to the
number of the living Creatures, is plain by comparing this Verſe with the 16 and 19; and with
Chap. x. 9. The Wheels are repreſented here as
ſtanding *upon the Earth,* or near the Earth: At
other times they appear'd as being lifted up above
it; ſee *ver.* 20, 21. and *Chap.* x. 17.

Verſe 16.

Ver. 16. *The Appearance of the Wheels was like
unto the Colour of a Beryl*] Azure, the Colour of
the Sky, mixed with a bright Green; compare *Dan.*
x. 6.

Ibid. *Their Appearance and their Work was as it
were a Wheel in the middle of a Wheel*] as it were
one Wheel put croſs within another, like two Cir-
cles in a Sphere cutting one another at right Angles; to ſignify the Stability and Uniformity of
their

their Motions, and the subserviency of one part of
Providence to another; see the following Verse,
and the Note upon *ver.* 9.

Ver. 17. *When they went, they went upon their
four sides*] Each Wheel consisted of four Semicircles, crossing one another, as appears by the foregoing Verse, and each of them had its proper
Motion.

Ibid. *They returned not when they went*] They never went backward; see *Chap.* x. 11. to signify
that Providence doth nothing in vain, but always
accomplishes its Ends: So God speaks of his Word
and Decree, *Isa.* lv. 11. *It shall not return unto me
void, but shall accomplish that which I please.* To
return by the way that he went, is a Proverbial
Speech signifying a Man's missing his aim, or not
accomplishing his designs; see 1 *Kings* xiii. 9.
2 *Kings* xix. 33.

Ver. 18 *As for their rings* [or strakes] *they were
so high that they were dreadfull*] their Circumfe-
rence was so vast as to cause a Terrour in the Prophet that beheld them: To signify the vast compass of Providence which *reacheth from one end to
another mightily, Wisd.* viii. 1. or as St. *Paul* expres-
seth it, the *Heighth and Depth both of the Wisdom
and Knowledge of God, how unsearchable his Judgments are, and his ways past finding out,* Rom. xi. 33.
Dr. *Lightfoot* translates it, *And they were Reverend,*
that is, they were observant of that Presence and
Glory upon which they waited, and watchfull to
obey it's Commands.

Ibid. *And their Rings were full of Eyes, about
these four*] and so were also the living Creatures
themselves; compare *Chap.* x. 12. to signify that all

C 2   the

Chapter the Motions of Providence are directed by a con-
I.   summate Wisdom and foresight. To the same sense
~~~~   the Angels who are the Instruments of Providence,
         are called the *Eyes of the* L O R D, *Zech.* iv. 10.
         Rev. v. 6.

Verse 19, Ver. 19, 20, 21.   *And when the living Creatures*
20, 21. *went, the Wheels went by them &c.*] Both the living
         Creatures and the Wheels were animated by the
         same Principle of Understanding and Motion, to
         signify, with what Readiness and Alacrity all the
         Instruments of Providence concurr in carrying on
         its great designs and purposes; compare *Chap.* x.
         16, 17.

         Ver. 20. *The Wheels were lifted up over against*
         them] That is, the Wheels, which were placed just
         by them; see *ver.* 15, 19. The word *Leummatham*
         is rendred *besides them.* *Chap.* x. 19. xi. 22.

         Ibid. *For the Spirit of the living Creatures was in*
         the Wheels] that is, the Spirit of each living Crea-
         ture, as the Word is used in the 22 ver.

Vrese 22. Ver. 22. *And the likeness of the Firmament upon*
         the Heads of the living Creatures, was as the Colour
         of the terrible Crystal] Over the heads of all the li-
         ving Creatures, or of this whole vision of living Crea-
         tures (compare *Chap.* x. 15, 20.) was the like-
         ness of a clear Sky or Firmament, where the
         divine Glory appear'd as upon a Throne ; see *ver.*
         26. and *Chap.* x. 1. and compare *Rev.* iv. 2, 3. By
         the *terrible Crystal* is meant such as dazles the Eyes
         with its Lustre.

Verse 23. Ver. 23. *And under the Firmament were their Wings*
         straight.] The Sense is the same with that of
         Verse 11. denoting that two of the Wings of
         each living Creature were stretcht upward; out
                                                          of

of Reverence to the Divine Presence, or to express Chapter their Readiness to obey his Commands : See ver. I. 11. and 24, and with the two other they covered their Bodies.

Verse 24. *And when they went, I heard the noise* Verse 24. *of their wings like the noise of many Waters, &c.*] To denote the Terribleness of the Judgments which they were to execute upon *Jerusalem*, and the whole Jewish Nation. Compare Chap. xliii. 2. *Dan.* x. 6. *Rev.* i. 15.

Ibid. *As the Voice of the Almighty.*] It resembled great and dreadful Thunder. Compare *Job* xxxvii. 4, 5. *Ps.* xxix. 3. lxviii. 33. St. *Jerom*, in his Note upon the Place, tells us, That the LXX. translate these Words Φωνὴ τῶ Λόγε, *The Voice of the Λόγος*, or Second Person in the Blessed Trinity : which Words are now in the *Alexandrian* Copy. The *Vatican* Copy is defective, but the *Alexandrian* Copy runs thus: ὡς φωνὴν ἱκανῦ· ἐν τῶ πορεύεσθαι αὐτὰ φωνὴ τῶ λόγε ὡς φωνὴ τῆς παρεμβολῆς. As the Voice of the Almighty. *When they went* [there was] *the Voice of Speech, like the Voice of an Host.* This Reading shews that the LXX. designed to translate the following Words by φωνὴ τῶ λόγε, where we read, *The Voice of Speech* : and then the Word λόγος may probably be taken in its ordinary Signification : Though we may certainly conclude, that this was the Appearance of the Second Person of the Blessed Trinity, both because he appears under the Resemblance of a Man, Verse 26. and from what hath been said upon this Subject in the Note upon *Isaiah*, vi. 1.

Ibid. *The Voice of Speech, like the noise of an Host.*] Like the confused Murmur of an Army : either

Chapter either to denote the Army of the *Babylonians* that
I. should besiege the City, or to signify the Angels,
who are called God's Host.

Ibid. *And when they stood, they let down their
wings.*] They put themselves in a Posture of hearkening to God's Voice ; and as it were quietly
waiting to receive his Commands. See the next
Verse.

Verse 25.   Ver. 25. *And there was a voice from the firmament when they stood.*] The *Vulgar* Latin renders
it, *When there was a voice they stood :* in an attentive Posture. Compare *Psalm* ciii. 20.

Verse 26.   Ver. 26. *And above the firmament was the likeness of a throne, as the appearance of a sapphire-
stone.*] God is described in Scripture, as *dwelling
in light,* and *cloathing himself with it.* Compare
Exod. xxiv. 10. *Rev.* iv. 2, 3. *Psalm* civ. 2. 1 *Tim.*
vi. 16. So the Throne of God here described was
made up of Light, resembling the Colours and
Brightness of a Sapphire.

Ibid. *And upon the likeness of the throne was
the likeness as of the appearance of a man above upon it*] When *Moses* and the Elders *saw the God of
Israel, Exod.* xxiv. 8. or the Glory of God, as the
Targum explains it, they saw no determinate
Figure, but an inconceivably resplendent Brightness, that they might not think God could be represented by any Image, *Deut.* iv. 16. But in this
Vision, the Form and Shape of a Man is directly
represented to *Ezekiel,* as a *Præludium* or Figure
of the Incarnation. see the Note on *Jerem.* i. 4.

Verse 27.   Ver. 27. *And I saw as the colour of Amber, as
the appearance of Fire round about within it, &c.*]
The upper part of this Appearance was of an Am-
                                                  ber

ber Colour outwardly, but appeared more flaming Chapter
inwardly; the lower part of a deeper Red, en- I.
compassed with a bright Flame, to represent God's
coming to take Vengeance of the *Jews*. See the
Notes on Verse 4.

In most of our English Bibles the Stops are placed wrong in this Verse; whereas the whole
Verse should be pointed thus, *And I saw as the*
colour of Amber, as the appearance of Fire round
about within it, from the appearance of his loyns
even upwards, and from the appearance of his loyns
even downwards, I saw as it were the appearance
of Fire, &c.] The Words should be thus pointed,
as appears by comparing them with Chap. viii.
2.

Ver. 28. *As the appearance of the Cloud, &c.*] Verse 28.
The Light reflected from this Vision had the appearance of a Rainbow, a Token of God's Covenant of Mercy, *Gen.* ix. 11, *&c.* to denote that
God in the midst of Judgment would remember
Mercy, and not utterly destroy his People. Compare *Revel.* iv. 3. Especially this Vision being an
evident Representation of the WORD *that was to*
be *made Flesh*, whose Incarnation is the Foundation of God's Covenant of Mercy with Mankind; a Rainbow, the Symbol and Token of
Mercy, was a very fit Attendant upon that Glorious Vision. Compare *Revel.* x. 1.

Ibid. *This was the appearance of the likeness*
of the Glory of the LORD] This is a Description of that Glorious Vision wherein God appeared, and whereby he made manifest his Attri-
butes and Perfections.

Ibid.

Chapter.   Ibid. *And when I saw it, 1 fell upon my Face.*]
I.   As struck down with Fear and Astonishment, compare Chap. xi. 2. iii. 23. *Dan.* viii. 17. *Revel.* i.
17. Prostration was also a Posture of Adoration
used upon any Token of the Divine Presence.
See *Gen.* xvii. 3. *Numb.* xiv. 5. xvi. 4.

CHAP.

CHAP. II.

Chapter II

The ARGUMENT.

This Chapter contains Ezekiel's *Commiſſion for executing his Prophetical Office, and Inſtructions given him for the diſcharge of it.*

Ver. 1.  N D he ſaid unto me, Son of Ver. 1.
Man.] This Expreſſion is commonly underſtood to ſignify the ſame with a common and ordinary Man, as it is uſually expounded in that Text, *Pſal.* viii. 4. *What is Man that thou art mindful of him, or the Son of Man that thou viſiteſt him?* So here moſt Commentators underſtand it as applied to the Prophet, to put him in Mind of his Frailty and Mortality, and of the infinite Diſtance between God and Man. In which ſenſe it is ſuppos'd to be taken when ſpoken of Chriſt in the New Teſtament, implying his great Humility in aſſuming our Nature, and appearing no otherwiſe than an ordinary Man:

D And

Chapter
II.

And so the Hebrew Phrase *Ben Adam* is plainly used when it is opposed to *Ben Iſh* : and is rightly tranſlated *Men of low degree, or mean Men* : *Pſal.* lxix. 2. *Iſa.* ii. 9.

But some Criticks have obſerved that the Phraſe *Son of Man* is likewiſe taken for a Man of Dignity or Character, as in *Pſal.* lxxx. 17. *The Man of thy Right Hand, and the Son of Man whom thou madeſt ſo ſtrong for thy ſelf.* And *Pſal.* cxlvi. 3. *Put not your truſt in Princes, nor in the Son of Man in whom there is no help.* And there is no incongruity in ſuppoſing that Chriſt himſelf may be called the *Son of Man* κατ᾿ ἐξοχὴν, by way of Eminence, as a Title denoting him to be that great Perſon whom God promiſed to raiſe up to be a *Prince aud a Saviour* of his People. And ſo the Title of *Son of Man* may be given to the Prophet in the Text, as one ſet apart for the Prophetical Office : in like manner as *Daniel* is called *Son of Man*, Chap. viii. 17. who in the next Chapters hath the Title of a *Man greatly beloved*, Chap. ix. 23. x. 11.

Ibid. *Stand upon thy Feet.*] Put thy ſelf into a Poſture of attending to what I ſay : See Ver. 2. and compare *Daniel* x. 11.

Ver. 2.

Ver. 2. *And the Spirit entred into me, &c.*] God's Spirit revived me and gave me new Life and Vigour, that I could attend to what was ſaid unto me. See the Note on Chap. iii. 24. and compare Ver. 12, and 14. of that Chapter.

Ver. 3.

Ver. 3. *To a rebellious Nation.*] The Hebrew Word is *Goiim, Nations*, the Word which is commonly uſed to denote the Heathens, intimating that the Jews had out done the wickedneſs of the Heathens. See Chap. v. 6, 7. Ver.

Ver. 4. *For they are impudent Children and* Chapter
stiff-hearted.] The Original might be more signi- II.
ficantly rendred, *They are Children Impudent in*
their Countenance, and hardened in their Hearts. Ver. 4.
They are so far harden'd in Wickedness as to have
cast off all Shame, and even the very outward
Shew of Modesty.

Ver. 5. *And they, whether they will hear, or* Ver. 5.
whether they will forbear, shall know that there
hath been a Prophet among them.] Whether they
will regard what is said by thee or not: See Chap.
iii. 27. Yet the Event answering thy Predictions
shall render thy Authority unquestionable, and
them inexcusable for not hearkening to the Warnings thou hast given them. See Chap. xxxiii. 33.

Ver. 6. *And thou Son of Man be not afraid of* Ver. 6.
them.] The Prophets and Messengers of God are
often exhorted to take Courage, and are promised
a proportionable Assistance in the discharge of
their Office without fearing any Man's Person,
or standing in awe of any Man's Greatness. See
Chap. iii. 8, 9. *Jerem.* i. 8, 18. *Mat.* x. 28. Such a
presence of Mind is expressed by Παῤῥησία *Boldness*
in the New Testament, and is spoken of as a peculiar Gift bestowed upon the first Preachers of the
Gospel. See *Act.* iv. 13, 29. *Eph.* vi. 19. *Phil.* i.
20. called *the Spirit of Might,* or Courage, *Col.* i.
11. 2 *Tim.* i. 7. And they had need of great Presence of Mind who were to reprove Men hardened
in Sin, who are always impatient of Reproof, and
become the Enemies of those who tell them such
Truths as they have no Mind to hear.

Ibid. *Tho' Briars and Thorns be with thee.*]
Such as study to vex and torment thee: Comp.

D 2 *Micah*

Chapter
II.

Micah vii 4. The Prophets often denote the Wicked by Briars and Thorns. See the Note on
Isa. ix. 18.

Ibid. *And thou dost dwell among Scorpions.*]
Who would sting thee to Death, and are as veno-
mous as the worst of Serpents : Compare *Mat.* iii,
7. xxiii. 33.

Ibid. *Be not afraid of their Words, neither be
dismayed at their Looks.*] Be not afraid of their
Threats wherewith they would affright thee :
neither be afraid of their Looks wherewith they
would Brow-beat thee.

Ver. 8.   Ver. 8. *Open thy Mouth, and eat what I give
thee.*] The Knowledge of Divine Truths is often
expressed by the Metaphors of bodily Food and
Nourishment : See *Isa.* lv. 1, 2. *Joh.* vi. 27. So to
eat the Words of this Prophecy, signifies to commit them to Memory, to meditate upon them and
digest them ; Compare *Revel.* x. 10.

Ver. 9.   Ver. 9. *Behold an Hand was sent unto me,* &c.]
I saw a Hand stretched out toward me as from
that Divine Person which appear'd to me in the
Shape of a Man, Chap. i. 26. Compare Chap. viii.
3. *Jerem.* i. 9. *Dan.* x. 10.

Ibid. *And lo a Roll of a Book was therein.*]
Wherein was contained the Contents of the following Prophecy. Compare *Rev.* v. 1.

The Antient way of Writing was upon long
Scrols of Parchment rolled upon Sticks : See *Isa.*
viii. 1. *Jerem.* 36. 1.

Ver. 10.   Ver. 10. *And he spread it before me.*] That I
might understand the Contents of it.

Ibid. *And it was written within and without.*]
It was written on both sides, both that which was
in-

innermoſt when it was rolled up, and on the outſide alſo.   To denote a large Collection of Prophecies.   Compare *Rev. v. 1.*

Ibid. *And there was written therein Lamentations, and Mourning and Woe.*]   All the Prophecies contained therein conſiſted of God's Judgments and Mournful Events, without any mixture of Mercy, at leaſt with reſpect to the Jews of the preſent Age.

CHAP.

CHAP. III.

The ARGUMENT.

The Prophet hath more particular Instructions given him for the discharge of his Office : and is encouraged to undertake it by a Promise of God's especial Assistance.

Ver. 1.   Ver. 1.   *AT this Roll.*] See Chap. ii. 8, 9.

Ver. 2.   Ver. 2. *So I opened my Mouth.*] I readily complyed with God's Command, which this Vision figuratively expressed. Compare *Jerem.* xxv. 17.

Ver. 3.   Ver. 3. *Cause thy Belly to eat, and fill thy Bowels with this Roll.*] The Belly often signifies in Scripture the Mind, or secret Thoughts ; See *Job* xxxii. 18. *Prov.* xviii. 8. xx. 27. *John* vii. 38. So here the Expressions denote the laying up this Prophecy in his Memory. See Ver. 10. and the Note on Chap. ii. 8.

Ibid. *It was in my Mouth as Honey for sweetness.*] I took Delight in having God's secret Counsels

sels communicated to me, and in delivering his Chapter
Commands to my Brethren: and was pleased III.
with the Hopes of being an Instrument of their
Conversion, and the Amendment of some of them:
But yet this Pleasure was afterwards very much
allayed by the heavy Tidings I was to be the Mes-
senger of, and the ill Treatment I was to expect.
See Ver. 14. Compare *Jer.* xv. 16, 17. *Rev.* x. 10.

Ver. 5. *For thou art not sent to a People of a* Ver. 5:
strange Speech.] It would be a great Addition to
the Burden of thy Office, if thou wert sent as a
Prophet to a Foreign Nation, and to a People
whose Language thou couldst not understand, nor
they thine, as *Jonah* was.

Ver. 6. *Surely had I sent thee to them, they* Ver. 6.
would have hearken'd unto thee.] And yet in all
Appearance those Strangers would have hearken-
ed to thy Preaching sooner than the House of *Israel*
will, as the *Ninevites* did to *Jonah*'s. Compare
Mat. xii. 41. xi. 21. The Particles *Im lo* are very
well rendred *surely:* They are the form of an
Oath, the Words, *As I live*, being understood.
Compare Chap. v. 11. xvii. 19. *Numb.* xiv. 28.

Ver. 7. *For they will not hearken unto me.*] Ver. 7.
They have so long resisted the means of Grace that
I have offered them by the former Prophets; See
Jerem. xxv. 4. that there is less Hopes of their Con-
version, than if they were Infidels. Compare
Mat. v. 13.

Ver. 8. *Behold I have made thy Face strong* Ver. 8.
against their Faces.] I have given thee Courage
and Assurance proportionable to the Hardiness and
Impudence of those thou hast to deal with. See
Chap. ii. 6. and *Isa.* l. 7.

Ver.

Chapter
III.

Ver. 10.
Ver. 12.

Ver. 13.

Ver. 14.

Ver. 10. *All the Words that I shall speak unto thee, receive in they Heart.*]See the Note on Chap. ii. 8.

Ver. 12. *Then the Spirit took me up.*] Carried me from the place where I was before, when I saw the Vision mentioned Chap. i. 3, 4. See the Note on Chap. viii. 3.

Ibid. *And I heard behind me the Voice as of a great rushing.*] I heard a Voice so loud that it shook the Earth like Thunder. See *Joh.* xii. 27, 28.

Ibid. *Blessed be the Glory of the* LORD *from his place.*] Whatever Place God honours with his especial Presence is equivalent to his Temple, and there the Angels always attend upon the Divine Majesty, to give him the Honour due unto his Name. Compare *Gen.* xxviii. 13, 16, 19. The Words imply that tho' God should forsake his Temple (see the Note on Chap. ix. 3.) and destroy the Place that is called by his Name, yet his Presence will make a Temple of every Place, and Multitudes of the heavenly Host will always be ready to do him Service.

Ver. 13. *I heard also the noise of the Wings of the living Creatures.*] See the Note on Chap. i. 20.

Ibid. *The noise of the Wheels over against them;*] That is, besides them, as the *Hebrew* Phrase is elsewhere rendred: See the Note on Chap. i. 20.

Ver. 14. *So the Spirit lifted me up.*] See Ver. 12. and the Note upon Chap. viii. 3. xxxvii. 1.

Ibid. *And I went in bitterness, in the heat of my Spirit.*] The Joy that I first conceived in receiving the Divine Message, was quickly turned into Grief and Anguish of Mind. See Ver. 15.

Ibid.

Ibid. *And the Hand of the* Lord *was strong* Chapter *upon me.*] I was unable to resist the Impulses of III. God's Spirit. See Chap. i. 4. viii. 1. *Jer.* xx. 9.

Ver. 15. *Then I came to them of the Captivity of* Ver. 15. *Telabib, that dwelt by the River of Chebar.*] These seem to be a distinct Colony of Captives from those that are mentioned Chap. i. 3. See Ver. 23. of this Chapter. The King of *Babylon* carried away the *Jews* by several Captivities: some in the first Year of his Reign, *Dan.* i. 1. Some in the seventh, *Jerem.* lii. 28. then followed *Jechoniah*'s Captivity in the eighth Year of *Nebuchadnezzar*, 2 *Kings* xxiv. 12. when *Ezekiel* himself was carried Captive.

Ibid. *And I remained there among them astonished seven Days.*] Having my Spirit wholly cast down and amazed under the Apprehension of these terrible Judgments, which were to come upon my Nation, and of which I was to be the Messenger. Compare *Jer.* xxiii. 9. *Habak.* iii. 16. *Seven Days* was the space of time appointed for Mourning. See *Gen.* l. 10. 1 *Sam.* xxxi. 13. *Job* ii. 3. *Ecclus.* xxii. 12.

Ver. 17. *I have made thee a Watchman to the* Ver. 17. *House of Israel.*] Prophets have the Title of Watchmen given to them: See *Isa*, lvi. 10. *Jerem.* vi. 17. like Watchmen placed on the Tower, (see *Habak.* ii. 1.) They by their Prophetical Spirit foresee the Evils coming upon the Ungodly, and are bound to give People timely notice to avoid them by a sincere Repentance. See the following Verse.

Ver. 18. *When I say unto the Wicked, Thou shalt* Ver. 18. *surely die.*] That is, unless he Repent, a Conditi-

E on

Chapter
III.

on generally to be underſtood in ſuch like Threatnings. See Chap. xviii. 27.

Ibid. *And thou giveſt him not warning, &c.*] We are to diſtinguiſh a Prophet's immediate Commiſſion to go to any particular Perſon in God's Name, from ſuch a General Charge to inform others of their Duty, which is incumbent upon all Paſtors and Teachers. Theſe latter can only give Men General Warnings, unleſs where they have received ſuch Informations as are a ſufficient ground for a particular Reproof.

Ibid. *The ſame wicked Man ſhall die in his Iniquity.*] He ſhall die in a ſtate of Sin, and be condemned to thoſe Puniſhments to which Death tranſlates Sinners. See *John* viii. 24 and the Note upon Chap. xviii. 4.

Ibid. *But his Blood will I require at thy Hand.*] Thou ſhalt be accountable for the loſs of his Soul, juſt as a Man's Blood is laid to the Charge of him that is any way acceſſary to his Death. Compare *Gen.* ix. 5.

Ver. 19.

Ver. 19. *But thou haſt delivered thy Soul.*] Thou art clear from the Guilt of his Sin. Compare *Act.* xx. 26.

Ver. 20.

Ver. 20. *And I lay a ſtumbling block before him.*] I cauſe his Iniquity to become his *Ruin*, as the Word *Micſhol* is tranſlated. Chap. xviii. 30.

Ver. 22.

Ver. 22. *And the Hand of the* LORD *was there upon me.*] See Ver. 14. and Chap. i. 3.

Ibid. *Ariſe, Go into the Plain.*] As a Place more retired and fitter for Contemplation.

Ver. 23.

Ver. 23. *The Glory of the* LORD *ſtood there.*] See Chap. i. 28.

Ibid.

Ibid. *As the Glory which I saw by the River* Chapter
of Chebar.] This part of that River seems distant III.
from that Place where the former Vision was
shewed him. Comp. Ver. 15. with Chap. i. 3.

Ver. 24. *Then the Spirit entred into me, and set* Ver. 24.
me upon my Feet, and spake with me.] The Words
are literally to be translated thus : *Then the Spirit
entred into me, and set me upon my Feet ; and he
spake unto me :* for the last Verb is in the *Masculine* Gender, and the two former in the *Feminine.*
In like manner, the fifth Verse of the Eleventh
Chapter should be read, *And the Spirit of the
Lord fell upon me, and he said unto me.* The
Spirit or Power of God which the Prophet felt
within him, (called likewise the Hand of the
Lord, Ver. 14, and 22. of this Chapter, and
Chap. viii. 1.) being distinguish'd here from the
Divine Glory or *Shekinah*, which the Prophet saw,
as it is very plainly Chap. ii. 2. *And the Spirit
entred into me, when* He *spake unto me.*

Ibid. Go shut thy self within thy House.] Here-
by to represent the Siege of *Jerusalem.* See Chap.
iv. 1, &c.

Ver. 25. *They shall put Bands upon thee, &c.*] Ver. 25.
Thou shalt be confin'd to lie so many Days upon
thy right Side, and so many upon thy left, as if
thou wast bound and not able to stir : See Chap.
iv. 8. The LXX. and the *Vulgar Latin* read,
Bands shall be put upon thee : and it is very common in the *Hebrew* Language to take the Verb
Transitive in an *Impersonal* Sense. See the Notes
on *Isa* xliv. 18.

*Ibid. Thou shalt be dumb, and shalt not be to
them a Reprover.*] *Ezekiel's* Dumbness might pro-

E 2   ceed

Chapter III. ceed from two Caufes: Excefs of Grief, as we read Ver. 15. of this Chapter, that he *remained aftonied feven Days* : wherein he was a Type or Figure of the Condition of the *Jews* when they were to be *aftonied one with another* : Chap. iv. 17. Another caufe of his filence might be by way of Reproof to them for disbelieving what he had before delivered by the commands of God. See the Note on Chap. xxxii. 22. xxiv. 17. And becaufe they regarded not the Words, which God commanded him to fpeak to them, he was directed to inftruct them only by Signs, fuch as are thofe Emblems of the Siege contained in the next Chapter.

Ver. 27. Ver. 27. *But when I fpeak with thee* [or to thee] *I will open thy Mouth*] But when I bid thee declare my Commands by Word of Mouth, thou fhalt have free Liberty to fpeak. See Chap. xi. 25.

Ibid. *He that heareth, let him hear ; and he that forbeareth, let him forbear.*] The fum of what thou fhalt fay unto them is this : to let them know that this is the laft Warning God will give them, and therefore let them take it as fuch, and either give heed to what is faid to them, or neglect it at their utmoft Peril. Compare 1 *Cor.* xiv. 38. *Revel.* xxii. 11.

CHAP.

CHAP. IV.

The ARGUMENT.

*Under the Emblem of a Siege, and of the ſtraitneſs
of Proviſion during the Siege, is ſhewed the Miſeries the Jews ſhall ſuffer when the City is beſieged: and by the Prophets lying upon his Right
and Left ſide a certain number of Days, is declared of how long continuance thoſe Sins were
which God did viſit upon that People.*

Ver. 1.
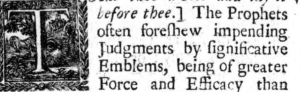
Ake thee a Tile and lay it
before thee.] The Prophets
often foreſhew impending
Judgments by ſignificative
Emblems, being of greater
Force and Efficacy than
Words. So *Jeremy* was commanded to go down
to the Potters Houſe, and ſee how frequently Veſſels were marred in his Hands, Chap. xviii. and
to take one of thoſe Earthen Veſſels and break it
in the ſight of the Elders of the *Jews.* Chap. xix.
that they might thereby be ſenſibly taught the
greatneſs of God's Power, and their own Frailty.
So

Ver. 1.

Chapter IV.

So here God commands the Prophet to take a Tile, or such a Slate as the Mathematicians draw Lines or Figures upon, and there make a Pourtraiture of *Jerusalem*, thereby to represent it as under a Siege. We may observe that God often suits Prophetical Types and Figures to the Genius and Education of the Prophets themselves. So the Figures which *Amos* makes use of are generally taken from such Observations as are proper to the Imployment of a Shepherd or an Husbandman. *Ezekiel* had a peculiar Talent for Architecture, so several of his Representations are suitable to that Profession. And they that suppose the Emblem here made use of to be below the Dignity of the Prophetical Office, may as well accuse *Archimedes* of Folly for making Lines in the Dust.

Ver. 2.

Ver. 2. *And lay Siege against it*, &c.] Make a Portraiture of a Siege, and of such warlike Preparations as are necessary to it.

Ver. 3.

Ver. 3. *Moreover take thou unto thee an Iron Pan.*] A Plate or Slice, as the Margin reads. This may either represent the Walls of *Jerusalem* which were to be broken down, in order to the taking of it, as the following Words may be thought to imply: or else some of those Works which the Besiegers cast up for their own defence; so this is another Representation of the Siege mentioned Ver. 1.

Ibid. *This shall be a Sign to the House of Israel.*] *Ezekiel* often expressed God's Purposes by Signs. See Chap. xii. 2--12. xxiv. 24, 27. and the Notes upon the 17th Ver. of this Chapter.

Ver.

Ver. 4. *Lie also on thy left Side.*] Lie on that Chapter Side, without stirring or moving thy self: See IV. Ver. 8.

Ibid. *According to the Number of the Days thou* Ver. 4. *shalt lie upon it, thou shalt bear their Iniquity.*] By lying on one side thou shalt signify *God's* Forbearing their Punishment for so many Years: So the Words are commonly explained; but in my Opinion not agreeably to the Genuine Sense of the Phrase, *To bear ones Iniquity:* which never signifies, that I can find, to forbear the Punishment of Sin, but on the contrary, always denotes the Bearing or suffering the Punishment due unto it: As also that other Expression of *Laying Iniquity upon* any, imports the Imputing the Guilt of it, or inflicting the Punishment due unto it. So here the Prophet does in Vision bear the Punishment due to the Idolatry of *Israel* and *Judah,* which had continued, the one for Three hundred and ninety, the other for Forty Years.

The Circumstances of this Vision prove that the Prophet did really perform what is here related: or else it could not have been a *Sign unto the House of Israel,* Ver. 3. unless they themselves had been Eye-Witnesses of it. Compare Chap. xii. 7, 11. The chief Objection against this Opinion is, that there is not the Distance of Four hundred and thirty Days between this Vision, and that which is next related, Chapter viii. 1. but that may be answered by supposing this to be an *Intercalary* Year, which may be supposed to have happened often in the Jewish Computation of time, whose Years consisted at most but of Three hundred and sixty Days, or as some think, were Lunar Years,

reduced

Chapter reduced by Intercalations to the Solar Form. See
IV. Dr. *Prideaux*, *Script. Hist. Par.* 1. p. 281.

Ver. 5.   Ver. 5. *Three hundred and ninety Days.*] The
most probable Computation of this time is, to date
its beginning from *Jeroboam*'s first setting up
the Idolatrous Worship of the Golden Calves, to
the last Captivity of the Jews, in the Twenty-
third Year of *Nebuchadnezzar*'s Reign; See *Jer.*
lii. 30. This seems to have made an entire riddance
of the Natives of the Land, and consequently to
be the finishing Stroke of the Jewish Captivity.
Both *Judah* and *Israel* being now intirely carried
away, whereas before that time many of the Ten
Tribes lived in their own Habitations. See 2 *Chron.*
xxix. 14. xxxi. 11, 18. xxxii. 33. *Ezra*, vi. 17.

Ver. 6.   Ver. 6. *Thou shalt bear the Iniquity of the House
of Judah Forty Days.*] This Series of Time may
probably be computed from the Eighteenth Year
of *Josiah*, at which time the King and People entred into a solemn Covenant to serve and worship God, so that the Idolatry they were afterward
guilty of received a new Aggravation, as being a
breach of this Solemn Covenant, the greater Part
of the People being still Idolatrous in their Hearts;
See the Notes on *Jeremiah* iii. 6---10. The *Thirtieth Year* mentioned in the beginning of this Prophecy is supposed to take its Date from the Eighteenth Year of *Josiah*, which makes it probable
that the Prophet refers to the same *Æra* in this
Place.

Scaliger and some others begin those Forty
Years from *Jeremiah*'s Mission as a Prophet,
which was in the Thirteenth Year of *Josiah*, from
which time till the last Year of *Zedekiah*, when the
City

City and Temple were deftroyed, is juft Forty
Years.

Ibid. *I have appointed each Day for a Year.*]
Days frequently ftand for Years in the Prophetical
Accounts of Time. See *Numb.* xiv. 34. *After
the Number of Forty Days, each Day for a Year,
fhall you bear your Iniquities, even Forty Years,
Dan.* ix. 24. The Days of the *Seventy Weeks* muft
necefſarily be underftood in the fame Senfe, fo as
to make up the Sum of Four hundred and ninety
Years; And the One thoufand two hundred and
fixty *Days* mentioned *Revel.* xi. 3. are according
to the Genius of the Prophetical Style, to be underftood of fo many Years.

Ver. 7. *Therefore thou fhalt fet thy Face toward* Ver. 7.
the Siege of Jerufalem.] When thou lieft in one
Pofture, as is commanded thee, Ver. 4, 6. thou
fhalt ftill have the Portraiture of the Siege of *Jerufalem* before thy Face, Ver. 1. or *fetting thy
Face toward the Siege of Jerufalem,* may fignify
looking earneftly, or with a threatning Vifage toward it: as the Prophet is faid to *fet his Face againft*
a Place, when he Prophecies againft it. See Chapter vi. 2.

Ibid. *And thy Arm fhall be uncovered.*] or
ftretched out. Their Habits were anciently contrived fo that the Right Arm was difengaged from
the Upper Garments, that they might be the more
ready for Action. So ancient Statues and Coins
reprefent Heroes with their right Arm bare, and
out of the Sleeve of their Garments. Thus God
is faid to *make bare his Arm, Ifa.* lii. 10. where
he is reprefented as fubduing his Adverfaries, and
bringing Salvation to his People.

F   Ibid.

Ibid. *And thou shalt Prophecy against it.*] By Signs, and not by Words. See the Note on Chapter iii. 26.

Ver. 8. *I will lay Bands upon thee.*] See Chapter iii. 25.

Ibid. *Till thou hast ended the Days of thy Siege.*] The Three hundred and ninety Days mentioned Verse 5, and 9, were designed not only to signify the Years of *Israel*'s Sin, but the Continuance of the Siege of *Jerusalem.* That Siege lasted, from the beginning to the ending of it, Seventeen Months, as appears from 2 *Kings* xxv. 1--4. But the King of *Egypt* coming to relieve the City was the occasion of raising the Siege for some time, as appears from *Jeremiah* xxxvii. 3. So that it may reasonably be gathered from the Authority of the Text joined to the Circumstances of the Story, that the Siege lasted about Thirteen Months, or Three hundred and ninety Days. See Archbishop *Usher*'s *Annals, ad Annum Mundi* 3415.

Ver. 9.

Ver. 9. *Take thou also unto thee Wheat and Barley, &c.*] In time of Scarcity 'tis usual to mix a great deal of the coarse kinds of Grain with a little of the better sort, to make their Provisions last the longer. Thus *Ezekiel* was commanded to do, to signify the Scarcity and coarse Fare the Inhabitants should endure in the Siege of the City.

Ibid. *According to the number of the Days thou shalt lie upon thy side, Three hundred and ninety Days* shalt thou *eat thereof.*] During which time the Siege lasted, see Ver. 8. The Forty Days mentioned Ver. 6. seem not to be reckoned into this Account. These denoted *Judah*'s Sin of Forty Years Continuance, from the Eighteenth Year of

Josiah

Josiah, Ver. 6. And as they were superadded to the Three hundred and ninety Days of the Siege, they may signify the Days spent in plundering the City, and burning the Temple, and carrying away the Remnant of the People : *Jerusalem* was taken on the *Ninth Day of the Fourth Month, Jeremiah* lii. 6. and on the *Tenth Day* of the *Fifth Month,* the Temple was Burnt, Ver. 12. and so we may reasonably conjecture by the Eighteenth of that Month which was the Fortieth from the taking of the Place, the whole City was Burnt, and the few Jews which were left, were carried into Captivity.

Chapter IV.

Ver. 10. *And the Meat which thou shalt eat shall be by weight, twenty Shekels a Day.*] In Sieges 'tis common to stint every one to a certain allowance, by which Means they can guess how long their Provisions will last ; Twenty Shekels is but Ten Ounces, a short Allowance for a Days Sustenance. See Ver. 16. and *Jeremiah* xxxvii. 21.

Ver. 10.

Ibid. *From Time to Time shalt thou eat it.*] This shall be thy daily Allowance during the whole Three hundred and ninety Days.

Ver. 11. *The sixth part of an Hin.*] which is something above a Pint and an Half of our Measure. See Bishop *Cumberland's* Account of *Jewish Weights* and *Measures,* placed at the End of many *English* Bibles.

Ver. 11.

Ver. 12. *And thou shalt eat it as Barley Cakes.*] Such as People make in haste, when they have not time for preparing a set Meal : See *Exod.* xii. 39. This represents the Hurry and Disorder of a Siege.

Ver. 12.

Ibid. *And thou shalt bake it with Dung, &c.*] To signify the Scarcity of all sorts of Fewel : See Ver. 15.

F 2

Ver. 13.

Ver. 13. *Even thus shall the Children of Israel eat their defiled Bread among the Gentiles, &c.*] Their Circumstances in their Captivity shall not permit them to observe the Rules of their Law relating to Unclean Meats, and they will be constrained to partake of Meats, part of which hath been offered unto Idols. Compare *Hof.* ix. 1. *Dan.* i. 8. Bread is often used in the *Hebrew* for all sorts of Food. See *Gen.* xliii. 31.

Ver. 13.

Ver. 14.

Ver. 14. *Behold my Soul hath not been polluted, &c.*] I have always carefully observed the Distinction between Meats Clean and Unclean: I beseech thee command me not now to eat any Thing so contrary to my former Practice.

Ibid. *Neither came there abominable Flesh into my Mouth.*] The *Hebrew* Word *Piggut abominable*, is properly used of such Meats as are forbidden by the Law. See *Levit.* vii. 18. xix. 7. *Isa.* lxv. 4. Such are those here mentioned. See the Texts quoted in the Margin of our Bibles.

Ver. 16.

Ver. 16. *I will break the Staff of Bread in Jerusalem.*] The Siege shall produce a Scarcity of Bread in *Jerusalem*, 2 *Kings* xxv. 3. and deprive you of the chief Support of Man's Life. Compare *Levit.* xiv. 13. xxvi. 26. *Isa.* iii. 1.

Ibid. *They shall eat their Bread by Weight and with Care, &c.*] See Ver. 10, 11. When they have consumed their last Allowance, they shall be in great Care where to get more for the next Meal: and some of you be forced to eat the Flesh of their nearest Relations: See Chapter v. 10.

Ver. 17.

Ver. 17. *And be aftonied one with another, and confume away in your Iniquities.*] Look one upon another as Persons under astonishment for the

Great-

Greatneſs of your Calamities, and pining away or dying a lingring Death thro' Famine and other Hardſhips. See Chapter xxiv. 23.

CHAP. V.

The ARGUMENT.

The Prophet is commanded to ſhave his Hair, and then conſume it, to ſignify thereby God's Judgments upon Jeruſalem for her repeated Provocations, by Famine, Sword and Diſperſion.

Ver. 1. Ake thee *a ſharp Knife, take thee a Barber's Raſor.*] The latter Expreſſion explains the Former: Hair being an Ornament, and Baldneſs a token of Sorrow, thereupon Shaving denotes a great Calamity or Deſolation. Compare *Iſa.* vii. 20. *Maimonides Moreh Nevoch. l. 2. c.* 46. obſerves upon this Place, that the Prieſts were forbidden to ſhave their Heads; ſee Chapter xliv. 20. and not allowed to do it in the time of Mourning, *Levit.* xxi. 5. From whence that Author concludes that what the Prophet is here commanded, was performed only

in

in Vision. But there is no need of such an Evasion to answer that Difficulty. For the immediate Command of God to any Prophet is a sufficient Discharge from any Obligations of the Ceremonial Law. So *Elijah* offered Sacrifice upon Mount *Carmel* : 1 *Kings* xviii. 20. contrary to the Rule of the Law, *Deut.* xii. 5.

Ibid. *Then take thee Balances,* &c.] To signify the Exactness of the Divine Justice.

Ver. 2.　　Ver. 2. *And thou shalt burn a third part in the midst of the City.*] Of that Portraiture of the City which the Prophet was commanded to make, Chapter iv. 1. This signifies the Destruction of the Inhabitants within the City by Famine and Pestilence. See Ver. 12. and Chapter vii. 12.

Ibid. *And thou shalt take a third Part, and smite it about with a Knife.*] To shew that a third Part of the Inhabitants shall be slain with the Sword, just after they have escaped out of the City : See Ver. 12. This was remarkably fulfilled in the Slaughter of *Zedekiah*'s Sons, and the rest of his Retinue. *Jeremiah* lii. 10.

Ibid. *And a third part thou shalt scatter in the Wind, and I will draw out a Sword after them.*] The rest shall be dispersed to all the Four Winds : See Chapter vi. 8. and even my Vengeance shall pursue many of them in their Dispersions; see Ver. 12. and Compare *Levit.* xxvi. 33. *Jeremiah* xxiv. 10. xliv. 12. *Amos* ix. 4.

Ver. 3.　　Ver. 3. *And bind them in thy Skirts.*] The *Hebrew* reads, *in thy Wings :* to signify that they should be placed under the Divine Protection : See *Ps.* xci. 4. This denotes those that should be left in the Land under *Gedaliah, Jeremiah* xl. 5, 6.

Ver.

Ver. 4. *Then take of them again, and caſt them into the midſt of the Fire.*] This denotes the Conſpiracy with *Iſmael* formed againſt *Gedaliah*, and the Calamities that followed thereupon.

Ibid. *For thereof ſhall come a Fire forth into all the Houſe of Iſrael.*] This was the Occaſion of the utter Ruin of that poor Remainder of the *Jews* which were left in their Native Country. Thereupon ſome of them went down into *Egypt*, where they were all conſumed, according to *Jeremiah*'s Prophecy againſt them : See Chapter xliv. 11, &c. and the reſt that remained in the Land were entirely carried away Captive by *Nebuzaradan.* See *Jeremiah* lii. 30.

Ver. 5. *This is Jeruſalem, I have ſet it in the midſt of the Nations.*] This Jeruſalem thou doſt now Prophecy againſt, was placed in the midſt of the Heathen Nations ; it made a Figure among them for the ſake of my Temple, and the viſible Tokens of my Preſence there. See Chapter xvi. 14. 1 *Kings* viii. 41, 42. It was a *City ſet on a Hill*, on purpoſe that it might be a pattern of Religion and Vertue to them. Compare *Matt.* v. 14.

Ver. 6. *And ſhe hath changed my Judgments into Wickedneſs.*] or, *ſhe hath rebelled againſt my Judgments, for the ſake of Wickedneſs* ; that is, to fulfil her wicked Deſires : for ſo the Verb *Marah* is rightly tranſlated Chapter xxx. 8.

Ibid. *More than the Nations.*] She hath ſinned againſt a clearer Light and greater Convictions. Compare Chap. xvi. 48. and Matt. xii. 41, 42.

Ibid. *For they have refuſed my Judgments.*] The Reaſon why the Heathen have rejected my Laws, is becauſe they have kept conſtant to the Religion

of

Chapter
V.

Ver. 7.

Ver. 9.

of their Forefathers: whereas the *Jews* have forsaken that Religion which their Forefathers Received from me. See the next Verse.

Ver. 7. *Because you have multiplied more than the Nations.*] The *French* Translation reads, *Because thou haft multiplied thy Wickednesses:* Some such Word ought to be added to supply the Sense.

Ibid. *Neither have done according to the Judgments of the Nations round about you.*] or rather, *According to the manner of the Nations round about you:* as the very fame Phrase is tranflated, Chapter xi. 12. You have not been fo conftant and zealous for the true Religion as they are in a Falfe one. Compare Chapter xvi. 47. *Jeremiah* ii. 10, 11. *Micah* iv. 5.

Ver. 9. *And I will do unto thee that which I have not done.*] As your Sins have particular Aggravations above thofe of other Nations, fo your Punifhment fhall be proportionably greater. See *Dan.* ix. 12. *Lam.* iv. 6. *Amos* iii. 2.

Ibid. *And I will not do any more the Like.*] The Punifhments you fhall fuffer fhall be more remarkable for their Greatnefs than thofe I fhall at any time inflict upon other Nations. The Punifhment due to the Sins of *Ifrael* and *Judah*, which the Prophet was to bear for Four hundred and thirty Days by way of Type or Vifion, may probably fignify a Judgment to continue for fuch a length of time as is not yet expired: according to God's Threatnings, that for their Obftinacy and Irreclaimablenefs, he would go on to *punifh them feven times more for their Sins*, *Levit.* xxvi. 18, 28. Multiplying the length of their Calamities by a Seven fold Proportion. And taking the Words

in

in this large extent, so as to comprehend all the Chapter
Marks of God's Indignation, which have already   V.
lain upon that People for above Sixteen Hundred
Years, and how much longer they may continue
we know not, it may truly be said that none of
God's Judgments have been like it.

Ver. 10. *Therefore the Fathers shall eat the Sons* Ver. 10.
in the midst of thee.] A terrible Judgment threatned by *Moses*, *Levit.* xxvi. 29. *Deut.* xxviii. 53.
and afterwards by *Jeremy*, Chap. xix. 9. and actually fulfilled in the Famine that attended the
Siege of *Jerusalem*. See *Lament.* ii. 20. iv. 10.

Ibid. *And the whole remnant of them will I
scatter into all the Winds.*] This is another Judgment threatned against them by *Moses: Deut.*
xxviii. 65. and remarkably fulfilled in this their last
Dispersion, when every known part of the World
hath some Share of them, and yet they live every
where like Strangers, only upon sufferance.

Ver. 11. *Because thou hast defiled my Sanctuary* Ver. 11.
*with all thy detestable things, and with all thy
Abominations.*] Thou hast profaned my Temple,
by placing Idols in it: See Chap. vii. 20. viii. 5.
xxiii. 38. 2 *Chron.* xxxvi. 14. *Detestable things*
and *Abominations* are Words of the same signification, denoting Idols: See Chap. xi. 21.

Ibid. *Therefore will I also diminish thee, neither
shall mine Eye spare, &c.*] or, *I will destroy thee*
(for so this Word is used, *Numb.* xxvii. 4.) *without shewing any pity or compassion:* See Chap. vii.
4, 9. viii. 18. ix. 10. xxiv. 14.

Ver. 12. *A third part of thee shall die by the* Ver. 12.
Pestilence, (See Chap. xiv. 22.) *and with the Fa-*
G *mine,*

Chapter *mine*, &c.] See Ver. 2. and Chap. vi. 12. *Jerem.*
V. xv. 2. xxi. 9.

Ibid. *And I will draw out a Sword after them.*]
And thereby fulfil that Threatning denounced
against them, *Levit.* xxvi. 33. Compare likewise
Deut. xxviii. 65. *Amos* ix. 4. All which Places
import, that God's Anger should still pursue them
even into the Countries whither they were bani-
shed and carried Captive. This was particularly
fulfilled in those that went into *Egypt :* See *Jerem.*
xliv. 7. and it was remarkably verified in the several Persecutions and Massacres they have undergone at different times, in most of the Countries
of *Europe* in latter Ages : Of which see an Account in *Basnage's Continuation of Josephus.*

Ver. 13. Ver. 13. *I will cause my Fury to rest upon them.*]
See the Note on Chap. viii. 18. The Words may
be rendred thus, *I will cause my Fury toward them
to rest*, as the Phrase is translated, Chap. xvi. 42.
that is, my Anger shall be appeased toward them,
after I have executed due Punishment upon their
Sins.

Ibid. *And I will be comforted.*] This and the
former Expression is borrowed from Men's Passi-
ons, who find some Ease and Rest in their Minds
upon their venting them, and bringing Offenders
to condign Punishment. So God is here described
as feeling Ease and Satisfaction in executing his Justice upon obstinate and incorrigible Sinners. Comp.
Chap. xvi. 42. xxi. 17. *Isa.* i. 24.

Ibid. *They shall know that I the* LORD *have spoken it in my Zeal.*] Out of a just Concern for mine
own Honour and Authority which they have
slighted and despised. See Chap. xxxvi. 5, 6.

xxxviii.

xxxviii. 17. The Word may likewife be taken Chapter
here for that Paffion of Jealoufy that is proper to a V.
Husband when his Wife proves falfe to him, and is
applied to God when his People forfake his Worfhip and ferve Idols, Chap. xvi. 35, 42 xxiii. 25.

The Covenant between God and his People, is
often reprefented under the Notion of a Marriage
Contract: See Chap. xvi. 8. whereupon Idolatry
is called *Going a Whoring after other Gods,* and
committing Adultery with Stocks and Stones: Jerem. iii. 9.

Ver. 14. *I will make them wafte and a reproach* Ver. 14.
among the Nations, &c.] See *Deut.* xxviii. 37.
1 *Kings* ix. 7. *Pfal.* lxxix. 4. *Jerem.* xxiv. 9. *Lam.*
ii. 15.

Ver. 15. *So it fhall be---an inftruction to the Na-* Ver. 15.
tions.] They fhall learn from fuch an Example of
Vengeance, to hear me and be afraid of my Judgments.

Ibid. *In furious rebukes.*] See Chap. xxv. 17.

Ver. 16. *When I fhall fend upon them the evil* Ver. 16.
Arrows of Famine, &c.] God's Judgments are
elfewhere expreffed by Arrows: See *Deut.* xxxii.
23. *Pfal.* vii. 13. lxiv. 7. xci. 5.

Ibid. *And I will break the ftaff of your Bread.*]
See Chap. iv. 16.

Ver. 17. *So I will fend upon you Famine and evil* Ver. 17.
Beafts.] Wild Beafts multiply in a Land when it
is become uninhabited, *Exod.* xxiii. 29. This is
likewife a Punifhment threatned againft the *Jews*
among other Defolations. See *Levit.* xxvi. 22.
Deut. xxxii. 24. and Comp. Chap. xiv. 21. xxxiii.
27. xxxiv. 25. of this Prophecy.

44

Chapter
V.

Ibid. *And Peſtilence and Blood ſhall paſs through thee.*] Blood ſignifies any unuſual ſort of Death, and denotes here ſuch a Peſtilence as will deſtroy Multitudes. Comp. Chap. xiv. 19. Or it may be equivalent to the Sword which is joyned with the Peſtilence, Ver 12. See Chap. xxxviii. 22.

CHAP.

CHAP. VI.

The ARGUMENT.

The Prophet continues to denounce God's severe Judgments upon the Jews for their Idolatry: but tells them that a Remnant shall be saved, and by their Afflictions shall be brought to a sense of their evil doings.

Ver. 2.  ET thy Face towards the *Mountains of Israel.*] Direct thy Face and thy Speech toward the Mountains in the Land of *Judea:* Compare Chap. iv. 7. xx. 46. xiii. 17. xxi. 2. xxv. 2. xxxviii. 2.

Ibid. *Toward the Mountains of Israel.*] *Judea* was an hilly Countrey, See *Josh.* xi. 21. xx. 7. So the whole Land of *Judea* is expressed here and elsewhere by the *Mountains of Israel:* See Chap. xix. 9. xxxiii. 18. xxxiv. 14. xxxv. 12. xxxvi. 1. xxxvii. 22. *Isa.* lxv. 9. *Micah* vi. 1. The Prophets sometimes direct their Discourse to the ina-

nimate

Chapter VI. nimate Parts of the Creation, thereby to upbraid the Stupidity of Men: See *Ifa.* i. 2.

Ibid. *And Prophecy againft them.*] As the moft confpicuous Parts of the Land : But the Judgments denounced extend to all the other Parts of the Country, as appears in the following Verfe.

Ver. 3. Ver. 3. *Thus faith the Lord* GOD *to the Mountains and to the Hills, to the Rivers and to the Valleys.*] Every part of the Countrey had been defiled with Idolatry : The Altars built for Idol-Worfhip were commonly placed upon Mountains and Hills : See Chap. xvi. 16, 24. *Jerem.* ii. 20. iii. 6. The fhady Valleys and River fides were likewife made ufe of for the fame purpofe : Ibid. Ver. 23. particularly for the facrificing of Children offered to *Moloch.* See *Ifa.* lvii. 5. *Jerem.* vii. 31. So the Prophet denounces a general Judgment againft the whole Countrey.

Ver. 4. Ver. 4. *Your Altars fhall be defolate, and your Images fhall be broken,* &c.] The Verfe is plainly taken from *Levit.* xxvi. 30. where *Mofes* denounces the fame Judgments againft the *Jews* upon their Provocations. The Word *Hamannim, Images,* is generally fuppofed to fignify fuch as were erected to the Honour of the Sun, and is accordingly tranflated Sun-Images in the Margin. Comp. 2 *Chron.* xxxiv. 4. *Ifa.* xvii. 8.

Ibid. *I will caft down your flain Men before your Idols.*] So that their Sin may be read in the manner of their Punifhment. See *Levit.* xxvi. 30.

Ver. 7. Ver. 7. *And ye fhall know that I am the* LORD.] An *Epiphonema,* or Conclufion of a fevere Denunciation often repeated by this Prophet ; importing that the Judgments God intended to bring upon the

the *Jews*, would make the moſt hardned and ſtupid
Sinners ſenſible that this was God's Hand.

Ver. 8. *I will leave a remnant, &c.*] A gracious Exception that often occurs in the Prophets,
when they denounce general Judgments againſt
the *Jews:* Implying that God will ſtill reſerve a
Remnant of that People to whom he will fulfil the
Promiſes made to their Fathers. See Chap. **xiv.**
22. and the Notes upon *Iſa.* iv. 2. *Jerem.* xliv. 14.

Ver. 9. *And they that eſcape of you ſhall remem-*
ber me among the Nations.] Their Afflictions ſhall
bring them to the Senſe of themſelves, and their
Duty to me. See *Hoſ.* v. 15.

Ibid. *Becauſe I am broken with their whoriſh*
Heart.] My Patience is tired out with this People's
Idolatries, called in Scripture ſpiritual Whoredom.
See the Note on Chap. v. 13.

God is here introduced, as ſpeaking after the
manner of Men, whoſe Patience is tired out by the
repeated Provocations of others, eſpecially when
they ſee no hopes of Amendment. Compare *Iſa.*
xliii. 24.

Ibid. *And with their Eyes which go a whoring*
after their Idols.] The Eyes are the Seat of laſci-
vious Inclinations: See 2 *Pet.* ii. 14. So in purſuance of the ſame Metaphor, they are ſaid to be en-
ticed to Idolatry: being often tempted to Idolatrous Worſhip, by the Coſtlineſs of the Images,
and the fine Shew which they make. See *Jerem.*
x. 4, 9. *Dan.* xi. 38.

Ibid. *And they ſhall loath themſelves for the*
Evils which they have committed.] They ſhall *ab-*
hor themſelves, as *Job* ſpeaks Chap. **xlii.** 6. when
they

Chapter they reflect upon their manifold Provocations : See
VI   Chap vii. 16. xii. 16. xx. 43. xxxvi. 31.

Ver. 10.   Ver 10. *And that I have not said in vain.*] Or
        without cause, as the Word *Hinnam* is more fig-
        nificantly tranflated, Chap. xiv. 22.

Ver. 11.   Ver. 11. *Smite with thy Hand, and ftamp with
        thy Foot,* &c.] Join to thy Words the Geftures
        which are proper to exprefs Grief and Concern at
        the Wickednefs of thy People, and for their Cala-
        mities that will enfue. Comp. Chap. xxi. 12, 14.
        Numb. xxiv. 10.

        Ibid. *For they fhall fall by the Sword,* &c.] See
        Chap. v. 12.

Ver. 12.   Ver. 12. *He that is far off.*] He that is out of
        the reach of the Siege.

Ver. 13.   Ver. 13. *When their flain Men fhall be round
        about their Altars,* &c.] See Ver. 4, 5.

        Ibid. *Upon every high Hill in all the tops of the
        Mountains,* &c.] Thefe were the noted Places for
        Idolatrous Worfhip : See *Jerem.* ii. 20. *Hof.* iv. 13.
        and the Notes upon Ver. 3. of this Chapter.

        Ibid. *And under every green Tree, and under
        every thick Oak.*] The offering Sacrifice in Groves
        and fhady Places was another ancient Rite of Ido-
        latry : See the Note on *Ifa.* i. 29. upon which Ac-
        count Groves and Images are often joined together
        by the facred Writers.

Ver. 14.   Ver. 14. *Yea more defolate than the Wildernefs
        towards Diblath.*] *Diblath* was part of the De-
        fart in the Borders of *Moab* : See *Numb.* xxxiii. 46.
        Jerem. xlviii. 22.

C H A P.

CHAP. VII.

Chapter VII.

The ARGUMENT.

The Prophet denounces the irreversible Judgment of Captivity, and final Desolation upon the Jews for their Idolatry and other heinous Sins.

Ver. 2. *PON the Land of Israel.*] This Ver. 2. comprehends the whole Countrey of *Judea*: Comp. Chap. xii. 22. xiii. 9. xviii 2. *Israel* is often put for *Judah* after the Captivity of the Ten Tribes. See *Micah* i. 14. iii. 9, 10. *Malach.* i. 1. ii. 11. They that were left of the Ten Tribes, joining themselves to the Tribe of *Judah*. See 2 *Chron.* xxx. 11, 18. Dr. *Prideaux* supposes that *Manasses* and his Successors in the Kingdom of *Judah* had the Dominion of the whole Land of *Canaan*, formerly divided into the two Kingdoms of *Judah* and *Israel*, as Tributaries under the *Kings* of *Assyria*. See his *Connection of Scripture History*, Part 1. p. 34.

H   Ibid.

Ibid. *The End is come upon the Four Corners of the Land.*] Upon the whole Country : Compare *Numb.* xxiv. 17.

Ver. 4.   Ver. 4. *Mine Eye shall not spare thee &c.*] See Chapter v. 17.

Ibid. *And ye shall know that I am the* LORD.] See Chap. vi. 17.

Ver. 5.   Ver. 5. *An only Evil, behold, is come.*] Such an Evil as shall comprehend all other Calamities in it.

Ver. 6.   Ver. 6. *An End is come.*] A Destruction which shall be fatal to a great part of those that go into Captivity, as well as to those who are consumed in their own Country.   See Chapter v. 12.. vi. 8. *Jerem.* xliv. 27.

Ver. 7.   Ver. 7. *The Morning is come upon thee.*] God's Judgments shall overtake thee speedily and unexpectedly : Compare *Psal.* xlvi. 9. The Expression alludes to the time, when the Magistrates use to give Sentence against Offenders, which was in the Morning. See the Notes upon *Jerem.* xxi. 12.

Ver. 7.   Ver. 7. *The Time is come.*] The Time of God's Vengeance, called elsewhere the *Day of the* LORD. Compare Ver. 12. Chapter xxi. 25. xxx. 3. *Jerem.* xvii. 7.

Ibid. *And not the sounding again of the Mountains.*] The sound of War and Tumults : not such a joyful Sound as useth to eccho from the Mountains, by which the Treaders of Grapes express their Satisfaction at the time of the Vintage : which the *Hebrew* Word *Hed* or *Heidad* properly signifies : See *Isa.* xvi. 9. *Jerem.* xxv. 30. xlviii. 33.

Ver.

Ver. 10. *The Rod hath bloſſomed, Pride hath* Chapter
budded.] Wickedneſs daily ſpreads and increaſes, VII.
till it becomes ripe for Judgment.

Ver. 11. *Neither ſhall there be any wailing for* Ver. 10.
them.] In an utter Deſtruction there ſhall none Ver. 11.
eſcape to bewail the Calamities of their Brethren :
or they ſhall uſe no Expreſſions of Sorrow, as Perſons that are aſtoniſhed under the greatneſs of their
Afflictions. Compare Chapter xiv. 16, 22. *Deut.*
xxviii. 28, 34.

Ver. 12. *Let not the Buyer rejoice, nor the Seller* Ver. 12.
mourn.] The Buyer will have no Reaſon to rejoice,
becauſe he will not enjoy what he hath bought ;
nor the Seller cauſe to mourn for the loſs of his
Poſſeſſions, which the approaching Captivity will
for ever deprive him of.

Ver. 13. *For the Seller ſhall not return to that* Ver. 13.
which is ſold, altho' they were yet alive.] The
Year of Jubilee ſhall be no advantage to the Sell-
ers, when once they are gone into Captivity : For
tho' they ſhould live ſo long, yet they ſhall not
enjoy the Benefit of the Law, *Levit.* xxv. 13. nor
return any more to their Poſſeſſions.

Ibid. *Neither ſhall any ſtrengthen himſelf in the*
Iniquity of his Life.] And tho' they harden themſelves in Sin, and ſhut their Eyes againſt the Judgments which hang over their Heads, theſe will at
laſt unavoidably overtake them.

Ver. 14. *They have blown the Trumpet* [See *Je-* Ver. 14.
remiah vi. 1.] *but none goeth to the Battle.*] Mens
Hearts fail them, as looking upon themſelves as
given up to Deſtruction. See Ver. 17.

Ver. 15. *The Sword is without, the Peſtilence* Ver. 15.
and the Famine within.] See Chapter v. 2, 12.

H 2 Ver.

Chapter
VII.

Ver. 16.

Ver. 16. *But they that are escaped of them shall escape.*] Some few of them shall have the Favour of escaping the common Calamity, called elsewhere the *Escaped* or the *Remnant*, from whence is derived the Phrase οἱ Σωζόμενοι in the New Testament, *such as are or should be saved:* See the Note on *Isa.* i. 9. and *Jeremiah* xliv. 14.

Ibid. *And shall be upon the Mountains like Doves in the Vallies,* &c.] When they flee from the Enemy to the Mountains [Compare *Psal.* xi. 1. *Matth.* xxiv. 16.] and are escaped out of the imminent Danger that threatned them, they will then reflect upon their former Provocations, and bemoan themselves and their Calamities the Effects of them. See Chapter vi. 9. and compare *Isa.* xxxviii. 14. lix. 11.

Ibid. *All of them mourning.*] St. *Jerom* renders it, *All of them trembling :* an Epithet ascribed to Doves, *Hos.* xi. 11. who are by Nature exceeding timerous : This Interpretation implies, that their Guilt should make them very apprehensive of God's Judgments, and fearful of what should befal them.

Ver. 17.

Ver. 17. *All Hands shall be feeble, and all Knees shall be weak as Water.*] Weakness and failing of Spirits doth cause Feebleness in the Hands and Knees. Compare Chapter xxi. 7. *Isa.* xxxv. 3. *Job* iv. 3, 4.

Ver. 18.

Ver. 18. *Horror shall Cover them.*] or, *Overwhelm them,* as the Phrase is translated, *Psal.* lv. 6.

Ibid. *Shame shall be upon all Faces.*] The Marks of Confusion and Misery, covering the Face, or Shaving the Head, and making it bald; as it follows : See the Note on *Isa.* xv. 2.

Ver.

Ver. 19. *They ſhall caſt their Silver into the* Chapter
Streets, and their Gold ſhall be removed.] or, *Shall*   VII.
be accounted an unclean Thing ; ſo the Margin
renders the Word *Leniddah,* in the following Verſe : Ver. 19.
it ſhall be valued no more than Dung or Filthineſs, as being made a Prey to the Conquerors.

Ibid. *They ſhall not ſatisfy their Souls, nor fill
their Bowels.*] Their Wealth will not procure
them the Neceſſaries of Life under the Streights
of Famine, or Miſeries of Bondage.

Ibid. *Becauſe it is the ſtumbling Block of their
Iniquity.*] They laid out their Silver and Gold in
making Ornaments for their Idols : Compare
Chapter xiv. 2. xvi. 17. xliv. 12.

Ver. 20. *As for the Beauty of his Ornament, he* Ver. 20.
ſet it in Majeſty, &c.] The Expreſſions may moſt
probably be underſtood of the Glory and Magnificence of the Temple, called elſewhere the
Beauty of Holineſs : Compare Verſe 22. This very Place they have defiled with Idolatry. See
Chapter v. 11, therefore I have given it into the
Hands of the *Gentiles* to profane and pollute it.
For to that Senſe the Marginal reading rightly
tranſlates the following Words. The Preterperfect
Tenſe is often uſed by the Prophets for the Future ;
who to denote the Certainty of the Event, ſpeak
of what is to come, as if it were already done. See
the Note upon *Iſa.* xxi. 9. The ſame Senſe is expreſſed in the following Verſe, *I will give it into
the Hands of Strangers,* &c.

Ver. 21. *To the Wicked of the Earth.*] See Ver. 21.
Ver. 24.

Ver. 22. *My Face alſo will I turn from them,* &c.] Ver. 22.
I will not hear them when they cry to me in their
Di-

Chapter
VII.

Ver. 23.

Ver. 24.

Ver. 26.

Diſtreſs : See Chapter viii. 18. but will deliver up the Holieſt Part of the Temple, where none but the High Prieſt uſed to enter, into the Hands of the *Chaldeans* that ſhall profane and plunder it.

Ver. 23. *Make a Chain.*] The Prophets foretold Things by Actions as well as by Words. So *Jeremiah* is commanded to make Bonds and Yokes, *Jeremiah* xxviii. 2. and *Ezekiel* here to make a Chain, to foreſhew the approaching Captivity, when King and People ſhould be carried in Chains to *Babylon.* See 2 *Kings* xxv. 7. *Jerem.* xl. 1.

Ibid. *For the Land is full of bloody Crimes.*] The innocent Blood that has bin ſhed in it, cries aloud for Vengeance. See Chapter ix. 9. xxiii. 27. xxvi. 18.

· Ver. 24. *Therefore will I bring the worſt of the Heathen.*] The *Chaldeans*, who were at that time the great Oppreſſors of the World, and a Terror to all the Countries round about them. See Chapter xxviii. 7. xxx. 11.

Ibid. *I will make the Pomp of the Strong to ceaſe.*] All the State and Magnificence of the Mighty Men ſhall be brought to nothing. Compare Chapter xxxviii. 28.

Ibid. *And their Holy Places ſhall be defiled.*] The Word Holy Places being in the Plural Number, denotes the Temple and all its outward Courts, where the People aſſembled for the Worſhip of God, and thereupon were accounted Holy. Compare Chapter ix. 7. xxi. 2. *Pſal.* lxviii. 35. lxxiii. 17. *Jeremiah* li. 51.

Ver. 26. *Then ſhall they ſeek a Viſion from the Prophet.*] Men are deſirous to hear what the
Event

Event fhall be in Times of Perplexity : See Chapter xiv. 9. xx. 1. xxxviii. 17.

Ibid. *But the Law fhall perifh from the Prieft, and Counfel from the Ancients.*] *Jeremiah*, *Daniel* and *Ezekiel* himfelf fhall go into Captivity. So there fhall either be no Prophet left among you, or if there be any left, they fhall not be favoured with Divine Revelations. See *Lamen.* ii. 8.

Ibid. *And Counfel from the Ancients.*] or the *Elders*, as the Word is elfewhere tranflated ; Chapter viii. 1. xiv. 1. xx. 1. Men of Authority and famous for Wifdom, whofe Advice they asked in all Cafes of Difficulty : See *Pfal.* cxix. 100. *Ifa.* iii. 2. In like manner the *Prophet*, the *Prieft*, and the *Wife Men* are joined together, *Jeremiah* xviii. 18.

Ver. 27. *The King fhall mourn, and the Princes fhall be cloathed with Defolation, and the Hands of the People fhall be troubled.*] There fhall be a general Confternation of all Ranks and Degrees of Men. They that are in Authority fhall want Prefence of Mind to give Counfel and Directions, and the Inferiors fhall have no Heart to put them in Execution. The Word *Prince* is Synonymous with the King, as may appear by comparing Chapter xii. 10, 12. xxi. 25.

C. H. A. P.

CHAP. VIII.

The ARGUMENT.

The Prophet is carried in Vifion to Jerufalem, and there fhewed the Idolatries committed by the Jews within the Precincts of the Temple.

Ver. 1.

Ver. 1. *A*ND *it came to pafs in the fixth Year.*] of *Jehoiakin*'s Captivi- ty. See Chapter i. 2.

Ibid. *And the Elders of Judah.*] Men of Note for their Age or Authority, perhaps fuch as had been Members of the Greater or Leffer Confiftories before their Captivity. Thefe Elders came to me to inquire of the LORD concerning their prefent State of Affairs : Compare Chapter xiv. 1, 4. xxxiii. 31. It is probable that they together with the Priefts of the Captivity often met together to confult about the Publick Affairs, or to make Orders and Rules for the better Government of the People. So when *Sharezer* and *Regemmelech* came to *Jerufalem* to
ask

ask Counfel of the Prophets and Priefts about obfer- ving the Fafts relating to their former Calamities, *Zech.* vii. 2, 3. it is highly probable that they were fent by the Elders and Priefts that met in *Babylon* for this purpofe. See Dr. *Prideaux Connex. of Scrip. Hift.* Part i. p. 272.

Ibid. *Sat before me.*] This was the Pofture of thofe that came to hear the Inftructions of any Prophet or Teacher. Compare Chapter xiv. 1. xx. 1. xxxiii. 31. 2 *Kings* iv. 38. In after Times the Teachers fat in a Chair or eminent Seat, and the Hearers fat on lower Forms at the Feet of their Mafters : See *Luke* x. 39. *Act.* xxii. 3.

Ibid. *That the Hand of the* Lord *fell upon me.*] See Note on Chapter i. 3.

Ver. 2. *I beheld.*] A Divine of great Learning and Character thinks the *Hebrew* Words fhould be underftood of the time Paft, and tranflated *I had beheld:* and that we are not to fuppofe the Prophet began to fee this Vifion while the Elders were before him, but related to them by God's Direction what he had formerly feen in the Fourth Month, the Seafon fet apart for the Worfhip of the Idol *Tammuz:* See the Note on Verfe 14. This Senfe is confirmed by comparing the Place with Chapter xi. 25. *Then,* or, *Thus I fpake to them of the Captivity all the Things that the* Lord *had fhewed me.*

Ibid. *And lo, a Likenefs as the Appearance of Fire,* &c.] See the Note on Chapter i. 27.

Ver. 3. *He put forth the form of an Hand.*] Juft as the form of an *Hand* appeared *writing upon the Wall, Dan.* v. 5.

Ibid.

Chapter
VIII.

Ibid. *And the Spirit lift me up, and brought me in the Vision of God to Jerusalem.*] This Expreſſion in *the Visions of God*, (which is likewiſe uſed again at the End of the Recital of this Prophecy, Chapter xi. 24. and Chapter xl. 2.) may import that all this Repreſentation was performed only in Viſion: that is, by a lively Repreſentation to the Mind, as if the Prophet had been perſonally preſent at *Jeruſalem*. In the ſame manner *Eliſha* was preſent with *Gehazi* when he took *Naaman's* Preſent, 2 *Kings* v. 26. and heard the Words that were ſpoken in the King of *Syria's* Bedchamber: Ibid. Chap. vi. 12. and St. *Paul*, tho' he was *abſent in Body* yet was *preſent in Spirit* at the Church of the *Coloſſians*, beholding their Order, *&c. Coloſ.* ii. 5. But the Words may alſo ſignify a local Tranſlation of the Prophet from *Chaldea* to *Jeruſalem*; Compare Chapter iii. 14. xl. 1.

This latter Interpretation is confirmed *by the Spirit's lifting him up between Heaven and Earth, and bringing him to Jeruſalem,* and afterward *carrying him back into Chaldea,* Chap. xi. 24.

Ibid. *To the Door of the inner Gate.*] The Entrance that goes into the inner Court, called the *Court of the Prieſts,* where the Altar of Burnt-offerings ſtood: See Ver. 5. The Prophet ſtood at the outſide of this Door, and view'd the Image here mentioned, placed in ſome outward Verge of the Temple: which yet was all accounted Holy Ground, and called in Scripture the *Mount* of the Lord, or the *Holy Mountain.* See Chap. vii. 24.

Ibid. *Where was the Image of Jealouſy, that provoketh to Jealouſy.*] An Image ſet up within the

the Precincts of the Temple, to provoke God to
Jealousy, by setting up a Rival against him in the
place dedicated to his own Worship. See the
Note on Chap. v. 11.

Ver. 4. *And behold the Glory of the* GOD *of If-* Ver. 4.
rael was there.] To shew that that was the place
of his peculiar Residence.

Ver. 5. *Northward at the Gate of the Altar.*] Ver. 5.
Northward of the Gate or Entrance that was over-
against the Altar.

Ver. 6. *That I should go far off from my Sanctu-* Ver. 6.
ary.] That I should forsake it, and deliver it up
to be polluted by the Heathen, Chap. vii. 21, 22.
which is significantly represented by the *departing
of the Divine Glory from the Threshold of the Temple*, Chap. x. 18.

Ibid. *And thou shalt see greater Abominations.*]
Because committed by Persons of greater Authority,
and nearer the place of my immediate Presence. See
Verses 11. 14, 16.

Ver. 7. *And he brought me to the Door of the* Ver. 7.
Court.] This Dr. *Lightfoot, of the Temple,* Chap.
28. understands of the East Gate of the Inner
Court, called the *Gate of Nicanor*, over which
was the Council-Chamber where the *Sanhedrim*
used to meet, and in some of the Rooms near it
they secretly practised Idolatry, as God discovered
to the Prophet, Ver. 11.

Ibid. *Behold an Hole in the Wall.*] Thro' which
I could look in, and see what Abominations were
committing there.

Ver. 8. *Then said he unto me, Dig now in the* Ver. 8.
Wall.] This was done only by Vision, to give the
clearer Proof and Conviction of the Idolatries there

I 2

com-

Chapter committed, by thus introducing him into the
VIII. Rooms where they were practiſed.

Ibid. *And when I had digged in the Wall, be-*
hold a Door.] Which had been made up, and another more ſecret Entrance contriv'd, that they
might go in and out unobſerv'd.

Ver. 9.   Ver. 9. *And he ſaid unto me, Go in,* &c.] To
give me the fulleſt Conviction I did not only peep
thro' the Hole, mentioned Ver. 8. but went into
the very Room where theſe Idolatries were committed.

Ver. 10.   Ver. 10. *So I went in and beheld---every form of*
creeping things and abominable Beaſts pourtrayed
upon the Walls round about.] Pictures were as much
prohibited by the Law as Carved Images: See
Numb. xxxiii. 53.

The worſhipping Serpents and other brute Creatures were Idolatries practiſed in *Egypt,* and upon
that Account particularly forbidden by *Moſes:*
Deut. iv. 17, 18.

Ver. 11.   Ver. 11. *And there ſtood before them ſeventy*
Men of the Ancients of the Houſe of Iſrael.] Thoſe
probably were the Members of the *Sanhedrim,* or
great Council of the *Jews.* See the Note on *Je-*
rem. xxvi. 19. The place of this Idolatry was
near the Council-Chamber where they uſed to ſit:
See Ver. 7.

Ver. 12.   Ver. 12. *Haſt thou ſeen what the Antients of*
the Houſe of Iſrael do in the dark.] See Ver. 7. 8.

Ibid. *For they ſay, The* LORD *ſeeth us not, the*
LORD *hath forſaken the Earth.*] They either deny
the Being and Providence of GOD, See Chap. ix.
9. or elſe they ſay in their Hearts, God hath caſt
us off, and withdrawn his wonted Protection from
us.

us. They seem to have been of the same Mind Chapter
with King *Abaz*, who resolved to worship the   VIII.
Gods of the *Syrians* his Conquerors: 2 *Chron.*
xxviii. 23. So these Men worshipped the Idols of
their Neighbours whom they saw more prosperous
than themselves.

Ver. 14. *Then he brought me to the Door of the* Ver. 14.
Gate of the LORD's *House, which was toward the*
North.] Which was over-against the Temple:
Dr. *Lightfoot (ubi supra)* distinguishes this Door
from that mentioned Ver. 5. that this was the
Upper North-Gate, and that the Lower: this be-
ing just over-against the Temple it self, whereas
that was opposite to the Altar.

Ibid. *And behold there sat Women weeping for*
Tamuz.] St. *Jerom* by *Tamuz* understands *Adonis*,
which learned Men suppose the same with *Osyris:*
See *Vossius de Idololatriâ, lib.* 2. *c.* 4, 10. By *Osyris*
is generally understood the *Sun*, whom they be-
wailed when he was going to leave them at the
Winter Season.

This Idolatry was derived from the *Egyptians*,
and afterwards the *Phœnicians* and *Greeks* impro-
ved it by the Addition of a new Fable, *viz.* of *Ve-*
nus's mourning for the Death of *Adonis*.

The fourth Month of the *Jews*, which answered
part of our *June* and *July*, was called *Tamuz*, from
a Feast dedicated to this Idol in that Month. The
Egyptian Year consisted but of Three hundred and
Sixty five Days, without any *Bissextile*, which
was afterwards added in the *Julian* Year. By this
means they lost a Day every four Years, which in
process of time made a great change in the beginning of their Year, and a Variation in their Festivals,

Chapter VIII. vals which muſt conſequently remove fiom one Seaſon of the Year to another. It is therefore probable that under the Idolatrous Kings of *Judah*, who brought in the Worſhip of *Tamuz*, this Feſtival fell in the Month that anſwered the Fourth Month of the *Jews*, and gave that Month this Name: in which Month *Ezekiel* probably ſaw this Viſion : See the Note on Verſe 2. and *Selden de Diis Syris, Syntagm.* 2. *c.* 11.

Ver. 16.   Ver. 16. *At the Door of the Temple of the* LORD *between the Porch and the Altar.*] Near the Entrance into the Temple, where the Brazen Altar ſtood, in the middle of the Court before the Houſe of the LORD. See 2 *Chron.* viii. 7. 2 *Kings* xvi. 14.

Ibid. *Were about five and twenty Men with their Backs toward the Temple of the* LORD, *and their Faces toward the Eaſt*, &c.] So they turned their Backs to God Almighty, and their Faces toward the Sun. Perhaps *Hezekiah* may allude to ſome ſuch Idolatrous Practice, in that Confeſſion of his, 2 *Chron.* xxix. 6. *Our Fathers have done Evil in the Sight of the* LORD, *and have forſaken him, and turned away their Faces from the Habitation of the* LORD, *and turned their Backs.*

They turned their Back to God, and not their Face; as *Jeremy* expreſſes their Contempt toward him, Chap. ii. 27. xxxii. 33. Comp. Chap. xxiii. 35. of this Prophecy. For this Reaſon the People were commanded to come in at the North or Southern Gates of the outward Court of the Temple, when they came to Worſhip, that they might not at their Return turn their Backs upon God. See Chap. xlvi. 9. God ordered the Holy of

of Holies in his Temple to be placed toward the Chapter
Weſt, in Oppoſition to this Species of Heathen VIII.
Idolatry, which conſiſted in worſhipping the Riſing
Sun. And the *Jews* always turned their Faces to-
ward the Temple, when they worſhipped. See
Dr. *Spencer, De Legib. Hebr. lib. 3. c. 2. Sect. 4.*

· Ver. 17. *For they have filled the Land with Vio-* Ver. 17.
lence, and have returned to provoke me to anger.]
Or, *Again they provoke me to Anger.* See the
Note on *Iſa.* vi. 13. After their repeated Acts of
Injuſtice and Oppreſſion, (See Chapter xxii. 6, 7.)
They add new Aggravations to their Wickedneſs
by committing theſe heinous Provocations of Ido-
latry.

Ibid. *And lo they put the Branch to their
Noſe.*] Thoſe that tranſlate the Words to this
Senſe, ſuppoſe them to relate to ſome Cuſtom
among the Idolaters, of dedicating a Branch of
Laurel, or ſome other Tree, to the Honour of the
Sun, and carrying it in their Hands at the time of
their Worſhip. But this Text is one of thoſe
which the Rabbins reckon among the *Tikkun So-
pherim,* or ſuch as have been corrected by their
Scribes and learned Men : and the Original Reading, ſay they, was *Appi, to my Noſe,* or *Face,*
inſtead of the preſent Reading *Appam.* According to which Reading the Senſe will be, *And
they put a ſtink to my Noſe,* that is, they put an
open Affront upon me, by turning their back
Parts to me in the place dedicated to my Worſhip.

To this Senſe the LXX render it, αὐτοὶ ὡς μυκτηρί-
ζοντες, *They are as thoſe that mock me,* or *publickly
affront me.*

Dr.

Chapter VIII.

Dr. *Lightfoot* upon *John* xv. 6. renders the place, *They put the Branch to my Wrath*, or, *to their Wrath*: that is, they add more Fewel to my Wrath, which will burſt out like a Flame to conſume them: juſt as if one ſhould lay an Heap of dry Sticks upon a Fire. Compare Chap. xv. 6.

Ver. 18.

Ver. 18. *Therefore will I alſo deal in Fury.*] God's unalterable Decree of executing Vengeance upon them for their heinous Iniquities, is deſcribed like the Fury of an enraged Perſon, which cannot be appeaſed but by bringing the Offender to condign Puniſhment. See Chap. v. 13. xvi. 42. xxiv. 13.

CHAP.

CHAP. IX.

The ARGUMENT.

This part of the Vision reprefents the Deftruction of the Inhabitants of Jerufalem, beginning with thofe that were neareft the Temple.

Ver. 1. **H**E also cried in mine Ears with a loud Voice.] To denote the Terriblenefs of GOD's Judgments : See Chap. i. 24. *Rev.* xiv. 7, 9, 15.

Ibid. *Caufe them who have a Charge over the City to come near.*] The Angels who had the Charge of executing God's Judgments upon the City. Compare 2 *Kings* x. 24.

Ver. 2. *Six Men came from the Way of the upper Gate, which lieth toward the North.*] See the Note on Chapter viii. 14. There is mention of the Higher or Upper Gate of the LORD's Houfe which *Jotham* built or repaired, called the *New Gate*, *Jeremiah* xxvi. 10. 2 *Kings* xv. 35. But that is generally thought to be at the Eaft fide of the Temple, and the fame with that which was afterward called

K

Chapter
IX.
called the *Gate of Nicanor* : whereas this is fuppofed to be on the North fide of the Temple and
Altar, becaufe there the Sacrifices were ordered
to be flain. See *Levit.* i. 11. and the Note upon
the following Words. Six Slaughtermen came like
fo many Levites, expecting an Order from the
chief facrificing Prieft, which Beaft to flay, and
at what time.

Ibid. *And one Man among them was cloathed
with Linnen.*] That is, an Angel (See Ver. 4.
and compare Chap. xl. 3. xliii. 6.) who was to
fupply the Place of the chief facrificing Prieft. Angels as Miniftring Spirits always attending upon
God's Service, are fometimes defcribed in the Habit of Priefts, fee *Revel.* xv. 5, 6. As God's Mini-
fters for the fame Reafon have the Title of Angels
given them, *Revel.* i. 20.

Ibid. *With a Writers Inkhorn by his fide.*] To
fet a Mark on thofe that were to be faved from the
common Deftruction. But the LXX tranflate the
Words, *With a Girdle of Saphire, or Embroidery
upon his Loins :* which agrees better with what
goes before, as being part of the Prieft's Habit,
Exod. xxviii. 8. and the above-cited place in the
Revelation. And this Interpretation of the Phrafe
Dr. *Caftell* follows in his *Lexicon,* in the Word
Kefeth.

Ibid. *And they went and ftood by the brazen
Altar.*] To denote that the Men ordained to Deftruction were offered up as fo many Sacrifices, to
make an Atonement to God's Juftice. The deftruction of the Wicked is elfewhere expreffed by
the Name of a Sacrifice : See Chap. xxxix. 17.
Ifa. xxix. 2. xxxiv. 6.

Ver.

Ver. 3. *And the Glory of the God of Israel was*
gone up from the Cherub whereupon he was, to
the Threshold of the House.] *Ezekiel* saw the Glory of God depart out of the inner Sanctuary to the
Threshold, or Door of the Temple; to shew that
God would shortly forsake his Temple. Compare
Chap. x. 4, 18, 19. xi. 23. The Word *Cherub*
stands for *Cherubims*, as Chap. x. 2. We are to distinguish this Apparition of the Divine Glory,
which had its constant Residence in the Temple,
from that which was shewed particularly to *Ezekiel,* Chap. i. 26. iii. 23. viii. 24. x. 1.

Ibid. *And he called to the Man, &c.*] The *Logos,* or second Person of the Blessed Trinity gave
his Commands to the Angel mentioned Ver. 3.

Ver. 4. *Set a Mark upon their Foreheads.*] Com- **Ver. 4.**
pare *Revel.* vii. 3. The Expression alludes to the
Custom of the Eastern Nations to mark their Servants in the Forehead. See *Grotius* upon that place
of the *Revelations.* The *Vulgar Latin* renders
the Words, *Mark with the Letter Thau the Foreheads:* and 'tis very probable the ancient Reading
in the LXX was τὸν Σημεῖον, tho' the present Copies
read τὸ Σημεῖον. See *Huetius Demonst. Evang. Prop.*
9.

It was the general Opinion of the Fathers, that
the Ancient *Samaritan* Letter *Thau* was made in
the Form of a Cross: and St. *Jerom* (a very com-
petent Judge in this matter) does attest the same
in his *Commentary* on this place.

This Opinion *Scaliger* rejects in his Notes upon
Eusebius's *Chronicon,* p. 109. but Bishop *Walton*
defends it at large in his Third *Prolegomenon,* N.
36. and in the Dissertation upon the ancient *Hebrew*

Chapter *brew Sicles* in his *Apparatus* to the *Polyglot Bi-*
IX. *ble*, p. 36, 38. The *Ethiopick* Letter *Tawi* or *Tau*
still retains the Form of a Cross; and the learned
Ludolphus supposes, that the *Ethiopick* Letters
were borrowed from the *Samaritans*. The *Cop-*
tick Letter of that Sound is in the same Form.
The Modern Antiquaries do all agree, that the *Sa-*
maritan Thau was in the Form of a *Greek* X. But
whether their Authority be sufficient to outweigh
that of St. *Jerom*, must be left to the Learned to
judge. It is observable, that the High Priest was
anointed upon the Forehead, in the Form of a X,
as *Selden* assures us, *lib.* 2. *de Success. in Pontif.*
c. 9.

    Ibid. *Of the Men that sigh and cry for all the*
Abominations that are done in the midst thereof.]
The irreclaimable Temper of Sinners that hate to
be reformed, is just matter of Grief to good Men.
See *Psal.* cxix. 136. *Isa.* lvii. 18. *Jerem.* xiii. 17.
2 *Cor.* xii. 21. 2 *Pet.* ii. 8. And when the Number of such Mourners is not sufficient to divert
God's Judgments from a Nation, they shall at
least deliver their own Souls. See Chap. xiv. 14.

Ver. 5.　 Ver. 5. *Let not your Eye spare*, &c.] See Chap.
v. 11.

Ver. 6.　 Ver. 6. *Slay utterly old and young*, &c.] This
Denunciation was executed by the *Chaldeans*. See
2 *Chron.* xxxvi. 17.

    Ibid. *And begin at my Sanctuary.*] Judgment
often *begins at the House of God*, 1 *Pet.* iv. 17. because such Persons sin against greater Light and
clearer Convictions. See *Amos* iii. 2. *Luke* xii.
47.

                                Ibid.

Ibid. *Then they began with the ancient Men that* Chapter
were before the Houſe.] Who committed Idolatry IX.
in the ſeveral Courts and Apartments belonging
to the Temple. See Chap. viii. 11, 12, 16.

Ver. 7. *Defile the Houſe, and fill the Courts* Ver. 7.
with the ſlain.] God declares he will own the Temple no longer for his place of Reſidence. See Ver.
3. as having been polluted with Idolatry, Chap.
viii. 10, &c. and therefore delivers up both the inner and outer Courts belonging to it (Compare
Chap. x. 35.) to be polluted by Blood and Slaughter.

Ver. 8. *And I was left.*] The Prophet thought Ver. 8.
himſelf preſerved alone out of the common Deſtruction, the Slaughter was ſo great: altho' thoſe
who had a Mark ſet upon them were certainly preſerved, as well as he.

Ibid. *I fell upon my Face.*] In a poſture of ſup-
plication to deprecate God's Anger, (See *Numb.*
xii. 5. xvi. 4, 22, 45.) and to beſeech him not to
make an utter Deſtruction of thoſe ſmall Remains
that were left of the Nation: *Jeruſalem* being al-
moſt the only place which was not in the Enemies
Power. See Chap. xi. 13.

Ver. 9. *The Land is full of Blood, and the City* Ver. 9.
of Perverſeneſs.] See Chap. viii. 23.

Ibid. *The* LORD *hath forſaken the Earth,* &c.]
See Chap. viii. 12.

C H A P.

CHAP. X.

The ARGUMENT.

The Vision of the Cherubims, *which the Prophet saw at the beginning of this Prophecy, is here renewed: from whence Coals are scattered over the City, to denote its Destruction by Fire. At the End of the Chapter the Divine Glory is described as still removing further from the Temple.*

Ver. 1.   Ver. 1. N *the Firmament that was above the Head of the Cherubims,* &c.] See the Note on Chap. i. 26.

Ibid. *As the Appearance of the likeness of a Throne.*] And God fitting upon it. *Ibid.*

Ver. 2.   Ver. 2. *Go in between the Wheels, even under the Cherubims.*] Or, *Between the Cherubims, as* Noldius translates the Phrase, *N.* 3, 98. according to the Explication given of it Ver. 7.

Ibid. *And fill thine Hand with Coals of Fire from between the Cherubims, and scatter them over the City.*] For the Coals of Fire sparkled and ran

up

up and down between the Living Creatures : See Chapter
Chap. i. 13. This part of the Vifion was to repre- X.
fent the Burning of the City. Coals of Fire do
elfewhere denote the Divine Vengeance : See *Pfal.*
cxx. 4. cxl. 10. *Revel.* viii. 5.

  Ver. 3. *Now the Cherubims ftood on the right* Ver. 3.
fide of the Houfe.] The Cherubims which were
Part of the Vifion fhewed to *Ezekiel :* See Ver. 1.
and the Note upon Chapter ix. 3. they ftood now
in the Inner Court, on the *North Side* of the
Houfe. See Ver. 18. The *Chaldee* Paraphrafe
underftands it of the *South Side* of the Houfe, but
then it is fpoken with refpect to thofe that came out
of the Temple. See Chap. xlvii. 1.

  Ibid. *And the Cloud filled the Inner Court.*]
This bright Cloud feems to be an Attendant upon
that Glory which was reprefented in this Vifion to
Ezekiel, Chapter viii. 4. x. 1. Or elfe the Words
may be underftood of the Cloud or *Shekinah,* removing from the inner Sanctuary, and coming toward the Door of the Houfe : See the following
Verfe.

  Ver. 4. *The Glory of the* LORD *went up from* Ver. 4.
the Cherub, &c.] The Words may better be tranflated thus, *Now,* (or, *For*) *the Glory of the* LORD
was gone up, &c. For the Prophet repeats here
what he had related before, Chap. ix. 3.

  Ibid. *And the Houfe was filled with the Cloud,
and the Court was full of the Brightnefs of the*
LORD's *Glory.*] A bright Cloud was the Sign of
GOD's Prefence, which firft filled the Tabernacle,
Exod. xl. 35. afterward the Temple, 1 *Kings* viii.
10. where it fixed it felf upon the Mercy Seat,
Levit. xvi. 2. From whence God is faid fo often to
dwell

Chapter
X.

dwell between the Cherubims. This Glory now removed from that its Refidence in the Inner Sanctuary, and came down toward the Porch of the Temple, and fixt it felf partly in the Temple, and partly in the Inner Court adjoining to it : to denote God's being juft about to leave the Temple and difown any Relation to it. See the Note on Chapter viii. 3. The *Shekinah,* or Divine Glory is reprefented as a bright Flame breaking out of a thick Cloud : See the Note on *Ifa.* vi. 1. So both together make up the Defcription of it.

Ver. 5.

Ver. 5. *And the Sound of the Cherubims Wings was heard even to the utter Court,* &c.] See Chapter i. 24. The Cherubims in *Ezekiel's* Vifion feem to have moved to attend upon the *Shekinah,* which now had took it's Refidence at the Threfhold of the Houfe. Compare Verfes 18, 19. and Chapter xi. 22.

Ver. 7.

Ver. 7. *Who took it and went out.*] To fignify the putting the Command in Execution.

Ver. 8.

Ver. 8. *And there appeared in the Cherubims the form if a Man's Hand.*] See Chapter i. 8.

Ver. 9, 10, 11, 12. The fame in Subftance which was defcribed Chapter i. 16, 17, 12, 18.

Ver. 11.

Ver. 11. *To the Place where the Head looked, they followed it.*] Each Wheel confifted of four Semicircles (fee the Note on Chapter i. 16, 17.) in correfpondence to the Four Heads of each Animal.

Ver. 13.

Ver. 13. *It was cried to them in my hearing, O Wheel.*] Or, *Move round,* as fome render the Word. They are put in mind of continually attending upon their Duty : for the Wheels and living Creatures were animated with the fame Principle of

Under-

Underſtanding and Motion. See Chap. i. 19, 20,
21.

. Ver. 14. *And every one had four Faces, &c.*]
See Chap. i. 6, 10.

Ibid. *The firſt had the Face of a Cherub.*] That
is, of an Ox, as appears by comparing this Verſe
with Chap. i. 10. The Word *Cherub* does originally ſignify an Ox: See Dr. *Spencer de Legib.
Hebr. l. 3. c. 3. Sect. 1.* The ſeveral Faces
are here repreſented in a different Order from the
Deſcription given of them Chap. i. 10. of which
Difference this Reaſon may be aſſigned. In the
Firſt Chapter the Prophet ſaw this Viſion *coming
out of the North,* and advancing Southward, Ver.
4. where the Face of a Man being placed on the
South-ſide, was firſt in View: a Lion was Weſtward, an Ox Eaſtward, and an Eagle Northward.
Whereas in this Chapter, the living Creatures
are repreſented as they ſtood in View in the Inward Sanctuary, which being placed toward the
Weſt, the Ox was firſt in View looking Eaſtward;
the Man was toward the South, the Lion was
toward the Weſt, and the Eagle toward the
North.

Ver. 15. *And the Cherubims were lifted up.*] Ver. 15.
To attend upon the Divine Glory where ever it
went, and particularly at its Removal from the
Temple. See Ver. 5. and 19.

Ver. 16, 17. See Chap. i. 19, 20, 21.

Ver. 18. *Then the Glory of the* LORD *departed* Ver. 18.
*from off the Threſhold of the Houſe, and ſtood over
the Cherubims.*] The Divine Preſence here makes
a further remove from the Temple: See Ver. 4.
It now quite leaves the Houſe it ſelf, and ſettles

upon

Chapter
X.

upon the Cherubims which stood in the Court adjoining to it : Ver. 3.

Ver. 19.   Ver. 19. *The Cherubims lift up their Wings—the Wheels also were beside them.*] See Chap. i. 19, 26.

Ibid. *And every one of them stood at the Door of the East Gate of the* LORD's *House.*] This is still a further Remove of GOD's Presence from the Temple : for the East Gate was just at the Entrance into the Inner Court before the Temple. See the Note on Chap. viii. 7. and compare xliii. 4.

Ver. 20.   Ver. 20. *This is the likeness of the living Creatures that I saw under the God of Israel, &c.*] See Chap. i. 22, 23, 26.

Ibid. *And I knew that they were the Cherubims.*] Having often seen that Form, which was carved in several Places upon the Walls and Doors and Utensils of the Temple : 1 *Kings* vi. 29, 35. vii. 29, 36.

Ver. 21, 22.   Ver. 21, 22. See Chap. i. 8, 10, 12.

CHAP.

CHAP. XI.

The ARGUMENT.

God denounces his Judgments upon those Wicked
Men who remained in the City, and made a
Mock of the Judgment of the Prophets: He
promises to favour those who are gone into Cap-
tivity, and truly turn to him: Intimating like-
wise that there shall be a general Restoration of
the Nation in Aftertimes. Then the Divine
Glory leaves the City, denoting God's putting it
out of his Protection.

Ver. 1. **M**Oreover *the Spirit lift me up.*] Ver. 1.
See Chapter iii. 12, 14. viii. 3.
Ibid. *And brought me unto*
the East Gate of the LORD's
House.] Where the Divine Glo-
ry had then placed it self, Chapter x. 19.

Ibid. *Five and twenty Men.*] The same probably that came thither to worship the Sun : Chapter viii. 16.

Ibid.

Ibid. *Princes of the People*.] Members of the Great Sanhedrim. Compare Chapter viii. 11. and see the Note on *Jeremiah* xxvi. 10.

Ver. 3. *Which say, It is not near: Let us build Houses.*] They were such as put the *evil Day far from them: Amos* vi. 3. Were not willing to believe that the Judgments threatned would soon overtake them. Compare Chapter xii. 27. and so securely went on in Building new Houses, and making such like Improvements.

Ibid. *This City is the Caldron, and we are the Flesh.*] *Jeremiah* had foretold the Destruction of *Jerusalem* under the Figure of a *Seething Caldron: Jeremiah* i. 13. and *Ezekiel* himself uses the same Metaphor Chapter xxiv. 3, 4, &c. So these Infidels made use of the same Expression on purpose to deride the Menaces of the Prophets : as if they had said, If this City be a Caldron, we had rather take our Chance of being consumed in it, than leave our fine Houses and other Accommodations, and run the risque of War or Captivity. Compare Ver. 7, 8, 11.

Ver. 5. *And the Spirit of the* Lord *fell upon me, and said unto me.*] See the Note on Chap. iii. 24.

Ver. 6. *Ye have multiplied your Slain in this City.*] See Chapter xxii. 3, 4.

Ver. 7. *Your slain whom ye have laid in the midst of it, they are the Flesh, and this City is the Caldron.*] The comparing of the City to a Caldron may fitly be applied to the Slain, whom you have butchered in your Streets, and cut in Pieces in the midst of it, just as pieces of Flesh prepared for the Caldron. See Chapter xxiv. 6. and Compare *Micah* iii. 3.

Ibid.

○Ibid. *But I will bring you out of the midst of it.*]
You shall not die there, but I will reserve you for
another Punishment. See Ver. 9, 11.

Ver. 9, 10. *I will bring you out of the midst*
thereof, and deliver you into the Hands of Stran-
gers.] Ye shall be carried out of the City by the
Chaldeans, and afterwards be slain by them in the
Land of *Hamath*: See *Jerem.* xxxix. 6. 2 *Kings*
xxv. 19, 20, 21. Which is called the *entrance of*
Hamath, 1 *Kings* viii. 65. 2 *King's* xiv. 25. because it was just upon the Borders of *Judea*.

Ver. 12. *But have done after the Manners of the* Ver. 12.
Heathen.] Have defiled your selves with their Idolatries. See Chap. viii. 10, 14, 16.

Ver. 13. *Then I fell down upon my Face, and* Ver. 13.
cried with a loud Voice, &c.] The Prophet thought
this an Earnest of the common Destruction which
was coming upon all the Inhabitants of the City,
and thereupon he earnestly deprecated so severe a
Judgment. See Chap. ix. 8.

Ver. 15. *Thy Brethren, the Men of thy Kin-* Ver. 15.
dred] Those of thy Kindred and Acquaintance
who are carried away captive with thee.

Ibid. *To whom the Inhabitants of Jerusalem*
have said, Get ye far from the LORD, &c.] The
Jews who were left in their own Countrey,
thought themselves more in God's Favour, than
those who were carried away Captive: whom
they look'd upon as Out-casts, and such as had no
right either to the Priviledges of *Jews*, or the
Land of *Judea*: See the Note on *Jerem.* xxiv. 5.

Ver. 16. *Yet will I be to them a little Sanctu-* Ver. 16.
ary.] The *Jews* were under God's immediate Protection, expressed in Scripture by *dwelling under*
the

Chapter
XI.

~~~

the *Shadow of his Wings*. The Phrase alluding to the Wings of the *Cherubims*, covering the Mercy Seat, and signifying God's Presence among them, and Protection over his People. Therefore to comfort those who were under a State of Exile and Captivity, God tells them that altho' they were deprived of the Benefit of attending upon his Sanctuary, and being placed under that Protection his Presence there did import, yet he would supply that by being a constant Refuge and Defence to them in the Countries where they were scattered. Compare *Pfal.* xxxi. 20. xci. 1. *Ifa.* viii. 14.

Ver. 17.

Ver. 17. *I will even gather them from the People.*] This may be in some degree fulfilled in those that returned from Captivity, but the utmost Completion of this and the following Verses, must be expected at the general Restoration of the *Jewish* Nation. See the following Notes, and Compare Chap. xx. 4. xxviii. 25. xxxiv. 13. xxxvi. 24.

Ver. 18.

Ver. 18. *They shall take away all the detestable things thereof.*] They shall live pure from all the Pollutions of Idolatry, wherewith the Land had been formerly defiled. See Chap. xxxvii. 23.

Ver. 19.

Ver. 19. *And I will give them one Heart.*] They shall serve me *with one Consent, Zeph.* iii. 9. and not be distracted by the several Idolatrous Worships which were set up in opposition to God's true Worship, when the *Ten Tribes* separated themselves from *Judah.* Compare *Jeremiah* xxxii. 39. *Hos.* x. 2. *Pfal.* lxxxvi. 11.

Ibid. *I will put a new Spirit within them.*] These Promises chiefly relate to the general Conversion of the *Jews*: When God shall pour out upon them the *Spirit of Grace*, in order to their Conversion,

version, *Zech.* xii. 10. Compare Chap. xxxvi. 26, Chapter 27. and see the Notes upon *Jerem.* xxiv. 7. xxxi. **XI.** 33, 34. xxxii. 39. Conversion is commonly spoken of in Scripture as if it were a New Creation, because of the New Dispositions and Powers which accompany it. See *Psal.* li. 10. 2 *Cor.* v. 17. *Gal.* vi. 15. and the Note upon Chap. xviii. 31.

Ibid. *I will take the stony Heart out of their Flesh.*] Men's Insensibility as to religious Matters, is often ascribed to the hardness of their Hearts, being such as will receive no Impression. Here God promises to give them teachable Dispositions, and to take away the *Veil from their Hearts*, as St. Paul expresses it, speaking of this Subject, 2 *Cor.* iii. 16. The same Temper being indifferently expressed either by Blindness, or hardness of Heart.

Ver. 20. *They shall be my People.*] They shall Ver. 20. never Apostatize any more from me to serve Idols, but shall constantly adhere to my Worship; and I will own them as my People, those who are under my immediate Protection. Compare Chapter xiv. 11. xxxvi. 28. xxxviii. 27. *Jerem.* xxx. 22.

Ver. 21. *But as for them whose Heart goeth af-* Ver. 21. *ter the Heart of their detestable things, &c.*] The Prophet speaketh of Idols, called here their *detestable things*, as Ver. 18. the Prophet mentions the *Heart of their detestable things*, as if their Idols had an Understanding and Appetites, because their Worshippers applied to them as such, and because evil Spirits who were worshipped in and by them, were pleased with the Devotions in that manner paid to them.

Ibid.

Chapter
XI.

Ibid. *I will recompence their Way upon their own Heads.*] See Ver. 9, 10. and the Notes upon Chapter xx. 38.

Ver. 22.

Ver. 22. See Chapter i. 19, 26. x. 19.

Ver. 23.

Ver. 23. *And the Glory of the* LORD *went up from the midst of the City.*] God's Presence was before departed from the Temple, Chap. xi. 19. and now it quite left the City, to signify that he would acknowledge no longer his Relation to either, but deliver them up to be profaned by Heathens.

Ibid. *And stood upon the Mountain which is on the East side of the City.*] That is, the Mount of *Olives:* from whence it is described returning, when God shall again make the City and Temple the Seat of his Presence. See Chapter xliii. 2. *Zech.* xiv. 4.

Ver. 24.

Ver. 24. *Afterward the Spirit took me up,* &c.] See the Notes on Chapter viii. 3.

Ibid. *And brought me in Vision by the Spirit of* GOD *into Chaldea.*] Returned me back into *Chaldea,* in the same manner as it carried me away from thence, being still under the Power of a Divine Ecstasy, add the immediate Influences of God's Spirit.

Ver. 25.

Ver. 25. *Then I spake to them of the Captivity,* &c.] See the Note on Chapter viii. 2.

CHAP.

CHAP. XII.

The ARGUMENT.

Ezekiel *being commanded to remove his Houſhold*
Stuff, and to take his Suſtenance with Quaking
and Trembling, is a Type of the Captivity both
of King and People, and of the Conſternation
which their Calamities will bring upon them;
he afterwards reproves the Infidelity of thoſe who
disbelieved his Prophecies.

Ver. 2.   O N *of Man.*] See Chapter Ver. 2.
               ii. 1.

            Ibid. *Thou dwelleſt in the*
            midſt of a rebellious Houſe.]
            See Chapter ii. 3, 6, 7. The
            Prophet applies himſelf to
thoſe of the Captivity: among whom lie dwelt.
They ſaw *Jeruſalem* ſtill inhabited, and under the
Government of its own King. And as they that
were left at home inſulted over the Exiles: See
Chap. xi. 15. So theſe repin'd at their own ill
               M   Fortune,

Chapter. Fortune, and thought thofe who dwelt at *Jerufa-*
XII. *lem* in a much better Condition than themfelves.
Therefore the following Parables are defigned to
fhew, that they who are left behind to endure the
Miferies of a Siege, and the Infults of a Conque-
ror, will be in the worfe Condition of the two.

St. *Jerom* in his *Preface* to *Ezekiel*, obferves
this was the Temper of thofe Captives to whom
Ezekiel prophefied ; *Iis qui cum eo Captivi fuerant*
prophetavit, pœnitentibus quod ad Jeremiæ vatici-
nium fe ultro adverfariis tradidiſſent, & viderent
adhuc urbem Hierofolymam ſtare, quam ille caſuram
eſſe prædixerat.

Ibid. *Which have Eyes, and fee not,* &c.] Who
will not make ufe of that Senfe and Underftanding
that God hath given them. See *Ifa.* vi. 9. *Jerem.*
v. 21.

Ver. 3.　Ver. 3. *Prepare thee ſtuff for removing,* &c.]
Get all thy Goods together, and pack them up as
thofe do that move from one Houfe to another. Do
this openly and at Noon day, that they may all fee
and take Notice of it. The Prophets often prophefied by Signs, as being of greater Force and Efficacy than Words. See Chap. iv. 1.

Ver. 4.　Ver. 4. *Thou ſhalt go forth at Even in their*
Sight, as they that go forth into Captivity.] As
Men do that would go off by Stealth : To fignify
alfo that *Zedekiah* and his Retinue fhould efcape
out of the City by Night, 2 *Kings* xxv. 4.

Ver. 5.　Ver. 5. *Dig thou thro' the Wall in their Sight.*]
To fhew that the King fhall make his efcape by the
fame Means : See Ver. 12.

Ibid. and Ver. 6. *And carry out thereby. In*
their ſight thou ſhalt bear it upon thy Shoulders-----
in

Chapter
XII.

iu the Twilight.] This which the Prophet was commanded to carry out in the Twilight, was something different from the Goods he removed in the Day time, See Ver. 4, 7. and therefore muſt mean neceſſary Proviſion for his preſent Subſiſtance.

Ibid. *Thou ſhalt cover thy Face, that thou ſee not the Ground.*] As *Zedekiah* ſhall do, that he might not be diſcovered.

Ibid. *I have ſet thee for a Sign to the Houſe of Iſrael.*] See Ver. 12. and Chap. iv. 3.

Ver. 9. *Hath not the Houſe of Iſrael, the rebelli-* Ver. 9.
ous Houſe ſaid to thee, What doſt thou?] They enquire by way of Deriſion and Contempt, what theſe Signs mean. Compare Chap. ii. 5. xvii. 12. xx. 49. xxiv. 19.

Ver. 10. *This Burden concerneth the Prince in* Ver. 10.
Jeruſalem.] King *Zedekiah* : See Chap. vii. 27.

Ver. 12. *And the Prince that is among them* Ver. 12.
ſhall bear upon his Shoulder in the Twilight.] He ſhall be glad to carry what he can with him in the dusk of the Evening, and his Retinue ſhall make a private way to get out of the City, that they may not be diſcovered. See *Jerem.* xxxix. 4.

Ibid. *He ſhall cover his Face, &c.*] That no body may know or diſcover him, till he is got beyond his Enemies Camp.

Ver. 13. *My Net alſo will I ſpread upon him, &c.*] Ver. 13.
Tho' he thinks to eſcape, yet I will bring his Enemies upon him, who ſhall encompaſs him and ſtop his Flight, as when a wild Beaſt is entangled in a Net, 2 *Kings* xxv. 5, 6, 7. and compare Chapter xvii. 20. xix. 8. xxxii. 3. of this Prophecy.

Ibid. *Yet he ſhall not ſee it, tho' he ſhall die there.*] Having his Eyes put out before he came thither.

Ibid.

Chapter Ibid. *Josephus* tells us *Antiq. lib.* ii. *c.* 10. that
XII. *Zedekiah* thought this Prophecy inconsistent with
that of *Jeremiah*, Chap. xxxiv. 3. That *Zedekiah's*
Eyes should see the Eyes of the King of Babylon:
and therefore believed neither. But they both actually came to pass, as the sacred Story assures us:
The King of *Babylon* passing Sentence upon him
at *Riblah*, as one that had broke the Oath and Covenant he had made with him, and then putting
out his Eyes and carrying him to *Babylon.*

Ver. 14.   Ver. 14. *And I will scatter toward every Wind*
all that are about him to help him.] See 2 *Kings*
xxv. 4, 5.

Ibid. *And I will draw out the Sword after*
them.] See the Note upon Chap. v. 12.

Ver. 16.   Ver. 16. *But I will leave a few Men of them,---*
that they may declare their Abominations among
the Heathen.] And there justify my Proceedings
against them. See Chap. vi. 8, 9, 10.

Ver. 18.   Ver. 18. *Eat thy Bread with quaking, and drink*
thy Water with trembling and carefulness.] Shew
all the Signs of Anxiety and Consternation, whenever thou takest thy common Sustenance.

Ver. 19.   Ver. 19. *Thus saith the Lord* GOD *of the Inha-*
bitants of Jerusalem, and of the Land of Israel.]
This was designed to inform the Captives, that
they were not in a worse Condition than those that
were left behind in *Judea*. See the Note on Ver. 2.

Ibid. *They shall eat their Bread with carefulness,*
&c.] See Chap. iv. 16, 17.

Ver. 20.   Ver. 20. *And ye shall know that I am the* LORD.]
See Chap. vi. 7.

Ver. 22.   Ver. 22. *In the Land of Israel.*] See the Note on
Chap. vii. 2.

Ibid.

Ibid. *The Days are prolonged, and every Vision faileth.*] Words of the same import with those at Ver. 27. and Chap. xi. 3. Both of them the Words of Infidels who turn the Grace of God into Wantonness, and take Incouragement from his Patience and Long-suffering to despise his Threatnings, as if they would never be fulfilled. Comp. *Isa.* v. 19. *Amos* vi. 18. 2 *Pet.* iii. 3, 4.

Ver. 23. *The days are at hand.*] The same is elsewhere expressed by *the day of the* LORD *is at hand:* See *Joel* ii. 1. *Zeph.* i. 14. The time when GOD will *shew his Wrath,* and *make his Power* and Justice *known* to the World. See Ver. 25.

Ver. 25. *For there shall be no more any vain Vision,* &c.] The false Prophets who foretold Peace and Safety, shall see their Prophecies so confuted by the Events quite contrary to what they foretold, that they will never pretend any more to publish new Prophecies. Compare Chap. xiii. 23.

Ibid. *It shall be no more prolonged.*] My Threatnings shall come to pass in your own Days, and ye shall have ocular Demonstration of their Truth.

Ver. 27, 28. See Ver. 22, 23, 25.

Chapter XII.

Ver. 23.

Ver. 25.

CHAP.

CHAP. XIII.

The ARGUMENT.

The Prophet denounces God's Judgments against false Prophets who made a gain of their Profession, and encouraged Men to go on in their Sins, by giving them false Visions of Peace and Security: and at the same time disheartened the truly Pious, and discouraged them from continuing in the ways of Holiness.

Ver. 2.

Ver. 2. *AY thou unto them that Prophecy out of their own Hearts.*] The true Prophets often denounce God's Judgments against the false ones : laying to their Charge many Misdemeanors in their private Conversation, and upbraiding them for Unfaithfulness in the Office they undertook of guiding and directing Men's Consciences. See Chap. xxii. 25, 28. *Jeremiah* vi. 14. xxiii. 11, *&c.* xxviii. 14. xxix. 8, 22, 23. *Micah* iii. 5.

Ver. 4.

Ver. 4. *O Israel, thy Prophets are like the Foxes in the Desarts.*] *Deceitful Workers,* as the Apostle

..ftle ftyles fuch Perfons, 2 *Cor.* xi. 13. who craftily Chapter
infinuate falfe Doctrines into weak and unftable XIII.
Minds; and withal hungry and ravenous, and fuch
as greedily catch at any Appearance of Advantage.
Compare Chap. xxii. 25.

Ver. 5. *Ye have not gone up into the Gaps.*] Or, Ver. 5.
ftood in the Gap, or *Breach,* as it is expreffed Chap.
xxii. 30. *Pfal.* cvi. 23. Which place alludes to the
Interceffion which *Mofes* made for the *Ifraelites,*
whereby he withheld God's Hand, as it were, when
it was juft ftretched out to take Vengeance upon
the People for their heinous Sin, in making the
Golden Calf. See *Exod.* xxxii. 10, 11.

The Phrafe is taken from thofe that put a ftop·
to the Enemy when he is juft entring in at a Breach.
In like manner, it was the Office and Duty of thofe
Prophets, if they had truly been what they pretended, by their Prayers and Interceffions to put a
ftop to God's Vengeance when it was juft ready
to be poured out upon a finful People.

Ibid. *Nor made up a Fence for the Houfe of Ifrael.*] Or, *made up a Wall,* as the *Vulgar Latin*
tranflates it. Another Expreffion taken from thofe
that are befieged, and if a Breach be made in a
Wall, prefently make it up, or build up a new one
within it: to prevent the Enemy from entring,
and becoming Mafters of the City. The Word
Geder, Fence, fignifies another fort of Fortification:
See *Pfal.* lxii. 3. l·x ix. 40.

Ibid. *To ftand in the Battle in the day of the*
LORD.] When God fhall come like a Leader or
General, at the Head of his Army, *i. e.* his Judg-
ments, to execute Vengeance upon his Enemies..
Compare *Jer.* xxv. 30. *Joel* ii. 11.

Ver.

Chapter
XIII.

Ver. 6. *They have seen Vanity and lying Divinations.*] Concerning Peace and Prosperity: See Ver. 10. and Chap. xii. 23, 24.

Ver. 6.

Ibid. *And they have made others to hope that they would confirm the Word.*] Or, *that the Word should be confirmed:* the *Transitive* Verb being often taken in an Impersonal Sense: See the Note on *Isa.* xliv. 18. their speaking with so much Assurance made others confidently expect that the Event would answer their Predictions: and sometimes even impos'd upon the true Prophets for a time; as *Hananiah* did upon *Jeremiah*: See *Jer.* xxviii. 6.

Ver. 9.

Ver. 9. *They shall not be in the Assembly of my People.*] They shall not be Members of the Church here, nor partake of the Communion of Saints in Heaven. The *Hebrew* Word *Sôd,* signifies a secret Assembly or Privy Council: Such as are acquainted with the most inward Thoughts and secret Intents of a Prince: and from thence it is applied to God's chosen People, those that are acquainted with the *whole Counsel of God,* and whom he instructs by the secret Directions of his Holy Spirit. See *Psal.* xxv. 14. *Jerem.* xxiii. 18. So the Prophet tells these Men that pretended to know so much of the Secrets of the Almighty, that they should never be of the Number of those Favourites of Heaven, to whom God will reveal himself and his Counsels.

Ibid. *Neither shall they be written in the Writing of the House of Israel.*] The Sense is much the same with that of the foregoing Sentence: the Expressions being an Allusion to the Registers that use to be kept of the Members of any City or Corporation,

poration, the Privileges of which Society none can
pretend to, but they whofe Names are entred into
fuch Regifters. Comp. *Ezra.* ii. 62. *Pfal.* lxix. 28.
Exod. xxxii. 32. *Luke* x. 20. *Phil.* iv. 2. *Heb.* xii.
23. It may be thefe Falfe Prophets foretold a fpee-
dy return to the Exiles ; whereupon God tells them
that they fhall never live to fee it, nor fhall their
Names be entred into the Regifter of thofe that
Return Home. See *Nehem.* vii. 5.

Ibid. *Neither fhall they enter into the Land of
Ifrael.*] They fhall never fee their own Country
again, nor fhall they have a fhare among the *true
Ifraelites.* See the Note on Chap. xx. 38.

Ver. 10. *They have feduced my People, faying,*
Peace, and there were no Peace.] They have deceived my People by telling them that none of
thofe Judgments fhould overtake them which *Jeremy* and the other true Prophets threatened
them with, and they have fpoke Peace to Men's
Confciences upon falfe Grounds and Principles:
See *Jeremiah* iv. 10. vi. 14. xxiii. 14, 17.

Ibid. *And one built a Wall, and lo others daubed it with untempered Mortar.*] Inftead of provi-
ding fuch a Fence and Bulwark as might fecure
the People againft the Judgments that threaten
them, See Ver. 5. They have made a flight Wall
without any Mortar, or Cement to bind and
ftrengthen it: that is, they have applied flight
and palliating Remedies to publick Calamities,
which will never give true Peace to Mens Confciences, nor ftand them in any ftead when God vifits for their Iniquities. Juft as if an unfkilful
Builder fhould undertake to fet up a Wall, and his

N   Fellow-

Fellow-Workmen ſhould daub it with untempered Mortar. See Verſes 11, 12, 16.

Ver. 11. Ver. 11. *There ſhall be an overflowing Shower, and ye, O great Hail-ſtones ſhall fall, &c.*] God's Judgments are often compared to Storms and Tempeſts, the Artillery of Heaven : See Chapter xxxviii. 22. *Job* xxvii. 20. *Pſal.* xi. 6. xviii. 13, 14. Eſpecially when he executes his Judgments by a Victorious Army : See *Iſa.* xxviii. 2. xxix. 6. *Jeremiah* iv. 13. Compare *Ecclus.* xlix. 9.

Ver. 13. Ver. 13. *I will rent it with a ſtormy Wind in my Fury, &c.*] Under theſe Metaphors is probably foretold the Deſtruction of *Jeruſalem* by the *Chaldean* Army. Thus the *Chaldee Paraphraſe* expounds it : *I will bring a mighty King with the Force of a Whirlwind, and deſtroying People as it were an overflowing Storm, and powerful Princes like great Hailſtones.*

Ver. 14. Ver. 14. *So will I break down the Wall, and bring it down to the Ground, &c.*] The *Chaldee* explains this Verſe to the ſame Senſe : *I will deſtroy the City wherein ye have uttered theſe falſe Prophecies :* Which Expoſition is confirmed by the following Words, *And ye ſhall be conſumed in the midſt thereof,* that is, you ſhall be deſtroyed in the ſame common Calamity.

Ibid. *And ye ſhall know that I am the* LORD.] See Chapter vi. 7.

Ver. 15. Ver. 15. *The Wall is no more, nor they that daubed it.*] The *Chaldee* Expounds it, *The City is no more, nor the Falſe Prophets.*

Ver. 16. Ver. 16. *See Viſions of Peace, and there is no Peace.*] See *Jeremiah* vi. 10. viii. 11.

Ver.

Ver. 17. *Set thy Face against the Daughters of* Chapter *thy People, that prophesy.*] Direct thy Discourse XIII. against those She-pretenders to Prophecy : Comp. Chap. xx. 46. xxi. 2. God did sometimes bestow Ver. 17. the Gift of Prophecy upon Women : See *Exod.* xv. 20. *Judg* iv. 4, 2 *Kings* xxii. 14. This encouraged others of that Sex to pretend to the same Gift. Compare *Revel.* ii. 20.

Ver. 18. *Wo to the Women that sow Pillows to* Ver. 18. *all Armholes,* &c.] As the Prophet compares the deceitful Practices of the false Prophets to the daubing of a Wall, so he represents the Artifices of these Female Seducers by sowing Pillows under their Hearers Elbows, that they might rest securely in their evil Ways : and by covering their Faces with Veils, or Kerchiefs, Ornaments proper to Women, thereby to keep them in Blindness and Ignorance.

Ibid. *To the Head of every Stature.*] *Of every Age,* both great and small : So the *Greek* Word Ηλικία, used by the LXX here, signifies Age as well as Stature. See Dr. *Hammond* upon *Matth.* vi. 27.

Ibid. *To hunt Souls.*] That they may drive them into those Nets and Snares that they have laid for them, and make them their Prey. Comp. Chap. xxv. 25. *Micah* ii. 7. 2 *Pet* ii. 14.

Ibid. *Will ye hunt the Souls of my People, and will ye save the Souls alive that come to you?*] Or, *Will ye promise life unto those that come to you?* See Verses 19, 22. that is, will ye make a Prey of Men's Souls by deluding them with fair Hopes and Promises?

Ver. 19. *And will ye pollute me among my Peo-* Ver. 19. *ple.*] Will ye profane my Name by making use

Chapter
XIII.

of it to give Credit to your own Dreams and Lies?
See Ver. 7.

Ibid. *For handfulls of Barley, and for pieces of Bread.*] For the meaneſt reward: See *Prov.* xxviii. 21. So greedy are they of making gain to themſelves. Compare Chap. xxii. 25. *Micah* iii. 5.

Ibid. *To ſlay the Souls that ſhould not die,* &c.] Thus they threatned Death to thoſe that yielded themſelves to the *Chaldeans* in *Jechoniah*'s Captivity: and yet God preſerved them alive. See *Jerem.* xxix. 5, 6. and they have encouraged thoſe that remain at *Jeruſalem* with Promiſes of Peace and Safety, who ſhall all be deſtroyed. See Chap. v. 12. or the Words may be meant in general of diſcouraging the Godly and confirming the Wicked in their evil Ways. See Ver. 22. and compare *Jerem.* xxiii. 14, 17.

To *ſlay* and to *make alive*, ſignify here to promiſe Men Life, or threaten them with Death: See Ver. 22. So the Prophet ſaith he *came to deſtroy the City,* Chap. xliii. 3. that is, to pronounce the Sentence of Deſtruction upon it. And the Prieſt is ſaid to make the Leper unclean, *Levit.* xiii. 3. that is, to *pronounce him unclean,* as our Tranſlation rightly expreſſes the Senſe.

Ver. 20.

Ver. 20. *Wherewith ye hunt the Souls to make them fly.*] To make them run into thoſe Nets and Snares that you have laid for them: See Ver. 18. The Metaphor is continued from the manner of hunting and purſuing living Creatures, by that means to drive them into the Toils prepared for them.

Ibid.

Ibid. *I will tear them from your Arms.*] I will Chapter make your Cheats and Impostures appear so evi- XIII. dently, that no body shall be in danger of being seduced by you any more. See Ver. 23.

Ver. 22. *Because with Lies ye have made the* Ver. 22. *Heart of the Righteous sad,* &c.] As you have deluded the Wicked with vain Hopes (See Ver. 10.) so you have disheartned the Righteous with groundless Fears: Ver. 19. and compare Chapter xxii. 25.

C H A P.

Chapter
XIV.
〰️

CHAP. XIV.

The ARGUMENT.

The Prophet denounces God's Judgments against those Hypocrites who pretended to be his Worshippers, and at the same time secretly practiced Idolatry. He afterward sets forth God's Mercy toward the Jews in sparing a few of that sinful Nation, and those no better than the rest that were destroyed, when he might in Justice have involved all of them in one common Destruction.

Ver. 1.

Ver. 3.

Ver. 1. T HEN *came certain of the Elders of Israel,&c.*] See Chap. viii. 1.

Ver. 3. *These Men have set up their Idols in their heart, and put the Stumbling-block of their Iniquity before their Face.*] They are not only Idolaters in their Heart, but they have actually set up Idols and worshipped them : and thereby have fallen into that great Sin of Deserting me and my Worship. See Chap. vii. 19.

Ibid. *Should I be enquired of at all by them?*] Tho' they have the Impudence to come to ask
Counsel

Counfel of God, (See Chap. vii. 26.) they fhall not Chapter
receive a favourable Anfwer, but fuch a one as XIV.
their Hypocrify deferves. See the following Verfe,
and compare Chap. xxxvi. 37.

Ver. 5. *That I may take the Houfe of Ifrael in* Ver. 5.
their own Heart.] That I may deal with them
according to their Deferts, and thereby convince
them that I am a fearcher of Hearts, and know
the inward and fecret Wickednefs of their
Thoughts.

Ver. 6. *From all your Abominations.*] Your Ido- Ver. 6.
latries : See Chap. viii. 10. xvi. 2.

Ver. 7. *Or of the Stranger that fojourneth in If-* Ver. 7.
rael.] The Stranger within thy Gates, as it is expreffed in the Fourth Commandment. Thefe,
tho' they were not all of them circumcifed, yet devoted themfelves to the Service of the one True
God, for which Reafon they are ftyled the *Wor-*
fhippers of God, Act. xvi. 14. xviii. 7.

Ibid. *Who feparates himfelf from me.*] Who
turns Apoftate from me and my Service ; for Men
cannot ferve God and Idols : he having declared
himfelf a *Jealous God,* that will not admit any Rival in his Worfhip. See *Jofh.* xxiv. 19.

Ibid. *I the* LORD *will anfwer him by my felf.*]
I will punifh him immediately by my own Hand :
See the following Verfe.

Ver. 8. *And I will fet my Face againft that Man.*] Ver. 8.
I will make him a Mark of mine Indignation. See
Chap. xv. 7. *Jerem.* xliv. 11.

Ibid. *And will make him a Sign and a Proverb.*]
I will make him a fignal and remarkable Inftance
of my Vengeance. Comp. *Numb.* xxvi. 10. *Deut.*
xxviii. 38.

Ibid.

Chapter
XIV.   Ibid. *And will cut him off from the midst of my*
People.] By a sudden Death attended with Extraordinary Circumstances : See *Levit.* xx. 6, 17, 18.

Ver. 9.   Ver. 9. *And if a Prophet be deceived.*] This is to be understood of the False Prophets, whose Practices are reproved throughout the whole foregoing Chapter.

Ibid. *I the* LORD *have deceived that Prophet.*] I have suffered him to be deceived.: See the Note on *Isa.* lxiii. 17. I have given him up to *strong Delusions*, as a just Judgment upon him for going after Idols, and setting up false Pretences to Inspiration. See Chap. xiii. 2, 7, 23. *Jerem.* iv. 10. 1 *Kings* xxii. 23. and compare 2 *Thess.* ii. 11, 12. Or the Words may be explained to this Sense : I will disappoint the Hopes and Expectations of those Prophets who seduce my People by speaking *Peace* to them, Chap. xiii. 10. For I will bring upon them those Evils which they with great Assurance have declared should never come to pass. To this purpose it follows, *I will stretch out my Hand upon him*, &c. *i. e.* I will send such a Judgment upon him, as I inflicted upon *Hananiah* the False Prophet, *Jerem.* xxviii. 16, 17.

Ver. 10.   Ver. 10. *The punishment of the Prophet shall be even as the punishment of him that seeketh to him.*] Because both Parties are equally guilty of going astray from me, and seeking after Idols, and other unlawful Means of Divination. See Ver. 11. and compare 2 *Kings* i. 3, 4.

Ver. 11.   Ver. 11. *That the House of Israel may go no more astray from me.*] The Judgments I inflict upon the False Prophets and those that consult them, shall be an Instruction to my People to keep close to me
and

and my Worship, and not hanker after the Idola- Chapter
trous Practices of the Neighbouring Nations. XIV.

Ibid. *But that they may be my People,* &c.] See
the Note on Chap. xi. 20.

Ver. 13. *When the Land trespasseth grievously,* Ver. 13.
&c.] Or, *when a Land*----The design of this and
the following Verses is to shew, that when the Inhabitants of a Land have filled up the Measure of
their Iniquities, and God ariseth to execute Judgment upon them, the few Righteous that are left
among them shall not be able by their Prayers and
Intercessions to deliver the Nation from the Judgments decreed against it. *They shall but deliver
their own Souls:* as we see in the Case of *Sodom,*
where there was none Righteous but *Lot* and his
Family: those just Persons saved themselves, but
no Intercession could avail to save the City. See
the following Verse.

Ibid. *And break the Staff of the Bread thereof.*]
See Chap. iv. 16.

Ver. 14. *Tho' these three Men, Noah, Daniel,* Ver. 14.
and Job were in it.] All of them Persons eminent
for their Piety: *Noah* and his Family were saved
out of the Universal Deluge, and obtained a Promise from God that he would never destroy the
World so again, *Gen.* viii. 21. *Daniel* interceded
with God for the whole Nation of the *Jews,* and
obtained a Promise of their Restoration, *Dan.* ix.
Job was appointed by God to make Intercession
for his Three Friends, *Job* xlii. 8. But when God's
irreversible Decree is gone out against a Nation,
even the Prayers of such Men will be ineffectual
toward their Deliverance. Compare *Jer.* xv. 1.

We

We may obferve how early the Fame of *Dani-el*'s Piety was fpread over *Chaldea*, who was at this time not above Thirty Years of Age: it being but Thirteen Years ago fince he was carried Captive to *Babylon* when he was very young. See *Dan.* i. 1---4, &c.

Ver. 15.

Ver. 15. *If I caufe noifome Beafts to pafs thro' the Land.*] See Chap. v. 17.

Ver. 17.

Ver. 17. *Or if I bring a Sword upon the Land.*] If I deliver it into the Hands of a cruel and bloody Enemy. See Chap. v. 12. vii. 15. xxi. 9, 16. The Conqueror's Sword is often called the *Sword of the* LORD, in the Prophets; becaufe they are the Executioners of God's Judgments. See *Ifa.* x. 15. *Jer.* xxv. 9. xlvii. 6.

Ibid. *And fay, Sword go through the Land.*] So God is faid *to call for a Sword upon Gog*: Chap. xxxviii. 21.

Ibid. *So that I cut off Man and Beaft from it.*] The Men are deftroyed by the Sword, and the Cattle are drove away by the Enemy; Or elfe confumed by Peftilence, arifing from the Air's being corrupted thro' the Stench of dead Bodies. Compare xxv. 13. xxix. 8. xxxii. 13. *Hof.* iv. 3. *Zeph.* i. 3.

Ver. 19.

Ver. 19. *Or if I fend a Peftilence upon that Land.*] See Chap. v. 12.

Ibid. *And pour out my Fury upon it in Blood.*] With great Deftruction of Men's Lives, as the *Chaldee* Paraphrafe explains it. Compare Chap. xxxviii. 22.

Ver. 21.

Ver. 21. *How much more* [fhould there be an utter Deftruction] *when I fend my four fore Judgments upon Jerufalem,* &c.] See Chap. v. 12. vi. 12. xii. 16. *Jerem.* xv. 2. The Particles *Aph Ki,*

are

are very properly tranflated here, *How much more*: Chapter in which Senfe they are plainly taken, 2 *Sam.* iv. 11. XIV. *Prov.* xi. 31. xxi. 15.

Ibid. *The noifome Beaft.*] See Chap. v. 17. xxxiii. 27.

Ver. 22. *Yet behold therein fhall be left a Rem-* Ver. 22. *nant that fhall be brought forth.*] Notwithftanding thefe Four fore Judgments, fome fhall efcape, and be brought into *Chaldea* to be your Companions in Captivity. Compare Chap. vi. 8. *Jerem.* lii. 29, 30.

Ibid. *Both Sons and Daughters.*] See Ver. 16, 18, and 20. of this Chapter.

Ibid. *And ye fhall fee their Ways and their Do-ings.*] Their Afflictions fhall bring them to a due Senfe of their former Iniquities, and they fhall humbly confefs their own Sins, and the Sins of thofe who were confumed in the Deftruction of the City : whereby it will appear that I have not punifh-ed them beyond what their Sins have deferved. See Chap. vi. 9. xx. 43. xxxvi. 31.

Ibid. *And ye fhall be comforted concerning the Evil that I have brought upon Jerufalem.*] This will compofe your Minds and make you give Glory to God, and acknowledge his Judgments to be Righteous, tho' they touch you very nearly in the Deftruction of your Friends and Countrey.

Ver. 23. *And ye fhall know that I have not done* Ver. 23. *without Caufe, &c.*] See the Note on Chap. vi. 10.

O 2 CHAP.

CHAP. XV.

The ARGUMENT.

Under the Parable of a Vine, which when it is
Barren, is Unfit for any Use, is shewed the utter
Rejection of Jerusalem.

Ver. 2. *HAT is the Vine-tree more*
than any other Tree, or than
a Branch which is among the
Trees of the Forest? The
latter part of the Verse may
be better Translated thus, *If*
it be as a Branch which is among the Trees of the
Forest; i. e. if it prove unfruitful : See Dr. *Lightfoot*
upon *Joh.* xv. 6. The Jewish Church is often
compared to a Vine in the Sacred Writers. See *Isa.*
v. 1. *Psal.* lxxx. 8, &c.

Ver. 3.   Ver. 3. *Shall Wood be taken thereof to do any*
Work, &c.] The Wood of a Vine is of no use for
Building, or making any Utensil. The Works of
that Kind which *Pliny* takes notice of, *Nat. Hist.*
l. xiv. *c.* 1. are rather to be lookt upon as Rarities,
than as things of common Use.

Ver.

Ver. 4. *Behold it is caſt into the Fire for Fuel.*] Chapter
The only Uſe that Dead Vine-Branches can be put XV.
to: See *Joh.* xv. 6.

Ibid. *The Fire devoureth both the Ends of it, and* Ver. 4.
the Midſt of it is burnt.] A fit Repreſentation of
the preſent State of *Judea,* when both its Extremi-
ties were conſumed by the Ravages of a Foreign
Enemy, and the midſt of it, where the Capital City ſtood, is ready to be deſtroyed: Juſt as the Fire
ſtill ſpreads toward the Middle Part of a Stick,
when once both Ends are lighted.

Ver. 7. *And they ſhall go out from* one *Fire, and* Ver. 7.
another *Fire ſhall devour them.*] Flying from one
Evil, another ſhall overtake them. Fire ſometimes ſignifies any Judgment or Calamity inflicted
by God. See *Amos* i. 4, *&c.* and the Note upon
Jerem. vii. 20.

CHAP.

CHAP. XVI.

The ARGUMENT.

*God sets forth his Free Love toward the Church
and Nation of the Jews, represented here by Jerusalem, under the Emblem of a Person that
should take up an exposed Infant, breed her up,
and afterward Marry her. He then upbraids
their monstrous Ingratitude in departing from his
Worship, and being polluted with Heathenish Idolatries: which the Prophet illustrates by the
Resemblance of a Lewd Woman that proves False
to a Kind and Indulgent Husband. For which
God threatens to deal with her as abused Husbands use to deal with Wives convicted of Adultery. Notwithstanding all these Provocations,
he promises in the End to shew them Mercy. The
Metaphor of describing Idolatry as Spiritual A-
dultery, often made use of in the Prophets, is
here and in the xxiii. Chapter pursued with
great Force, and in a lively way of Representation: Both Chapters being a Remarkable Instance*

ftance of that Vehemence of Expreffion, which Chapter
the Rhetoricians call by the Name of Δεινόσις. **XVI.**

Ver. 2. *Aufe Jerufalem to know her A-* Ver. 2.
bominations.] This might pro-
bably be done by way of Letter, as *Jeremiah* fignified the
Will of God to the Captives
at *Babylon, Jerem.* xxix. 1. God particularly upbraids *Jerufalem* for her Iniquities, becaufe it was
the Place he had chofen for his peculiar Refidence,
and yet the Inhabitants had defiled that very Place,
nay, and the Temple it felf with Idolatry: the Sin
particularly denoted by the Word *Abomination.*
See Chap. viii. 10. xiv. 6.

Ver. 3. *Thy Birth and thy Nativity is of the* Ver. 3.
Land of Canaan.] As your Fathers fojourned in
the Land of *Canaan,* before they came to have
any Right or Property in it, fo you their Pofterity
have all along refembled the Manners of *Canaan,*
more than thofe of *Abraham, Ifaac,* and *Jacob*
your Anceftors.

Ibid. *Thy Father was an Hittite, and thy Mo-*
ther an Amorite.] Thofe are faid to be our Pa-
rents in the Scripture Dialect, whofe Manners we
refemble. See Ver. 45. of this Chapter: *Joh.* viii.
44. *Mat.* iii. 7. There is an Expreffion of the fame
import in the *Hiftory of Sufannah,* Ver. 56. that
feems to be copied from this Text, *O thou Seed of*
Canaan, and not of Juda, Beauty hath deceived
thee, and Luft hath perverted thy Heart.

Ver. 4, 5. *In the Day when thou waft born, &c.*] Ver. 4, 5.
The Prophet defcribes the forlorn Condition of the
Ifraelites in *Egypt* under the Similitude of a New-
born

Chapter
XVI. born Infant expofed in its Native Filthinefs, without any Friend to pity his Condition, or take the
leaft Care of it.

Ver. 6. Ver. 6. *I faid unto thee when thou waft in thy Blood, Live.*] Whilft as yet no Body took fo much care of thee as to wafh thee from thy Native Filthinefs, Ver. 4. I took pity on thee ; as a Traveller that paffes by, and fees an Infant lie expofed ; and I provided all Things neceffary for thy Support.

Ver. 7. Ver. 7. *I have caufed thee to Multiply, &c.*] The Prophet defcribes the Peoples increafing in *Egypt* under the Metaphor of a Child's growing to Woman's Eftate. Comp. *Exod.* i. 7.

Ver. 8. Ver. 8. *Behold thy Time was the Time of Love, &c.*] I thought it now a proper Time to betroth thee to my felf: The *Jews* Deliverance out of *Egypt* is elfewhere defcribed as the Time of God's Efpoufing them to himfelf: See *Jerem.* ii. 2, &c. *Hof.* ii. 15, 19. and his entring into Covenant with them, is commonly reprefented by a Marriage Contract: See *Ifa.* liv. 5. *Jerem.* iii. 1---14. and Bifhop *Patrick's Preface to his Commentary on the Canticles.*

Ibid. *I fpread my Skirt over thee.*] I took thee under my Protection, as a Husband doth the Wife. See *Ruth* iii. 9.

Ibid. *And covered thy Nakednefs.*] Inriched thee with the Goods and Poffeffions of the *Egyptians* and *Canaanites :* See Ver. 10, 11, &c.

Ver. 9. Ver. 9. *Then I wafhed thee with Water,----and anointed thee with Oil.*] I added every Thing that could contribute to thy Beauty and Ornament. The Anointing with Oil was reckoned a neceffary Ingredient in a Feftival Drefs. See *Ruth* iii. 3. *Ifa.* lxi. 3. *Mat.* vi. 17. Ver.

Ver. 10. *I shod thee with Badgers Skins, &c.*] Chapter Or, *with Sandals of a Purple Colour,* as *Bochart* XVI. expounds the Word *Tahash.* This and the following Ver. 10. Verses allude to those Parts of Womens Attire, which serve not only for Use, but for Ornament too; and import that God did not only provide the Jews with Necessaries, but likewise with Superfluities.

Ibid. *I girded thee with fine Linnen.*] This Manufacture *Egypt* was famous for; See Chapter xxvii. 7. it was one of the principal Ornaments of Women; See *Isa.* iii. 16. as well as of Great Men.

Ver. 11. *I put Bracelets upon thy Hands, and a* Ver. 11. *Chain about thy Neck.*] These were Ornaments that none but Persons of better Quality used to wear. See *Gen.* xxiv. 47. *Prov.* i. 9.

Ver. 12. *And I put a Jewel on thy Forehead.*] Ver. 12. The same which is called a *Nose-Jewel, Isa.* iii. 21. where the Words might as well be translated, *a Jewel for the Face,* or *Forehead.* Compare likewise *Gen.* xxiv. 47.

Ibid. *And a beautiful Crown upon thy Head.*] Crowns or Garlands were used in times of Publick Rejoicing; from whence is derived that Expression of St. *Paul, A Crown of Rejoicing,* 1 *Thes.* ii. 19. Compare *Isa.* xxxv. 10. Virgins were sometimes adorned with Crowns. See *Baruch* vi. 9. and they were commonly put upon the Heads of Persons newly Married. See *Cantic.* iii. 11.

Ver. 13. *Thou didst eat fine Flower, Honey, and* Ver. 13. *Oil.*] Thy Country afforded all manner of Plenty and Delicacies. Compare *Deut.* xxxii. 13, 14.

Ibid. *And didst prosper into a Kingdom.*] Thou wast advanced to be the Seat of a Kingdom, and the

P

the *City of the Great King* of Heaven and Earth, *Pſal.* xlviii. 2.

Ver. 14.

Ver. 14. *And thy Renown went forth among the Heathen for thy Beauty.*] For the Magnificence of the Temple, called the Beauty of Holineſs, and honoured with God's eſpecial Preſence. Compare *Lam.* ii. 15. *Pſal.* xlviii. 2.

Ver. 15.

Ver. 15. *But thou didſt truſt in thy own Beauty, and playedſt the Harlot, becauſe of thy Renown.*] Women that are proud of their Beauty, are eaſily tempted to Lewdneſs, if they have not a ſtrict Guard upon themſelves: So you abuſed thoſe Honours and Advantages which I had beſtowed upon you, and made them an Occaſion of forſaking me your Benefactor, and ſerving Idols. You preſumed upon that very Favour which I had ſhewed to *Jeruſalem* in chooſing it for the Place of my Reſidence: as if that would ſecure you from my Vengeance, let your Idolatries and other Wickedneſs be never ſo Great. See *Jerem.* vii. 4. *Micah* iii. 11.

Ibid. *And playedſt the Harlot.*] Idolatry is commonly deſcribed by the Metaphor of Spiritual Adultery, as hath been already obſerved. See the Note on Ver. 8. and compare Chapter xxiii. 3, 8, 11. *Iſa.* lvii. 8. *Jerem.* ii. 20. iii. 2, 6, 20.

Ver. 16.

Ver. 16. *And of thy Garments thou didſt take, and deckedſt thy High Places, &c.*] This was a great Aggravation of their Ingratitude, that they applied thoſe very Bleſſings which God had given them, to the Worſhip of Idols. Compare *Hoſ.* ii. 8.

Ibid. *And deckedſt thy High-Places with divers Colours.*] Or, *Madeſt High-Places,* or, *Images of divers Colours:* as the LXX explain the Senſe.

Thou

Thou madeſt little Shrines, Chappels or Altars for Chapter
Idols, and deckedſt them with Hangings of divers XVI.
Colours: Ver. 18. See 2 *Kings* xxiii. 7. The Word
Bamah is ſometimes uſed for an Altar, becauſe Al-
tars were commonly ſet upon Eminent Places; See
Ver. 24, 25. In that Senſe the *Chaldee Paraphraſe*
underſtands it, *Jerem.* xlviii. 35. and ſo it may be
beſt underſtood, Chap. xx. 29. of this Prophecy.

Ibid. *The like Things ſhall not come, neither ſhall
it be ſo.*] I will utterly deſtroy thoſe Idolatries, and
thoſe that commit them.

Ver. 17. *Thou haſt alſo taken thy fair Jewels of* Ver. 17.
*my Gold, and my Silver,--and madeſt to thy ſelf Ima-
ges of Men.*] The Wealth I had beſtowed upon
thee thou haſt laid out in doing Honour to Idols:
See Chapter vii. 19. *Hoſ.* ii. 8, 13. and particularly
in ſetting up Images to deified Heroes; See Chap.
xxiii. 14, 15.

Ver. 18, 19. *And thou haſt ſet mine Oil and* Ver. 18,19
*mine Incenſe before them, my Meat alſo which I
gave thee, fine Flour and Oil and Honey,* &c.]
Thou offeredſt theſe my Creatures as a Meat-offering unto Idols. The Meat-offering is called an
Offering *of a ſweet Savour,* becauſe of the Frank-
incenſe that was put upon it: See *Levit.* ii. 2. The
Oblation here mentioned, differs from thoſe offered to God in one Particular, *viz.* That Honey was
mixt with it, which God had expreſly forbidden
to be uſed in his Service, *Levit.* ii. 11.

Ver. 20. *Moreover thou haſt taken thy Sons and* Ver. 20.
*thy Daughters----and theſe thou haſt ſacrificed unto
them to be devoured.*] Theſe inhuman Sacrifices
were offered to the Idol *Moloch,* in the Valley of
Hin-

Chapter. *Hinnom :* See Ver. 36. xx. 26, 31. xxiii. 37. *Jer.*
XVI. vii. 31.

Ibid. *Whom thou haft born to me.*] Being Married to me by a Spiritual Contract, Ver. 8. Comp. Chap. xxiii. 4. The Children whom I bleffed thee with are mine, being entred into the fame Covenant with their Parent, and devoted to my Service : See *Deut.* xxix. 11, 12.

Ver. 21. Ver. 21. *Thou haft flain my Children to caufe them to pafs thro' the Fire,* &c.] See the Note on *Jerem.* xxxii. 35. By Children are meant here the Firft-born, who were fet apart to be God's Property in a peculiar manner, *Exod.* xiii. 2. and yet even thefe they fometimes facrificed to their Idols : See *Micah* vi. 7.

Ibid. *To caufe them to pafs thro' the Fire.*] The Verb *Henebir,* tranflated *to caufe them to pafs thro' the Fire,* fignifies alfo to dedicate, and denotes the confecrating the Firft-born unto God, *Exod.* xiii. 12. So the Words imply, that the *Jews* inftead of dedicating their Firft-born to God, as the Law required, offered them up a Sacrifice to the Devil that was worfhipped in their Idols.

Ver. 22. Ver. 22. *Thou haft not remembred the Days of thy Youth,* &c.] That miferable Condition from which I refcued thee, when I firft took Notice of thee, and fet thee apart for my own People : See Ver. 3, &c. and compare Ver. 43, 60.

Ver. 24. Ver. 24. *Thou haft alfo built to thee an eminent place in every Street.*] *Manaffeh* filled *Jerufalem* with Idols. See 2 *Chron.* xxxiii. 4, 5, 15. many of which were worfhipped upon high or eminent Places. Compare Ver. 16, 31. and 2 *Kings* xxiii.

5, 12,

5, 12, 13.] The LXX render the *Hebrew* Word Chapter
Gab, a *Brothel-house*: and 'tis certain, that the XVI.
Worſhip of ſome of the Heathen Idols conſiſted in
committing all manner of Uncleanneſs. See 2 *Kings*
xxiii. 7. and the Note upon Ver. 26.

Ver. 25. *Thou haſt alſo built thy high place at* Ver. 25.
the Head of every way, &c.] Theſe and the following Expreſſions allude to the Practices of common Harlots, who uſe to frequent the moſt publick
Places, to allure Paſſengers to them: See *Gen.*
xxxviii. 21. *Prov.* ix. 14, 15. Idolatry being in
this Chapter and elſewhere compared to the rage
of Luſt. See *Iſa.* lvii. 5. *Jerem.* ii. 23, 24. iii. 2.

Ver. 26. *Thou haſt alſo committed Fornication* Ver. 26.
with the Egyptians thy Neighbours.] While the
Iſraelites ſojourned in *Egypt*, they learned to practice their Idolatries. See Chap. xx. 7, 8. *Levit.*
xx. 3. *Deut.* xxix. 16, 17. *Joſh.* xxiv. 14 From *Jo-*
ſiah's time the *Jews* were in a ſtrict Confederacy
with the *Egyptians*, and to ingratiate themſelves
with them, practiſed their Idolatries. Compare
Chap. xxiii. 19, 20, 21, 40, 41. And the Worſhip of
Tamuz, the Idolatry they are upbraided with, Chap.
viii. 14. was derived from the ſame Country.

Ibid. *Great of Fleſh, and haſt increaſed thy*
Whoredoms.] Compare Chap. xxiii. 20. The Expreſſions may allude to the Whoredoms which
were committed in the Worſhip of ſome of their
Idols. See Chap. x iii 9. *Numb.* xxxi. 16. *Hoſ.*
iv. 4. *Baruch* vi. 43.

Ver. 27. *I have ſtretched out my Hand over thee*, Ver. 27.
and have diminiſhed thine ordinary Food.] I have
abridged thee of many Neceſſaries and Conveni-
ences,

Chapter ences, by giving thy Country into the Hand of
XVI. thine Enemies, as it follows.

Ibid. *And delivered thee into the Will of them
that hate thee, the Daughters of the Philistines.*]
As a Punishment of the Idolatries which King
Ahaz introduced among you: See Ver. 57. and
2 *Chron.* xxviii. 18, 19. The Daughters of the
Philistines are put here for the *Philistines*, as the
Daughters of *Samaria, Sodom* and the *Syrians*, stand
for the People of those Places, Ver. 46, 47, 57. to
carry on the Allegory and Comparison between
them and *Jerusalem*, being all of them described as
so many Lewd Women prostituting themselves
to Idols. See Ver. 41. By the same Metaphor
Samaria and *Sodom* are called Sisters to *Jerusalem*,
Ver. 46.

Ibid. *Which are ashamed of thy lewd Way.*]
Those have not forsaken the Religion of their Countrey as you *Jews* have done, nor have been so fond
of Foreign Idolatries: Compare Chap. v. 7. and
Jerem. ii. 11. The *Chaldee* Paraphrase explains
the Words to this Sense, *If I had sent my Prophets
to them, they would have been ashamed, but thou
art not converted.* See Ver. 47, 48.

Ver. 28. Ver. 28. *Thou hast played the Whore also with
the Assyrians.*] The *Jews* courted the Alliance of
their two potent Neighbours, the *Egyptians* and
Assyrians, as it served their present turn; and to
ingratiate themselves with them served their Idols:
See *Jer.* ii. 18, 36. This is particularly recorded of
Ahaz: See 2 *Kings* xvi. 10. 2 *Chron.* xxviii. 23.

Ver. 29. Ver. 29. *Moreover thou hast multiplied thy Fornication in the Land of Canaan unto Chaldea.*] Or,
with

with the Land of Canaan, as *Noldius* tranflates the Chapter
Particle *El*, in his *Concordance*, p. 59. The Senfe XVI.
is, thou haft defiled thy felf with all the Idolatries
of the Heathen, beginning with thofe which were
practiced by the former Inhabitants of *Canaan*, and
by degrees learning new Species of Idolatry derived
from diftant Countries, fuch as *Chaldea* was reckoned. See *Jerem.* v. 15. Compare this Verfe
with Chap. xviii. 16, 17. 2 *Kings* xvii. 16, 17.
xxi. 3, &c. xxiii. 5, &c.

Ver. 30. *How weak is thine Heart.*] Not only
unftable as to Good Refolutions, but even Reftlefs
and Unfettled in Evil Practices; ftill hankering after fome New kind of Idolatry? and refolved to
indulge a Wandring Appetite; See Ver. 28, 29.

Ver. 31. *In that thou buildeft thine eminent* Ver. 31.
Place.] See Ver. 16, 24.

Ibid. *And haft not been as an Harlot, in that
thou fcorneft Hire.*] Or, *To proftitute thy felf for
Hire :* as fome tranflate the Words.

Ver. 33. *But thou giveft thy Gifts to all thy* Ver. 33.
Lovers.] The Jews are often upbraided for making Leagues with Idolaters, and courting their Favours by Prefents, and by complying with their
Idolatries. See *Ifa.* xxx. 6. lvii. 5----9. *Jerem.* ii.
18, 25, 36. and the Notes upon thefe Texts.

Ver. 36. *And by the Blood of thy Children.*] See Ver. 36.
Ver. 20. *Jerem.* ii. 34.

Ver. 37. *Behold therefore I will gather all thy* Ver. 37.
Lovers.] Thofe Allies whofe Friendfhip thou haft
courted by complying with their Idolatries. See
Chapter xxiii. 9, 22. *Jerem.* ii. 25. iv. 30. xxii. 20.
Lament. i. 8. *Hof.* ii. 10.

Ibid.

Ibid. *With all them that thou haft hated.*] Compare
Ver. 41. fuch were *Edom, Moab,* and *Ammon:*
who always bore a Spight to the Jews, and infulted over their Calamities. See Chap. xxv. 3, 8, 12.

Ibid. *And will difcover thy Nakednefs unto them.*] They fhall fee thee carried away Captive, ftript and bare, (fee Ver. 39.) without any Covering to thy Nakednefs, according to the Barbarous Cuftom of Conquerors; See the Notes on *Ifa.* iii. 17. xx. 4. The Words allude to the Punifhment that ufed to be inflicted upon Common Harlots and Adulterefles; which was to ftrip them Naked, and expofe them to the World. Compare Chap. xxiii. 29. *Jerem.* xiii. 22, 26. *Hof.* ii. 3.

Ver. 38.   Ver. 38. *And I will judge thee as Women that break Wedlock.*] Whofe Punifhment was Death by the Law, *Levit.* xx. 10. *Deut.* xxii. 22.

Ibid. *And fhed Blood.*] See Ver. 20, 21, 26. This was likewife a Capital Crime. See *Exod.* xxi. 12. In thefe two Parts of *Jerufalem's* Character, fhe was a Type of the *Antichriftian* Whore, who was likewife *Drunk with the Blood of the Saints, Revel.* xvii. 5, 6.

Ibid. *And I will give thee Blood in Fury and Jealoufy.*] I will make an utter Deftruction of thine Inhabitants: See Chapter xiv. 19. Or, I will *pour out the Blood* of thy Slain *like Water, Pfal.* lxxix. 3. Jealoufy is the *Rage of a Man, Prov.* vi. 34. Such Indignation will God fhew againft the Idolatry of his own People, who hath declared himfelf a *Jealous* God, and very tender of his Honour, which is highly injured by the Worfhip of Idols, fet up as his Rivals. See the Note on Chap. v. 13.

Ver.

Ver. 39. *They shall throw down thine eminent* Chapter
Places.] They shall destroy all thy High Walls XVI.
and Fortifications: the Expression alludes to the
high Places dedicated to Idolatrous Worship. See Ver. 39.
Ver. 24, 31.

Ibid. *They shall strip thee of thy Clothes,* &c.]
They shall first plunder thee before they carry
thee away Captive. See Ver. 37. and Chap. xxiii.
26.

Ver. 40. *And they shall bring a Company against* Ver. 40.
thee, and they, shall stone thee with Stones.] The
Chaldean Army shall beat down thy Walls and
Houses with Stones slung out of Battering Engines.
See *Jer.* xxxiii. 4. The Expression alludes to the
Punishment inflicted upon Adulteresses, which was
stoning: See *Joh.* viii. 5. The particular sort of
Death which they were to suffer is not expressed
in the Law: so the Conjecture of *Grotius* upon
that Place of St. *John* is not improbable; that in the
latter times, as Wickedness increased, the *Sanhedrim* exchanged the milder Punishment of Stran-
gling used before, for the severer Death of stoning.

Ibid. *And thrust thee thro' with their Swords.*]
See Chap. v. 12. xxiii. 10, 47. xxiv. 21.

Ver. 41. *And they shall burn thy Houses with* Ver. 41.
Fire.] The Punishment allotted to an Idolatrous
City, *Deut.* xiii. 16. The Words may likewise
allude to the Punishment of Burning, anciently inflicted upon Harlots: See *Gen.* xxxviii. 24.

Ibid. *And execute Judgment upon thee in the*
sight of many Women.] The *Syrians, Philistines,*
and other Neighbouring Nations. See Ver. 37. and
the Notes upon Ver. 27. The Judgment I will
execute upon thee shall be for an Instruction to

Q other

Chapter other Nations, how they follow thine ill Practices.
XVI. See Chap. xxiii. 48.

Ibid. *And I will cause thee to cease from playing the Harlot.*] See Chap. xxiii. 27.

Ver. 42. Ver. 42. *So will I make my Fury toward thee to rest, and my Jealousy shall depart from thee, &c.*] See Ver. 38. and the Note upon Chap. v. 13.

Ver. 43. Ver. 43. *Because thou hast not remembred the Days of thy Youth.*] See Ver. 22.

Ibid. *And thou shalt not commit this Lewdness above all thine Abominations.*] Thou shalt not add these manifold and shameless Practices of Idolatry to all thy other Wickedness. But the Words may be rendred, *Neither hast thou laid to Heart all these thine Abominations.*

Ver. 44. Ver. 44. *Behold every one that useth Proverbs, shall use this Proverb against thee, &c.*] They that love to apply the memorable Sayings of former Ages to the present Times, shall apply that common Saying to thee, that the Daughter follows her Mother's Steps, and *Jerusalem* is no better than the *Amorites* whose Land they inhabit, and whose Manners they imitate : See Ver. 3.

Ver. 45. Ver. 45. *Thou art thy Mother's Daughter, that lotheth her Husband and her Children.*] Both these Qualities are the Property of an Harlot, and were verified in the *Jews,* who abhorred God their Husband, Ver. 8. and cast off all natural Affection to their Children, sacrificing them in the Fire to the Honour of their Idols : Ver. 20.

Ibid. *And thou art the Sister of thy Sisters.*] *Samaria* and *Sodom* : Ver. 46. The Worship of *Moloch* was generally practised by the Ten Tribes whose Metropolis was *Samaria,* See 2 *Kings* xvii.

17.

17. as it was by the *Ammonites*, who derived their Original from *Lot*, an Inhabitant of *Sodom*. See 1 *Kings* xi. 7.

Chapter XVI.

Ibid. *Your Mother was an Hittite*, &c.] See Ver. 3.

Ver. 46. *And thine elder Sister is Samaria, she and her Daughters that dwell at thy Left Hand,* &c.] *Samaria* is called the elder Sister to *Jerusalem*, as being the Capital City of the Kingdom of *Israel*, a more large and potent Kingdom than that of *Judah*, of which *Jerusalem* was the Metropolis. She likewise led the way to that Idolatry which afterward infected the whole Nation, forsaking the Worship which God had appointed in his Temple, and setting up the Idolatry of the Golden Calves. *Samaria* lay Northward of *Jerusalem*, and *Sodom* Southward, which two Quarters of the World are expressed by the Right and Left, in the *Hebrew* Language, being placed in such a Position to those that set their Faces Eastward. So the Phrase is to be understood, *Gen.* xiii. 9. *If thou wilt go to the Left Hand, I will go to the Right:* where the *Targum* expounds the Words, *If thou wilt go to the North, I will go to the South.* The same way of Speaking is still used in the ancient *British* or *Welsh* Language, as Archbishop *Usher* observes in his *Primord. Eccl. Britan.* p. 306. *Edit. Fol.*

Samaria and *Sodom* are described as *Metropoles,* or Mother Cities: So their Daughters may be expounded not only of the Inhabitants of each City, but likewise of the lesser Towns which were antiently under the Jurisdiction of the greater. Compare Chap. xxvi. 4, 6. *Jerem.* xlix. 2.

Q 2

Ver.

Chapter
XVI.

Ver. 47.

Ver. 48.

Ver. 49.

Ver. 51.

Ver. 47. *Yet thou haft not walked after their Ways, &c.*] See Chap. v. 7.

Ibid. *Thou waft corrupted more than they, &c.*] See Ver. 48, 51.

Ver. 48. *Sodom thy Sifter hath not done as thou haft done.*] Their Sins were not committed with fuch Aggravations of Ingratitude: nor did I ufe fuch powerful Methods to convince them of their Wickednefs, as I have done toward you. Comp. Chap. v. 6. *Math.* x. 15. xi. 24.

Ver. 49. *Behold this was the Iniquity of Sodom, Pride, fulnefs of Bread, and abundance of Idlenefs.*] *Sodom* abufed that Plenty which God gave them to Pride and Idlenefs, which gave rife to thofe Enormities which they afterward were guilty of. The Scripture takes Notice of the Fruitfulnefs of the Soil where *Sodom* ftood : *Gen.* xiii. 10.

Ibid. *Neither did fhe ftrengthen the Hand of the Poor and Needy.*] Pride and Luxury make Men expenfive in their own way of Living, and regardlefs of the Wants and Miferies of others. See *Luke* xvi. 20, 21.

Ver. 51. *Neither hath Samaria committed half thy Sins.*] The Ingratitude of *Jerufalem* was greater than that of *Samaria,* becaufe God had placed his Name there, whofe Worfhip fhe forfook, and profaned the Temple by placing Idols in it ; which was a Degree of Idolatry beyond any Thing the Ten Tribes had been guilty of. See Chapter v. 11. vii. 20. viii. 6, 15. xxiii. 38, 39. xliii. 8. 2 *Kings* xvi. 14. xxi. 7, 9.

Ibid. *Thou haft juftified thy Sifters in all thine Abominations.*] Thou haft made them appear lefs Guilty : See *Jerem.* iii. 11. Another Aggravation
of

of thy Sin confifts in this, that thou wouldeft not
take Warning by the Judgments God brought upon them : See ibid. Ver. 8.

Ver. 52. *Thou alfo which haft judged thy Sifters,*
bear thine own Shame.] Becaufe *wherein thou haft*
judged them, or declared them defervedly punifhed,
thoù haft condemned thy felf, having been Guilty
of the fame Sins, and thofe accompanied with greater Aggravations.

Ver. 53. *When I fhall bring again their Captivi-*
ty, the Captivity of Sodom, and her Daughters,
&c.]   When the *Fulnefs of the Gentiles* fhall come
into the Church, fome of whom may be compared
with *Sodom* for Wickednefs, (See *Ifa. i. 9.*) then
will I alfo remember you, who were my ancient
People. St. *Paul* tells us, that the *Jews* will be
provoked to Emulation by the *Gentiles* coming into the Church, and thereby induced to acknowledge the Truth.   See *Rom.* xi. 11, 12, 15, 25, 31.
The Converfion of the *Gentiles* is expreffed in *Je-*
remy, by returning the Captivity of *Moab, Am-*
mon and *Elam,* Chap. xlviii. 47. xlix. 6, 39. and
by the *Egyptians, Affyrians, Ethiopians* and *Syri-*
ans bringing Prefents to God, and acknowledging
themfelves his Servants, in the Prophecy of *Ifaiah,*
Chap. xviii. 7. xix. 24, 25. xxiii. 18.   And by the
fame Analogy we are to underftand the *returning*
of the Captivity of Sodom here, of the *Gentiles* coming into the Church.

Ver. 54. *That thou mayft bear thine own Shame,*
&c.] In the mean time thou fhalt bear the Shame
and Punifhment due to thy Sins, and fhalt be fome
fort of Comfort to thy Neighbours, in being a
Com-

Chapter
XVI.

〰
Ver. 55.

Companion with them in Punishment, as thou haft
been in Wickedneſs.

Ver. 55. *When Samaria and her Daughters ſhall
return to their former Eſtate, then thou and thy
Daughters ſhall return to your former Eſtate.*] When the Prophets foretel the General Converſion
and Reſtoration of the *Jewiſh* Nation, they always
join *Judah* and *Iſrael* together, as equal Sharers in
that Bleſſing. See Chap. xxxvii. 16---22. and the
Notes there.

Ver. 56, 57 Ver. 56, 57. *For thy Siſter Sodom was not mentioned by thy Mouth in the Day of thy Pride, Before thy Wickedneſs was diſcovered.*] Theſe Words
ſhould be joined together in the ſame Verſe or Sentence: God ſaith to *Jeruſalem*, that in the height
of her Proſperity, before her Wickedneſs ſo fully
appeared to the Eyes of the World, by the extraordinary Judgments brought upon her, ſhe did
not reflect upon the terrible Vengeance which befel *Sodom*, and was deſigned for an *Example* or
Warning *to thoſe that ſhould afterward live Ungodly*; 2 Pet. ii. 6.

Ver. 57, 58 Ver. 57, 58. *As at the time of thy Reproach of
the Daughters of Syria,* &c.] The Words begin a
New Sentence, which may be tranſlated more
perſpicuouſly thus, joining them to the following
Verſe: *But when it was the time of* thy *becoming
the Reproach of the Daughters of Syria,* &c. The
Particle *Kemo*, ſometimes ſignifies *When*: See *Noldius*, p. 431. The Words, with regard to what goes
before, import thus much: In thy Proſperity thou didſt
deſpiſe thoſe who are no worſe than thy ſelf: but
ſince thou haſt been inſulted and invaded by thy
Neigh-

Neighbours, both *Syrians* and *Philiftines*, whom
God hath made ufe of as Executioners of his Judgments upon thee, thou haft been a remarkable Inftance of his Vengeance, and God's Hand hath bin
heavy upon thee for all thine Idolatries and Abominations. The Words relate to the frequent In-
roads the *Syrians* and *Philiftines* made into *Judea*
in the time of King *Ahaz*. See 2 *Kings* xvi. 5.
2 *Chron.* xxviii. 18.

Ver. 59 *I will even deal with thee as thou haft
done, which haft defpifed the Oath in breaking the
Covenant.*] That folemn Oath and Covenant you
entred into with me to be my People, and ferve
no other God befides: See *Deut.* xxix. 12, 14.
which is likewife reprefented in this Chapter, and
many other Places under the Solemnity of a Marriage Contract. Hereupon God threatens her,
that fince fhe had broke her Oath and Promife, he
fhould not think himfelf obliged to make good any
of the Promifes of Favour and Protection which
he had made to her, but would give her up to Ruin and Defolation. See *Numb.* xiv. 34.

Ver. 60. *Neverthelefs I will remember my Covenant with thee in the Days of thy Youth.*] I will
have fome Regard for you, becaufe you were formerly my People, by Virtue of the Covenant that
I made with you at your coming out of *Egypt*.
Compare Ver. 4, and 22. of this Chapter, and *Hof.*
ii. 15. xi. 1. *Jerem.* ii. 2. at which time God chofe
them to be his peculiar People : See *Exod.* xix. 5, 6.

Ibid. *And I will eftablifh with thee an everlaft-
ing Covenant.*] Such a one as fhall never be abo-
lifhed, *viz.* that of the Gofpel : See *Jerem.* xxxii.
40. and the Note upon that Place.

Chapter
XVI.

Ver. 59.

Ver. 60.

Ver.

Chapter
XVI.

Ver. 61.

Ver. 61. *Then shalt thou remember thy Ways, and be ashamed.*] The Jews shall be touched with a deep Sense and Remorse for their former Provocations, as a necessary Preparation for their Conversion: Compare Chap. xx. 43. xxxvi. 31. *Jerem.* xxxi. 9. l. 5. and see the Notes upon those Places.

Ibid. *When thou shalt receive thy Sisters, thine Elder and thy Younger.*] See Ver. 53.

Ibid. *And I will give them to thee for Daughters*] *Jerusalem* thus restored shall be a Type of that Heavenly *Jerusalem*, *which is the Mother of us all*, *Galat.* iv. 26. And even in the Times of the Apostles there was a particular Deference paid to the Church of *Jerusalem*, as the Mother Church of the Christian World: See *Rom.* xv. 26, 27. Accordingly she is stiled the *Mother of all Churches*, by the *Second General Council*, in their *Synodical Epistle*: See *Theodorit. Hist. Eccles. lib.* 5. *c.* 9. A Title which the Church of *Rome* now assumes, without any Pretence from Scripture or Antiquity.

Ibid. *But not by thy Covenant.*] Not by Virtue of that Covenant mentioned Ver. 60. You having forfeited all your Title to its Privileges, Ver. 89. but by Virtue of that New Covenant which I will make with you, thro' the *Messias:* See *Jerem.* xxxi. 31.

Ver. 62.

Ver. 62. *And thou shalt know that I am the* LORD.] I will be then as conspicuous in my Mercies, as I was before in my Judgments. See the Note on Chap. vi. 7.

Ver. 63.

Ver. 63. *That thou mayst remember, and be confounded.*] Be Confounded at the Remembrance of thy former Wickedness: See Ver. 61.

Ibid.

Chapter
XVI.

Ibid. *And never open thy Mouth more becaufe of thy Shame.*] The Mercies of the Gofpel in *calling Sinners to Repentance*, and accepting them, notwithstanding their many Imperfections, do unanfwerably confute all Claim or Pretence to Merit. See *Rom.* iii. 19.

R

CHAP.

CHAP. XVII.

The ARGUMENT.

*Under the Parable of two Eagles and two Vine
Branches, the Prophet figuratively expresses the
carrying away* Jehoiakin *into Captivity by the
King of* Babylon, *who made* Zedekiah *King in
his Stead. He afterward revolted from the King
of* Babylon *whose Vassal he was, and entred into
an Alliance with the King of* Egypt. *For this
Breach of his Oath and Fidelity, God threatens
to make him Captive to that very King from
whom he had revolted.*

Ver. 2.

Ver. 2.  *UT forth a Riddle.*] *i. e.* A
continued *Metaphor* or figu-
rative Speech, ftill purfuing
the Allegory of an Eagle and
Vine in the feveral Parts of
the Parable: This perhaps
may make the Hearers more attentive to what thou
fpeakeft.

Ver.

Ver. 3. *An Eagle with great Wings.*] That is, Chapter
the King of *Babylon*: See Ver. 12. Conquerors XVII.
are elsewhere represented by Eagles, who are
Birds of Prey, and remarkable for their Swiftness. Ver. 3.
See *Deut.* xxviii. 49. *Jer.* iv. 13. *Hof.* viii. 1.

Ibid. *Long wing'd.*] The LXX and other Interpreters translate the Word from the *Chaldee* Senfe
of it, *Of a great fize:* to avoid the Repetition of
the fame Senfe over again.

Ibid. *Came to Lebanon, and cropt off the higheft
Branch of the Cedar.*] i. e. Invaded *Judea,* or in-
vefted *Jerufalem* and took King *Jehoiakin* Captive: See Ver. 12. and compare *Jer.* xxii. 23.

Ver. 4. *And carried it into a Land of Traffick.*] Ver. 4.
Babylon and the Countrey about it, being the Seat
of an Univerfal Monarchy, muft needs have been
a place of great Trading. *Strabo* takes notice,
that the Merchants who travelled by Land to *Babylon,* went thro' the Countrey of the *Arabians*
called *Scenitæ: lib.* xvi. p. 747. and Veffels of great
Burden came up to the Walls of it from the *Perfian*
Gulph up the River *Euphrates.* See *Pliny*'s *Nat.
Hift. l.* vi. *c.* 26.

Ver. 5. *He took alfo of the Seed of the Land.*] Ver. 5.
Of the King's Seed, as it is explained Ver. 13. *i. e.
Zedekiah.*

Ibid. *And planted it in a fruitful Field, he pla-
ced it by great Waters, and fet it as a Willow Tree.*]
Judea was a fruitful Countrey, and well watered,
See *Deut.* viii. 7. where *Zedekiah* flourifhed as a
Willow Tree that thriveth beft in a moift Ground.
See *Ifa.* xliv. 4.

Ver. 6. *And it grew and became a fpreading* Ver. 6.
Vine of low Stature, whofe Branches turned to-

R 2 *ward*

Chapter
XVII.

ward him; and the Roots thereof were under him.] Tho' he flourished, yet he enjoyed but a Tributary Kingdom under the King of *Babylon*, and acknowledged him as his Lord and Sovereign: See Ver. 14.

Ver. 7.

Ver. 7. *There was also another great Eagle,&c.*] *Pharaoh* King of *Egypt*, with whom *Zedekiah* made an Alliance: whereupon that King sent an Army to raise the Siege of *Jerusalem*: See 2 *Chron.* xxxvi. 13. *Jerem.* xxxvii. 5, 7.

Ibid. *This Vine did bend her Roots toward him, and shot forth her Branches toward him, &c.*] *Zedekiah* desired the King of *Egypt*'s Assistance and Protection. Some render the Words thus, *Shot forth her Branches under him from the Furrows where she was planted, that he might water it.*

Ver. 8.

Ver. 8. *It was planted in a good Soil, &c.*] The Words are to the same Purpose with Ver. 5. to shew that *Zedekiah*'s Condition was so good under the King of *Babylon*, that he needed not to have broke his Oath, out of a Desire to better it: whereby he involved himself and his Countrey in Ruin. See 2 *Kings* xxiv. 20. and the Note upon *Jer.* xvii. 25.

Ver. 9.

Ver. 9. *Shall he not pull up the Roots thereof,&c.*] *Nebuchadnezzar* in return for this Perfidiousness, shall destroy him and his Family. See 2 *Kings* xxv. 7.

Ibid. *Even without great Power.*] God will appear visibly on the *Chaldeans* Side, so there will be no need of great Force to subdue their Enemies. See *Jer.* xxi. 4. xxxvii. 10.

Ver. 10.

Ver. 10. *Shall it not utterly wither when the East Wind toucheth it?*] The Prophet compares the
Chal‑

Chaldean Army to a parching Wind that blasts Chapter
the Fruits of the Earth, withers the Leaves of the XVII.
Trees, and makes every thing look naked and bare.
See Chap. xix. 12. *Iſa.* xxvii. 8. *Jerem.* iv. 11. *Hoſ.*
xiii. 15.

Ver. 12. *Say now to the rebellious Houſe.*] See Ver. 12.
Chap. ii. 5. xii. 9.

Ibid. *Know ye not what theſe things mean?*]
Will ye not apply your Minds to underſtand what
God ſpeaks to you? And that whether he directs
his Speech to you in plain Words, or delivers his
Mind in Riddles and Parables? See Chap. xii. 2, 9.
xx. 49.

Ibid. *And hath taken the King thereof, and the
Princes thereof.*] *Jechoniah* and all his Princes and
Officers. See 2 *Kings* xxiv. 12.

Ver. 13. *And hath taken of the King's Seed,--* Ver. 13.
and hath taken an Oath of him.] Hath made *Ze-*
dekiah ſwear an Oath of Fealty to him. See
2 *Chron.* xxxvi. 13.

Ibid. *He hath alſo taken the mighty of the Land.*]
As Hoſtages for the Performance of the Covenants
agreed between him and *Zedekiah.*

Ver. 14. *That the Kingdom might be baſe, &c.*] Ver. 14.
Zedekiah by this Means became only a Tributary
King (Compare Chap. xxix. 14.) and conſequently
not in ſo honourable a Condition as his Predeceſſors
had been: but yet this was the only Means under
the preſent Circumſtances to ſupport himſelf and
his Government.

Ver. 15. *But he rebelled againſt him in ſending* Ver. 15.
*his Ambaſſadors into Egypt, that they might give
him Horſes and much People.*] See the Note on
Ver. 7. *Egypt* was a Country that abounded in
Horſes,

Chapter Horſes, of which there was great Scarcity in *Ju-*
XVII.] *dea.* See 1 *Kings* ix. 28. *Iſa.* xxxi. 1. xxxvi. 9.

　Ibid. *Shall he proſper, &c.*] This was not only a
Violation of his Oath and Covenant, but likewiſe
a Breach of that part of the *Jewiſh* Law, *Deut.*
xvii. 16. which expreſly forbad their King to *fetch*
Horſes out of Egypt, or ſtrengthen himſelf with the
Alliance of that People.

Ver. 16.　　Ver. 16. *In the midſt of Babylon he ſhall die.*]
Whither he ſhall be carried Priſoner.　See Chapter
xii. 13.

Ver. 17.　　Ver. 17. *Neither ſhall Pharaoh with his mighty*
Army make for him.] See *Jer.* xxxvii. 7.
　　Ibid. *By caſting up Mounts.*] See *Jer.* xxxii. 14.

Ver. 18.　　Ver. 18. *When lo he hath given his Land.*] In
token of entring into a mutual League and Covenant, See *Iſa.* xli. 13.　Particularly it was a Ceremony uſed when an Inferior made Profeſſion of his
Subjection to his Superior :　See *Jerem.* l. 15. *Lam.*
v. 6. 1 *Chron.* xxix. 24. where we read that the
Princes and mighty Men ſubmitted themſelves to So-
lomon the King : but in the Original, it is, *They*
gave the Hand under Solomon.

Ver. 20.　　Ver. 20. *And I will ſpread my Net upon him.*]
See Chap. xii. 13.
　　Ibid. *And will plead with him there for his Treſ-*
paſs.] God is ſaid to *plead with Men,* when he
places their Sins before their Eyes, and convinces
them of their Diſobedience by manifeſt Tokens of
his Vengeance.　See Chap. xx. 36. xxxviii. 22.

Ver. 21.　　Ver. 21. *And all his Fugitives with all his*
Bands ſhall fall by the Sword.] See Chap. xii. 14.

Ver. 22.　　Ver. 22. *I will alſo take of the higheſt Branch of*
the high Cedar, and will ſet it.]　The Prophet
pursuing

pursuing the same Metaphor, foretels the Restoration of the Royal Family of *David*, in such Terms as might in some Degree be fulfilled at the Return from the Captivity, when *Zorobabel* of the Lineage of *David* had a Shadow of Kingly Authority among the Jews, and by his Means their Church and Constitution was again restored. But the Words do more properly belong to *Christ* and his Kingdom, which shall be extended over all the World.

Ibid. *I will crop off from the young Twigs a tender one.*] This Description may fitly be applied to our Saviour, in respect to the low Estate to which the Family of *David* was then reduced, with great Humility acknowledged by his Mother, *Luke* i. 48. The meanness of his outward Condition and Appearance is represented by the Prophet *Isaiah*, under the same Expressions, Chap. liii. 2.

Ver. 23. *In the Mount of the height of Israel will I plant it.*] The Temple stood upon Mount *Moriah*, 2 *Chron.* iii. 1. thence styled God's *Holy Mountain:* which Expression is often used in the Prophets to denote the Christian Church: which is described as a *City set on an Hill*, and conspicuous to all the World. See Chap. xx. 40. and the Note upon *Isa.* ii. 2.

Ibid. *And it shall bring forth Boughs and bear Fruit.*] The living Members of the Church are compared to fruitful Trees, and flourishing Branches: See *Joh.* xv. 5, 8. *Psal.* i. 3. xcii. 2.

Ibid. *And under it shall dwell all Fowl of every Wing.*] *i. e.* Of every Kind. A powerful, especially if it be an easy Government, is a Shelter and Security to all its Subjects. Comp. Chap. xxxi. 6.

Dan.

Chapter
XVII.

Ver. 24.

Dan. iv. 12. Such shall be the Kingdom of Christ to all that submit themselves to his Laws.

Ver. 24. *And all the Trees of the Field shall know that I the* LORD *have brought down the high Tree, have exalted the low Tree,* &c.] Christ's Kingdom shall by degrees exalt it self above all the Kingdoms of the World: and shall at length put an end to them, and it self continue unto all Eternity. See *Dan.* iv. 35, 44. vii. 27. *Luke* i. 33. 1 *Cor.* xv. 24.

Ibid. *I the* LORD *have spoken it, and have done it.*] The Prophets often speak of Future Events as if they were already accomplished, to assure us that they shall certainly come to pass. See the Note upon *Isa.* xxi. 9.

CHAP.

C H A P. XVIII.

The ARGUMENT.

*The Calamities which uſhered in and attended the
Captivity of the Jews, were expreſly threatned as
Puniſhments of the Idolatries and other Sins of
their Anceſtors: See* Jerem. xv. 4. *This made
the Jews of the preſent Age complain of God's
dealing hardly with them in puniſhing them for
the Sins of their Forefathers. This Chapter contains an Anſwer to the Objection, importing
that even under their Captivity they ſhould find
their Condition Better or Worſe, according as
they behaved themſelves: and withal laying before them God's Eternal Rules of Juſtice, with
Regard to the Rewards and Puniſhments of the
next Life, when he will Judge every Man according to his Works, and every Man ſhall
bear his own Burden.*

Chapter
XVIII. Ver. 2.

Ver. 2.

H ∝*AT* *mean ye that ye ufe this Proverb concerning the Land of Ifrael?*] With re-fpect to the Defolations made in it by Sword, Famine and Peftilence. See Chap. vi. 2, 3, &c. vii. 2.

Ibid. *The Fathers have eaten fower Grapes, and the Children's Teeth are fet on Edge.*] i. e. The prefent Generation is punifhed for the Offences committed by their Forefathers, particularly for the Sins committed in the time of *Manaffeh* King of *Judah:* See *Jerem.* xv. 4, xxxi. 29. *Lament.* v. 7. 2 *Kings* xxiii. 26. This Proverb had likewife a profane Senfe implied in it, and infinuated that the prefent Age was not remarkably worfe than thofe that had gone before it, and fo did not deferve to be made an extraordinary Example of God's Vengeance.

Ver. 3.

Ver. 3. *As I live, faith the* LORD, *ye fhall not have* occafion *to ufe this Proverb any more in Ifrael.*] I will make fuch a vifible Difcrimination between the Righteous and the Wicked, between thofe that tread in the Steps of their Forefathers, and thofe who take warning by their Examples, that you fhall not have any farther Occafion to ufe this Proverb among you. God exprefly threatens to *Vifit the Sins of the Fathers upon the Children* both in the Old and New Teftament; See *Exod.* xx. 5. *Matth.* xxiii. 35. But this is to be underftood only with refpect to the temporal Punifhments of this World, (and thefe he doth not always inflict in an exact Proportion to the Demerits of thofe that

fuf-

Chapter
XVIII.

suffer) not with respect to the Eternal Punishments of the next. See Bishop *Sanderson's Third
Sermon upon* 1 *Kings* xxi. 29. " The Scripture
" takes notice of a certain *Measure of Iniquity,*
" which is filling up from one Generation to ano-
" ther, 'till at last it makes a Nation or Family
" ripe for Destruction. And altho' those Persons
" on whom this Vengeance falls, suffer no more
" than their own Personal Sins deserved; yet be-
" cause the Sins of former Generations which they
" equal or out-do, make it time for God utterly to
" destroy them, the Punishments due to the Sins of
" many Ages and Generations are said to fall upon
" them. See *Matth.* xxiii. 35, 36. Dr. *Sherlock of*
" *Providence,* Chap. 8.

Ver. 4. *Behold all Souls are mine.*] As they are Ver. 4.
all equally my Creatures, so my Dealings with
them shall be without Prejudice or Partiality.

Ibid. *The Soul that sinneth, it shall die.*] *Death
is the Wages of Sin,* and all Men being Sinners,
the Sentence of Temporal Death passes equally upon them all. But as *Life* signifies in general all
that Happiness which attends God's Favour, so
Death denotes all those Punishments which are the
Effects of the Divine Displeasure. See 2 *Sam.* xii.
13. under which are comprehended the Miseries of
the next World; and these shall be allotted to Men
according to their Deserts, without any regard to
the Faults of their Ancestors, which shall not then
be laid to their Charge, or taken into Account to
aggravate their Guilt.

As the Prophets instruct Men in the Practice of
Inward and Evangelical Righteousness, and in order to it speak slightingly of the meer External Du-

ties

Chapter
XVIII.

ties of Religion : See *Ifa.* i. 11, &c. *Jer.* vii. 22, 23.
fo they raife Men's Minds to look beyond the Temporal Promifes and Threatnings of the Law, to the Eternal Rewards and Punifhments of another Life : See *Ifa.* lxvi. 24. *Dan.* xii. 2. In both which Refpects they prepared Mens Minds for the Reception of the Gofpel, when it fhould be Revealed.

Ver. 6.

Ver. 6. *And hath not eaten upon the Mountains.*] Idolatrous Worfhip was commonly performed upon Mountains or High Places : See Chap. vi. 13. xvi. 16, 24. xx. 28. and eating part of the Sacrifice was properly maintaining Communion with the Idol to whom it was offered. See *Exod.* xxxiv. 15. 1 *Cor.* x. 20, 21.

Ibid. *Neither hath lift up his Eyes to the Idols of the Houfe of Ifrael.*] Lifting up the Eyes is a Pofture of Religious Worfhip or Adoration : See *Deut.* iv. 19. *Pfal.* cxxi. 1. cxxiii. 1.

Ver. 7.

Ver. 7. *Hath reftored to the Debtor his Pledge.*] God commanded the Jews not to detain any Pledge they took from a poor Man all Night : which was in effect to enjoyn them to lend to the Poor without either Pawn or Ufury. See *Exod.* xxii. 25, 26. *Deut.* xxiv. 12, 13.

Ver. 8.

Ver. 8. *He that hath not given upon Ufury, neither hath taken any increafe.*] Ufury when it is exacted from the Poor, hath bin generally cried out upon as no better than Oppreffion : and is particularly forbidden by the Law : See *Exod.* xxii. 15. *Levit.* xxv. 35, 36. *Nehem.* v. 1---7. *Jerem.* xv. 10. It is probable that this fort of Ufury is chiefly here meant, becaufe it is joined with Oppreffion, Violence, and want of Charity.

Ver.

Ver. 9. *He shall surely live.*] See the Note on Chap. xx. 11.

Ver. 13. *His Blood shall be upon him.*] His Destruction is owing wholly to himself. See Chap. xxxiii. 4.

Ver. 19. *Yet say ye, why? doth not the Son bear the Iniquity of the Father?*] The *Jews* still appealed to their own Experience, as the Ground of their Complaint mentioned Ver. 2.

Ibid. *When the Son hath done that which is lawful and right,----he shall surely live.*] In like manner if ye had forsaken your Fathers Sins, you might have escaped those Judgments I denounced against your Fathers: See the Note upon *Jerem.* xvii. 25. But since ye have continued in their Abominations, the Punishments due to them justly come upon you.

Ver. 20. *The Soul that sinneth, it shall die.*] See the Notes upon Ver. 3, 4.

Ver. 22. *They shall not be mentioned to him.*] Or, *Remembred against him.*: God is said in Scripture to remember Men's Sins, when he punishes them: See *Jer.* xiv. 10. *Hos.* viii. 13. and to forget them when he pardons them: *Amos* viii. 7. *Jeremiah* xxxi. 34.

Ver. 23. *Have I any pleasure at all that the Wicked should die, &c.*] In conformity to this Doctrine the New Testament instructs us, that *God would have all Men to be saved,* and *is not willing that any should perish,* 1 *Tim.* ii. 4. 2 *Pet.* iii. 9.

Ver. 24. *All his Righteousness that he hath done shall not be mention'd.*] For *better had it been for him not to have known the way of Righteousness, than after he hath known it, to turn aside from the holy Commandment,* 2 *Pet.* ii. 21. Such a one sins

against

Chapter
XVIII.

Ver. 9.
Ver. 13.

Ver. 19.

Ver. 20.

Ver. 22.

Ver. 23.

Ver. 24.

Chapter against a clearer Light and greater Convictions, XVIII. and withal is guilty of the highest Ingratitude in doing despite unto the Spirit of Grace.

Ver. 25.   Ver. 25. *Yet ye say, The way of the* LORD *is not equal, &c.*] The Declarations I have so often repeated concerning the eternal Rewards and Punishments allotted to the Righteous and the Wicked, are sufficient to vindicate the Justice of my Proceedings, against all your Objections.

Ver. 26, 27   Ver. 26, 27. *When a righteous Man turneth away from his Righteousness, &c.*] It is an Opinion that prevails among the *Jews* even till this Day, that at the Day of Judgment a considerable Number of good Actions shall overballance Men's evil ones. See Chap. xxxiii. 13. So they thought it a hard Case for a Man who had been Righteous the far greatest part of his Life, if he did at last commit Iniquity, that his former Righteousness should avail him nothing. In opposition to this Doctrine, God here declares, that a righteous Man sinning, and not repenting, should die in his Sins; and that a wicked Man upon his Repentance should save his Soul alive.

Ver. 30.   Ver. 30. *Therefore I will judge you, O House of Israel, every one according to his Ways.*] You complain of the Injustice of my Ways, or Proceedings; but if I judge you according to the Desert of your Ways, you will certainly be all found guilty : and nothing but Repentance and true Contrition can avert that Ruin your Sins threaten you with.

Ver. 31.   Ver. 31. *And make you a new Heart and a new Spirit.*] The Prophets often exhort the *Jews* to an inward Purity and Holiness, thereby to take them off from relying upon an outward legal Righteousness,

neſs, and an Exactneſs in the Obſervance of the Chapter
ritual Parts of the Law : See the Note upon Ver. XVIII.
4. By thus inſtructing them in a more excellent
way of ſerving God, than the Ceremonial Law did
directly preſcribe, they prepared their Minds for
receiving thoſe Truths which the Goſpel would
more fully diſcover. God promiſes Chap. xxxvi.
26. *to give them a new Heart, and to put within
them a new Spirit* : here he exhorts them to *make
themſelves a new Heart and a new Spirit.* Which
difference of Expreſſion, is thus to be reconciled,
that altho' God *works in us to will and to do,* and
is the firſt Mover in our Regeneration, yet we
muſt *work together* with his Grace, at leaſt wil-
lingly receive it, and not *quench* or *reſiſt* its Motions. See the Note upon *Jer.* xxxi. 18.

more fully discover

| Chapter
XIX. | # C H A P. XIX. |

The Argument

Under the Parable of a Lion's Whelps, the Prophet describes the sad Catastrophe of the two Kings of Judah, Jehoahaz and Jehoiakim : and under the Figure of a Vine he represents the Desolation and Captivity of the whole People.

Ver. 1.

Ver. 1. *Ake thou up a Lamentation for the Princes of Israel.*] The Expression alludes to the mournful Ditties used at Funerals : Compare Chap. xxvi. 17. xxvii. 2. Such a Lamentation the Prophet is directed to apply to the mournful Estate of the Royal Family of *Judah*: particularly with respect to *Jehoahaz* and *Jehoiakim.*

Ver. 2.

Ver. 2. *What is thy Mother ?*] The Prophet proposes a Question that may be applied to each Prince distinctly.

Ibid. *What is thy Mother ? a Lioness, &c.*] The Land of *Judea* thy native Country, See Ver. 10.

is

is become cruel and bloody, compare *Pfal.* xxxiv. Chapter
10. *Nahum* ii. 11, 12. and hath taught her Princes XIX.
and Rulers to govern by Cruelty and Oppreſſion.
See Chap. vii. 23. xxii. 27. *Jerem.* xxii. 17. *Zeph.*
iii. 3.

Ver. 3. *She brought up one of her Whelps, it* Ver. 3.
became a young Lion.] Compare Ver. 6. This is
meant of *Jehoahaz,* who followed not the good
Example of his Father *Joſiah,* but the evil Practices
of the wicked Kings his Predeceſſors. See 2 *Kings*
xxiii. 32.

Ver. 4. *The Nations alſo heard of him, &c.*] Ver. 4.
Pharaoh Necoh King of *Egypt* hearing his ill Cha-
racter, depoſed him, and made him a Priſoner:
See 2 *Kings* xxiii. 33. 2 *Chron.* xxxvi. 4.

Ibid. *He was taken in their Pit.*] The Expreſſion alludes to thoſe Pit-falls and Snares which
are made to take wild Beaſts.

Ver. 5. *Then ſhe took another of her Whelps.*] Ver. 5.
Jehoiakim was ſet up King in his Brother's Stead
by the King of *Egypt,* who by his Victory over
Joſiah had made himſelf Maſter of *Judea*: 2 *Kings*
xxiii. 33, 34. But yet *Pharaoh* ſeems to have
done this by the joint Conſent of the People, who
had before ſet up *Jehoiakim*'s younger Brother without aſking the King of *Egypt*'s Conſent.

Ver. 6. *He went up and down among the Lions,* Ver. 6.
&c.] He learned and practiſed all the Methods of
Tyranny and Oppreſſion: See *Jerem.* xxii. 13--17.
xxxvii. 2.

Ver. 7. *And he knew their deſolate Places.*]
Or, *He knew their Palaces,* as the Word *Armenoth*
is tranſlated, *Amos* i. 7. And the Word *Alme-
noth* here uſed is equivalent to *Armenoth.* See

T   *Iſa.*

Chapter *Iſa.* xiii. 22. *Jehoiakim* made himſelf Maſter of the
XIX.   Riches and pleaſant Seats of the Great Men of the
ᴗᴡᴗ   Land.

Ver. 8, 9.   Ver. 8, 9. *Then the Nations ſet againſt him on*
every ſide, &c.] The *Chaldeans,* and their Neighbours and Allies invaded *Judea,* and afteward beſ-
ſieged *Jeruſalem,* and took *Jehoiakim* Priſoner:
See 2 *Kings* xxiv. 2. 2 *Chron.* xxxvi. 6.

Ibid. *And ſpread their Net over him, he was*
taken in their Pit.] See Ver. 4. and Comp. Chap.
xii. 13.

Ver. 9.   Ver. 9. *That his Voice ſhould no more be heard*
upon the Mountains of Iſrael.] The Words allude
to a Lion's ſeeking his Prey upon the Mountains.
Ezekiel often expreſſes the Land of *Iſrael,* by the
Mountains of Iſrael. See the Note upon Chapter
vi. 2.

Ver. 10.   Ver. 10. *Thy Mother is like a Vine in thy Blood,*
&c.] The Country of *Judea* from whence the Roy-
al Family have their Original, was like a fruitful
Vine in a very flouriſhing Condition. See Chap.
xvii. 5, 6.

Ver. 11.   Ver. 11. *And ſhe had ſtrong Rods for the Scep-*
ters of them that bare Rule.] From her ſprung Sovereign Princes, who were themſelves very powerful, and made their People appear conſiderable,
among their Neighbours. A Rod or Scepter is an
Emblem of Authority. See *Iſa.* ix. 4. x. 5. *Je-*
rem. xlviii. 17.

Ibid. *Her Stature was exalted among the thick*
Branches.] Compare Chap. xxxi. 3. *Dan.* iv. 11.

Ver. 12.   Ver. 12. *But ſhe was plucked up in Fury.*] God
in his Anger removed her out of her Land: Compare *Jer.* xii. 14. *Pſal.* lii. 5.

Ibid.

Ibid. *The East Wind dried up her Fruit.*] See
Chap. xvii. 10.

Ibid. *Her strong Rods were broken and wither-*
ed.] Her Kings and Princes were subdued and
made Captives.

Ibid. *The Fire consumed them.*] God's Anger
destroyed them, as Fire consumeth the Branches of
a Tree when it is withered. See Chap. xv. 4. God's
Wrath is often compared to Fire. See Chap. xxx. 8.

Ver. 13. *And now she is planted in the Wilder-*
ness, in a dry and thirsty Land.] A great Part of
her People are carried Captive, where their Condition is as much different from what it was formerly, as the Condition of a Tree is when it is
removed out of a rich Soil into a dry and barren
Ground. The Jews suffered several Captivities before that Final one which ended in the Destruction
of their Temple and Government. See *Dan.* i. 3.
2 *Kings* xxiv. 12. *Jer.* lii. 28.

Ver. 14. *And Fire is gone out of a Rod of her*
Branches, which hath devoured her Fruit, &c.]
Zedekiah's breaking his Oath of Fealty to the King
of *Babylon,* hath been the Occasion of the utter
Destruction of the Royal Family, and the entire
Ruin of the Government. See Chap. xvii. 18, 19.
2 *Kings* xxiv. 20.

Ibid. *This is a Lamentation, and shall be for a*
Lamentation.] This is Matter of present Lamentation, and shall be so to after Times.

Ver. 13.

Ver. 24.

T 2   CHAP.

CHAP. XX.

The ARGUMENT.

*This Chapter contains a Rehearfal of the Rebellions
and Idolatries of the Jews from their going out
of Egypt to that very Day. The Prophet afterwards foretels their Converfion and Reftaura-
tion. The laft Five Verfes contain a Prophecy
againft Jerufalem.*

Ver. 1.

Ver. 1. A*ND it came to pafs in the fe-
venth Year*, &c.] Of *Jehoiakin*'s
Captivity : Compare Chap. i.
2. viii. 1. All the Prophecies
recorded from the Eighth Chap-
ter to this, probably belong to the fixth Year of that
Captivity.

Ibid. *Certain of the Elders of Ifrael came to enquire of the* LORD, &c.] See the Note on Chap.
viii. 1.

Ver. 3.

Ver. 3. *I will not be enquired of by you.*] You
fhall not receive fuch an Anfwer as you expect,
but fuch as your Hypocrify deferves. See Ver. 31.
and Chap. xiv. 3, 4.

Ver. 4.

Ver. 4. *Wilt thou judge them?*] *Wilt thou plead
for them* as our Margin reads, or defend their
Caufe?

Caufe? But the Words may perhaps be more fig-
nificantly tranflated, *Wilt thou not judge them?*
i. e. Wilt thou not reprove, or condemn them?
Noldius obferves in his *Concordance,* p. 233. that
He the Particle of Interrogation, which anfwers
the *Latin* Particle *An?* is often equivalent to the
Negative *Annon,* and is to be tranflated, *Is it not?*
See Ver. 30. of this Chapter, and Chap. xxxviii.
17. In which Senfe it is underftood by our Tran-
flators, 2 *Sam.* xxiii. 17. and fo it fhould be rendred 1 *Sam.* ii. 27. *Did I not plainly appear to the*
Houfe of thy Father, &c.

Ibid. *Son of Man.*] See Chap. ii. 1.

Ver. 5. *In the Day when I lifted up my Hand*
to the Seed of the Houfe of Jacob.] When I entred
into a folemn Covenant with them, purfuant to the
Oath which I had fworn to their Fathers: See
Exod. vi. 8. *Lifting up the Hand* was a Ceremony
ufed in taking an Oath. See *Gen.* xiv. 22. and
thereupon applied to God himfelf, *Deut.* xxxii. 40.
The fame Expreffion is ufed Ver. 6, 15, 23, 42. of
this Chapter. The fame Ceremony in taking an
Oath, is mentioned by *Homer,* Εὔχελο χεῖρας ἀναχών.

Ibid. *And made my felf known unto them.*] By
appearing unto *Mofes,* and fhewing my felf prefent
among them by the Wonders I wrought for their
Deliverance.

Ibid. *Saying, I am the* LORD *your God.*] I am
the God whom you ought to ferve, and, none elfe.
See *Exod.* xx. 2, 3.

Ver. 6. *Into a Land which I had efpied for*
them.] I performed the Office of a Spy, before
thofe that were fent to fearch out the Land, *Numb.*
xiii. 16. and chofe it out of all others to beftow it
upon

Ver. 5.

Ver. 6.

Chapter upon them. So God is said *to go before them to*
XX. *search out a place to pitch their Tents in,* Deut.
i. 33. Numb. x. 33. The Expreſſions in both Places import, that every Step the People took till
their Settlement in the Land of *Canaan,* was
under the immediate Care and Conduct of Providence.

Ibid. *Flowing with Milk and Honey, which is
the Glory of all Lands.*] *Judea* is often called a
Land *Flowing with Milk and Honey,* both upon
Account of its own Fruitfulneſs, the Seed ſown
frequently bringing forth an Hundred Fold: See
Gen. xxvi. 1.2. *Matth.* xiii. 8. and alſo from God's
particular Bleſſing upon it : See *Deut.* xi. 12. The
great Numbers of Inhabitants which it nouriſhed
is an evident Proof of its Fertility. See the Note
on *Jerem.* xxxiii. 22. It might juſtly be called the
Glory of all Lands becauſe it was the Place of God's
eſpecial Reſidence. See *Pſal.* xlviii. 2. *Dan.* xi.
16, 41, 45.

Ver. 7. Ver. 7. *Caſt ye away every Man the Abominations of his Eyes.*] Lift not up your Eyes to Idols:
See Chap. xviii. 6. One of the chief Allurements
to the Worſhip of Images is, that by way of In-
dulgence to Men's Imaginations, they exhibit a
viſible Object of Adoration. This was what the
Iſraelites were ſo fond of when they ſaid to *Aaron,
Make us Gods to go before us,* Exod. xxxii. 1.

Ibid. *And defile not your ſelves with the Idols of
Egypt.*] The *Iſraelites,* while they dwelt in *Egypt,*
learned the Idolatries of that Countrey. See Chap.
xxiii. 3, 8. *Levit.* xvii. 7. xviii. 3. *Deut.* xxix. 16.
Joſh. xxiv. 14. Some Learned Men ſuppoſe that
the

the *Golden Calf* was copied from the *Egyptian* Idolatry: See *Selden de Diis Syris, Syntagm. l.* 1. *c.* 4.

Ver. 8. *Then I said, I will pour out my Fury upon them,----in the midst of the Land of Egypt.*] Such a Threatning as this, is no where recorded in Scripture, no more than that which follows Ver. 23. of this Chapter. Without Question God might have justly cut them off in *Egypt*, for the Idolatries and other Sins they had there committed, and never exerted his Power for their Deliverance.

Ver. 9. *But I wrought for my Name's sake, that it should not be polluted,* &c.] This is elsewhere assigned as the Reason why God did not punish the *Israelites* according to their Deserts: *viz.* Because it would turn to God's Dishonour in the Judgment of the Heathen World, as if he were not able to make good those gracious Promises he had given them. See Chap. xxxvi. 21, 22. *Exod.* xxxii. 12. *Numb.* xiv. 13, &c. *Deut.* ix. 28. This was a proper Consideration to check the vain Presumption of the Jews, who imagined that God's gracious Dealings with them were owing to their own Deserts. See Ver. 44. of this Chapter, and Chap. xxxvi. 22.

Ver. 11. *And I gave them my Statutes.*] A Favour not afforded to other Nations: See *Deut.* iv. 8. *Psal.* cxlvii. 20. Such a Treasure as *David* prizes above *Thousands of Gold and Silver*: *Psal.* cxix. 72.

Ibid. *Which if a Man do, he shall even live in them.*] By *Life* is meant in the Old Testament all that Happiness which is contained in the Literal Sense of the Promises belonging to that Covenant: Comp. Ver. 25. and *Deut.* xxx. 15, &c. *Psal.* lxix. 32. *Amos* v. 4. Under these were Mystically comprehended

prehended

prehended the Promiſes of a Better Life, wherein
God will beſtow upon his Servants the peculiar
Marks of his Favour. See *Pſal.* xvi. 11. Theſe
Promiſes were made over to the Jews upon Condition of their punctual Obedience to the whole Law :
Levit. xviii. 5. xxvi. 3, &c. *Deut.* xxvii. 26. And ſeveral Perſons under that Diſpenſation are ſtyled
Blameleſs by reaſon of the Sincerity of their Obedience, tho' it was not Perfect or Unſinning : See *Luke*
i. 6. *Philip.* iii. 6. But if we underſtand the forementioned Condition in its rigorous Senſe, as implying an Exact and Unſinning Obedience, and as
the Word *Life* contains the Promiſe of Eternal Life
under it : which Promiſe the Jews expected and
hoped to obtain : See *Matth.* xix. 16, 17. *Act.*
xxvi. 6, 7. I ſay the Condition of the Old Covenant thus expounded, as it was impoſſible to be
performed, ſo no Perſon could lay claim to Eternal
Life by Virtue of any Promiſe therein contained.
From whence St. *Paul* infers the Neceſſity of ſeeking to Chriſt, and laying hold of the Promiſes of his
Goſpel for the obtaining Juſtification and Eternal
Life : *Gal.* iii. 12, 21.

Ver. 12.   Ver. 12. *Moreover I gave them my Sabbaths, to
be a Sign between me and them,* &c.] The ſetting
apart the Seventh Day for God's Worſhip, was a
Sign of his ſetting apart the Jews to be his peculiar
People, and the Worſhippers of the true God, who
*in Six Days made Heaven and Earth, and reſted
the ſeventh Day.* See *Exod.* xxxi. 13, 17. *Nehem.*
ix. 14.

Ver. 13.   Ver. 13. *But the Houſe of Iſrael rebelled againſt
me in the Wilderneſs.*] See *Numb.* xiv. 22. *Pſal.*
lxxviii. 40. xcv. 8, 9, 10.

Ibid.

Ibid. *And my Sabbaths they greatly polluted.*] Chapter Particularly in their going to gather *Manna* on that XX. day against my expreſs Command, confirmed by an extraordinary Deſcent of the Manna on the Day foregoing ; *Exod.* xvi. 25, &c.

Ver. 14. *But I wrought for my Name's ſake*, &c.] Ver. 14. See Ver. 9.

Ver. 15. *Yet alſo I lifted up my Hand to them in* Ver. 15. *the Wilderneſs, that I would not bring them into the Land which I had given them.*] I ſolemnly ſwore, (ſee Ver. 5.) they ſhould not enter into that Reſt which I had deſigned for them. See *Numb.* xiv. 28. *Pſal.* xcv. 11. cvi. 26.

Ver. 16. *For their Heart went after their Idols.*] Ver. 16. They ſtill had a hankering after the Idolatries they had learned in *Egypt*, to which they added new Idols which they had ſeen in the Countries thro' which they traveled, *viz.* the Idols of the *Midianites, Amorites,* &c. See *Numb.* xv. 39. xxv. 2. *Deut.* xxix. 16, 17. *Amos* v. 25, 26. Compared with *Acts* vii. 42.

Ver. 17. *Nevertheleſs mine Eyes ſpared them,* Ver. 17. &c.] See *Pſal.* lxxviii. 38.

Ver. 18. *But I ſaid unto their Children in the* Ver. 18. *Wilderneſs, Walk ye not in the Statutes of your Fathers,* &c.] This refers to the many Pathetical Exhortations contained in the Book of *Deuteronomy,* particularly thoſe in xxix, xxx, xxxi, and xxxii, Chapters, which were uttered after that rebellious Generation were all conſumed, according as God had threatned them : (See *Numb.* xiv. 32, 33. xxvi. 64, 65.) and were deſigned as Warnings to ſucceeding Generations. See *Deut.* xxxi. 16---21.

U Ver.

Ver. 21. *Notwithstanding the Children rebelled against me.*] See *Numb.* xxi. 5. xxv. 2. *Deut.* ix. 24. xxix. 18, 19. xxxi. 27. *Psal.* lxxviii. 32.

Ibid. *They polluted my Sabbaths.*] Profaning the Sabbath and committing Idolatry are often joined together: See Ver. 16, 24. Chap. xxii. 8, 9. xxiii. 37, 38. 1 *Maccab.* i. 45. one great End of instituting the Sabbath being to preserve the *Jews* from falling into Idolatry. See Ver. 12.

Ibid. *Then I said, I will pour out my Fury upon them,* &c.] God did punish the Posterity of that rebellious Generation very severely for their Sins, particularly for their Idolatry aud Fornication in the matter of *Peor, Numb.* xxv. 5, 9.

Ver. 23. *I lifted up my Hand unto them also in the Wilderness, that I would scatter them among the Heathen,* &c.] St. *Jerom* observes upon the place, that we do not read of any particular Threatning denounced against the Children of that rebellious Generation. But the Words may relate to those general Denunciations against their Disobedience which we find recorded *Levit.* xxvi. *Deut.* xxviii, xxix. 20, &c. xxxi. 17. xxxii. 22, &c.

Ver. 25. *Wherefore I gave them also Statutes that were not good,* &c.] This some understand of the Ceremonial Law, as if it were given purely to be a Check and Restraint to that perverse People, consisting of numerous Rites and Observances, many of which had no intrinsick Goodness in them. But I conceive the Statutes here spoken of, to be of a different Nature from those mentioned Ver. 11. because they have a quite contrary Character given them; therefore I take the Words to import, that God in a just Judgment for their Disobedience

to

tò his own Laws, gave them up to a reprobate
Mind, and fuffered them to walk after the idolatrous and impious Cuftoms of the Heathens round
about them. And whereas by obeying the Laws
and Ordinances which he had given them, they
might have lived happily, Ver. 11. they became
Slaves to the vile and cruel Practices of the Heathen Idolatries, fo as to offer up their very Children in Sacrifice to Idols, to the utter Deftruction
of themfelves and their Pofterity, Ver. 26. This
will appear to be the Senfe of the 'Text, if we compare it with Ver. 39. and with *Deut.* iv. 28. xxviii.
36. *Jerem.* xvi. 13. in which Texts God threatens
them as a Punifhment for their Neglect of his
Worfhip, to difperfe them into the Heathen Countries, and thereby deprive them of an Opportuni-
ty of ferving him in Publick, and expofe them to
the Peril of being feduced to Idols. Juft as *David*
complains to *Saul* of the Hardfhip of his Exile, that
it did lay him open to the Temptation of ferving
the Heathen Gods, 1 *Sam.* xxvi. 19.

Ver. 26. *And I polluted them in their own* Ver. 26.
Gifts.] I fuffered them to pollute themfelves (fo
the Form *Hiphil* is elfewhere ufed in the Senfe of
Permiffion : See the Note on *Ifa.* lxiii. 17.) in thofe
very Gifts which by the Law they were to dedicate to my Service. See Ver. 31. and Chap. xvi.
20, 21.

Ibid. *In that they caufed to pafs thro' the Fire all*
that opens the Womb.] In offering their Firftborn
Sons in Sacrifice to *Moloch* : the Expreffion of
paffing thro' the Fire, is explained in the Note upon
Jerem. xxxii. 35.

Ibid.

Chapter   Ibid. *That I might make them desolate.*] Their
XX.   Sin brought its own Punishment along with it,
destroying the Hopes of Families, and bringing
them to utter Desolation.

     Ibid. *To the end that they might know that I
am the* LORD.] See the Note upon Chap. vi. 7.

Ver. 27, 28   Ver. 27, 28. *Yet in this your Fathers have blafphemed me,* &c.] Or, *Moreover in this,* &c. The
Prophet proceeds to speak of other Instances of Idolatry which their Fathers were guilty of after their
Settlement in the Land of *Canaan:* and in which
their Posterity imitated them.

     Ibid. *Then they saw every high Hill and all the
thick Trees,* &c.] Offering Sacrifice upon Mountains or high Places was a piece of Service at first
performed by the *Jews* to the true God, before
the Temple was built: See 1 *Kings* iii. 2. and afterwards was permitted for that Purpose by godly
Kings who were zealous in putting down all sorts
of Idolatry: See 1 *Kings* xv. 14. xxii. 43. 2 *Chron.*
xxxiii. 17. But by degrees those Places became
appropriated to idolatrous Worship, and upon that
Score are severely condemned. See Chap. vi. 13.
xviii. 6. *Isa.* lvii. 5. 2 *Kings* xxiii. 5.

     Ibid. *There they presented the Provocation of
their Offering : there also they made their sweet
Savour.*] This is to be understood of their Meat-
offerings, being distinguished from their Sacrifices
already mentioned. The Word in the *Hebrew* is
Min-chah, which might more properly be render'd
Bread-offering, as appears by the several kinds of
it reckoned up *Levit.* ii. and answers to the *Mola*
or *Fartum* of the *Romans.* The Meat-offering was
particularly styled, an *Offering of a sweet Savour.*
                                See

See Chap. xvi. 19. but being offered to Idols, it
became abominable, and was turned into a Provo-
cation.

Ver. 29. *What is the high place whereunto ye*
go,. &c.] The Word *Bamah* signifies an Altar as
well as an high place : See the Note on Chap. xvi.
16. So the Sense seems to be, What Name is this
Altar called by, which you frequent? meaning, it
is likely, the very Altar belonging to the Temple :
is it not called *Bamah* at this very time, which
Word properly denotes an high place? An evident
Token that Idolatry is so much practised among
you, that it hath occasioned the changing the very
Names of the Places and Things dedicated to God's
Worship. So that instead of the Word *Mizbeach*,
the Name which God appropriated to his own
Altar, the place is usually called *Bamah*, a Name
taken from an idolatrous Custom.

Ver. 30. *Are ye polluted after the manner of*
your Fathers, &c.] The Reproof would be more
vehement if the Words were render'd thus, *Are*
ye not polluted after the manner of your Fathers,
and do ye not commit Whoredom, &c.] i. e. Do ye
not walk in your Fathers Sins and Idolatries?
Notwithstanding all the Warnings I have given
you, and the severe Instances of my Displeasure
against their Practices, which ought to have terri-
fied you from following their ill Example. The
Particle of Interrogation often implies a Negative
in it, as hath been observed upon the Fourth Verse
of this Chapter : to which Sense the *Vulgar Latin*
renders this Verse,

Certe in viis patrum vestrorum polluimini, &c.

Ver.

Chapter XX.

Ver. 31. Ver. 31. *For when you offer your Gifts, &c.*] See Ver. 26.

Ibid. *And shall I be enquired of by you?*] See Ver. 3.

Ver. 32. Ver. 32. *And that which comes into your Mind shall not be at all, &c.*] We find by the Scripture History that the *Jews* had all along a fond Desire of worshipping the Gods of their Neighbours, and could not bear that Imputation of Singularity which their peculiar way of Worship exposed them to. They thought likewise by this means to live more undisturbedly among the Heathens whither they were led Captive. God tells them here that he will prevent this Purpose of theirs from taking effect. And we find from the very time of their Return from the *Babylonish* Captivity, they have been very cautious of committing Idolatry, and scrupulous of making the least Approaches toward it.

Ver. 33. Ver. 33. *Surely with a mighty Hand and stretched out Arm, and with Fury poured out will I rule over you.*] I will no longer try to reclaim you by the gentle Methods of Patience and Forbearance, but will govern you as Masters do ill Servants by Stripes and Corrections, and by this Means cure you of your hankering after the Heathen Customs and Idolatries.

Ver. 34. Ver. 34. *And I will bring you out from the People, and gather you out of the Countries wherein ye are scattered, with a mighty Hand, &c.*] This some understand of God's bringing his People out of the Countries of the *Moabites, Ammonites,* and other Neighbouring Nations, whither many of them were carried Captive, or went as voluntary Exiles before the general Captivity by the *Chaldeans:*

ans: See *Jerem.* xii. 14. xl. 11. But I conceive it is rather to be understood of the general Restoration of the *Jewish* Nation from the several Parts of the World where they are dispersed: an Event often spoken of in the Prophets: See Ver. 38, 41. and compare this and the following Verses with several Passages in the xxxiv, xxxvi, and xxxvii Chapters of this Prophecy.

Ver. 35. *And I will bring you into the Wilderness of the People.*] The *Wilderness of the People* may be equivalent *to the Countrey where they sojourn,* Ver. 38. so as to signify either the several Dispersions of the *Jewish* Nation; or rather some particular Place or Countrey thro' which they are to pass, in order to their Return into their own Land. The Dissolution of a Government is expressed in Scripture by a Wilderness State: See Chap. xix. 13. The *Jews* going into Captivity are said to *go out of the City, and dwell in the Field,* Micah iv. 10. And the Church under Persecution is represented as *flying into the Wilderness,* Revel. xii. 14. The Phrase does likewise allude to the Wilderness thro' which the *Jews* passed to the Land of *Canaan,* in order to the Tryal of the Obedient, and the Destruction of the Rebellious. Compare Ver. 36, 38. Chap. xxxviii. 8. and *Hos.* ii. 14.

Ibid. *And there will I plead with you Face to Face.*] I will convict you of your Crimes, so that you shall not be able to deny your Guilt, but shall humbly acknowledge that you have deserved those Punishments I have, or shall bring upon you. Compare Chap. xvii. 20. xxxviii. 22. and see the Note upon *Jerem.* ii. 9.

Ver.

Chapter
XX.

Ver. 36.

Ver. 36. *Like as I pleaded with your Fathers in the Wilderness of the Land of Egypt.*] This relates to that solemn Sentence confirmed by an Oath, whereby God irreversibly doomed the Rebellious *Israelites* to perish in the Wilderness, and never to enter into the Land of Promise: *Numb.* xiv. 28, &c.

Ver. 37.

Ver. 37. *And I will cause you to pass under the Rod.*] I will take an exact Account of you as a Shepherd does of his Flock, and will sever between the Good and the Bad, between the Sheep and the Goats; See Chap. xxxiv. 17. The Expression alludes to the Custom of the Shepherds who Number their Cattle by striking every one of them with a Rod. See *Levit.* xxvii. 32. *Jerem.* xxxiii. 13.

Ibid. *And I will bring you into the Bond of the Covenant.*] I will make you sensible that I have not forgotten my Promises to your Fathers, tho' you have forgotten your Obligations to me, and the Engagements implied in your entring into Covenant with me. The Words may be rendred, *I will bring you into the Discipline of the Covenant*; the *Hebrew* Verbs *Yasar* and *Asar* being of promiscuous Signification: and then the Sense will be, I will revenge upon you the *Quarrel of my Covenant*, *Levit.* xxvi. 25. and assert my Authority over you by bringing you under Chastisement in order to your Correction. See *Amos* iii. 2.

Ver. 38.

Ver. 38. *And I will purge out from among you the Rebels.*] I will separate the Righteous from the Wicked, (See Ver. 37.) in order to destroy the latter, as I did the rebellious *Israelites* in the Wilderness: *Numb.* xiv. 29, 30. Compare *Ezek.* xi. 21. xxxiv. 17, 20.

Ibid.

Ibid. *I will bring them forth out of the Country where they Sojourn, and they shall not enter into the Land of Israel.*] See the Note on Ver. 35. The Word *Country* in the Singular Number may be equivalent to *Countries* in the Plural. Ver. 41. The Sentence alludes as the former does, to the Judgment denounced upon the rebellious *Israelites*, that their Carcasses should fall in the Wilderness, and themselves never enter into the Land of *Canaan*: which shall be only a Portion for the Righteous among them. This Text among many others favours the Opinion maintained by several Authors both Ancient and Modern, that the Jews upon their Conversion shall return into their own Land. Comp. Chap. xi. 14. xxviii. 25. (See the Note there) xxxiv. 13. xxxvi. 24.

Ver. 39. *As for you, O House of Israel.*] You of the present Generation.

Ibid. *Go ye, serve ye every one his Idols, &c.*] An *Ironical* Permission full of Indignation and Rebuke, sharply upbraiding them for despising those many Warnings God had given them : and implying that he was now resolved to forsake them, and give them up to *strong Delusions,* as a just Judgment for their abuse of the Means of Grace so long offered to them, and still rejected by them. Compare *Amos* iv. 4. *Psal.* lxxxi. 11, 12. *Rom.* i. 28. 2 *Thes.* ii. 11. and see the Note upon Ver. 25. of this Chapter.

Ibid. *But pollute ye my Name no more with your Gifts, and with your Idols.*] Whilst you offer your Gifts, and make a Present of your Children to Idols, See Ver. 26, 31. do not call your selves any longer my Servants, nor pretend to pay your De-

X   votions

Chapter XX.

Chapter votions in my Temple, and thereby bring a Re-
XX. proach upon my Name and Worſhip. See Chap.
xxiii. 37, 38, 39.

Ver. 40.   Ver. 40. *For in my holy Mountain, in the Mountain of the height of Iſrael.*] In the Chriſtian
Church, called God's holy Mountain in alluſion to
the Temple at *Jeruſalem,* built upon Mount *Moriah:* See the Notes upon Chap. xvii. 23. and *Iſa.*
ii. 2. The Prophet ſpeaks here of the *Jews* as converted and united to the Chriſtian Church: tho'
ſome Learned Men are willing to believe that upon their Converſion and Return to their own
Countrey, certain Privileges ſhall belong to the
Earthly *Jeruſalem,* as the Metropolis of that Nation. See *Iſa.* lxv. 18, 19. lxvi. 20. *Jerem.* iii. 17.
Joel. iii. 17, &c.

Ibid. *There ſhall all the Houſe of Iſrael, all of
them in the Land ſerve me.*] There ſhall be no more
any ſuch Separation among you, as was when the
Ten Tribes forſook the Worſhip of God at *Jeruſalem.* See Chap. xxxvii. 22, 23.

Ibid. *There will I accept them, and there will
I require your Offerings and the Firſt-Fruits of your
Oblations,* &c.] *Requiring* ſignifies the ſame with
Accepting, by a *Metonymy* of the Cauſe for the
Effect: juſt as *Seeking* is ſometimes uſed for *Finding:* See *Iſa.* lxv. 1. In the ſame Senſe God is ſaid
not to *require* ſuch Inſtances of Worſhip, in which
he takes no delight: *Iſa.* i. 11. Offerings ſignify
in general every thing devoted to God's Service,
ſo as to comprehend Tithes under it, *Numb.* xviii.
21, 26. The Firſt-Fruits were offered out of the
Fruits of the Earth which were firſt ripe: Of this
kind was a Sheaf of the Corn which was firſt
reaped,

reaped, *Levit.* xxiii. 10. part of the Dough which was first baked, *Numb.* xv. 20. and in general, the first of all the ripe Fruits, *Numb.* xviii. 12, 13. compare Chap. xliv. 30. with this Text. This was computed to amount to the Sixtieth part of the whole Produce, See *Ezek.* xlv. 13. The Prophet here expresses the Christian Worship by those religious Oblations which were proper to his own time: as the other Prophets frequently describe the State of the Christian Church by Representations taken from the Jewish Temple and Service. See *Isa.* xix. 19. lvi. 7. lx. 7. lxvi. 23. And even the primitive Christians brought Oblations out of the First Fruits of their Increase, for the Support of God's Ministers and Service, out of which the Elements of the Eucharist and the Love Feast which followed it, were provided: as appears from several Testimonies of the ancient Fathers, particularly of *Irenæus, lib.* 4. *c.* 32, and 34. who generally interpret those Words of Christ, *Matth.* v. 23. *If thou bring thy Gift to the Altar,* &c. of the Sacrament of the Lord's Supper.

Ver. 41. *I will accept you with your sweet Savour.*] This is mention'd in Opposition to the sweet Savour of their Offerings to Idols: Ver. 28.

Ibid. *When I bring you out of the People, and gather you out of the Countries wherein ye have been scattered.*] Or as it may better be translated, *When I have brought you out of the People,* &c. Compare Chap. xi. 17. xxxiv. 13. xxxvi. 24. xxxviii. 8.

Ibid. *And I will be sanctified in you before the Heathen.*] I will procure Honour to my Name by the wonderful Works whether of Justice or Mercy,

Ver. 41.

which

Chapter which I will shew toward you. Compare Chap.
XX. xxviii. 22, 25. xxxvi. 23. xxxviii. 23. xxxix. 27.

Ver. 42.   Ver. 42. *And ye shall know that I am the* LORD.]
An *Epiphonema* often used in this Prophet by way
of Conclusion of some severe Denunciation : See
Chap. vi. 7.   But in this and the 44th Verse, and
some other Places added after the Promises of Grace
and Favour, by which God makes his Power
known unto the World, as well as by his Judgments.   See Chap. xxxvi. 23. xxxviii. 23.

Ibid. *When I shall bring you.* [or shall have
brought you] *into the Countrey for which I lifted
up my Hand.*] See Ver. 5.

Ver. 43.   Ver. 43. *And there shall ye remember your Ways
and your Doings.*] The Prophets suppose, that the
Conversion and Restoration of the *Jews* shall be
accompanied with a general Repentance, and a
deep Remorse for their former Misdoings. See
Chap. xvi. 61. and the Note there.

Ibid. *And ye shall lothe your selves in your own
sight.*] See Chap. vi. 7. xvi. 63. xxxvi. 31.

Ver. 44.   Ver. 44. *When I have wrought with you for my
Name's Sake,* &c.] When I have exerted my Power in your Deliverance, moved thereto not by any
Deserts of yours, but purely out of regard to my
own Honour, and the Promises made to your Fathers. See Chap. xxxvi. 22.

Ver. 46.   Ver. 46. *Set thy Face toward the South.*] Direct
thy Looks, and thy Speech (See Chap. iv. 7. vi. 2.)
toward the Land of *Israel,* and particularly toward
Jerusalem, which lay Southward of *Chaldea.* See
Chap. i. 4. xxi. 2.

Ibid. *Drop thy Word toward the South.*] The
Gift of Prophecy is compared to Rain, or the Dew
of

of Heaven, which makes every thing fruitful: See *Deut.* xxxii. 2. Such is the Benefit of found Doctrine where-ever it is received. Compare *Micah* ii. 6. *Job* xxix. 22, 23.

Ibid. *And prophecy against the Forest of the South Field.*] By the *Forest of the South Field* is meant *Jerusalem:* the Word *Forest* being taken metaphorically in the Prophets for a City: because its stately Buildings resemble tall Cedars standing in their several Ranks. Compare *Jer.* xxi. 14. xxii. 7. *Zech.* xi. 1.

Ver. 47. *I will kindle a Fire in thee, and it shall devour every green Tree in thee, and every dry Tree.*] Fire is often taken in a general Sense for God's severe Judgments. Compare Chap. xix. 13. xxii. 21, 31. xxx. 8. But it may here particularly denote the Destruction of *Jerusalem* by Fire: which the Text faith shall devour both the *green Trees* and *the dry:* i. e. the Righteous as well as the Wicked. See Chap. xxi. 3. The Righteous are elsewhere compared to green and flourishing Trees, and the Wicked to dry and wither'd ones, such as are only fit for the Fire. See *Psal.* i. 3. *Luke* xxiii. 31. *Joh.* xv. 5, 6.

Ibid. *And all Faces from the South to the North shall be burnt therein.*] The Destruction shall reach from one End of the Land to the other. See Chap. xxi. 2, 4.

Ver. 49. *Ah Lord* God, *they say of me, Doth he not speak Parables?*] They make this an Argument for disregarding what I say, that I use so many Similitudes and metaphorical Expressions, that they can't discover my Meaning. Comp. Chap. xii. 9. Whereupon God commands him in the next Chapter to speak the same thing in plain Terms.

Ver. 47.

Ver. 49

CHAP.

CHAP. XXI.

The Argument.

The Prophet under the Emblem of a sharp Sword,
foretells the Destruction of Judea, *and particu-*
larly of Jerusalem, *and the Country of the Am-*
monites, by the Armies *of* Nebuchadnezzar.

Ver. 2.

Ver. 2. S ET *thy Face toward Jerusa-*
lem.] See Chap. xx. 46.

Ibid. *Drop thy Word to-*
ward the Holy Places.] i. e.
Toward the Sanctuary or
Temple, and the several
Courts belonging thereto. See the Note on Chap.
vii. 24.

Ver. 3.

Ver. 3. *I will draw forth my Sword out of his*
Sheath.] The Sword of the King of *Babylon,* the
Instrument of my Vengeance. See Ver. 19. and
Chap. xiv. 17.

Ibid. *And will cut off from thee the Righteous*
and the Wicked.] The Command given by God,
Chap. ix. 6. is to *Slay Young and Old, both Maids,*
little Children and Women: i. e. those that have
not

not bin guilty of Idolatry and the other National Sins, as well as thofe that have. Only the Few *Mourners* mentioned Chap. ix. 4. have a Promife to efcape. God's abfolute Dominion will juftify any Temporal Calamity he thinks fit to bring upon Men: and every Man is fo much a Sinner, that no Evil which befals him in this World can be thought unjuft with refpect to God that inflicts it. But yet when God punisheth Men immediately by himfelf, as he did in the Deftruction of the *Old World*, and of *Sodom*, it may be expected he fhould put a Difference between the Righteous and the Wicked: as *Abraham* argues with him upon this Subject, *Gen.* xviii. 23, 25.

Ver. 4. *Againft all Flefh from the South to the North.*] See Chap. xx. 47. Ver. 4.

Ver. 5. *It fhall not return any more.*] *Into its Sheath*, as the Senfe is more fully expreffed, Ver. 30. till it has executed my Commands. Ver. 5.

Ver. 6. *Sigh therefore with the breaking of thy Loins*, &c.] Shew all the Tokens of Grief and Concern: Compare Ver. 13, and 17. and let the Senfe of thefe impending Judgments fo deeply affect thee, as to make thee ftoop, like one that is perfectly bowed down under the Weight of them. Comp. *Ifa.* xxi. 3. *Pfal.* xxxv. 14. xxxviii. 5. God's Judgments, as they were reprefented to the Minds of the Prophets, did very often affect them with dreadful Apprehenfions: efpecially when they concerned their own People. See *Jer.* xxiii. 9. *Dan.* viii. 28. *Habak.* iii. 16. Ver. 6.

Ibid. *Before their Eyes.*] Before the Eyes of the Elders of *Ifrael*, mentioned Chap. xx. 1. or of the Jewifh Captives, who could not but be touched with

a ten-

Chapter a tender Senfe of the Calamities ready to befal their
XXI. Brethren in *Judea.*

Ver. 7. Ver. 7. *Every Heart fhall melt, and all Hands
fhall be feeble, &c.*] Men's Hearts and Strength
fhall fail them for Fear: See Chap. vii. 17.

Ver. 10. Ver. 10. *Should we then make Mirth?*] Men
that are hardened in Sin are apt to laugh at God's
Judgments, and at thofe who give warning of
them. This may be applied to thofe who fpeak
Peace unto the People, *when there was no Peace,*
Chap. xiii. 10.

Ibid. *It contemneth the Rod of my Son, as every
Tree.*] It makes no Diftinction between the Scepter and common Wood: between the Branches of
the Royal Family, defcended from *David* and *Solomon,* whom I honoured with the Title of being
my Sons, *Pfal.* lxxxix. 26. 2 *Sam.* vii. 14. and the
meaneft of the People: See Ver. 12, 25, 26, 27.
and Chap. xix. 11----14.

Ver. 11. Ver. 11. *It is furbifhed, to give it into the Hand
of the Slayer.*] of the King of *Babylon,* the Exe-
cutioner of God's Judgments upon *Judea:* Ver. 19.

Ver. 12. Ver. 12. *It fhall be upon my People, it* fhall be
upon all the Princes of Ifrael.] Both Princes and
People fhall be involved in one common Deftruction. Concerning the Princes of *Ifrael,* fee the
Note upon Chap. xxii. 6.

Ibid. *Smite therefore upon thy Thigh.*] Ufe all
the outward Expreffions of Grief and Mourning.
Compare Ver. 6, 14, 17. Chap. vi. 11. xxxi. 19.

Ver. 13. Ver. 13. *Becaufe it is a Trial.*] As all great Calamities are ftyled, *Job* ix. 23. 2 *Cor.* viii. 2. *Heb.*
xi. 36.

Ibid.

Ibid. *And what if the Sword contemn even the* Chapter
Rod?] The Scepter and Royal Family : See Ver. XXI.
10.

Ibid. *It shall be no more, saith the* LORD.] See
Ver. 27.

Ver. 14. *Smite thy Hands together.*] See *Numb.* Ver. 14.
xxiv. 10. and Ver. 12, of this Chapter.

Ibid. *And let the Sword be doubled the third
time.*] The Expreſſion may import, Firſt the
Slaughter made at the Siege : then thoſe that were
ſlain at the taking of the City ; in which number
may be reckoned the Sons of *Zedekiah*, as alſo the
Chief Prieſts and principal Officers of State, who
were taken and put to Death immediately afterward : See Ver. 14. and 2 *Kings* xxv. 7, 18, 19,
20, 21. To theſe may be added in the third Place,
thoſe who were ſlain with *Gedaliah*, *Jerem.* xli. 2,
3. But perhaps the Expreſſion, *Let the Sword be
doubled a third time*, may mean no more than if the
Prophet had ſaid, *Let the Stroke be repeated twice
and thrice*, i. e. often times. So that Phraſe is
uſed *Job* xxxiii. 29. *All theſe Things worketh God
twice and thrice with Man*, where our Tranſlation
very fitly expreſſes the Senſe *Oftentimes*. A Form
of Speech much like thoſe elſewhere uſed, *For three
Tranſgreſſions and for four*, *Amos* i. 3. *Give a
Portion to ſeven, yea alſo to eight*, *Eccleſ.* xi. 2.

Ibid. *It is the Sword of the Great* Men that
are *Slain, which entreth into their Privy Chambers.*] Whither they went to hide themſelves.
See 1 *Kings* xxii. 25.

Ver. 15. *I have ſet the point of the Sword* Ver. 15.
againſt all their Gates.] The Word *Ibchath*, tranſlated the *Point*, is to be found but in this one
Y Place

Chapter Place of the Bible, and ſo is variouſly rendred by
XXI. Interpreters. Dr. *Caſtell* underſtands it of the De-
ſtruction made by the Sword, from the uſe of the
Word in the *Ethiopick* Language.

Ibid. *It is made bright.*] The *Hebrew* reads
here and Verſe 10. *It is made like Lightning :* the
ſame Metaphor which we read in *Virgil, Æn.* 4.

---*Vaginaque eripit enſem Fulmineum.*

He drew his Sword, which did like Lightning blaze.

Ibid. *It is wrapt up for the Slaughter.*] Or rather, *It is ſharpened for the Slaughter,* as the
Chaldee tranſlates *Menuttah,* which is derived from
the Noun *Nèt,* ſignifying, an Iron Pen or Styletto.

Ver. 16.   Ver. 16. *Go thee one Way or other.*] The Words
are directed to the Sword, implying that God hath
given it a large Commiſſion to go through the
Land without any Reſtraint. See Chap. xiv. 17.

Ibid. *On the Right Hand, or on the Left.*] Either to the South, or to the North, Ver. 4. Thoſe
two Quarters of the World being expreſſed in the
Hebrew Language by the *Right* and *Left.* See
the Note on Chap. xvi. 46.

Ver. 17.   Ver. 17. *I will alſo ſmite my Hands together.*]
To expreſs my juſt Indignation at their Provocations. See Ver. 14. Chap. xxii. 13.

Ibid. *And I will cauſe my Fury to reſt.*] See the
Note on Chap. v. 13.

Ver. 19.   Ver. 19. *Appoint thee two Ways that the Sword
of the King of Babylon may come*] God fore-
ſhews his Prophet that the King of *Babylon* coming with his Army into *Syria,* and finding that the
Ammonites had entred into a Confederacy with
Egypt,

Egypt, as well as *Zedekiah*, he was in doubt a- Chapter
gainſt which of the two People he ſhould firſt XXI.
make War, and committed the Deciſion of this
Matter to his Arts of Divination, deſcribed Ver.
21.

Ver. 20. *That the Sword may come to Rabbath* Ver. 20.
of the Ammonites.] *Rabbath*, otherwiſe called
Rabbah, Chap. xxv. 5. was the chief City of the
Ammonites. See 2 *Sam.* xii. 26. *Jerem.* xlix. 2.

Ibid. *In Jeruſalem the defenced.*] Which had
been ſtrongly fortified, firſt by *David*, 2 *Sam.* v.
9. then by *Solomon*, 1 *Kings* ix. 24. afterward by
Hezekiah, 2 *Chron.* xxxii. 5. and then by *Manaſ-*
ſeh, ibid. Chap. xxxiii. 14.

Ver. 21. *For the King of Babylon ſtood at the* Ver. 21.
parting of the Way---to uſe Divination; *he made his*
Arrows bright.] This way of Divining by Arrows is thus deſcribed by St. *Jerom* in his Commentary upon this Place : " They wrote on ſeveral Ar-
" rows the Names of the Cities they intended to
" Aſſault, and then putting them altogether pro-
" miſcuouſly in a Quiver, they drew them out
" thence as Lots are drawn : and that City whoſe
" Name was writ on the Arrow firſt drawn, was
" the City they firſt made War upon. Perhaps
from this Cuſtom the Verb *Hatſah* or *Hatſats*,
from whence *Hets* an *Arrow*, is derived, comes
to ſignify the Parting or Dividing any thing by
Lot, in which Senſe it is uſed *Job* xli. 6. *Prov.*
xxx. 27.

Ibid. *He made his Arrows bright.*] Or rather,
He mingled his Arrows, as the *Vulgar Latin* tranſlates it.: which Senſe of the Verb *Kilkal* agrees
better with the Deſcription of this Kind of Divi-
Y 2 nation

Chapter
XXI.

nation already given; and therefore is preferred by Dr. *Pocock*, who confirms this Exposition from the *Arabick* use of the Word: See his Notes *In Specim. Hist. Arab.* p. 329. where he treats at large of this manner of Divination.

Ibid. *He consulted with Images.*] The *Hebrew* reads *Seraphim*, which Word as it signifies some Image or visible Representation of a Deity, so consequently it must be taken in an ill Sense, for an Idolatrous Worship, in which Sense it is certainly used 1 *Sam.* xv. 23. 2 *Kings* xxiii. 24. *Zech.* x. 2. Dr. *Spencer* takes a great deal of Pains to prove that the Word is sometimes taken for a sort of Divine Oracle, and is equivalent to the *Urim*, by which the High Priest received an Answer when he consulted God upon Emergent Occasions. See his Third Book *De Legibus Hebr. Dissert. ult. de Urim & Thummim.*

Ibid. *He looked in the Liver.*] This was another noted sort of Divination, which was taken from Lucky or Unlucky Tokens which appear'd in the Entrails of the Sacrifices when they were slain, called *Aruspicina* by the *Romans.*

Ver. 22.   Ver. 22. *At his right Hand was the Divination for Jerusalem.*] When the King of *Babylon* stood at the Head of two Ways, Ver. 21. to consult which of the Two he should take, the Tokens that were shewed him, perswaded him to March with his Army to the Right, *i. e.* toward *Jerusalem.*

Ibid. *To appoint Captains to open the Mouth in Slaughter, to lift up the Voice with Shouting.*] Whose Office it was to encourage the Army to fall upon their Enemies, and destroy them. See *Jerem.* l. 15.   Ibid.

Ibid. *To caſt up a Mount.*] See *Jerem.* xxxii. 24.

Ver. 23. *And it ſhall be unto them as a falſe Divination in their Sight, to them that have ſworn Oaths.*] The King of *Judea* and his Courtiers will deſpiſe all theſe Preparations of War, tho' directed againſt them, as if they were grounded upon the falſe Arts of Divination: whereas it is indeed God himſelf that directs the March of the *Chaldean* Army to revenge the Perjury which *Zedekiah* and his Counſellors were guilty of, in breaking that ſolemn Oath of Fealty which he made to the King of *Babylon.* See Chapt. xvii. 13, 15.

Ibid. *But he will call to remembrance Iniquity, that they may be taken.*] *Nebuchadnezzar* will remember *Zedekiah*'s Breach of his Oath, and revenge himſelf by taking the City, and making him and his Subjects Priſoners of War.

Ver. 24. *Becauſe ye have made your Iniquity to be remembred—ye ſhall be taken with the Hand.*] Becauſe your Sins cry to Heaven for Vengeance, ye ſhall fall into the Hands and Power of the King of *Babylon.*

Ver. 25. *And thou profane wicked Prince of Iſrael.*] The Words are directed to *Zedekiah,* whom the Prophet calls *prophane* and *wicked,* chiefly with reſpect to his breaking that ſolemn Oath uttered in the Name of God, whereby he had engaged himſelf to be Tributary to the King of *Babylon.* See Chap. xvii. 19. *With God is no reſpect of Perſons:* in like manner, when the Prophets ſpeak to Kings in the Name of God, they lay aſide thoſe Titles and Expreſſions of Reſpect which are otherwiſe due to the regal Dignity. See

1 *Sam.*

Chapter **1** *Sam.* xiii. 13. **1** *Kings* xviii. 18. **2** *Kings* iii. 13, **XXI.** 14.

Ibid. *Whose Day is come, when Iniquity shall have an end.*] The Day of whose Calamity is near at hand, when his and his People's Iniquity shall receive their just Doom. Compare Chap. vii. 6. xxx. 3. xxxv. 5.

Ver. 26.

Ver. 26. *Remove the Diadem and take off the Crown.*] The Words *Crown* and *Diadem* are equivalent, and put to signify the Kingly Ornaments of Dignity. See *Isa.* lxii. 3. Indeed the Crown is elsewhere taken for the Emblem of Sovereignty, and the Diadem or Miter for the proper Ornament of the Priesthood, and so the *Chaldee* Paraphrase expresses the Sense of the Verse in these Words, *Remove the Miter from* Seraiah *the chief Priest, and I will take away the Crown from* Zedekiah *the King.* But I conceive this Sense does not so well agree with the Design of the place where the Judgment threatned is spoken only of *Zedekiah.*

Ibid. *This shall not be the same: exalt him that is low, and abase him that is high.*] Things shall not continue in their present State: as *Zedekiah* shall be brought down from his Kingly Dignity, so another Branch of that Family, *viz.* CHRIST, (See Ver. 27.) shall be advanced from an obscure Original and low Condition, to the supreme Degree of Sovereignty. Compare Chap. xvii. 24.

Ver. 27.

Ver. 27. *I will overturn----it, and it shall be no more, until he come whose right it is, and I will give it him.*] After that *Zedekiah* is deprived of his regal Authority, there shall be no more Kings of that Family till Christ come, the King so often foretold

foretold and promised, who in due time shall *reign* Chapter
upon the Throne of his Father David, and of whose XXI.
Kingdom there shall be no End: Luke i. 32, 33.
After the Captivity some of the Priests of the
Assamonean Race did assume the Style and Title
of Kings, but they not being of the Tribe of *Judah*,
could have no just Right to that Honour.

Ibid. *Until he come whose right it is.*] In this
Sense the LXX understand the Word *Shiloh*, *Gen.*
xlix. 10. translating it there, ῟Ω ἀπόκειαι, *To whom
it is reserved:* as if that *Hebrew* Word were equivalent to *Sheloh*, *Whose it is*, as the Learned P. *Fa-
gius* hath observed in his Notes upon the *Targum*
of that Text.

Ver. 28. *Thus saith the Lord* GOD *concerning* Ver. 28.
the Ammonites, *and concerning their reproach.*]
They insulted over the Calamities of their Brethren
the *Jews*, for which they are often reproved very
severely by the Prophets, and threatned with the
like Judgments. See Chap. xxv. 2, 6. *Zeph.* ii.
8, 10.

Ver. 29. *While they see Vanity unto thee, while* Ver. 29.
they divine a Lie unto thee.] While the Sooth-say-
ers and Pretenders to Divination foretel nothing
but happy Events. See Chap. xiii. 23. xxii. 28.

Ibid. *To bring thee upon the Necks of them that
are slain.*] To add thee to the Number of those
who are slain in *Judea:* Ver. 14, 15. and make
thy Condition like theirs.

Ibid. *Of the Wicked whose Day is come.*] See
Ver. 25.

Ver. 30. *Shall I cause it to return into his* Ver. 30.
Sheath?] See Ver. 4, 5.

Ibid.

Chapter
XXI.

Ibid. *I will judge thee in the place where thou wast created.*] Thou shalt not be carried Captive, but shalt be destroyed in thine own Land: See Ver. 32.

Ver. 31.

Ver. 31. *I will blow against thee in the Fire of my Wrath.*] Compare Chap. xxii. 20, 21, 22.

Ver. 32. *Thou shalt be no more remembred.*] See Chap. xxv. 10.

CHAP.

CHAP. XXII.

The ARGUMENT.

*This Chapter contains a Catalogue or Recital of the
Sins of Jerusalem, and of all Orders and Degrees
of Men in it : for which God threatens to inflict
his severest Judgments upon it.*

Ver. 2. Wilt thou judge the bloody City?] See the Note upon Chap. xx. 4.

Ibid. *The bloody City*] See Chap. xxiii. 37, 45. xxiv. 6, 9. 2 *Kings* xxi. 16.

Ver. 3. *That her time may come.*] See Chapter vii. 7.

Ver. 4. *Thou hast caused thy Days to draw near, and art come even to thy Years.*] Thou hast filled up the Measure of thine Iniquities, and brought the time of Vengeance upon thy self. See Chap. vii.

Z   Ibid.

Chapter XXII.

Ibid. *Therefore I have made thee a Reproach unto the Heathen,* &c.] See Chap. v. 14. xxi. 28. *Deut.* xxviii. 37. 1 *Kings* ix. 7.

Ver. 5.

Ver. 5. *Those that be near, and those that be far off, mock thee.*] See Chap. xvi. 57.

Ver. 6.

Ver. 6. *Behold the Princes of Israel,* &c.] These were probably the Members of the *Great Sanhedrim:* or the King's Counsellors and chief Officers of State: See *Jerem.* xxvi. 10. xxxvi. 12.

Ver. 7.

Ver. 7. *In thee they have set light by Father and Mother.*] Against which Sin there is a solemn Curse pronounced, *Deut.* xxvii. 16.

Ver. 8.

Ver. 8. *Thou hast despised my holy Things, and profaned my Sabbaths.*] Thou hast profaned the Things dedicated to my Service, and the Times and Places set apart for the same Purpose. Compare Ver. 26. Chap. xxiii. 38. and *Levit.* xix. 30.

Ver. 9.

Ver. 9. *In thee are Men that carry Tales to shed Blood.*] That bear false Witness against Men in Capital Cases. See *Levit.* xix. 16.

Ibid. *And in thee they eat upon the Mountains.*] See Chap. xviii. 6.

Ver. 10.

Ver. 10. *In thee have they discovered their Father's Nakedness.*] Took their Mother in Law to Wife: which St. *Paul* calls *such Fornication as is not named among the Gentiles:* 1 *Cor.* v. 1.

Ver. 12.

Ver. 12. *In thee they have taken Gifts to shed Blood.*] The Judges have taken Bribes not only to pervert Justice, but even to take away the Lives of the Innocent.

Ver. 13.

Ver. 13. *Therefore I have smitten my Hand at thy dishonest Gain.*] I have expressed mine Indignation at these unjust Practices. See Chapter xxi. 14, 17.

Ver.

Ver. 14. *Can thy Heart endure, or can thine* Chapter
Hands be strong in the Days that I shall deal with XXII.
thee?] On the contrary, *All Hearts shall melt,* ◠◠
and all Hands shall be feeble at the Approach of Ver. 14.
God's Judgments: Chap. xxi. 7.

Ibid. *I the* LORD *have spoken it, and will do*
it.] See Chap. xxiv. 14.

Ver. 15. *And will consume thy filthiness out of* Ver. 15.
thee.] I will purge thee *in the Furnace of Afflic-*
tions, and take that Method to consume thy Dross,
and put an End to thy Idolatrous Practices. Compare Ver. 18, 19, &c. Chap. xxiii. 27.

Ver. 16. *And thou shalt take thine Inheritance* Ver. 16.
in thy self in the Sight of the Heathen.] Instead of
being mine Inheritance, and under my peculiar
Care and Protection, thou shalt be cast out among
the Heathen, and there eat the Fruit of thine own
Ways, and receive the just Reward of thy Wickedness. The Margin of our Bibles reads, *Thou*
shalt be profaned in thy self, &c. Which I think
expresses the Sense much better; taking the Verb
Nihal in the same Sense wherein it is used Chap.
vii. 24. and Chap. xxv. 3. of this Prophecy. *i.e.*
Thou shalt no longer enjoy the Privileges of a City
called by my Name, and set apart for my Residence, but shalt be laid open as common Ground,
to be profaned by Infidels. Compare *Isa.* xlvii. 6.

Ver. 18, 19, 20. *The House of Israel is become*
to me Dross, &c.] Their Filthiness may fitly be
compared to the Mixture of Dross and baser Me-
tals with the pure Silver: and as that is purified
by being melted in a Furnace, or Crucible, so *Jeru-*
salem when it is set on Fire, shall be the Furnace
wherein I will cast them and their Wickedness to

Z 2   be

Chapter be confumed. Compare *Jerem.* vi. 28, 30. God's
XXII. fevere Judgments are expreffed by the *Furnace of*
Affliction, Ifa. xlviii. 10. and compared to *a Re-*
finer's Fire, Malach. iii. 2. *Ifa.* i. 25. becaufe they
are defigned to purge Men from that Drofs and
Corruption which is too often the Effect of Eafe
and Profperity.

Ver. 21. Ver. 21. *I will gather you, and blow upon you in*
the Fire of my Wrath.] God's Vengeance is often compared to Fire: See Chap. xx. 47. But here it was
fo in a literal Senfe, when both City and Temple
were confumed by Fire: 2 *Kings* xxv. 9.

Ver. 24. Ver. 24. *Thou art the Land that is not cleanfed*
nor rained upon, in the Day of Indignation.] God
had in the foregoing Verfes compared his Anger to
Fire; in purfuance of which Metaphor he adds,
That if the wholfom Advice and Admonition of
the Prophets (compar'd to the Dew or Rain coming from Heaven, Chap. xx. 46.) had bin but duly received, they would have fupplied the place of
Rain, and wafh'd away the filth of the Land:
So that it needed to have bin purged or cleanfed by
Fire. The *Chaldee Paraphrafe* expounds the Senfe
thus, *Thou art the Land in which there have been*
no good Works done, to protect it in the Day of
God's Curfe or Indignation.

Ver. 25. Ver. 25. *There is a Confpiracy of the Prophets in*
the midft of her.] i. e. of the Falfe Prophets: See
the Note upon *Jerem.* xxix. 1. Thefe are often reproved for making a gain of their Profeffion: See
Jerem. vi. 13. *Micah* iii. 5, 11.

Ibid. *They have devoured Souls; they have ta-*
ken the Treafure and precious Things, &c.] They
make Merchandife of Men's Souls: or elfe they
take

take away their Lives by false Accusations, and
then seize upon their Substance. Compare Ver.
27. and *Matth.* xxiii. 14.

Ver. 26. *Her Priests have violated my Law, and*
have profaned my Holy Things.] The Gifts and
Sacrifices offered in my Service, either by offering
them in an undue manner, as the Sons of *Eli* did,
1 *Sam.* ii. 15. or without due Purification of themselves; or else eating them as Common Meats,
without regard to the Rules prescribed in the Law,
Levit. xxi, xxii.

Ibid. *They have put no Difference between the
Holy and Profane,* &c.] They have not shewed
any regard to the Rules the *Levitical* Laws lay
down, whereby to distinguish betwixt what is Holy or Unholy, Clean or Unclean, and that both
with respect to Persons and Things. And they are
guilty of this Neglect, in contradiction to an express Charge given them concerning this Matter,
Levit. x. 10.

Ibid. *And have hid their Eyes from my Sabbaths.*] They have not attended upon my Publick
Worship on the Sabbath Days, See 2 *Chron.* xxix.
7. and thereby have encouraged my People in the
Neglect and Profanation of that Day. See Ver. 8.

Ver. 27. *Her Princes in the midst of her are
like Wolves, ravening the Prey,* &c.] The chief
Officers of State under the King: See *Jerem.* xxxvi.
12. xxxviii. 4. not excluding the Kings themselves,
whose Oppressions of their Subjects the Prophet
elsewhere severely reproves: See Chap. xix. 3, 6.
xlv. 9. All those, the Text saith, stick at no Method of Injustice and Oppression, whereby they
may increase their Substance, tho' it be by taking

away

Chapter XXII.

away the Lives and Estates of the Innocent. Compare *Isa.* i. 23. *Micah* iii. 1, 2, &c. *Zeph.* iii. 3.

Ver. 28. Ver. 28. *And her Prophets have daubed them with untemper'd Mortar,* &c.] Have daubed over the evil Practices of the great Men by palliating Devices. See Chap. xiii. 6, 10.

Ver. 29. Ver. 29. *The People of the Land have used Oppression.*] See *Jerem.* v. 26. vi. 13.

Ibid. *Yea, they have oppressed the Stranger wrongfully.*] Contrary to an express Prohibition of God's Law, frequently repeated and urged upon them from the Consideration, that they themselves were Strangers in *Egypt.* See *Exod.* xxii. 21. xxiii. 9. *Levit.* xix. 33, 34.

Ver. 30. Ver. 30. *And I sought for a Man among them that should make up the Hedge----but I found none.*] This general Complaint may be expounded with some Restriction, (such as is commonly understood in unlimited Expressions.) For we read Chap. ix. 4. that there were some that did *sigh* and *cry to God,* by way of deprecating his Wrath, *for the Abominations done in Jerusalem.* See the like Expression *Jerem.* v. 1. and the Note upon that place.

Ibid. *That should make up the Hedge, and stand in the Gap,* &c.] See Chap. xiii. 5.

Ver. 31. Ver. 31. *Their own Way have I recompenced upon their Heads.*] See Chap. ix. 10. xi. 21. xvi. 43.

CHAP.

CHAP. XXIII.

The ARGUMENT.

The Idolatries of Samaria *and* Jerusalem *are here
represented under the Metaphor of the lewd
Practices of two Common Harlots: For which
Crimes God denounces severe Judgments against
them both. The same Metaphor is here made
use of, which was pursu'd at large in the Six-
teenth Chapter. See the Argument there.*

Ver. 2. Here were two Women, the
Daughters of one Mother.] Countries are commonly represented as Mothers of their People, and the Inha-
bitants as their Children : So the *Daughters of Syria* signify the Inhabitants of that Country, Chap. xvi. 57. Thus *Samaria* and *Jerusalem* are described in this Chapter as Sisters, the Offspring of the same Land or Country. Compare Chap. xvi. 46. *Jerem.* iii. 7, 8, 10.

Ver. 3. *And they committed Whoredoms in E-
gypt.*] They learned to commit Idolatry there.

See

See Chap. xx. 7, 8. It has been already observed
that Idolatry is often represented as spiritual Adultery. See Chap. xvi. 15, &c.

Ibid. *They committed Whoredoms in their Youth.*]
The time when the *Israelites* were in *Egypt*, or
were lately departed out of it, is called their *Youth*
in the Prophets, because that was the time when
God first owned them for his People. See Ver. 8,
19. Chap. xvi. 8, 22, 60. *Jerem.* ii. 2. *Hos.* ii. 15.

Ibid. *There were their Breasts pressed, &c.*]
*There they served Idols, and there they corrupted
their Ways*, as the *Chaldee Paraphrast* expresses
the Sense. The Scripture commonly calls Idolatrous Churches and Nations by the Name of *Harlots*: and in like manner honours those who preserve their Allegiance to God pure and undefiled,
with the Title of *Chast Wives* or *Virgins*. See
2 *Cor.* xi. 2. *Revel.* xix. 7. xxi. 2. xiv. 4.

Ver. 4.
Ver. 4. *And the Names of them were Aholah
the Elder, and Aholibah her Sister,——Samaria is
Aholah, and Jerusalem Aholibah.*] The Word
Aholah signifies, *Her Tent* or *Tabernacle*: *Aholibah* denotes, *My Tent* or *Tabernacle is in her.*
These two different Appellations imply, that *Samaria* had indeed a Tabernacle or Place for Publick
Worship, but of her own Devising : *viz.* the Cities of *Dan* and *Bethel* where the Golden Calves
were set up : whereas God's Tabernacle first, and
afterward his Temple was placed in *Jerusalem.
He placed his Name there,* or chose it for the Place of
his peculiar Residence : 1 *Kings* viii. 29. Why *A-
holah* is called the *Elder Sister,* See the Note on
Chap. xvi. 46.

Ver. 5. *And Aholah plaid the Harlot when she* Chapter
was mine.] After she had lived in Covenant with XXIII.
me, and attended upon my Service and Worship
all the time of the Judges, and of *David* and *So-* Ver. 5.
lomon, she fell off from my Service, and was the
first that established Idolatry by a Law, and con-
sented to *Jeroboam's* wicked Device of setting up
the Golden Calves.

Ibid. *And she doated on her Lovers.*] i. e. Her
Foreign Allies, whose Idolatries she was fond of,
and hoped by that means to procure their Friendship and Assistance. See the Note on Chap. xvi.
33, 37.

Ibid. *On the Assyrians her Neighbours.*] The
King of *Assyria* was a very Potent Prince, and
thereupon his Alliance was courted both by the
Kings of *Israel* and *Judah.* See 2 *Kings* xv. 29.
xvi. 7. and Ver. 12. of this Chapter.

Ver. 6. *Which were cloathed with Blew, Cap-* Ver. 6.
tains and Rulers.] As Women are apt to fall in
Love with comely Young Men, well Mounted and
richly Cloathed : so the *Israelites* were enamoured
with the State and Bravery of the *Assyrians,* and
thought themselves secure if they could but procure their Alliance and Friendship : and in order
to it embraced their Idolatries.

Ibid. *Horsemen riding upon Horses.*] Horses
were scarce in *Judea,* which made the Jews apply
themselves to the neighbouring Countries for
Troops of Horse in the time of any Hostile Invasi-
on. See *Isa.* xxx. 16. xxxi. 2. xxxvi. 8.

Ver. 7. *Thus she committed Whoredoms with* Ver. 7.
them.] She defiled her self with their Idols, as the

A a   Sense

Chapter
XXIII.

Sense is more plainly expressed at the end of the Verse.

Ver. 8.

Ver. 8. *Neither left she her Whoredoms brought from Egypt.*] She added New Idolatries to those she had formerly committed. See Ver. 3.

Ver. 9.

Ver. 9. *Wherefore I delivered her into the Hand of her Lovers.*] God made these very *Assyrians* the Executioners of his Judgments upon the Ten Tribes: many of them being carried away Captive by *Pul* King of *Assyria*, 1 *Chron.* v. 25, 26. afterward by *Tiglath-Pileser*, 2 *Kings* xv. 29. and at length the whole Country was subdued and depopulated by *Salmaneser*, 2 *Kings* xvii. 6. The Kings of *Babylon* were likewise stiled Kings of *Assyria*: See 2 *Kings* xxiii. 29. 2 *Chron.* xxxiii. 11. *Lovers* mean the same with Allies, those whose Friendship and Assistance the Jews courted by complying with them in their Idolatries. See Chap. xvi. 37.

Ver. 10.

Ver. 10. *These discovered her Nakedness, they took her Sons and her Daughters.*] They carried her and her Children away Captive, stript and bare: Comp. Ver. 29. and Chap. xvi. 37, 39.

Ibid. *And slew her with the Sword.*] Comp. Ver. 47. and Chap. xvi. 40. Those that were not led Captive were slain in the Field of Battle, or in the Siege of *Samaria*, 2 *Kings* xvii. 5.

Ibid. *And she became famous among Women.*] The *Hebrew* reads, *She became a Name among Women*: As she had been formerly *renowned among the Heathen* for her *Beauty*, Chap. xvi. 14. So now she was every where talked of as a remarkable Instance of God's Vengeance, and set forth for an

Ex-

Example to other Cities and Nations to deter them
from the like Abominations. See Ver. 48. and
Chap. xvi. 41.

Ibid. *For they had executed Judgment upon her.*]
See Ver. 24.

Ver. 11. *And when her Sister Aholibah saw*
this, she was more corrupt in her inordinate Love
than she.] *Jerusalem* was so far from taking Warning by the Judgments inflicted upon *Samaria*,
that she advanced to greater Degrees of Idolatry.
See Ver. 14. Chap. xvi. 47, 51. *Jerem.* iii. 8. and
the Notes upon those Places.

Ver. 12. *She doated upon the Assyrians her*
Neighbours, &c.] Comp. Ver. 1. The King of
Judah, Ahaz, entred into a Confederacy with
the King of *Assyria,* hoping for Relief from his
Power and the Bravery of his Army, and serving
his Idols to that End. See 2 *Kings* xvi. 7----11.
2 *Chron.* xxviii. 16---23.

Ver. 13. *They took both one way.*] Both of them
were like Common Harlots, impudent in their Idolatries, and irreclaimable. Compare *Jerem.* iii. 13.

Ver. 14. *When she saw Men pourtrayed upon the*
Wall, Images of the Chaldeans, &c.] These were
probably the Pictures of those Deified Heroes whom
the *Chaldeans* worshipped as Gods: Such were
Bel, Nebo, and *Merodach,* mentioned *Isa.* xlvi. 1.
Jerem. l. 2.

Ver. 15. *Girded with Girdles upon their Loins.*]
A Girdle was a Mark of Dignity, and worn as
such by Princes and Men in Authority. See 1 *Sam.*
xviii. 4. *Isa.* xxii. 21.

Ibid. *In died Attire upon their Heads.*] The
Chaldeans, and afterward the *Persians,* wore a

Chapter
XXIII.

Ver. 11.

Ver. 12.

Ver. 13.

Ver. 14.

Ver. 15.

A a 2   sort

Chapter sort of Turbans upon their Heads, with different
XXIII. Degrees of Ornaments according to their different
Qualities.

Ver. 16.   Ver. 16. *And as soon as she saw them with her Eyes, she doted upon them, and sent Messengers unto them into Chaldea.*] These Images pleased her so much, that she sent to *Babylon* to learn the manner how their Idols were to be worshipped. See Ver. 40, 41. and Chap. xvi. 17. This probably relates to those Times when a Correspondence was maintained between the Cities of *Babylon* and *Jerusalem*: after that *Nebuchadnezzar* had conquered *Judea*, and made it a tributary Kingdom, in the Beginning of the Fourth Year of *Jehoiakim*. See *Dan.* i. 1, 2. 2 *Kings* xxiv. 1. and the Notes upon *Jerem.* xxii. 19.

Ver. 17.   Ver. 17. *And the Babylonians came to her into the Bed of Love,* &c.] The Metaphor of representing Idolatry by the inordinate Lust of Adultery is still carried on.

    Ibid. *And her Mind was alienated from them.*] She quickly grew weary of these too, as lewd Women are of their former Gallants, and look out for new ones. She broke her League and Covenant with them, as St. *Jerom* very well expresses the Sense: meaning that Covenant which *Jehoiakim* made with *Nebuchadnezzar* to be his Tributary. Compare Ver. 16, 22, 28. and was afterward renewed by *Zedekiah*: See Chap. xvii. 15.

Ver. 18.   Ver. 18. *So she discovered her Whoredoms,* &c.] The Sense might better be expressed, *After she had discover'd,* &c. the Sense being still continued with the foregoing Verse.

                                    Ibid.

Chapter
XXIII.

21 Ibid. *Then my Mind was alienated from her,&c.*]
As she by her Idolatries had broken all the Bonds
of Duty and Allegiance whereby she was engaged
to me, a Sin often compared to a Wife's Disloyal-
ty toward her Husband: So I withdrew my Love
and Affection from her, and resolved to give her
a Bill of Divorce, as the Prophet *Jeremy* expresses
it, and not own her any more as mine, as I had
cast off her Sister *Samaria.* Compare *Jerem.* iii. 8.
vi. 8. *Hof.* ii. 2.

Ver. 19. *Yet she multiplied her Whoredoms, in* Ver. 19.
calling to remembrance the Days of her Youth, &c.]
Tho' she was fond of new Idolatries, she did not
forget her old ones, even those which she had
learn'd in *Egypt.* See Ver. 3.

Ver. 20. *For she doted upon their Paramours,* Ver. 20.
&c.] Upon the Idols of *Egypt*, and the impure
Rites which accompany their idolatrous Worship.
See the Notes upon Chap. xvi. 26. This may relate to the time when *Zedekiah* entred into a New
Confederacy with *Egypt*, See Ver. 21. and Chap.
xvii. 15. which made the People fond of admitting
the *Egyptian* Idolatries.

Ver. 22. *I will raise up thy Lovers against thee,* Ver. 22.
from whom thy Mind is alienated.] I will execute
my Judgments upon thee by those very *Babylonians*, whose Alliance and Idolatries thou hast been
so fond of: See Ver. 9. but since hast broken the
League thou madest with them, contracting a new
one with *Egypt*, and thereby hast provoked them
to revenge thy Perfidiousness. See Ver. 17.

Ver. 23. *The Babylonians, and all the Chalde-* Ver. 23.
ans, Pekod, and Shoa, and Koa, and all the Af-
fyrians with them.] The Inhabitants of the several
Pro-

Chapter
XXIII.

Provinces of the *Babylonish* Monarchy. *Pekod* is
mentioned as a Province of *Babylon*, *Jerem.* l. 21.
St. *Jerom* upon the place underſtands theſe three
Words *Pekod*, *Shoa*, and *Koa*, in an *Appellative*
Senſe, to denote ſo many Titles or Degrees of Honour, as much as to ſay, Governors, Princes, and
great Men. In which Senſe the two former
Words, *Pekod*, (or *Pakud*) and *Shoa*, are confeſ-
ſedly taken in Scripture : and *Koa* is ſuppoſed to be
derived from the Verb *Kaàng*, which ſignifies
Printing Marks in the Fleſh. *Levit.* xix. 28. and
it was the Cuſtom of great Men to diſtinguiſh
themſelves from their Inferiors by ſuch Marks or
Prints: See Dr. *Spencer de Legib. Hebr. lib. 2. c.*
14. *Sect.* 1.

    Ibid. *All of them deſirable young Men*, &c.] As
their Riches and Bravery made them appear ami-
able in your Eyes when you firſt courted their Alliance, Ver. 12. So they ſhall appear in the ſame
ſplendid Equipage when they come to invade your
Country, and to beſiege your City : but then their
gallant Appearance ſhall ſtrike a Terror and Conſternation into you.

Ver. 24.

    Ver. 24. *And they ſhall come againſt thee with
Chariots, Waggons, and Wheels*, &c.] A like De-
ſcription of warlike Preparations may be ſeen
Chap. xxvi. 10. *Jerem.* xlvii. 3. *Nahum* iii. 2, 3.
Chariots are mentioned both in ſacred and profane
Writers, as of principal Uſe in the ancient way of
Fighting.

    Ibid. *And I will ſet Judgment before them, and
they ſhall judge thee according to their Judgments.*]
I will deliver thee into their Power as the Miniſters
of my Juſtice, who ſhall make thy Puniſhments
bear

bear a Correspondence with thy Guilt. See Ver. 45.

Ver. 25. *And I will set my Jealousy against thee,* *and they shall deal furiously with thee.*] They shall punish thee with that Fury, with which a Man in the Rage of Jealousy shall treat a Wife that hath been unfaithful to him. Compare Chapter xvi. 38.

Ibid. *And they shall take away thy Nose, and thine Ears,* &c.] As Husbands in that Case render those Women deformed, whose Beauty hath been too pleasing to Strangers: so shall the *Chaldeans* deface all the Glories and Ornaments of *Jerusalem*, and after they have slain and carried Captive its Inhabitants, shall set the City on Fire, and reduce it to an Heap of Ashes. Compare Chap. xvi. 41.

Ver. 26. *They shall also strip thee of thy Clothes,* &c.] See ibid. Ver. 37, 39.

Ver. 27. *Thus will I make thy Lewdness cease from thee.*] These severe Judgments shall effectually deter thee from Idolatry, and make thee abhor the least Approaches toward it. See Chapter xxii. 15. Accordingly we find, that after the Captivity the *Jews* never returned to their former idolatrous Practices.

Ibid. *And thy Whoredoms brought from the Land of Egypt.*] Where thou didst first learn Idolatry, and ever since hast had an Inclination toward it. See Ver. 3, 19.

Ibid. *So that thou shalt not lift up thine Eyes unto them.*] See Chap. xviii. 6.

Ver. 28. *I will deliver thee into the Hand of them whom thou hatest,* &c.] The *Chaldeans* that were thy Lovers formerly: Ver. 22. But since thou hast broken thy League and Friendship with them,

Chapter XXIII. Ver. 25.

Ver. 26.

Ver. 27.

Ver. 28.

them,

them, thy Love is turned to Hatred. See Ver. 17.

Ver. 29. *And they shall deal with thee hateful-
ly, and shall take away all thy Labour.*] As thou
haft requited their Love with Hatred, so shall
they deal with thee: their Hatred against thee
shall be greater than their former Love toward
thee, which was the Conclusion of *Ammon's* unlawful Love to his Sifter, 2 *Sam.* xiii. 15. This
shall prompt them to take a full Revenge upon thy
Perfidioufnefs, to consume all the Fruits of thy Labours, and to take away all the Wealth thou haft
gather'd by thine Industry.

Ibid. *And shall leave thee naked and bare.*] See
the Note on Chap. xvi. 37.

Ver. 31, 32, 33. *Therefore will I give her Cup
into thine Hand: Thou shalt be laught to fcorn and
had in derision----Thou shalt be filled with Drunken-
nefs and Sorrow, &c.*] God's Judgments are often
compared to a Cup of intoxicating Liquors, becaufe they aftonifh Men, and bereave them of
common Judgment and Difcretion, and likewife
expofe them to the Scorn and Contempt of their
Enemies. See *Jerem.* xxv. 15, &c. xlviii. 26. *Habak.* ii. 16.

Ver. 34. *Thou shalt even drink it, and fuck it
out.*] The foreft and heavieft of God's Judgments
shall fall to thy Share: like thofe that drink a Po-
tion off to the Bottom, where the moft naufeous
part of it is fettled. See *Pfal.* lxxv. 8. *Jeremiah*
li. 17.

Ibid. *Thou shalt break the Sherds thereof, and
pluck off thine own Breasts.*] Thou shalt behave
thy felf as drunken People do, who firft throw
away, or break in Pieces the Cup, and then are
angry

angry with themselves as the Cause of their own
Misfortunes. The Text mentions her *Breasts*,
as the Parts which had a principal Share in her
Guilt, according to the allegorical Description here
given of her Idolatries. See Ver. 3, 21.

Ver. 35. *Because thou hast forgotten me, and*
cast me behind thy Back.] Because thou hast not
only forsaken my Worship, but hast shewed the
utmost Contempt and Aversion toward me, (See
the Note upon Chap. viii. 16.) thou shalt deser-
vedly bear the Punishment due to thine Idolatries.
Compare Ver. 17, 19, 30, 49.

Ver. 35.

Ver. 36. *Wilt thou judge Aholah and Aholi-*
bah?] See the Note on Chap. xx. 4.

Ver. 36.

Ver. 37. *That they have committed Adultery,*
and Blood is in their Hands, &c.] They have committed Adultery with their Idols, as it follows, and
have slain their Children in Sacrifice to them. See
Chap. xvi. 20, 21.

Ver. 37.

Ver. 38. *They have defiled my Sanctuary in the*
same Day, &c.] By coming within the Precincts
of it polluted with Idolatry. See the following
Verse, and Chap. xxii. 8.

Ver. 38.

Ver. 39. *And lo, thus have they done in the*
midst of mine House.] The Words may be expounded of their setting up Idols in the very Temple,
and worshipping them there. See 2 *Kings* xxi. 4.

Ver. 39.

Ver. 40. *And furthermore that ye have sent for*
Men to come from far, to whom a Messenger was
sent, &c.] See Ver. 16. Their courting the Alli-
ances of Foreign Nations, by complying with their
Idolatries, is set forth under the Representation of
the several Arts which Harlots use to recommend
themselves to new Lovers. Compare *Isa.* lvii. 7, 9.

Ver. 40.

B b

Ibid.

Chapter XXIII.

Ibid. *For whom thou didſt waſh thy ſelf.*] A Cuſtom generally practiſed by Women before the time of their Nuptials : See *Ruth* iii. 3.

Ibid. *And paintedſt thine Eyes.*] Or *thy Face,* as the Phraſe is tranſlated 2 *Kings* ix. 30. See the Note upon *Jerem.* iv. 30.

Ver. 41.

Ver. 41. *And ſatteſt upon a ſtately Bed, and a Table prepared before it.*] The Expreſſions denote their ſitting down with Idolaters, and partaking of their Sacrifices : The Words *Altar* and *Table,* are uſed promiſcuouſly in the Prophets. See *Malachi* i. 7. becauſe all Sacrifices were Feaſts made of Offerings dedicated to God's Service : ſo that he was properly the Entertainer, and thoſe that did partake of the Sacrifices were his Gueſts, that did eat at his Table in token of their being in Covenant and Friendſhip with him. What was conſumed upon the Altar, was God's Meſs or Portion, and is therefore called, the *Bread of God,* See Chapter xliv. 7. *Levit.* xxi. 6. and *the Food of the Lord,* ibid. Chap. iii. 11. The Remainder of the Sacrifices, his Gueſts were entertained with, either by themſelves, as in Peace-offerings, or elſe by their Proxies the Prieſts, as in Sin-offerings. See Mr. *Mede's Diſcourſe of the Chriſtian Sacrifice,* Chap. 7. The *Jews* as well as the *Romans* lying upon Beds or Couches at their Meals. See *Iſa.* lvii. 7. So did other Eaſtern Nations : See *Eſth.* i. 6.

Ibid. *Whereupon thou haſt ſet mine Incenſe, and mine Oyl.*] See Chap. xvi. 18.

Ver. 42.

Ver. 42. *And the Voice of a Multitude being at eaſe was with her.*] All ſorts of Expreſſions of Joy were heard at theſe her Meetings : Such as Muſick and

and Dancing, which ufually accompanied idolatrous Feftivals. See *Exod.* xxⱴii. 6, 18, 19.

Ibid. *And with the Men of the common fort
were brought the Sabeans from the Wildernefs.*]
The Prophet perfifts in comparing the Idolatries
of the *Jews* to the Practices of lewd Women who
proftitute themfelves to all Comers, even thofe of
the meaneft Condition. Such were the *Sabeans*
that came *from the Wildernefs :* i. e. from *Arabia*
called *the 'Defart,* where dwelt the Pofterity of
Seba mentioned *Gen.* x. 7. Thefe were probably
fome of thofe idolatrous People dwelling in the
Wildernefs, whom *Jeremy* mentions, Chap. ix. 26.
who polled the Corners of their Heads in honour
of fome Idol whom they worfhipped. See the Note
upon that place.

Ibid. *Which put Bracelets upon their Hands,
and beautiful Crowns upon their Heads.*] i. e. Upon the Hands and Heads of thefe two lewd Women, *Aholah* and *Aholibah,* See Ver. 45. Bracelets and Crowns were Ornaments proper to Brides,
See Chap. xvi. 11, 12. and were likewife prefented
by Lovers to their Miftreffes. Crowns were likewife worn at publick Feftivals and Times of Rejoicing : See *Ifa.* xxxv. 10. Whereupon the *Hebrew* Phrafe is tranflated here and Chap. xvi. by
the LXX, Στέφανον καυχήσεως, *a Crown of Rejoicing :*
an Expreffion probably taken from hence by St.
Paul, 1 *Thef.* ii. 19.

Ver. 43. *Then faid I unto her that was grown*
old in Adulteries, &c.] The Words import, that
it was time for her to leave off her ill Courfes, that
Age and Experience might fufficiently convince
her of the Follies of them : but withal they imply,

Ver. 43.

that

Chapter
XXIII.

that Age and Time feldom correct ill Habits. The Word *Her*, is taken collectively in this and the following Verfe, fo as to include both the Sifters. So the Singular Number is ufed *Pfal.* xii. 7. *Thou fhalt preferve* him *from this Generation for ever:* where our Interpreters rightly obferve in the Margin, that the Word *Him*, fignifies *every one of them.*

Ver. 44.

Ver. 44. *Yet they went in unto her,* &c.] Both *Samaria* and *Jerufalem* defiled themfelves with the Idolatries of all the Heathen round about them. Compare Ver. 7, 17.

Ver. 45.

Ver. 45. *And the righteous Men they fhall judge them.*] By *righteous* or juft *Men*, fome underftand the *Babylonians*, who tho' a wicked and idolatrous People, were the Executioners of God's Juftice upon a Nation that had finned againft a clearer Light and greater Convictions. So *Nebuchadnezzar* and other Heathen Princes are called *God's Servants*, as being Inftruments of his Providence. But the Expreffion may in a more proper Senfe be underftood of the Prophets who foretold the Judgments God would inflict upon *Samaria* and *Jerufalem:* fuch as *Hofea, Amos, Jeremiah*, &c. The Prophets are faid to execute thofe Judgments which they foretel: So *Ezekiel* faith of himfelf, that *he was fent to deftroy the City:* Chap. xliii. 3. *i. e.* to Prophecy its Deftruction. To the fame Senfe we read *Hof.* vi. 5. *I have hewed them by my Prophets, I have flain them by the Words of my Mouth.* See the Notes upon *Ifa.* vi. 10. *Jerem.* i. 10. v. 14.

Ibid. *After the manner of Adultereffes, and after the manner of them that fhed Blood.*] See Ver. 37. and Chap. xvi. 38.

Ver. 46. *I will bring a Company upon them, and give them to be removed and spoiled.*] This is meant chiefly of the *Babylonians*, who should plunder and carry away Captive a great part of the Inhabitants of *Jerusalem.*

Ver. 47. *And the Company shall stone them with Stones, and dispatch them with their Swords.*] See Chap. xvi. 40.

Ibid. *They shall slay their Sons and their Daughters,* &c.] See Ver. 25.

Ver. 48. *Thus will I cause Lewdness to cease out of the Land.*] See Ver. 27.

Ibid. *That all Women may be taught not to do after your Lewdness.*] See the Notes upon Ver. 10. and upon Chap. xvi. 41.

Ver. 49. *And ye shall bear the Sins of your Idols.*] Ye shall bear the Punishment due to your Sins of Idolatry. *To bear Sin* or *Iniquity,* is a noted Expression in Scripture, signifying the undergoing the Punishment due to it. Compare Ver. 35.

Chapter
XXIII.
Ver. 46.

Ver. 47.

Ver. 48.

Ver. 49.

C H A P.

CHAP. XXIV.

The ARGUMENT.

By the Figure of a Boiling Pot *is shewed the Destruction of* Jerusalem *and its Inhabitants, and by* Ezekiel's *being forbidden to mourn for his Wife is signified, that the Calamities of the Jews shall be so astonishing as to be beyond all Expressions of Sorrow.*

Ver. 1.

Ver. 2.

Ver. 3.

Ver. 1. ***A**GAIN in the ninth Year of* Jehoiakin's *Captivity.*] See Chap. i. 2.

Ver. 2. *The King of Babylon set himself against Jerusalem this same day.*] See *Jer.* lii. 4. 2 *Kings* xxv. 1.

Ver. 3. *And utter a Parable unto the rebellious House.*] Add this Emblem or Parable concerning a Boiling Pot, to the rest thou hast delivered to them : tho' they seem resolved not to give heed to
what

what thou deliverest, either in plain Words or fi- Chapter
gurative Expressions. Compare Chap. xvii. 12. XXIV.
xx. 49.

Ibid. *Set on a Pot, set it on*, &c.] The Destruction of *Jerusalem* is represented by a Boiling Pot
or Caldron, both by *Jeremiah* Chap. i. 13. and by
Ezekiel Chap. xi. 3.

Ver. 4. *Gather the Pieces into it, even every* Ver. 4.
good piece, &c.] Meaning the chief of the Citizens, who should be destroyed together with the
City : See Chap. xi. 3.

Ver. 5. *Take the choice of the Flock.*] This be- Ver. 5.
longs in Sense to the former Verse, so the LXX
translate the Words, joining them with the foregoing Sentence, *With the choice Bones taken out of
the Flock.*

Ibid. *Burn also the Bones under it.*] The Bones
of those who have been unjustly slain in the midst
of the City. See Chap. xi. 7. whose Blood cries
for Vengeance against it, and kindles God's Anger like Fire.

Ibid. *And make it boil well.*] To denote the
City's being set on Fire : See Ver. 10, 11.

Ver. 6. *Wo to the bloody City.*] See Chap. xxii. Ver. 6.
3. xi. 6. xvi. 30. xxiii. 37.

Ibid. *Even to the Pot whose Scum is therein.*]
Whose Filthiness is not purged out of it : See
Ver. 13.

Ibid. *Bring it out piece by piece.*] The principal
Men of the City (See Ver. 4.) shall be carried out
of the City by the *Chaldeans*, and afterwards slain :
See Chap. xi. 7, 9.

Ibid. *Let no Lot fall upon it.*] Conquerors used
to cast Lots what Share of the Vanquish't they
would

Chapter
XXIV.
〰️

would fave :. See 2 *Sam.* viii. 2. *Joel* iii. 3: *Nahum* iii. 10.   Here there will be no ufe of Lots, for all the principal Inhabitants fhall be flain. See *Jerem.* xxxix. 6.

Ver. 7.

Ver. 7. *She fet it upon the Top of a Rock,* &c.] In a prefumptuous manner and with an high Hand fhe fhed it, as the *Chaldee* Paraphrafe expreffes the Senfe : She was impudent and barefac'd in her Cruelties : She did not feek to cover or excufe them.

Ibid. *She poured it not upon the Ground, to cover it with Duft.*] The Words allude to the Command of the Law, *Levit.* xvii. 13. that they cover the Blood of any Beaft or other living Creature which was flain, with Duft : which Precept was not only intended to prevent their eating of Blood, but alfo to give Men a fort of Horror or Averfion to the fight of Blood-fhed.

Ver. 8.

Ver. 8. *I have fet her Blood on the Top of a Rock.*] Her Punifhment fhall be as notorious in the Sight of the World as her Sin was.

Ver. 9,10.

Ver. 9, 10. *I will even make the Pile for the Fire great,* &c.] The Inhabitants fhall be the Materials prepared by their Sins to be confumed like Fuel in the Fire.

Ver. 10.

Ver. 10. *Spice it well.*] The Expreffion imports, that the *Chaldeans* fhall be as much fet upon deftroying the City and Inhabitants, as hungry People are greedy of devouring Meat well fpiced and dreffed.

Ibid. *And let the Bones be burnt.*] The Words denote an utter Deftruction, that the Fire fhall be fo fierce as to confume the very Bones as well as the Flefh put into the Caldron.

Ver.

Ver. 11. *Then set it empty upon the Coals there-* Chapter
of, &c.] After an entire Riddance of the Inhabi- XXIV.
tants, the City it self shall be set on Fire, and the
Place and its Wickedness be consumed together in Ver. 11.
the Flames.

Ver. 12. *She hath wearied her self with Lies.*] Ver. 12.
The Word *Teunim,* never met with but in this
place, is commonly derived from *Aven,* which
signifies Trouble or Vanity, and is a Word frequently applied to Idols, as particularly when *Bethel* is stiled *Bethaven,* upon the account of the
Golden Calf there set up, *Hos.* iv. 15. For these
Reasons I understand the Expression here, *She
hath wearied her self with Lies,* of the People's
multiplying their Idolatries, Idols being elsewhere
called Lies, and seeking Relief sometimes from one
Idol, sometimes from another, but all in vain. See
Chap. xvi. 29, 30. xxiii. 16, 19, 40.

Ibid. *And her great Scum went not forth out of
her, &c.*] All the Admonitions I gave her by my
Prophets, availed nothing to the purging her from
her Idolatries and other Wickedness: so that now
the Fire must purge and consume her and her Sins.

Ver. 13. *In thy Filthiness is Lewdness.*] Thou Ver. 13.
hast shewed thy self shameless and incorrigible in
thine Idolatries. Compare Chap. xxiii. 29, 35.

Ibid. *Because I have purged thee, and thou wast
not purged, &c.*] I did what was requisite on my
part toward thy Conversion, but thou refusedst to
comply with those frequent Calls and Exhortations
I gave thee, (See the Note on *Jer.* xxxi. 18.) and
therefore my Spirit shall not strive with thee any
longer, but I will proceed to execute my Judgments upon thee.

C c   Ibid.

Chapter
XXIV.

Ver. 14.

Ver. 16.

Ver. 17.

Ver. 18.

Ibid. *Till I cause my Fury to rest upon thee.*] See the Note on Chap. v. 13. Chap. viii. 18.

Ver. 14. *According to thy Doings shall they judge thee.*] See Chap. xxiii. 24.

Ver. 16. *Behold I take away the Desire of thine Eyes with a stroke.*] Thy Wife the Object of thy Love and thy Affection. See Ver. 18.

Ver. 17. *Bind the Tire of thine Head upon thee.*] Use the ordinary Dress upon thine Head: whereas in the time of Mourning it was customary sometimes to shave the Head. See *Levit.* xiii. 45. *Jer.* vii. 29. xvi. 6. sometimes to cast Dust upon it. See *Josh.* vii. 6. 1 *Sam.* iv. 12. The Priests were particularly forbid to uncover their Heads in the time of Mourning: See *Levit.* x. 6.

Ibid. *And put on thy Shoes upon thy Feet.*] Going bare-Foot was another Expression of Sorrow. See 2 *Sam.* xv. 30.

Ibid. *And cover not thy Lips.*] Covering the Lips or Face was another Token of Mourning. See *Levit.* xiii. 45. *Micah* iii. 7. 2 *Sam.* xv. 30. *Jerem.* xiv. 4.

Ibid. *And eat not the Bread of Men,*] Partake not of the Mourning Feast that Relations use to prepare for the Funerals of their Friends. See the Note on *Jer.* xvi. 5, 7. Such were the περιδειπνα and *Parentalia* among the *Greeks* and *Romans.*

Ver. 18. *So I spake to the People in the Morning, and at Even my Wife died.*] My Wife died in the Evening, and the next Morning I declared what Commands God had laid upon me, not to make any outward Shew or Sign of Mourning upon that Occasion. Compare Chap. xxxiii. 22. The Evening was the Beginning of the Day according

to

to the *Jews* reckoning. See *Gen.* i. 5. *Levit.* Chapter
xxiii. 32.

XXIV.

Ver. 19. *Wilt thou not tell us what these things
are to us?*] They enquire by way of Derision and
Contempt what these Signs mean : Comp. Chap.
xii. 9. xvii. 12. xx. 49.

Ver. 21. *Behold I will profane my Sanctuary,
the Excellency of your Strength.*] I will deliver my
Temple into the Hands of the Heathen, and they
shall profane and destroy it. See Chap. vii. 19, 20.
That Temple wherein you placed your Glory, and
thought my Residence there your greatest Protection. Compare Ver. 25. and see *Psal.* lxxviii. 61.
xcvi. 6. cv. 4. cxxxii. 8.

Ibid. *The desire of your Eyes, and that which
your Soul pitieth.*] The Beauty of Holiness, as the
Temple is often called, whose Destruction will affect you with a most tender Compassion.

Ibid. *And your Sons and your Daughters whom
ye have left, shall fall by the Sword.*] Whom ye
left behind you in the City when ye were carried
Captives. Or, who were left by the Famine and
Pestilence : See Chap. v. 12. xxiii. 47.

Ver. 23. *Ye shall not mourn nor weep.*] These
terrible Judgments shall strike you with Astonishment, and such a Grief as is too great to be expressed by Words or Actions: according to the
Verse of the Poet,

Curæ leves loquuntur, ingentes stupent.

Small Evils we complain of, greater strike us dumb.

C c 2   Ibid.

Chapter
XXIV.

Ibid. *But ye shall pine away for your Iniquities, and mourn one towards another.*] Ye shall waste away by a lingring Grief, and by a silent Lamentation over each others Calamities. See Chap. iv. 2, 17. *Levit.* xxvi. 39.

Ver. 24.

Ver. 24. *Thus Ezekiel is unto you a Sign.*] His Actions foreshew you what shall be your Condition. Compare Chap. iv. 3. xii. 6. The Holy Writers in several Places speak of themselves in the Third Person. See *Exod.* vi. 26. 1 *Sam.* xii. 11. *Matth.* ix: 9. So that this is an Argument of very little Force, when it is urged against *Moses* being the Author of the *Pentateuch.*

Ibid. *And when this cometh, ye shall know that I am the* LORD.] Comparing the Prediction with the Event, will convince the most Obstinate, that the immediate Hand of God is in the Judgments which are come upon you. See Chap. vi. 7. and compare *Joh.* xiii. 19. xiv. 29. xvi. 4.

Ver. 25.

Ver. 25. *When I shall take from them their Strength, the Joy of their Glory, the Desire of their Eyes,* &c.] When I shall take from them all that is dear and valuable to them : their Temple, an Emblem of my special Residence among them, and Protection over them, whose Beauty and Magnificence was their peculiar Glory, and the most grateful Object of their Sight: together with their Sons and Daughters whereon they placed their Affection. See Ver. 21.

Ver. 26.

Ver. 26. *That he that escapeth in that Day,* &c.] See Chap. xxxiii. 21, 22.

Ver. 27.

Ver. 27. *In that Day shall thy Mouth be opened to him that is escaped, and thou shalt speak and be no more dumb.*] From this time to the time when

the

the News comes of the City's being taken, thou Chapter
fhalt not prophecy any more to thine own People, XXIV.
but then will I give thee a new Commiffion to
fpeak: See Chap. xxxiii. 22. and that not by Signs
as thou doft at prefent, but with Freedom and
Plainnefs; the Event fo exactly anfwering thy Predictions, fhall give a new Authority to what thou
fpeakeft. See Chap. iii. 26. xxix. 21. and compare
Ephef. vi. 19.

Ibid. *And thou fhalt be a Sign unto them,* &c.]
They fhall then be convinced by Experience, that
thou didft forefhew by thy Actions and Behaviour
all that fhould befal them. And this will likewife
convince them of my Foreknowledge and Providence.

CHAP.

CHAP. XXV.

The ARGUMENT.

This Chapter contains God's Judgments against the Ammonites, Edomites, and Philiftines, for their Hatred against the Jews, and infulting over them in the time of their Diftrefs. Archbifhop Ufher in his Annals ad A. M. 3419. and Jofephus Antiq. lib. x. c. 11. place thefe Events five Years after the Deftruction of Jerufalem.

Ver. 2.

Ver. 3.

Ver. 2. 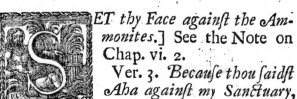 ET thy Face against the *Ammonites.*] See the Note on Chap. vi. 2.

Ver. 3. *Becaufe thou faidft Aha against my Sanctuary,* &c.] The *Ammonites, Moabites,* and *Edomites,* tho' related in Blood to the *Jews,* yet bore a conftant Hatred towards them, which they took all Opportunities to fhew, when the *Jews* were under any Diftrefs, and particularly at the time of their general Captivity, and the Deftruction of their City and Temple. For this they are often reproved by the Prophets, and threatned

with

with the like or feverer Judgments, and particularly the *Ammonites :* See the Note on Chap. xxi. 28.
 Ver. 4. *I will deliver thee to the Men of the*
Eaft for a Poffeffion.] By the Men of the Eaft muft
be meant the *Chaldeans :* See Chap. xxi. 19, 20.
Ammon is likewife reckoned among thefe Countries, which God foretold by *Jeremy* fhould be delivered into the Hands of the King of *Babylon.*
See *Jer.* xxv. 21. By the Eaft Country is commonly meant *Arabia* in Scripture, as hath been
obferved in the Notes upon *Ifa.* xi. 14. But *Syria*
and *Chaldea* and the Countries beyond it, are likewife called the Eaft : See *Numb.* xxiii. 7. *Ifa.* ii. 6.
Gen. xi. 2. *Chaldea* indeed lay Northward of *Ju-*
dea and the adjacent Countries, See Chap. l. 4.
but withal lying with a Point towards the Eaft,
the *Chaldeans* and their Confederates may not improperly be reckoned among the Men of the Eaft ;
juft as *Cyrus* is fometimes defcribed as coming from
the Eaft, and fometimes from the North, *Ifa.* xli.
25. with refpect to his Forces, that confifted both
of *Medes* that lay Northward, and *Perfians* that
lay Eaftward of *Babylon.*

Ibid. *And fhall drink thy Milk.*] Milk was the
chief Suftenance of thofe People, whofe Riches confifted chiefly in their Stocks of Cattle. Hence the
Scythians are called *Galactiophagi* by *Homer, Iliad*
3. and *Galactopotæ* by other Writers. The LXX
render the Senfe very well, *Shall drink or fwallow*
thy Fatnefs. The Word *Heleb* fignifying not only
Milk, but likewife the fatteft or choiceft Parts of
any Flefh or Fruits. So it is ufed *Gen.* xlv. 18. *Ye*
fhall eat the Fat of the Land. and *Pfal.* lxxxi. 16.
where

Chapter where our Tranflation reads, *The fineft of the Wheat,*
XXV.   it is in the *Hebrew, The Fat of the Wheat.*

Ver. 5.   Ver. 5. *And I will make Rabbah* (See Chap. xxi.
20.) *a Stable for Camels,* &c.] Inftead of being a
City inhabited by Men, it fhall be a place for Cattle, and particularly for Camels to feed in, of
which that and the neighbouring Countries had
great Store.   It is a Proverbial Expreffion for utter
Deftruction, to fay that Grafs grows where a
Town ftood. Compare *Ifa.* xvii. 2. xxii. 10. xxxii.
14. *Zeph.* ii. 14, 15.

Ver. 6.   Ver. 6. *Becaufe thou haft clapped thine Hands,
and ftamped with thy Feet.*] Geftures that fometimes fignify Grief and Indignation: See Chap. vi.
11. but are likewife ufed to exprefs our Joy and
Satisfaction: Compare *Job* xxvii. 23. *Lam.* ii. 15.
Jer. xlviii. 27.

Ibid. *With all thy defpite againft the Land of Ifrael.*] See Ver. 3.

Ver. 8.   Ver. 8. *Becaufe that Moab and Seir do fay.*] Seir
is the fame with *Edom.* See Chap. xxxv. 2. The
Prophet joyns them together as guilty of the fame
Crime, and then denounces particular Judgments
againft each of them.

Ibid. *Behold the Houfe of Judah is like unto all
the Heathen.*] They are no longer diftinguifhed
from their Neighbours by the vifible Protection of
the God whom they worfhip.

Ver. 9.   Ver. 9. *Therefore will I open the fide of Moab
from the Cities,* &c.] I will make a Paffage for his
Enemies to invade his Frontier Cities, and from
thence to poffefs themfelves of the beft of his Countrey. Some tranflate the Middle of the Verfe,
From the Cities, even from Ar his [City] *upon*
his

his Frontiers. Ar was the Coast or *Border of Moab,* Deut. ii. 18.

Ibid. *The Glory of the Countrey.*] The best part of all the Countrey of *Moab:* the *Hebrew* Word is *Tsebi,* frequently spoken of *Judea,* as being in many Respects the Glory of all Lands: See Chap. xx. 6.

Ibid. *Beth-jesimoth, Baal-meon, and Kiriatha-im.*] See *Numb.* xxxii. 38. *Josh.* xiii. 20. *Jer.* xlviii. 25. *Baal-meon* is called *Beth-meon* in that place of *Jeremy,* and more fully *Beth-baal-meon, Josh.* xiii. 17. *i. e.* the *House* or *Temple of the Idol Meon,* by which Bishop *Cumberland* understands *Menis* or *Osyris,* the great Deity of the *Egyptians:* in the first Book and the second Chapter of his *Treatise concerning Sanchoniatho's Phœnician Hist.*

Ver. 10. *Unto the Men of the East.*] See Ver. 4. Ver. 10.

Ibid. *That the Ammonites may not be remem-bred among the Nations.*] May make no Figure among their Neighbours, their Strength being entirely broken.

Ver. 12. *Because that Edom hath dealt against the House of Judah by taking Vengeance.*] The *Idumeans* being the Posterity of *Esau,* bare an ancient Grudge against the *Jews,* upon the account of their Ancestor's losing his Right of Primogeniture, and the subduing of *Edom* by *David* afterwards, 2 *Sam.* viii. 14. Upon both these Accounts they took hold of all Opportunities of venting their Spite toward the *Jewish* Nation, particularly see 2 *Chron.* xxviii. 17. For this their Behaviour they were in former Times reproved by *Amos,* Chap. i. 11. and afterward by *Obadiah,* Ver. 10. and by *Ezekiel* in this place, and Chap. xxxv. 5. The ill will that

Ver. 12.

D d   they

Chapter
XXV.
〰

they fhewed toward them at the time of their Captivity, was very remarkable, as appears by thofe pathetical Words of *Pfal.* cxxxvii. 7. *Remember the Children of Edom O* LORD *in the Day of Jerufalem, how they faid, Down with it, down with it, even to the Ground.*

Ver. 13.

Ver. 13. *I will ftretch out my Hand upon Edom, and cut off Man and Beaft from it.*] See Chap. xxxv. 7, 8, 9. *Jer.* xlix. 17, 18. *Zeph.* ii. 9. *Mal.* i. 3, 4.

Ibid. *And I will make it defolate from Teman, and they of Dedan fhall fall by the Sword.*] *Teman* is a noted place in *Idumea:* See *Amos* i. 12. *Jer.* xlix. 7. to which *Dedan* is joyned, ibid. Ver. 8. Compare *Ifa.* xxi. 13, 14. The *Dedanites* were originally *Arabians,* the Pofterity of *Dedan, Abraham's* Grandfon, but they feem afterward to have been incorporated with the *Idumeans.* See the Note upon that place of *Jeremiah.*

Ver. 14.

Ver. 14. *And I will lay my Vengeance upon Edom by the Hand of my People Ifrael.*] The *Jews* themfelves whom the *Edomites* have fo often infulted, fhall be the Inftruments of my Vengeance upon *Edom,* and fhall requite the Wrongs they have received by fubduing *Idumea,* which they did under the Conduct of *Judas Maccabæus:* See 1 *Macc.* v. 3. 2 *Macc.* x. 16, 17. Compare *Jer.* xlix. 2. And afterward the High Prieft *Hyrcanus* made an entire Conqueft of this Countrey. See Dr. *Prideaux Part* 2. *p.* 307.

Ver. 15.

Ver. 15. *Becaufe the Philiftines have dealt by Revenge, &c.*] The *Philiftines* being Borderers upon the *Jews,* were their ancient Enemies from the very time of the Judges downward, more particularly

ticularly in the time of *Abaz:* See 2 *Chron.* xxviii. Chapter
18.

Ver. 16. *Behold I will ſtretch out my Hand up-*
on the Philiſtines.] I will ſubdue them by *Nebu-* Ver. 16.
chadnezzar: See *Jer.* xxv. 20. xlvii. 1.

Ibid. *And I will cut off the Cherethims.*] The
Cherethims or *Cherethites* are the ſame with the
Philiſtines, or a Tribe of that People : See 1 *Sam.*
xxx. 14. *Zeph.* ii. 5. and the Notes upon *Jer.* xlvii.
4.

Ibid. *And deſtroy the Remnant of the Sea Coaſt.*]
The ſame who are called the *Remnant of the Phi-*
liſtines, *Amos* i. 8. the Remnant of *Aſhdod,* *Jer.*
xxv. 20. and *the Remnant of the Countrey of Caph-*
thor, Chap. xlvii. 4. See the Notes upon theſe two
laſt Places.

D d 2   C H A P.

C H A P. XXVI.

The ARGUMENT.

*This and the following Chapter with part of the
Twenty eighth, foretell the Destruction of* Tyre
by Nebuchadnezzar, *who took it after a thirteen
Years Siege, (as* Josephus *relates out of* Philostra-
tus *and the* Phœnician Annals: *See his* Antiq.
l. x. c. 11. ad fin. l. 1. contr. Appion. p. 1046.)
and in the Thirty second Year of Nebuchadnezzar's *Reign according to the* Babylonish *Account. See the Note on Chap.* xxix. 17. *By reason of which hard Service,* every Head was made
bald, and every Shoulder was peeled, *as our
Prophet speaks Chap.* xxix. 18. *The same Calamity is foretold by* Isaiah, Chap. xxiii. *This Siege
forced the Inhabitants to remove their Effects into an Island half a Mile distant from the Shore,
where they built another City called* New Tyre.
The Learned Dr. Prideaux, *in his Connect. of*
Script. Hist. Part 1. p. 91. *and* 484. *hath observed,*

ved, that this Prophecy of Ezekiel as well as the former one of Isaiah, was fulfilled in the Destruction of Old Tyre, a City that stood upon the Continent, and which Nebuchadnezzar utterly destroyed: tho' he grants some Expressions in both Prophesies are applicable only to the last Siege of that City, when it was conquer'd by Alexander the Great.

Ver. 1. I *N the Eleventh Year in the First Day of the Month.*] The particular Month not being named, some supply the Word *Fifth* (as the Word *Fourth* is supplied, 2 *Kings* xxv. 3.) and understand it of the Month following the taking of *Jerusalem*, at whose Desolation *Tyre* rejoiced, Ver. 2. But as Archbishop *Usher* observes *ad A. M.* 3416. the Fifth Month belongs to the Twelfth Year of *Jehoiakin*'s Captivity. So we may more probably understand the Expression of the *First* Month of the Year As the Year of *Evil-Merodack*'s Reign, 2 *Kings* is rightly understood by our Interpreters of the Year *when he begun to reign,* so the Tenth *Day of the Month* is necessarily to be understood of the First Month, Chap. **xl. 1.** of this Prophecy. And the Inhabitants of *Tyre* may very well be supposed to insult over *Jerusalem* at any part of the time of her Siege, which they saw must inevitably end in the taking of that City.

Ver. 2. *She is broken that was the Gates of the People.*] There was a great Confluence of People to *Jerusalem* from all Parts at the solemn Feasts of

the

Ibid. *She is turned unto me.*] Her Wealth is come into my Stores. Compare *Isa.* lx. 5.

Ibid. *I shall be replenished now she is laid waste.*] *Tyre* was a noted Market for all sorts of Trade: So when *Jerusalem* was taken and sackt, the Spoil of the City was carried thither for sale, and probably several of the Inhabitants being made Captives, were sold there for Slaves, a Traffick the *Tyrians* dealt in very much, Chap. xxvii. 13. This Interpretation may be confirmed by comparing it with *Joel* iii. 4, 5, 6. where the Prophet upbraids the *Tyrians* for making Merchandise both of the Persons and Substance of the *Jews*, when they came into their Hands. To the same Purpose we read *Maccab.* iii. 41. that when *Lysias came with great Forces to subdue the Jews, the Merchants of the Countrey took Silver and Gold and came into the Camp to buy the Children of Israel for Slaves.*

Ver. 3.

Ver. 3. *I will cause many Nations to come up against thee, as the Sea causeth his Waves to come up.*] The *Chaldeans* and their Confederates: Compare *Jer.* xxxiv. 1. li. 27. whom the Prophet compares to the Waves of the Sea, which come up with an irresistible Force: See *Jer.* li. 42. Armies are elsewhere represented by an Inundation that carries all before it: See *Isa.* viii. 7. *Dan.* ix. 26. xi. 22.

Ver. 4, 5.

Ver. 4, 5. *I will scrape her Dust from her, and make her like the Top of a Rock. It shall be a place for the spreading of Nets in the midst of the Sea.*] I will make an entire Riddance of her Buildings, so that not so much as any Dust or Rubbish

of

of them shall be left. Compare Ver. 12. and nothing shall be seen but the Rocks upon the Sea Shore, in the place where the City formerly stood. *Nebuchadnezzar* quite demolished *Old Tyre*, and the Stones and Rubbish of it were afterward made use of by *Alexander* to carry on a Causey from the Continent to the Island where *New Tyre* stood, by which means he took that. See Dr. *Prideaux, ubi supra.* This latter City is since so decayed, that there are no Remains of it left, but a few Huts for Fishermen to hang out their Nets a drying upon the Rocks, as it is related by Travellers that have been upon the place. See *Maundrel's Travels, p.* 48. and *Huetius, Demonst. Evangel. Prop.* 6. *ad finem.*

Ver. 6. *Her Daughters which are in the Field shall be slain with the Sword.*] By the *Daughters of Tyre* are meant the lesser Towns which were under her Jurisdiction, as the Mother City and Seat of the Kingdom. Compare Chap. xvi. 46. and *Jer.* xlix. 2.

Ver. 7. *Nebuchadnezzar a King of Kings.*] Who hath Kings for his Vassals and Tributaries. See Chap. xvii. 14, 16. *Dan.* ii. 37. The Kings of *Persia* affected the same Title afterward: See *Ezra* vii. 12. as the Kings of *Assyria* had done before. See *Isa.* x. 8. *Hos.* viii. 10.

Ver. 8, 9. *He shall make a Fort against thee, and cast a Mount against thee, &c.*] This Expression of a Siege properly relates to *Old Tyre,* which stood upon the Continent, and was besieged and taken by *Nebuchadnezzar.*

Ver. 9. *And with his Axes he shall break down thy Towns.*] The Word we render *Axes,* signifies

Chapter XXVI. fies any Instrument used in demolishing Buildings: See the Note on _Jer._ xxxiii. 4.

Ver. 10, 11, 12. _By reason of the abundance of his Horses their Dust shall cover thee,_ &c.] A lively Description of the Tumult and Desolation that attends a conquering Army making themselves Masters of a great City: Compare _Nahum_ ii. 3, 4, 9. iii. 2, 3.

Ver. 11. Ver. 11. _And thy strong Garrisons shall go down to the Ground._] Some render the Word _Matseboth, thine Images,_ and understand it of the Images of their Tutelar Gods.

Ver. 12. Ver. 12. _They shall lay thy Stones, thy Timber, and thy Dust, in the midst of the Water._] The Sea shall overflow thy Ruins: See Ver. 19.

Ver. 13. Ver. 13. _And I will cause the Noise of thy Songs to cease,_ &c.] Great Cities are full of all kind of Gaiety and Luxury: this shall be turned into a melancholy Silence. Compare _Isa._ xiv. 11. xxiii. 7, 16. _Jer._ vii. 34. xxv. 10.

Ver. 14. Ver. 14. _I will make thee like the Top of a Rock, thou shalt be built no more._] This part of the Prophecy was fulfilled upon _New Tyre,_ whose Inhabitants were quite destroyed by _Alexander_ when he took the City, and afterward the City it self became desolate: See Ver. 5.

Ver. 15. Ver. 15. _Shall not the Isles shake at the Sound of thy Fall?_] All those that are upon the Sea Coast near thee, shall be frightened at the News of thy Destruction. Compare Chap. xxvii. 28. xxxi. 16. _Jer._ xlix. 21.

Ver. 16, 17 Ver. 16, 17. _Then all the Princes of the Sea shall come down from their Thrones,_ &c.] All the Princes and rich Merchants of _Sidon, Carthage,_ and
other

other Maritime Cities that maintained a Trade Chapter with *Tyre,* and got great Wealth by that Means: XXVI. they *whose Merchants are Princes,* as *Isaiah* speaks of the Merchants of *Tyre,* Chap. xxiii. 8. Compare Ver. 2, 6, 10. of that Chapter: They shall express a deep Sense and Concern for her Misfortunes. Compare Chap. xxvii. 30, 31, 32. xxxii. 10. *Rev.* xviii. 11, 17, 19.

Ibid. *Shall come down from their Thrones, and lay away their Robes.*] Such was the Behaviour of the King of *Niniveh* at the time of his solemn Humiliation: *Jonah* iii. 6.

Ibid. *They shall clothe themselves with Trembling, &c.*] They shall put on the Habit of Mourners, and sit upon the Ground in a disconsolate Condition: See *Job* ii. 13. Compare Chap. vii. 17.

Ver. 17. *The renowned City which was strong* Ver. 17. *at Sea, &c.*] *Tyre* is called the *Strength of the Sea, Isa.* xxiii. 4. being strong at Sea, both by its Situation and the Strength of its Naval Forces, upon which Account it was formidable to all that had any Trading upon the Sea.

Ver. 18. *Now shall the Isles tremble at the Day* Ver. 18. *of thy Fall.*] See Ver. 15. St. *Jerom* translates it, Now shall the Ships tremble, *&c. i. e.* all Seafaring Men: Compare Chap. xxvii. 29, 30. *Isa.* xxiii. 14.

Ibid. *The Isles that are in the Sea shall be troubled at thy Departure.*] When thy People shall be carried Captive: See *Isa.* xxiii. 7.

Ver. 19. *When I shall bring up the Deep upon* Ver. 19. *thee, and great Waters shall cover thee.*] Thy Walls being demolished, the Sea shall come up and cover thy Ruins: See Ver. 12. or else the

E e   Prophet

Chapter Prophet compares the Destruction of *Tyre* to a
XXVI. Shipwrack : See Chap. xxvii. 26.

Ver. 20.

Ver. 20. *When I shall bring thee down with them*
that descend into the Pit, &c.] When thou shalt
be *thrust down into Hell*, as our Saviour speaks concerning *Capernaum, Luke* x. 15, and brought to
utter Desolation, like Cities which have been long
ago buried in Ruins and Oblivion : Compare Chap.
xxxii. 18, 24.

Ibid. *When I shall set Glory in the Land of the Li-*
ving.] Compare this and the following Verse with
Chap. xxxv. 14. When I shall restore other Cities
conquered by the King of *Babylon*, to that flourishing Condition they formerly enjoyed among the
Inhabitants of this World : so the *Land of the Li-*
ving signifies----Chap. xxxii. 23, 26, 27, 32. The
Word *Tsebi* is in many places appropriated to *Ju-*
dea, as being in several Respects the Glory of all
Lands, Chap. xx. 6. but is sometimes applied to
other Countries : See Chap. xxv. 9. Some Expositors understand it here of *Judea*, to this Sense ;
that when God should return the Captivity of the
Jews, and restore them to those Marks of his Grace
and Favour, which distinguished them from all
other Nations, and made them the nearest resemblance of Heaven that could be found upon Earth :
yet even then as it follows----

Ver. 21.

Ver. 21. *I will make thee a Terror, and thou*
shalt be no more] Thou shalt be left in utter Ruins and Desolation, and a terrible Example of my
Vengeance. The Word *Balaloth* which our Interpreters translate *Terrors*, is generally joined
with Words importing utter Destruction, and so
the

the LXX underſtood it here, and in other places of this Prophecy : See Chap. xxviii. 36. xxviii. 19. and compare *Iſa.* xvii. 14. *Pſal.* lxxiii. 19.

Ibid. *Tho' thou be ſought for, thou ſhalt never be found again.*] An Expreſſion denoting utter De-ſtruction : See *Pſal.* xxxvii. 36. and compare Ver. 5. and 14.

Chapter XXVI.

E e 2 CHAP.

CHAP. XXVII.

The ARGUMENT.

*The fame Subject is continued, where the Prophet
ſetting forth the great Trade and Riches of Tyre,
foretels the irrecoverable Fall thereof.*

Ver. 2.

Ver. 2. *A K E up a Lamentation for
Tyrus.*] This alludes to the
mournful Ditties uſed at Funerals, wherein the *Præficæ*
or Mourning Women, re-
counted every thing that
was valuable or praiſe-worthy belonging to the De-
ceaſed, and then lamented his Loſs : See the Notes
upon *Jer.* ix. 17, 18. In like manner thoſe that
traded with *Tyre* ſhould mourn over her, and bewail the Loſs of her Riches and Greatneſs : Comp.
Chap. xxvi. 16, 17. and ſee Ver. 32.

Ver. 3.

Ver. 3. *Thou that art ſituate at the Entry of
the Sea.*] A Seaport fitted by Situation for carrying
on Trade with many Countries : See *Iſa.* xxiii. 1.

Ibid. *Thou haſt ſaid, I am of perfect Beauty.*]
Thou haſt ſaid in the Pride of thy Heart, (See
Chap.

Chap. xxviii. 2.) the Strength of my Navy and Chapter
Fortreſſes are every way compleat and beautiful: XXVII.
See Ver. 4, 11. and I am furniſhed with all Accommodations that can make me conſiderable in
theEyes of the World. See Ver. 10, 11. and Chap.
xxviii. 12.

Ver. 4. *Thy Borders are in the midſt of the* Ver. 4.
Seas.] Taking the Words in a ſtrict Senſe, they
are a Deſcription of *New Tyre*, which ſtood in an
Iſland: Compare Chap. xxvi. 5. The *Tyrians* are
called the Inhabiters of the Iſland, *Iſa.* xxiii. 2.
But in the *Hebrew* Phraſe all Places are called
Iſlands which lie upon the Sea Coaſt. See the Note
on *Iſa.* xi. 11.

Ibid. *Thy Builders have perfected thy Beauty.*]
The following Verſes ſhew, that the Words are
chiefly to be underſtood of the Builders of their
Ships, wherein the chief Strength and Glory of the
Tyrians was placed.

Ver. 5. *They have made all thy Ship-boards of* Ver. 5.
Fir-Trees from Shenir.] The Decks of thy Ships
were made of Firr fetcht from Mount *Hermon*,
called anciently *Shenir.* See iii. 9.

Ver. 6. *The Company of the ſavorites have made* Ver. 6.
thy Benches of Ivory.] The *Tyrians* have made
the Seats for the Rowers of ivoy in a very coſtly
manner.

This is the Senſe of the Verſe, if we follow the
common Reading: But *Bochart* not without Reaſon ſuppoſes, that the Word *Bath aſhurim* is pointed wrong, and ſhould be read *Bith-aſſhurim*, and
then the Sentence muſt be tranſlated, *They have
made thy Seats of Ivory incloſed in Box*, the Expreſſion being parallel to that of *Virgil, Æn.* 10.

---*Quale*

Chapter
XXVII.

> ----*Quale per artem*
> *Inclufum buxo aut Orycia terebintho*
> *Lucet ebur.*

This Senfe the *Chaldee* follows.

Ibid. *Brought out of the Ifles of Chittim.*] The *Ifles of Chittim* are the Countries lying upon the Coaft of the *Mediterranean* Sea. See *Jer.* ii. 10.

Ver. 7.

Ver. 7. *Fine Linnen with broider'd Work from Egypt was that which thou fpreadeft out for thy Sail.*] Fine Linnen was one of the principal Commodities of *Egypt*: See 1 *Kings* x. 28. *Prov.* vii. 16. *Ifa.* xix. 9. and was an Habit ufed for Perfons of the beft Quality: See *Gen.* xli. 42. *Eft.* viii. 15. which fhews to what an Excefs of Vanity the *Tyrians* were come, to ufe fuch coftly Manufactures for Sails to their Ships. *Sueton* in his Life of *Caligula, c.* 37. reckons this among feveral Inftances of that Emperor's Extravagance, that he furnifhed his Pleafure-Boats with *Coftly Sails* and other expenfive Ornaments.

Ibid. *Blew and Purple from the Ifles of Elifha was that which covered thee.*] Blew and Purple are elfewhere reckoned among thofe Colours which fet off the richeft Attire: See *Exod.* xxv. 4. *Jer.* x. 9. The common Clothing of the *Tyrians* was of thefe kinds, which were brought from the Iflands of the *Egean* Sea, particularly *Coös,* famed for Purple among Heathen Authors. *Elifha* denotes the Countries upon the Coaft of *Greece*: a part of *Peloponnefus* retains the Name of *Elis* among the *Greek* Writers.

Ver.

Ver. 8. *The Inhabitants of* Zidon *and* Arvad Chapter *were thy Mariners,* &c.] Thou madeſt uſe of the XXVII. People of other Cities and Countries, to undergo the Servile Office of being Mariners or Rowers, Ver. 8. whilſt thy own Citizens pretended to the Skill of Steering thy Ships, and profeſſed the Art of being Pilots. Zidon was a famous Seaport Town, the Mother of *Tyre:* See the Note on *Iſa.* xxiii. 12. and Arvad the ſame with Arpad or Arphad, 2 *Kings* xviii. 33. *Iſa.* x. 9. *Jer.* xlix. 23. called Aradus by the *Greek* and *Latin* Authors, was an Iſland and Town in the Neighbourhood of *Tyre.*

Ver. 9. *The* Antients *of* Gebal *were thy Cal-* Ver. 9. *kers.*] Thou employeſt the Inhabitants of *Gebal* for calking thy Ships, as being remarkably ſkilful in that Trade: *Gebal* was a Province of *Phœnicia* near *Tyre:* See *Pſal.* lxxxiii. 8. 1 *Kings* v. 18. The LXX Interpreters ſuppoſe it the ſame with the City *Byblos,* with whom agree *Euſebius* and St. *Jerom, de locis Hebraicis.*

Ver. 10. *They of* Perſia, *of* Lud *and* Phut.] Ver. 10. Thy Citizens being all given to Trading, thou madeſt uſe of Foreign Souldiers for thine Army when thy City was beſieged. *Lud* and *Phut* are two Nations elſewhere mentioned together. See Chap. xxx. 5. *Jer.* xlvi. 9. Our Interpreters underſtand by them in theſe two Places, the People of *Libya* and *Lydia.* But *Phut* and *Lubim* being mentioned as diſtinct People, *Nahum* iii. 9, *Phut* probably ſignifies ſome part of *Africa* near *Egypt,* and *Lud* or *Ludim,* the Abyſſines. Theſe People, tho' Africans, are joined with the *Perſians,* Chap. xxxviii. 5.

Ibid.

Chapter
XXVII.

Ver. 11.

Ver. 12.

Ibid. *They hanged up the Shield and Helmet in thee.*] In thy Garrisons, which they kept in time of Peace.

Ver. 11. *The Men of Arvad,* (see Ver. 8.) *were with thine Army upon the Walls round about.*] They defended thy Walls when they were assaulted by the King of *Babylon*'s Army : See the Note upon Chap. xxvi. 8, 9.

Ibid. *The Gammadims were in thy Towers.*] It is very uncertain what People are here meant by this Name. Our learned Mr. *Fuller* supposes them People of *Phœnicia.* See his *Miscellanies, Lib.* vi. *c.* 3. *Ludolphus* conjectures they were *Africans,* in his *Comment. in Histor. Æthiop. l.* 1. *c.* 22. The *Chaldee* Paraphrase takes them to be *Cappadocians.* The *Vulgar Latin* renders the Word *Pygmies :* but if we should grant there were such a People, as *Ludolphus* takes a great deal of Pains to prove there were, yet they would not be fit to make use of for Soldiers.

Ibid. *They have made thy Beauty perfect.*] See Ver. 3.

Ver. 12. *Tarshish was thy Merchant.*] *Tarshish* probably signifies a Port of *Spain* called by the *Greek* and *Latin* Authors *Tartessus,* situate not far from the Place where *Cadiz* now stands; famous of old for *Hercules Pillars,* being the utmost Boundary of the Ancient Navigation. It comes from thence to signify any Merchant Adventurers who Traded in the *Mediterranean* Sea. See the Note upon *Isa.* ii. 16. The Commodities here mentioned which these Merchants traded in, being the Product of *Spain,* confirm this Exposition.

Ver.

Ver. **13.** *Javan, Tubal and Meſhech were thy* Chapter
Merchants.] By *Javan* is to be underſtood *Greece,* XXVII.
in which Senſe *Alexander* is ſtyled King of *Javan* ∿
or *Greece, Dan.* viii. 21. So the LXX tranſlate Ver. 13.
it here, and in that place of *Daniel.* And all
Greece, except *Peloponneſus,* was anciently called
Jonia. *Tubal* and *Meſhech* are Names uſually
joined together in Scripture: *Bochart* ſuppoſes them
to be the ſame with thoſe People afterward called
Moſchi and *Tibareni,* whoſe Habitation was near
the *Euxine* Sea.

Ibid. *They traded in the Perſons of Men.*] In
buying and ſelling Slaves in the Markets. The
Hebrew reads *In the Souls of Men,* the Word *Ne-*
pheſh Soul, ſometimes ſignifying a Slave. Comp.
I *Chron.* v. 21. *Numb.* xxxi. 35. *Revel.* xviii. 13.
In which Senſe ſome underſtand the Word *Gen.*
xii. 15.

Ibid. *And Veſſels of Braſs in thy Markets.*]
Criticks obſerve that the Word *Nehoſheth,* commonly tranſlated *Braſs,* does likewiſe ſignify Steel,
and ſo it is rendered by our Interpreters, *Pſal.* xviii.
34. a *Bow of Steel is broken by my Arms.* And
we may very well underſtand it ſo here, for the
Chalybes, a People ſo called from their Steel Manufactures, lived near *Pontus,* in the Neighbourhood of the *Moſchi* and *Tibareni*; for which Reaſon Steel is called the *Northern Iron, Jer.* xv. 12.

Ver. **14.** *They of the Houſe of Togarmah traded* Ver. 14.
in thy Fairs.] By *Togarmah Bochart* underſtands
Cappadocia: The LXX read the Word Θοϱγαμὰ,
Gen. x. 14. which comes near in Sound to *Trogma*
or *Trocma,* a part of *Cappadocia.*

F f Ver.

Chapter
XXVII.
Ver. 15.

Ver. 15. *The Men of Dedan were thy Mer-chants.*] The same learned Person distinguisheth this *Dedan* from that mentioned Ver. 20. this latter was of *Abraham*'s Posterity, whereas *Dedan* here spoken of, was derived from that *Dedan* mentioned *Gen.* x. 7. the Son of *Raamah* or *Regma.* The Posterity of this *Dedan* is probably placed near the *Persian* Gulph, where there was a City called afterwards *Rhegma :* and so is fitly joined with many Islands, or Countries lying upon the Sea Coast, which are usually called *Islands* in the *Hebrew* Phrase : See the Note on *Isa.* xi. 11.

Ibid. *Many Isles were the Merchandise of thy Hand,* &c.] Those Countries exported thy Manufactures, *the Wares of thy making,* as they are called in the following Verse : and by way of Return for them, brought thee in Ivory and other Rarities from *India,* whither they traded. They brought these *for a Present,* says our Translation, or rather by way of Price or Return for the Commodities exported. The Noun *Eshear* commonly signifies a Present or Gift, but it is near in Sound to the Word *Sacar,* that signifies a Price or Reward, and Words of such near Affinity are often used in a promiscuous Sense. See the Note upon *Jer.* xxiii. 39. Chap. xx. 37. xxix. 7. and xxxvi. 15. of this Prophecy.

Ver. 16.

Ver. 16. *Syria was thy Merchant,* &c.] The *Syrians* imported into thy Haven precious Stones, and all sorts of curious Apparel, in lieu of which they carried abroad the Wares of thy own making.

Ver. 17.

Ver. 17. *They traded in thy Market Wheat of Minith,* &c.] These were the Commodities which the Jews imported to *Tyre,* chiefly the necessary Pro-

Provisions for Food; the *Tyrians* having none of Chapter
their own Growth, the Jews supplied them there- XXVII.
with from their own, or the neighbouring Countries. See 1 *Kings* v. 9, 11. *Ezra* iii. 7. *Acts* xii.
20.

Ibid. *Wheat of Minnith.*] This was a place belonging to the *Ammonites*, See *Judg.* xi. 33. noted
for excellent Wheat, great Quantities of which the
Jews brought to *Tyre*.

Ibid. *With Pannag.*] A Word never elsewhere
to be found: supposed by some to be the Name of
a place; by others more probably taken for some
rich Ointment or Gum.

Ibid. *And Balm.*] For which *Gilead* was famous: See *Jer.* viii. 22. There were Balsam-trees
about *Jericho* too, which *Josephus* describes, *Antiq. l. 4. c. 6.* and *de Bello Jud. l. 5. c. 4.* tho' some
doubt whether that Balsam were the same with the
Balm of *Gilead.*

Ver. 18. *In the Wine of Helbon.*] *Helbon* is sup- Ver. 18.
posed the same part of *Syria* which is called *Chaly-
bonitis* by *Ptolemy*.

Ibid. *And white Wool.*] The Word *Tsachar* is
never met with but here, and *Judg.* v. 10. where
our Translation reads *White Asses.* *Bochart* explains the Word here to signify Wool of a bright
Purple Colour, from the *Arabick* use of it. So
Purpureus in *Latin* is used for a bright Colour in
Virgil, Æn. 1. *Lumenque juventæ Purpureum.*---
The LXX and *Chaldee* render it Wool from *Mile-
tus,* a place famous for that Commodity.

Ver. 19. *Dan also and Javan, going to and fro,* Ver. 19.
&c.] By *Dan* St. *Jerom* understands the Town
which was afterwards called *Cæsarea Philippi,* be-

F f 2   longing

Chapter longing to the Tribe of *Dan*, which was near
XXVII. *Tyre:* whereas *Javan*, which likewise traded with
〰〰〰 *Tyre*, lay further off. This is the Sense of the
Words, if we follow the common Translation, but
Bochart thinks the Words might be better translated, *Dan also and Javan coming from Uzal occu-*
pied in thy Fairs: to distinguish this *Javan* which
he supposes to be in the Southern part of *Arabia*,
from *Greece*, more commonly called by that Name.
See Ver. 13. In conformity to this Interpretation,
the Copies of the LXX which we have now, read
from Asel: tho' St. *Jerom* informs us, that the
former part of the Verse was wanting in the *Sep-*
tuagint, and supplied from *Theodotion*'s Translation.

    Ibid. *Bright Iron* [i. e. Steel] *and Calamus were*
in thy Market.] *Bochart* confirms the foregoing
Interpretation from hence, that those of *Javan* are
said to deal in Aromatick Gums, which are known
not to grow in *Greece*, but in *Arabia*.

Ver. 20.   Ver. 20. *Dedan was thy Merchant.*] This is probably to be understood of the Posterity of that *De-*
dan who was *Abraham*'s Grandson: See Ver. 15.
and Chap. xxv. 13.

Ver. 21.   Ver. 21. *Arabia and all the Princes of Kedar*
they occupied with thee.] The *Hebrew* reads, *They*
were the Merchants of thy Hand: i. e. they took
off thy Manufactures (see Ver. 15.) in exchange for
Cattle, in which their Substance did chiefly con-
sist: See *Isa*. lx. 7. *Kedar* is a Countrey in *Ara-*
bia, often mentioned in Scripture, which received
its Name from *Kedar*, *Ishmael*'s Son, who settled
there, *Gen*. xxv. 13.

Ver.

Ver. 22. *The Merchants of Sheba and Raamah.*] Chapter
Thefe were People of *Arabia Felix*, dwelling near XXVII.
the *Perfian* Gulph : See Ver. 15. and Chap. xxiii.
42. They traded in the rich Products of their own Ver. 22.
Countrey, which were Spices, precious Stones, and
Gold. Compare 1 *Kings* x. 2, 11. *Pfal.* lxxii. 15.
Ifa. lx. 6. *Bochart* places *Ophir* fo famous for Gold,
in *Arabia Felix*. See his *Phaleg. l.* 11. *c.* 27.

Ver. 23. *Haran and Canneh and Eden.*] *Haran* Ver. 23.
is the place where *Abraham* dwelt when he came
out from *Ur* of the *Chaldees, Gen.* xi. 31. called
Charræ by the *Romans,* and noted for the Defeat of
Craffus. Canneh fome fuppofe to be the fame
place that is called *Calneh, Amos* vi. 2. or *Calno,*
Ifa. x. 9. a City near *Euphrates.* Others take it
for *Ctefiphon,* a noted City fituate upon the River
Tigris. Eden is join'd with *Haran,* 2 *Kings* xix.
12. as it is here. *Huetius* fuppofes *Paradife* was
called the Garden of *Eden,* from the Name of the
Countrey where it was placed, which was where
the two Rivers *Tigris* and *Euphrates* meet. See
his Tract, *De fitu Paradifi, c.* 2. *n.* 7.

Ibid. *The Merchants of Sheba.*] There were
two *Sheba's,* as there were two *Dedans :* one defcended from *Raamah, Gen.* x. 7. the other from
Jockfhan, Abraham's Son, *Gen.* xxv. 3. As the
Twenty fecond Verfe is explained of the former,
fo the latter may be underftood here : They were
both Inhabitants of *Arabia.*

Ibid. *Chilmad.*] Both the *Chaldee* and LXX explain this by *Carmania.*

Ver. 24. *In Chefts of rich Apparel.*] The Word Ver. 24.
in the Original tranflated *Chefts,* is *Ginzé,* which
is elfewhere render'd *Treafuries :* See 1 *Chron.*

Chapter xxviii. 11. *Eſt.* iii. 9. From which Word the *La-*
XXVII. *tin. Gaza* is derived.

⟡ Ibid. *Bound with Cords, and made of Cedar.*]
Carefully packed up in Cheſts of Cedar to give
theſe Clothes a fine Scent, and preſerve them from
Putrefaction.

Ver. 25. Ver. 25. *The Ships of Tarſhiſh did ſing of thee in*
thy Market.] Ships of *Tarſhiſh* ſignify ſometimes in
Scripture any Trading or Merchant Ships, See the
Note on *Iſa.* ii. 16. and here I take it in this general Senſe: The Prophet having already reckon'd
up the principal Countries which Traded with
Tyre, now adds in comprehenſive Terms, that all
Merchant Adventurers ſung or ſpake great things
of her Riches, or as the Word *Sharoth* may be render'd, *They ruled or governed in thy Markets.*

Ibid. *In the midſt of the Seas*] See Ver. 4.

Ver. 26. Ver. 26. *Thy Rowers have brought thee into*
great Waters.] The Prophet compares the Condition of *Tyre* beſieged by the Enemy, to a Ship over-
ſet by the Winds, and juſt ready to ſink under Water. See the like Compariſon *Iſa.* xxxiii. 23. Great
Numbers are ſometimes ſignified by great Waters:
See *Pſal.* xviii. 16. cxliv. 7. *Jer.* li. 42.

Ibid. *The Eaſt Wind hath broken thee in the*
midſt of the Seas.] As the Violence of the Eaſt
Wind occaſions many Shipwracks in the Sea, See
Pſal. xlviii. 7. ſo the *Chaldean* Army, compared
elſewhere to an Eaſt Wind, ſhall ruin thy Strength
and Glory, and leave thee like a Wrack caſt upon
the Shore: Compare Chap. xvii. 10. xix. 12.

Ver. 27. Ver. 27. *Shall fall into the midſt of the Seas.*]
Shall be as utterly ruined and deſtroyed, as if they
were ſunk in a Shipwrack. See Chap. xxvi. 5, 14,

21. Or shall be killed in a Sea Fight while they Chapter defend the City. See the following Verse, and XXVII. Chap. xxix. 8.

Ver. 28. *The Suburbs shall shake at the sound of* Ver. 28. *the Cry of thy Pilots.*] The Cry of thy Wounded Seamen shall make the Inhabitants of the Suburbs shake for Fear, Chap. xxvi. 15.

Ver. 29. *All that handle the Oar----shall come* Ver. 29. *down from their Ships,* &c.] Sea-faring Men finding no Encouragement to follow their Employment, now thy Traffick is destroyed, shall lay aside their Trade and mourn over thee: Compare Chap. xxvi. 16.

Ver. 30. *They shall cause their Voice to be heard* Ver. 30. *against thee.*] Or rather, *over thee,* as the LXX and *Vulgar Latin* translate it: in which Sense the Preposition *Nal* is taken where Persons are said to mourn over the Dead, or the calamitous: See Chap. xxviii. 12. 1 *Kings* xiii. 30. *Hof.* x. 5.

Ibid. *And shall cast Dust upon their Heads, they shall wallow themselves in the Ashes.*] Expressions of the deepest Mourning and Lamentation. See 1 *Sam.* iv. 12. *Job* ii. 12. *Revel.* xviii. 19. *Jerem.* vi. 26.

Ver. 31. *And they shall make themselves utterly* Ver. 31. *bald for thee.*] Another Expression of publick Sorrow: See *Jer.* xlvii. 5. *Mich.* i. 16.

Ver. 32. *And in their Wailing they shall take up* Ver. 32. *a Lamentation for thee,* &c.] The Words allude to the publick Lamentations made at Funerals. See the Notes upon *Jer.* ix. 17, 18. xxii. 18. and compare *Rev.* xviii. 18.

Ver.

Chapter XXVII.

Ver. 34.
Ver. 35.
Ver. 36.

Ver. 34. *When thou shalt be broken by the Seas in the Depth of the Waters.*] See Ver. 26, 27. and Chap. xxvi. 19. xxix. 8.

Ver. 35. *All the Merchants of the Isles shall be astonished at thee,* &c.] See Chap. xxvi. 15, 16.

Ver. 36. *Thy Merchants among the People shall hiss at thee.*] By way of insulting and Derision, See 1 *Kings* ix. 8. As Men are apt to despise those in Adversity, whom they courted and respected in Prosperity. But the *Chaldee Paraphrase* renders it, *They shall be astonished:* and this Sense agrees better with the Lamentations of the Sea-faring Men mentioned in the foregoing Verses.

Ibid. *Thou shalt be a Terror,* &c.] See Chapter xxvi. 21.

C H A P.

C H A P. XXVIII.

The Argument.

*In this Chapter the Prophet denounces God's Judg-
ments against the King of* Tyre, *for his Pride
and Insolence : He likewise foretels the Destruction of* Sidon, *and that the Judgments threatned upon those and other Heathen Countries,*
Ammon, Moab, *&c. shall in the End turn to
the Benefit of God's People.*

Ver. 2. *AY to the Prince of* Tyrus.] Ver. 2.
Whose Name was *Ithobalus,*
according to the *Phenician*
Annals, Extracts out of which
may be seen in *Josephus, Lib.*
1. *Contr. Appion.* p. 1046.

Ibid. *I am a God, I sit in the Seat of God, in
the midst of the Seas.*] Some Princes have been so
Extravagant as to affect Divine Honours : This
seems to have been the Temper of this Vain
Man. The Words are an insolent Boast of self-
G g suffi-

Chapter ſufficiency, as if he had ſaid, I fear none, nor
XXVIII. ſtand in need of any: I am ſeated in a Place of
impregnable Strength: The Seas ſurround me·that
no Enemy can aſſault me. So they repreſent the
Exceſſive Pride and Carnal Security of this Prince,
who truſted in his own Strength, and· forgot his
Dependance upon God. The ſame Crime was in
like manner puniſhed in the King of *Egypt*, Chap.
xxix. 3. and afterward in *Nebuchadnezzar* himſelf,
Dan. iv. 30, 31. So *Babylon* is repreſented as
aſcribing ſelf-ſufficiency to her ſelf, and ſaying in
her Heart, *I am, and there is none elſe beſides me,*
Iſa. lvii. 10.

Ibid. *In the midſt of the Seas.*] See Chapter
xxvii. 4.

Ibid. *Yet thou art a Man, and not God.*] A
weak Mortal Man: an unequal Match for the
King of *Babylon*'s Forces; See Ver. 9. and *Iſa.*
xxxi. 3.

Ver. 3.   Ver. 3. *Behold thou art wiſer than Daniel.*]
The Fame of *Daniel*'s Wiſdom was quickly ſpread
over *Chaldea*, upon his being advanced to ſeveral
Poſts of Honour and Dignity by *Nebuchadnezzar.*
See *Dan.* ii. 48. ſo here the Prophet in an Ironical
Manner upbraids the vain Boaſts which the
Prince of *Tyre* made of his Wiſdom, and the Poli-
cy of thoſe about him, as if it exceeded the En-
dowments of *Daniel*, ſo famous, though a Young
Man, for his Skill in the ſeveral Parts of Know-
lege, and the Arts of Government. The *Phenici-*
ans of whom the *Tyrians* were a Colony, (ſee the
Note on *Iſa.* xxiii. 12.) valued themſelves for their
Wiſdom and Ingenuity, as being the Inventers of
                                                  Navi-

Navigation, of Letters and Sciences. Comp. *Zech.* Chapter
ix. 2. XXVIII.

Ver. 4. *With thy Wisdom and thy understanding* Ver. 4.
thou hast gotten thee Riches, &c.] Thy Skill in
Navigation and Trade has encreased thy Wealth;
See Ver. 5. and *Zech.* ix. 3.

Ver. 7. *Behold, I will bring Strangers upon* Ver. 7.
thee, the terrible of the Nations.] The *Babyloni-*
ans, who by their Conquests have made themselves terrible to all the Countries round about
them: See Chap. xxx. 11, 12.

Ibid. *They shall draw their Swords against the*
Perfection of thy Beauty.] They shall Deface
and Destroy every thing which thou valuest as Or-
namental, or Useful. Comp. Ver. 12.

Ver. 8. *Thou shalt die the Deaths of them that* Ver. 8.
are slain in the midst of the Seas.] Thou and
thy Mariners shall be slain in a Sea-Fight, or shall
be destroyed as those that are swallowed by the
Sea in a Tempest. See Chap. xxvi. 15. xxvii. 27,
28, 34.

Ver. 9. *Wilt thou yet say to him that slayeth thee,* Ver. 9.
I am as God?] Mortality will certainly convince
thee of thy Folly in pretending to Divinity.
Compare Chapter xxxii. 19. So *Plutarch* tells us
of *Alexander,* that he vainly affected to be
thought *Jupiter's* Son, and next in Honour to
Bacchus and *Hercules:* yet when he saw the
Blood run out of a Wound he had received,
which at the same time gave him much Pain, he
confess'd that was not such Blood as *Homer* said issued from the Immortal Gods: *Lib.* 2. *De Alex-*
andri Fortuna.

Chapter
XXVIII.

Ver. 10.

Ver. 10. *Thou shalt die the Death of the Uncircumcised.*] Thou shalt die by such a remarkable Judgment as God usually inflicts, upon Notorious Offenders: thou shalt come to the same Ill End as befals the other Enemies of God and of his Truth. Compare Chap. xxxi. 18. xxxii. 19, 21, 23, 24, &c. Circumcision being the Rite which distinguished God's People from the Heathen, *Uncircumcised* is equivalent in Sense to Wicked or Profane. So the *Chaldee* Paraphrase renders it here, *Thou shalt die the Death of the Wicked,* and to the same purpose again Chap. xxxi. 18. In the same Sense we are to understand that Expression, *Levit.* xxvi. 41. *If their Uncircumcised Heart be humbled,* and those of *Jeremy,* Chap. vi. 10. *Their Ear is uncircumcised:* And Chap. ix. 26. *The House of Israel is uncircumcised in their Heart.*

Ver. 12.

Ver. 12. *Take up a Lamentation upon the King of Tyrus.*] See Chap. xxvii. 32.

Ibid. *Thou sealest up the full Sum of Wisdom and perfect Beauty.*] In thine own Opinion thou art the perfect Pattern of Wisdom, and all other Excellencies: Compare Ver. 7. The Expression is taken from Vessels and other Repositories, which when they are full, used to be sealed up in order to the preserving of what is contained in them: See *Deut.* xxxii. 4. *Job* xiv. 17. The LXX and *Vulgar Latin* render the former Part of the Verse, *Thou art the Seal of Likeness,* i. e. Thou art the Image of God, or an Exact Impression taken from that great Copy. The following Verse shews that the Expression alludes to *Adam,* when he

was

was first created, and came pure out of the
Hands of his Maker. And then the following
Words in this Verse are to be translated, *Full of*
Wisdom, and perfect in Beauty : An exact De-
scription of the State of Innocence. The Word
Tacnith is translated *Pattern*, Chap. xliii. 10. of
this Prophecy, and so it signifies *Exod.* xxx. 32.
to which Sense the *Targum* there explains it :
But our Translation renders it *Composition*.

Ver. 13. *Thou haft been in Eden, the Garden of*
God.] As thy Situation was pleafant, so thou wast
plentifully supplied with every Thing that could
contribute to make thy Life pleafant and Happy.
A State of Paradise does in common Speech denote a Condition every way Complete and Happy. See *Ifa.* li. 3. But this Expreffion as well as
the whole Context alludes to the Complete Happinefs which *Adam* enjoyed in Paradise before his
Apoftacy and fearful Fall.

Ibid. *Every precious Stone was thy Covering,*
&c.] Like a great Prince or Monarch, thy
Crown was adorned with the choiceft Jewels, and
thou wast arrayed with Royal Robes, enriched
with Gold and Precious Stones of all forts. The Stone
probably alludes to the Precious Stones which
were placed in the High Priefts Breaftplate, as the
next Verfe alludes to the Cherubims over the
Mercy-Seat. Accordingly the LXX enlarge the
Number of the Stones here mentioned from
Nine to Twelve, and place them in the fame
Order in which they are ranked, *Exodus* xxviii.
17, &c.

Chapter XXVIII.

Ver. 13.

Ibid.

Chapter XXVIII. Ibid. *The Workmanſhip of thy Tabrets, and of thy Pipes, was prepared in thee* [or for thee] *in the Day thou waſt created.*] The higheſt Expreſſions of Joy, ſuch as are the ſounding of all ſorts of Muſical Inſtruments, uſhered thee into the World, according to the uſual Practice at the Birth of Great Princes, and ever ſince thou haſt been brought up in the choiceſt Delicacies, which a Royal Palace or a Luxurious City could furniſh. See Chap xxvi. 13. *Iſa.* xiv. 11.

Ver. 14.

Ver. 14. *Thou art the anointed Cherub that covereth.*] Anointing is the Ceremony wherewith Kings are Inaugurated; ſo the Prophet compares the Prince of *Tyre* to a Ruling or Principal *Cherub*, one of the chief of the Angelical Order, who attend upon God in Heaven, and are repreſented by the *Cherubims* in the Temple overſhadowing the Mercy Seat. To this Senſe St. *Jerom* tranſlates it, *The extended Cherub that covereth:* i. e. whoſe Wings were ſtretched out to cover the Mercy Seat: See *Exod.* xxv. 20. reading *Memuſſhak* inſtead of *Mimſhak.* The Words allude to the High Advancement of *Satan* in Heaven, before his Fall, where he was placed in one of the Higheſt Orders of Angels, ſuch as were neareſt in Attending upon the Divine Majeſty. So *Iſaiah*'s Deſcription of the Fall of the King of *Babylon* does plainly allude to the Downfal of Satan out of Heaven: *Iſa.* xiv. 12, &c.

Ibid. *Thou waſt upon the Holy Mountain of God.*] The Temple is often ſtyled God's Holy Mountain, ſee Chap. xx. 43. and the Temple being the Place of God's peculiar Reſidence, is now

and

and then put for Heaven it felf, fee *Pfal.* xi. 4.' Chapter xviii. 6. *Jonah* ii. 7. So the Phrafe denotes that XXVIII. this Prince might be compared to the Cherubims overfhadowing the Mercy-Seat, or the Angels who ftood before the Throne of God, typified by the Cherubims in the Temple: The Expreffions ftill alluding to the high Station of Satan before his Apoftacy.

Ibid. *Thou haft walked up and down in the midft of the Stones of Fire.*] Thy Dominion was in the upper Region of the Sky, where Hailftones and Lightning are formed; or as *Tertullian* Paraphrafes the Expreffion, *Lib.* 2. *Contr. Marcion.* cap. 10. *Inter gemmantes fiderum radios demoratus:* Thou hadft thy abode among glittering Stars: as the Angels are fometimes called: See *Job* xxxviii. 7. *Ifa.* xiv. 13.

Ver. 15. *Thou waft perfect in thy Ways----till Iniquity was found in thee.*] An exact Defcription of the Angelical Purity in which the Devil was created, and in which he continued till being lifted up with Pride, he fell from his firft Eftate. Ver. 15.

Ver. 16. *By the Multitude of thy Merchandife, they have filled the midft of thee with Violence, &c.*] Thy Skill in Trading hath degenerated into Violence, Cheating and Extortion; for which I will degrade thee from the Honour of being nearly related to me, as my Minifter and the Executor of my Commands, by whi h thou d'dft refemble the Dignity of the Angelick Order. See Ver. 14. Ver. 16.

Ver. 17. *Thine Heart was lifted up becaufe of thy Beauty.*] Compare Ver. 9, 13. Chap. xxxi. 10. So the Devil was *lifted up with Pride* upon Ver. 17.

on

Chapter on the Account of his Perfections: See 1 *Tim.* XXVIII. iii. 6.

〰️ Ibid. *Thou haft corrupted thy Wifdom by reafon of thy Brightnefs.*] That height of Glory and Authority to which I had advanced thee, has perverted thy Judgment, and made thee abufe thy Wifdom to Craft and Deceit. See Ver. 16.

Ibid. *I will lay thee before Kings, that they may behold thee.*] I will make thee a Spectacle to other Princes, expofe thee as a miferable Object before their Eyes, that thou mayeft be an Example to them to deter them from the like Practices. See Chap. xvi. 41. xxiii. 48. xxxi. 14.

Ver. 18. Ver. 18. *Thou haft defiled thy Sanctuaries by the Multitude of thine Iniquities,* &c.] The Word *Mikdafh* does fometimes fignify a Palace, in which Senfe it is probably taken *Amos* viii. 13. where our Tranflation renders it *the Kings Chappel:* thus Bifhop *Patrick* underftands it, *Exod.* xxv. 8. where the *Englifh* reads, *Let them make me a Sanctuary,* but it may probably mean a Palace: for God commanded himfelf to be ferved and attended upon in the Tabernacle, as a King is in his Court. The *Cherubims* were his Throne, the Ark his Footftool, the Altar his Table, and therefore called by that Name, Chap. xli. 22. *Malac.* i. 7. the Priefts his Attendants, and the Shew-bread and Sacrifices his Provifions. Thus the Word may moft probably be taken here to this Senfe: that fince their Palaces and ftately Buildings are filled with the Iniquity and Injuftice which they have practifed in their Trade and Commerce, therefore God will utterly deftroy them by *Nebuchadnezzar,* who reduced the whole City

City to an Heap of Afhes and Rubbifh, which
Alexander afterward made ufe of to make a Bank
or Caufey, by means of which he affaulted the
New City of *Tyre* and took it.   See Dr. *Prideaux*,
Part 1. p. 484.   If we follow the common Tranflation, it imports a Denunciation of God's Judgments for filling their idolatrous Temples with Riches and Prefents gotten by Injuftice.   So God often punifhes the Contempt of Religion in general
in thofe who are miftaken in their own way of
Worfhip.

Chapter XXVIII.

Ver. 19. *Thou fhalt be a Terror,* &c.] See Chap.
xxvi. 21.

Ver. 19.

Ver. 21. *Set thy Face againft Zidon,* &c.] Direct thy Face and thy Speech towards *Zidon,* See
Chap. vi. 2. and foretel its Deftruction by the King
of *Babylon:* See Chap. xxxii. 30. *Jer.* xxv. 22.
xlviii. 4. *Tyre* and *Sidon* were Neighbours and
Partakers of the fame Fate both in Profperity and
Adverfity.   *Sidon* was afterwards utterly deftroyed by *Ochus* King of *Perfia.*

Ver. 21.

Ver. 22. *I will be glorified in the midft of thee,*
&c.] I will make my Power and Juftice known by
the Judgments I will execute upon thee.   In the
fame Senfe God faith *Exod.* xiv. 17. *I will get me
Honour upon Pharaoh:* where the Word in the
Original is the fame.

Ver. 22.

Ibid. *And will be fanctified in her.*] God is faid
to be fanctified in thofe for whofe Prefervation or
Deftruction he exerts his Power in a remarkable
Manner, Compare Ver. 25. and fee Chap. xx. 41.

H h

Ver.

Ver. 23. *And I will send unto her Pestilence
and Blood into her Streets.*] The Pestilence which
often accompanies long Sieges, shall destroy her Inhabitants as well as the Sword.   See Chap. v. 12.
xxxviii. 22.

Ver. 24.
Ver. 24. *And there shall be no more a pricking
Briar unto the House of Israel, &c.*] My People
shall dwell in their Land quietly and securely, when
the rest of their ill Neighbours are destroyed : who
were a continual Vexation to them, and as so many Thorns in their Sides.   Compare *Numb.* xxxiii.
55. *Josh.* xxiii. 13.   So *a Thorn in the Flesh* 2 *Cor.*
xii. 7. signifies a cruel Enemy or Persecutor, as appears by comparing that place with the Context,
Ver. 9, 10.   The following Verse shews, that this
Promise chiefly relates to the General Restauration
of the Jews, when all the Enemies of God's Church
and Truth are vanquished and subdued, often denoted in the Prophetical Writings, by the Names
of *Edom, Moab,* and other Neighbouring Countries, who upon all Occasions shewed their Spite
and ill Will against the Jews.   See the Note upon
Chap. xxxviii. 17. and upon *Isa.* xi. 14. and compare *Jer.* xii. 14. with this place.

Ver. 25.
Ver. 25. *When I shall have gathered the House
of Israel from among the People among whom they
were scattered, &c.*] This, if we follow the literal
Sense of the Words, is a plain Prophecy of the general Restoration of the Jews and their Return into their own Land, as will appear, by comparing
the Words with the Parallel Texts in this Prophet,
viz. Chap. xi. 17. xx. 38, 41. xxxiv. 13. xxxvi.
24. xxxvii. 12, 14, 21, 25. xxxix. 27. and the Rules
laid

laid down concerning the Divifion of the Land Chapter among the Twelve Tribes, Chap. xlvii, and xlviii, XXVIII. do very much favour this Interpretation. Compare ⌇⌇ *Ifa.* lxv. 9, 10. *Jer.* xxx. 18. xxxii. 41. in which Predicion moft of the other Prophets agree with him. See the Note on *Ifa.* xi. 11.

Ibid. *And fhall be fanctified in them.*] See Ver. 22. and Chap. xxxvi. 23.

Ver. 26. *And they fhall dwell fafely therein.*] Ver. 26. This denotes outward Peace and Freedom from the Annoyance of Enemies. Compare Chap. xxxvi. 28. xxxviii, 11. *Jer.* xxiii. 6.

Ibid. *And fhalt build Houfes and plant Vine-yards.*] Building and planting are commonly join-ed together. Compare *Ifa.* lxv. 21. *Jer.* xxxi. 4, 5. *Amos* ix. 14.

Ibid. *When I fhall have executed Judgments upon all thofe that defpifed them.*] See Ver. 24. The Prophets conclude their Threatnings againft Infi-dels with gracious Promifes to God's People, imply-ing, that he will not make an utter Deftruction of them as of other People, but referve a Remnant to whom he may fulfil his Promifes made to their Fa-thers. Compare *Jer.* xlvi. 27, 28.

CHAP.

CHAP. XXIX.

The ARGUMENT.

In this and the three following Chapters, is foretold
the Conqueſt of Egypt *by* Nebuchadnezzar,
which came to paſs in the Third Year of Nebuchadnezzar's *Reign, which was the Twenty ſe-*
venth of Jehoiakin's *Captivity :* See Ver. 17. *This*
was the ſame Judgment upon Egypt *which was*
foretold by Jeremiah, *Chap. xlvi.* 13, &c.

Ver. 2.

V er. 2. ET *thy Face* [See Chap. vi. 2.]
againſt Pharaoh King *of* E-
gypt.] Pharaoh *being a com-*
mon Name to all the Kings
of *Egypt*, this Prince was
called Pharaoh Hophra, by
way of Diſtinction by *Jeremy*, Chap. xlvi. 30. and
Apries by *Herodotus*.

Ver. 3.

Ver. 3. *The great Dragon that lies in the midſt*
of his Rivers.] The Word *Tannim* ſignifies any
great

great Fish, such as a Whale, as it is translated
Chap. xxxii. 2. where it is applied to the same Subject as here. See the Note on *Isa.* xxviii. 1. *Bo-*
chart in his *Hierozoicon, lib.* 5. *c.* 16, 18. not improbably understands it here of a Crocodile, (See
the following Note) a Fish in a manner peculiar to
the River *Nile*, to which he likens the King of
Egypt, because he valued himself so much upon his
Dominion over that River. The same learned
Author observes, that the Word *Pharaoh* signifies
a *Crocodile* in the *Arabick* Tongue. The Kings
of *Egypt* are elsewhere compared to Whales or some
such great Fishes, sporting themselves in the Waters, and exercising a sort of Dominion over the lesser Fry : See *Psal.* lxxiv. 13, 14. *Isa.* li. 9.

Ibid. *Which hath said, My River is my own, and*
I have made it for my self.] The Prophet having
described this Prince as bearing Rule over the Waters, in pursuance of the same Metaphor, speaks of
his Kingdom as if it were a great River, and he
priding himself in having established his Government so firmly over it, *That it was not in the*
power of God himself to dispossess him of it, as *He-*
rodotus tells us, *Lib.* ii. *c.* 169. he profanely boast-
ed, affecting to be a God, as the Prince of *Tyre*
did, Chap. xxviii. 2.

Ver. 4. *But I will put Hooks in thy Chaws.*] In
pursuance of the same Metaphor, God tells him
that he will put a stop to all his vainglorious Designs and Boastings : having the same absolute
Power over him as a Fisherman hath over a Fish,
when he has fastened his Hook in his Jaws : Compare 2 *Kings* xix. 28.

Ver. 4.

Ibid.

Chapter
XXIX.

Ibid. I will cause the Fish of thy River to stick to thy Scales, and I will bring thee out of the midst of thy Rivers, &c.] Thou shalt send a great Number of thy Subjects upon an Expedition into *Libya* against the *Cyrenians*, where his Army having ill Success, the *Egyptians* entertaining an Opinion that the Army was sent upon this Expedition on purpose to be destroyed, thereupon Mutinied against him, and set up *Amasis* to be their King.

Ibid. I will bring thee out of the midst of thy Rivers.] By this is Metaphorically expressed his undertaking a foreign Expedition: The Expression alludes to the Nature of a Crocodile, who is not confined to the Water, but useth to come upon the Land, where he is frequently taken.

Ver. 5.

Ver. 5. *And I will leave thee thrown into the Wilderness, thee and all the Fish of thy Rivers.]* Thy Army shall be discomfited, and fall in the Desarts of *Libya* and *Cyrene: Apries* himself did not perish there, but the King and People being like the Head and Body, whatever Calamity befals either part is common to Both. So the King of *Assyria* is said to be involved in that Destruction which consumed his Army. *Isa.* xxx. 33. *Apries* himself was afterward strangled in his Palace at *Sais*, by *Amasis* that overcame him.

Ibid. They shall not be brought together, nor gathered.] Their Bones or Carcasses shall not be brought together in order for Burial. See *Jer.* viii. 2. xxv. 33.

Ibid. I have given thee for Meat to the Beasts of the Field, &c.] See Chap. xxxix. 17.

Ver.

Ver. 6. *Because they have been a Staff of Reed* Chapter *to the House of Israel.*] The Expreſſion alludes XXIX.
to the Canes or Reeds that grow on the Bank of
the River *Nile*; on which if a Man leaned they Ver. 6.
brake, and the Splinters ran into his Hand. Compare 2 *Kings* xviii. 21. The Prophets often upbraid
the Jews with their vain Confidence in *Egypt*,
which would certainly diſappoint them : See *Iſa.*
xx. 5, 6. xxx. 3, 5, &c. xxxi. 3. *Jer.* ii. 36.

Ver. 7. *When they took hold of thee by the Hand,* Ver. 7.
thou didſt break and rent all their Shoulder.] Or
their Arm : The King, who was *Zedekiah*'s
Confederate, came with a great Army to raiſe
the Siege of *Jeruſalem* ; but durſt not engage a
Battle with the *Chaldeans*, but in a little time retired again into his own Country, treacherouſly
leaving *Zedekiah*, whom they had engaged to rebel againſt *Nebuchadnezzar* ; whereby they became the occaſion of his own, and his Peoples
Ruin : See Chap. xvii. 15. *Jer.* xxxvii. 5, 7.

Ibid. *And madeſt all their Loyns to be at a*
ſtand.] Or *to ſhake,* as Men do when they are
tottering and ready to fall. The *Hebrew* Verb
Hanamadhta, ſignifies properly to ſtand, but it is
probably here taken in the ſame Senſe with the
Verb *Hamanadhta :* Words of a near Sound being
often taken one for the other : See the Note on
Chap. xxvii. 15.

Ver. 8. *Behold I will bring a Sword upon thee,* Ver. 8.
and cut off Man and Beaſt from thee.] See Chap.
xiv. 17. This is to be underſtood of *Nebuchadnezzar*'s Conqueſt of *Egypt,* who taking Advantage of
Amaſis Revolt againſt *Apries,* overran that
Country,

Chapter
XXIX.

Ver. 9.

Country, and made a Prey of the whole Kingdom : See Ver. 19. and Chap. xxxii. 13.

Ver. 9. *Becauſe he hath ſaid, The River is mine,*
&c.] *Hophra* himſelf ſhall be ſlain, and his Countrey deſtroyed for his Impiety and Inſolence : See
Ver. 3.

Ver. 10.

Ver. 10. *Behold I am againſt thee and thy Ri-*
vers.] Since thou haſt oppoſed me, I will ſet my
ſelf againſt thee, and bring down the Strength and
Glory of thy Kingdom, wherein thou magnifieſt
thy ſelf ſo much : See the Note on Ver. 3.

Ibid. *From the Tower of Syene unto the Border*
of Ethiopia.] If we follow this Tranſlation, we
muſt underſtand the Word *Cuſh* rendered here
Ethiopia, of *Arabia,* as it is often taken : See the
Note on *Jer.* xiii. 23. For *Syene* was the Border
of *Egypt* toward *Ethiopia :* (See *Pliny's Nat. Hiſt.*
l. v. *c.* 9.) which lay Weſtward of *Egypt,* as *Ara-*
bia did Eaſtward. But the Words may be tranſlated thus, *From Migdol to Syene, even to the Bor-*
ders of Ethiopia. Compare Chap. xxx. 5, 9. *Mig-*
dol was a Town near the *Red Sea,* mentioned *Ex-*
od. xiv. 2. *Jer.* xliv. 1. xlvi. 14. ſo it lay at the
Entrance of *Egypt* from *Paleſtine :* whereas *Syene*
was at the other End of the Country upon the Borders of *Ethiopia.* The Parallel Text Chap. xxx.
6. confirms this Interpretation, where our Tranſlation reads, *From the Tower of Syene, they ſhall*
fall in it by the Sword : but the Senſe would be
much more perfect, if we tranſlate it, *From Migdol*
to Syene, &c.

Ver. 11.

Ver. 11. *No Foot of Man ſhall paſs through it,*
neither ſhall it be inhabited Fourty Years.] The in-
teſtine

testine Wars between *Apries* and *Amasis*, Chapter and the Conquest of the whole Country by XXIX. *Nebuchadnezzar*, will make *Egypt* a Desolation, the greatest part of Fourty Years, nor shall it recover its former Settlement till those are ended: See Chap. xxx. 10. xxxii. 13. Compare Chap. xxxv. 7.

Ver. 12. *And I will make the Land of Egypt* Ver. 12. *desolate.*] Many of the Jews which fled into *Egypt* upon the Murder of *Gedaliah*, were involved in the common Destruction of the Country and its Inhabitants: See *Jer.* xliv. 27, 28.

Ibid. *Among the Countries which are desolate.*] *Egypt* shall have its Share of Calamities with its Neighbours, who shall be a Prey to *Nebuchadnezzar*, according to the Prophesies of *Jeremy*, Chap. xxv, xliv, xlvi, &c. and of *Ezekiel*, Chap. xxv, &c.

Ibid. *I will scatter the Egyptians among the Nations.*] Some of them shall flee for Refuge into Foreign Countries, and some shall be carried away Captive by the *Babylonians.* Compare *Jer.* xlvi. 19.

Ver. 13. *At the end of fourty Years, I will* Ver. 13. *gather the Egyptians from the People whither they were scattered.*] Archbishop *Usher* supposes this to have been fulfilled when upon *Cyrus*'s having married *Apries*'s Daughter, as *Herodotus* tells the Story, *Lib.* 2. *Amasis* revolted from *Cyrus*, and no longer continued a Tributary, as he had been under the Kings of *Babylon*: See his *Annals, ad A. M.* 3473.

Chapter
XXIX.
〰〰
Ver. 14.

Ver. 14. *And I will cauſe them to return into the Land of Pathros.*] That Part of *Egypt* which is called *Thebais*, as *Bochart* proves by ſeveral Arguments: See his *Phaleg. Lib. iv. c. 27.*

Ibid. *And they ſhall be there a baſe Kingdom.*] i. e. a Tributary Kingdom. See Chap. xvii. 14.

Ver. 15.

Ver. 15. *It ſhall be the baſeſt of Kingdoms,&c.*] Notwithſtanding *Amaſis*'s ſhaking off the *Perſian* Yoke, *Egypt* was not able to keep up its former Grandeur, but was entirely conquered by *Cambyſes*, *Cyrus*'s Son, who made it a Province to the *Perſian* Empire; and upon its revolting from under that Government, it was finally ſubdued by *Ochus* the *Perſian* Emperor, and has been governed by Strangers ever ſince. " For on the failure of the *Perſian* Empire, it " became ſubject to the *Macedonians*, after " them to the *Romans*, after the *Romans* to the " *Saracens*, then to the *Mammalukes*, and is " now a Province of the *Turkiſh* Empire." As Dr. *Prideaux* obſerves in his *Connect. of Script. Hiſt. Part* 1. *p.* 79.

Ver. 17.

Ver. 16. *And it ſhall be no more the Confidence of the Houſe of Iſrael, which bringeth their Iniquity to Remembrance, &c.*] At the ſame time that the *Jews* put confidence in *Egypt*, they diſtruſted the Promiſes and Aſſiſtance of God, and forſook him to comply with the Idolatries of their Allies; thereby to recommend themſelves to their Protection. See Ver. 7. *Iſa.* lvii. 8, 9. *Jer.* ii. 18, 36. *Hoſ.* xii. 1.

Ver.

Ver. 17, *In the seven and twentieth Year, in* Chapter
the first Month.] The following Prophecy is re- XXIX.
lated here, not with respect to the Order of
time (for there is near Seventeen Years distance Ver. 17.
between the Date of the foregoing Prophecy
and this) but because both Prophecies relate to
the same Subject, *viz.* The Conquest of *Egypt*
by *Nebuchadnezzar*, which fell out this Year:
The City *Tyre* having been taken by him the
Year before, after Thirteen Years Siege. Concerning which Event, Dr. *Prideaux* hath observed that the Chronology of the *Phenician Annals*, (the Extracts of which may be seen in
Josephus Lib. 1. *Contr. Apion.*) exactly agrees
with the Time the Prophet *Ezekiel* assigns for
the taking of *Tyre*. See his *Connect. of Script.
Hist. Par.* 1. *p.* 92, 93.

Ver. 18. *Nebuchadnezzar caused his Army to* Ver. 18.
serve a great Service against Tyrus, &c.] The
Siege lasted Thirteen Years, as hath been already observed; till the Heads of their Soldiers became bald with continual wearing their Hel-
mets, and the Skin was worn off their Shoul-
ders with carrying Earth to raise Mounts and
Fortifications against it. See Chap. xxvi. 8.

Ibid. *Yet had he no Wages, nor his Army for
Tyrus.*] Before the Town came to be close-
ly besieged, the Inhabitants had removed their
Effects into an Island about half a Mile distant from the Shore, and there built another City called *New Tyre*, which was afterwards besieged and taken by *Alexander* the
Great: (See the Argument to Chap. xxvi.) so

that

Chapter
XXIX.

Ver. 19.

Ver. 20.

Ver. 21.

that there was no body left there when *Nebuchadnezzar*'s Army took the City.

Ver. 19. *He shall take her Multitude, and take her spoil.*] He and his Army shall have the Advantage of the Captives and Spoil of *Egypt*, which they shall utterly pillage and lay waste. See Ver. 10, 12. Chap. xxx. 12.

Ver. 20. *Because they wrought for me, saith the* Lord.] The Destruction of Cities and Countries is a Work of God's Providence, for the effecting of which He makes use of Kings and Princes as his Instruments. Upon this Account he calls *Nebuchadnezzar* his Servant, *Jer.* xxv. 9. *because he wrought for him*, as it is here expressed, i. e. executed his Judgments upon *Tyre* and the other Cities and Countries which God delivered into his Hand.

Ver. 21. *In that Day.*] This Phrase frequently denotes in the Prophets not the same time which was last mentioned, but an Extraordinary Season, remarkable for some signal Events of Providence: See the Note on *Isa.* iv. 2. In this Sense it is to be understood here.

Ibid. *I will cause the Horn of the House of Israel to bud forth.*] The Word Horn signifies Strength, from whence it comes to denote Prosperity, or a flourishing Condition. See 1 *Sam.* ii. 1. *Job* xvi. 15. From whence it is applied to express Kingly Power and Majesty. See *Psal.* lxxxix. 24. xcii. 10. cxxxii. 17. So here it signifies that after the Destruction of God's and his Churches Enemies, denoted by *Tyre, Egypt,*
and

and other Oppreſſors of the *Jews,* (See the Chapter
Note on Chap. xxxviii. 17.) the Kingdom and XXIX.
State of the *Jews* ſhould again flouriſh under the
Meſſias, as it is more clearly foretold Chap. xxxiv.
and xxxvii. Compare likewiſe Chap. xxxiii.
25, 26.

Ibid. *And I will give thee the opening of the*
Mouth in the midſt of them.] When thy Propheſies are made good by the Event, this ſhall
add a New Authority to what thou ſpeakeſt.
See Chap. xxiv. 27.

CHAP.

CHAP. XXX.

See the ARGUMENT *of the fore-going Chapter.*

Ver. 2.   Ver. 2. HOWL *ye, Wo worth the Day.*] The Prophet directs his Speech to the *Egyptians.* Compare *Isa.* xiii. 6.

Ver. 3.   Ver. 3. *The Day is near, even the Day of the* LORD, &c.] The time of Gods Vengeance. See Chap. vii. 7, 12.

Ibid. *The cloudy Day.*] When the Calamities that are coming upon *Egypt,* shall make every thing look dark and dismal. See Ver. 18. Chap. xxxii. 7, 8. xxxiv. 12. *Joel* ii. 2. *Amos* v. 18.

Ibid. *It shall be the time of the Heathen.*] Of the Punishment of the *Egyptians* and their Allies. See Ver. 4, 5. Chap. vii. 7, 12. God's

Judg-

Judgments upon particular Places and Nations are an Earneſt of that General Judgment, when he ſhall execute Judgment upon all the Ungodly. See the Note upon *Iſa.* xiii. 10.

Ver. 4. *Great pain ſhall be in Ethiopia.*] See Ver. 5, and 9.

Ibid. *And her Foundations ſhall be broken down.*] Her ſtrong Forts and Citadels: Compare *Iſa.* xvi. 7. *Jer.* l. 15.

Ver. 5. *Ethiopia, and Libya, and Lydia.*] The Names in the *Hebrew* are *Cuſh Phut,* and *Lud:* Who are mentioned together as the *Egyptian* Allies, *Jer.* xlvi. 9. See the Note there, and Comp. *Nahum* iii. 9. *Cuſh* probably ſignifies *Ethiopia* here (See Chap. xxix. 10.) as being joined with *Phut* and *Lud:* which were People of *Africa.* *Phut* is rendered *Libya* by our Interpreters here and in that place of *Jeremy;* but *Phut* and *Lubim* were a diſtinct People, as hath been obſerved upon Chap. xxvii. 10. *Phut* may denote ſome part of *Africa* near *Egypt,* and *Lud* probably ſignifies ſome part of the *Abyſſines* Country.

Ibid. *And all the mingled People.*] All their Auxiliaries: Compare *Jer.* l. 37. If we diſtinguiſh theſe from the *Men of the League* which follow, they may mean that mixture of *Carians, Ionians* and other Nations lying upon the *Mediterranean* Sea, which *Apries* got together to encounter *Amaſis,* who together with him were deſtroyed. See Dr. *Prideaux, ubi ſupra;* and the Note on *Jer.* xxv. 20.

Ibid. *And Chub.*] The *Cubij* are mentioned in *Ptolemy* as a People of *Mareotis,* a Province of *Egypt.*

Chapter. Ibid. *The men of the land that is in League.*]
XXX. The LXX tranflate it, *The men of my League,*
or Covenant: i. e. the Jews: Many of whom
flying into *Egypt*, were deftroyed there with
the *Egyptians*: See the Note on Chap. xxix.
12.

Ver. 6.   Ver. 6. *They alfo that uphold Egypt fhall fall*]
The Governours of the feveral Provinces, thofe
who are called *the ftay of the Tribes thereof,*
Ifa. xix. 13. i. e. of the feveral *Nomi* or Divifi-
ons of *Egypt.*

Ibid. *From the Tower of Syene they fhall fall*
in it.] The Senfe would be more complete if
the Words were tranflated, *From Migdol to*
Syene. See the Note on Chap. xxix. 12.

Ver. 7.   Ver. 7. *And they fhall be defolate in the midft*
of the Countries that are defolate, &c.] See
Chap. xxix. 10.

Ver. 8.   Ver. 8. *When I have fet a fire in Egypt.*]
God's Judgments are often compared to Fire.
See Chap. xix. 14. xxii. 21, 31. *Jer.* vii. 20.
Amos i. 4. &c. *Pfalm* lxxviii. 63.

Ibid. *And when all her Helpers fhall be de-*
ftroyed.] All her Allies and Auxiliaries: Compare Chap. xxxi. 7. xxxii. 21.

Ver. 9.   Ver. 9. *In that Day fhall Meffengers go from*
me in Ships to make the carelefs Ethiopians
afraid.] The *Ethiopians* were the Confederates
of the *Egyptians* in former times, and fharers
with them in their Good or Ill Fortune. See
Ifa. xviii. 1, 2. xx. 3, 4. and the Notes upon
thofe places. The Verfe may be likewife thus rendered; *In that Day fhall Meffengers go from me to*
the

the People *in the Wilderness to make the* care- Chapter
less *Ethiopians afraid:* The word *Tziim* is XXX.
tranflated *the People in the Wilderness,* Ifa.
xxiii. 13. and that Appellation is particularly
given to the *Ethiopians,* Pfalm lxxii. 9. and
lxxiv. 14. as the LXX tranflate the Word.

Ibid. *And great* Pain *fhall come upon them,*
as in the Day of Egypt.] The *Egyptians* and
Ethiopians being Confederates, the ill News of
the Conqueft of *Egypt* fhall fenfibly affect them.
Compare xxiv. 16. xxxiii. 9, 10. xxvii. 35. *Ifa.*
xix. 17. xxiii. 5.

Ver. 11. *The terrible of the Nations.*] See Ver. 11.
Chap. xxviii. 7.

Ver. 12. *And I will make the Rivers dry.*] Ver. 12.
I will deftroy the Strength of *Egypt*; the Metaphor is taken from the Decreafe or Failing of
the *Nile,* upon whofe Overflowing all the Plenty and Prolperity of *Egypt* depended. Compare Chap. xxix. 3. *Ifa.* xix. 5, 6.

Ibid. *And fell the Land into the Hand of the*
Wicked, *and I will make the Land wafte by the*
Hand of Strangers.*] See Chap. vii. 24. To *Sell,*
fignifies here to deliver up, as Men do Goods
that they fell. Compare *Deut.* xxxii. 30. *Judg.*
ii. 14. iv. 9.

Ver. 13. *I will alfo deftroy the Idols.*] Idolatry being one of the Principal Sins for which
God vifits the Infidel Nations, he will take particular Vengeance upon the Idols, thereby fhewing how much he is fuperior to them in Power.
Compare *Ifa.* xix. 1. *Jer.* xliii. 12. xlvi. 25.
Exod. xii. 12.

K k   Ibid.

Ibid. And I will cause their Images to cease out of Noph.] *Noph*, or *Memphis* was one of the Principal Cities of *Egypt*, a Seat of their Kings where their Sepulchres stood : One of which is still remaining. Upon which Account it is often mentioned in Scripture. See *Isa.* xix. 3. *Jer.* ii. 16. xliv. 1. xlvi. 14. In *Hosea* it is called *Moph*, Chap. xi. 6. which comes near in sound to *Memphis*. This Place was famous for the Worship of *Apis* and *Osiris* ; whereupon the Prophet in a particular manner denounces Destruction to the Idolatry of that Place.

Ibid. And there shall be no more a Prince in the Land of Egypt.] It shall no more have a Natural Prince of the *Egyptian* Race to rule over it as formerly, but shall be subject to Foreigners. See the Note on Chap. xxix. 15.

Ibid. And I will put a Fear in Egypt.] Will make them Faint-hearted, and not able to defend themselves. Compare *Isa.* xix. 16. *Jer.* xlvii. 5.

Ver. 14.

Ver. 14. *And I will make Pathros desolate.*] See Chap. xxix. 14.

Ibid. And I will set Fire in Zoan.] *Zoan*, or *Tanis*, was one of the ancient Cities in *Egypt*. See *Numb.* xiii. 20. and the Metropolis of the Kingdom in *Moses*'s time. See *Psalm* lxxviii. 12, 43.

Ibid. And I will execute Judgments in No.] Called the *Multitude of No*, or *Hamon No*, in the next Verse ; and probably the same with the City *Thebes*, famous for its Hundred Gates. See the Note on *Jer.* xlvi. 25.

Ver.

Ver. 15. *And I will pour my Fury upon Sin,* Chapter *the Strength of Egypt.*] It is generally agreed XXX. that *Sin* is the fame with *Pelufium,* one of the Seven Mouths of *Nile,* which was commonly Ver. 15. called the Key of *Egypt,* as *Suidas* obferves, and therefore was ftrongly fortified, that no Enemy might gain Admittance.

Ibid. *And I will cut off the Multitude of No.*] Or *Hamon No,* as the Original reads. The Name is generally fuppofed to be derived from *Hamon* who was the *Egyptian Jupiter.* *Mizra-im* the Son of *Ham* was the Founder of *Egypt,* which is called the *Land of Ham, Pfal.* cvi. 22. And this *Hamon* was probably either *Ham* him-felf, or one of his Pofterity advanced to Divine Honours. *Plutarch* informs us in his Book *De Ifide & Ofiride,* that *Ammon* in the *Egyptian* Language is equivalent to Ζευς in *Greek, p.* 354. *Edit. Francof.*

Ver. 16. *And I will fet Fire in Egypt.*] See Ver. 16. Ver. 8.

Ver. 17. *The Young Men of Aven and Pi-* Ver. 17. *befeth fhall fall by the Sword.*] *Aven* is the fame with *On,* mentioned *Gen.* xli. 45. in after times called *Heliopolis,* as our Margin explains it here, becaufe of a Temple or Image there de-dicated to the Sun. Compare *Ifa.* xix. 18. *Jer.* xliii. 13. The Word is fo tranflated by the LXX Interpreters, both here, and *Gen.* xli. 45. who were very well acquainted with *Egypt,* and the principal Places of it. *Pibefeth* was afterward with very little Variation called *Bubaftum,* and fo tranflated here by the LXX.

Chapter
XXX.

Ver. 18.

Ver. 18. *At Tehaphnehes the Day shall be darkened.*] Compare Ver. 3. *Tehaphnehes* elsewhere writ *Tahpanhes*, is supposed to be the same place which was afterwards called *Daphnæ Pelusiaca.* See the Note on *Jer.* xliii. 7.

Ibid. *When I shall break there the Yokes of Egypt.*] When I shall set those at Liberty that are oppressed by the Bondage of *Egypt.* Compare Chap. xxxiv. 27.

Ibid. *A Cloud shall cover her.*] See Ver. 3.

Ver. 21.

Ver. 21. *I have broken the Arm of Pharaoh, &c.*] I have broken his Strength, so that he will never be able to recover his former Power. Compare *Jer.* xlviii. 25. It is usual for the Prophets to speak of a Thing future, as if it were already accomplished. See the Note on *Isa.* xxi. 9.

Ver. 22.

Ver. 22. *And I will break his Arms, the Strong, and that which was broken.*] The King of *Babylon* had before dispossessed the King of *Egypt* of all his new Conquests, from the River of *Egypt* to the River *Euphrates*, 2 *Kings* xxiv. 7. So that this Part of his Strength was already taken away, and never to be recovered; and now God threatens to destroy the Remainder of his Power, the Kingdom of *Egypt* it self.

Ibid. *And I will cause the Sword to fall out of his Hand.*] He shall have no more Strength to defend himself, than a Man hath to use his Sword when his Arm is broken.

Ver. 23.

Ver. 23. *And I will scatter the Egyptians among the Nations, &c.*] See Chap. xxix. 13.

Ver.

Ver. 24. *And I will strengthen the Arm of the* Chapter
King of Babylon.] The same Promise God af- XXX.
terwards made to *Cyrus, Isa. xlv. 1.* Compare
Psal. xviii. 39.
Ver. 24.

Ibid. *And he shall groan with the Groans of
a deadly wounded Man.*] His Strength shall
perfectly fail, as a Man's who is dying of his
Wounds.

C H A P.

C H A P. XXXI.

The ARGUMENT.

*A Continuation of the Judgments denounced a-
gainst* Pharaoh *and his Kingdom; whose Pride
God humbles by putting him in mind of the
dreadful Fall of the King of* Niniveh, *much
superior to him in Power and Greatness;
whose Ruin the Prophet elegantly describes
under the Metaphor of a Fair flourishing Tree
cut down and withered.*

Ver. 2.   Ver. 2. *HOM thou art like to in
Greatness.*] Thou pridest-
thy self as if there never
was any Prince or King that
could compare with thee.

Ver. 3.   Ver. 3. *Behold the Assyrian was a Cedar in
Lebanon,* &c.] By the *Assyrian,* Archbishop
Usher, ad A. M. 3378, and Dr. *Prideaux,* P. 1.
p. 47. do most probably understand that King
of *Assyria* whom some call *Chyniladanus,* others
                              Saracus;

Saracus; 'tis of this King of *Assyria* the Words of the Prophet *Nahum* are to be understood Chap. iii. 18. In like manner *Zephaniah* joins the Destruction of *Assyria* and the Desolation of *Niniveh* together, Chap. ii. 13. *Nabupolassar* the King of *Babylon*, and *Cyaxares* the King of *Media*, called by the Names of *Nebuchadonosor* and *Assuerus* in *Tobit*, Chap. xiv. 15. joining their Forces together against him, besieged *Niniveh*, took it, and after having slain the King, utterly destroyed that great and famous City; and put an End to that part of the *Assyrian* Empire. *Nabupolassar* having before possessed himself of the other part which was properly called the *Babylonian* Empire. See Dr. *Prideaux*, p. 45. In this remarkable Catastrophe, the Prophecies of *Jonah*, *Nahum*, and *Zephaniah*, foretelling the Destruction of *Niniveh*, were fulfilled.

The King of *Niniveh* is compared here to a Fair and Tall Cedar, such as grow in Mount *Lebanon*: See the like Comparison *Isa.* x. 34. xxxvii. 24. *Zech.* xi. 2. The Greatness of *Nebuchadnezzar*'s Power and Kingdom is set forth under the same Resemblance, *Dan.* iv. 10, &c. Ibid. *His Top was among the thick Boughs.*] He overtopped all the other flourishing Trees. Compare Chap. xvii. 3. xix. 11.

Ver. 4. *The Waters made him great, &c.*] Ver. 4. As Trees flourish by a River Side, (Compare Chap. xvii. 5.) so the Traffick of the several Branches of the River *Tigris*, upon which *Niniveh* was situate, made that City and Kingdom rich and populous, and she imparted her Wealth

and

Chapter and Stores among the Neighbouring Provinces.
XXXI. Compare *Nahum* ii. 6.

Ver. 5. Ver. 5. *Therefore his Height was exalted a-*
bove all the Trees of the Field.] He became
greater than all the Kings about him : Compare
Dan. iv. 11.

Ver. 6.   Ver. 6. *All the Fowls of Heaven made their*
Nests in his Boughs, &c.] Several Nations applied to him for Protection, and thought themselves and all their Concerns safe under his Government.   Compare Chap. xvii. 23. *Daniel*
iv. 12.

Ver. 8.   Ver. 8. *The Cedars in the Garden of God*
could not hide him.] He overtopped the goodly
Cedars, called in the *Hebrew, the Cedars of*
God: Psal. lxxx. 10. such fair ones as might be
supposed to have grown in Paradise. Compare
Chap. xxviii. 13.

Ver. 9.   Ver. 9. *So that all the Trees of Eden---envied*
him.] *All the Kings of the East envied him and*
his Greatness : as the *Chaldee* Paraphrast expres-
seth the Sense.

Ver. 10.   Ver. 10. *Because thou hast lifted up thy self*
in Height, &c.] Because thy Pride hath still increased with thy Prosperity : Compare Chapter
xxviii. 17.

Ver. 11.   Ver. 11. *I have therefore delivered him into*
the Hand of the mighty one of the Heathen] Or,
The mighty one of the Nations, as the Word *Go-*
jim is render'd in the next Verse. The Word
El, tho' commonly spoken of God, yet is sometimes applied to Heroes, See Chapter xxxii. 21.
sometimes to Angels, as being mighty in
Strength,

Strength, as *Pſal.* lxxxix. 6. So God here ſaith, Chapter
he delivered the *Aſſyrian* into the Hand of *Na-* XXXI.
bupolaſſar King of *Babylon*, who joining his Forces with *Cyaxares* King of *Media* his Confederate, made themſelves Maſters of *Niniveh*, and
the King of *Aſſyria*, whoſe Seat it was.

Ver. 12. *And Strangers, the terrible of the* Ver. 12.
Nations, have cut him off and have left him,
&c.] Compare Chap. xxviii. 7. xxx. 11. The
Armies of the Kings of *Babylon* and *Media*, ſhall
utterly deſtroy him and his Empire, and leave
him without Life or Strength, like a Tree that
is cut down dried up and withered.

Ibid. *Upon the Mountains and in all the Val-*
leys his Branches are fallen, &c.] As the Limbs
of ſuch a Tree are Broke by the fall, and thoſe
that reſted under its ſhadow are frighted away
and have forſook the place: So the *Aſſyrian*
Army lies Slain here and there: Compare Chap.
xxxii. 5. xxxv. 8. and thoſe that lived under his
Protection and Government withdrew their O-
bedience from him: Compare *Dan.* iv. 14.

Ver. 13 *Upon his ruin ſhall all the fowls of* Ver. 13.
the Heaven remain, &c.] As the Birds ſit up-
on the Boughs of a Tree cut down, and the
Beaſts browze upon its Branches: So his Domi-
nions ſhall be a Prey to the Conquerors: Or his
Armies that are ſlain, ſhall become Meat to the
Birds and Beaſts. Compare Chap. xxix. 5. and
Iſa. xviii. 6.

Ver. 14. *To the end that none of the Trees* Ver. 14.
by the Waters exalt themſelves, &c.] Thy Deſtruction ſhall be a Warning to other Kings and

Potentates

Chapter Potentates to deter them from Priding them-
XXXI. selves in the time of their Prosperity : See Chap.
xxviii. 17.

Ibid. *For they are all delivered unto Death,*]
Whatever distinction there is between them and
the inferior sort, Death shall make them all
equal : See *Psal.* lxxxii. 7. and particularly to
Egypt and those other Countries against which
God hath denounced his Judgments, the same
Fate is allotted which this *Assyrian* Monarch
has already undergone : See Chap. xxxii. 18. *&c.*

Ver. 15. Ver. 15. *In the day when he went down to
the Grave.*] This and the following Verse are
an Elegant Description of that Consternation
that seized the King of *Assyria*'s Allies at the
suddeness of his Downfal : the same Metaphor
being still pursued.

Ibid. *I caused a Mourning, I covered the Deep
for him.*] The Sense might better be expressed
thus, *I covered the Deep with Mourning.* For
when two Verbs are joined together in the *Hebrew,* one is usually taken in the Sense of a Noun
or an Adverb. The Deep that Nursed up this
fair Tree Ver. 4. is described as Mourning at its
Downfal.

Ibid. *I restrained the Floods thereof, and the
great Waters were stayed.*] As if the Streams
had stopped their usual Course, on purpose to
lament his Fate.

Ibid. *I caused Lebanon to mourn for him,* &c.]
The Forrest of *Lebanon* and all the stately Trees
in it, sympathized with his Misfortunes : *i. e.*
all his Confederates and Allies.

Ver.

Ver. 16. *I made the Nations to shake at the*
Sound of his Fall.] See Chap. xxvi. 15.

Ibid. *When I cast him down to Hell* [or the
Grave] *with them that descend into the Pit.*]
See Chap. xxxii. 18, 21. and *Isa.* xiv. 15.

Ibid. *All the Trees of Eden, the Choice of Le-*
banon, all that drink Water [See Ver. 14.] *shall*
be comforted in the nether parts of the Earth.]
The deceased Princes, Confederates to the *Assy-*
rians, described here as so many stately Trees
and Cedars, shall feel some Mitigation of their
Calamities, when they see thee brought down
as low as themselves. Compare Chap. xxxii. 31.
and *Isa.* xiv. 8, 9, 10. a Place exactly parallel to
this.

Ver. 17. *They also went down to Hell* [or the
Grave] *with him.*] His Allies underwent the
same Fate with himself, and were cut off in the
common Destruction. See Chap. xxxii. 20, &c.

Ibid. *Even they that were his Arm, that*
dwelt under his Shadow in the midst of the Hea-
then.] Or, *the Nations,* See Ver. 11. his Auxiliaries. See Chap. xxx. 8. xxxii. 21. who lived
under his Protection in several Countries and
Provinces : Compare *Lament.* iv. 20.

Ver. 18. *To whom art thou thus like in Glory*
and Greatness among the Trees of Eden.] The
Prophet now applies himself to the King of *E-*
gypt : q. d. Wilt thou still boast thy self as if no
Prince were thine Equal? See Ver. 2. yet thou
shalt undergo the same Fate with this fair flourishing Cedar, the King of *Assyria.* See Ver.
14. and compare Chap. xxxii. 19.

Ibid.

Chapter
XXXI.

Ibid. *Thou shalt lie in the midst of the Uncircumcised, &c.*] See Chap. xxviii. 10. xxxii. 19,
20.

Ibid. *This is Pharaoh, and all his Multitude,
saith the Lord* GOD.] The Judgment that befel
the King of *Assyria* here described, is an exact
Representation of the Destruction that remains
for *Pharaoh* and his People : The Word *Is* commonly denotes the same as to signify or represent,
especially in Prophesies, Parables, and such like
figurative Descriptions. See Chap. xxxiv. 31.
xxxvii. 11. *Gen.* xli. 26. *Exod.* xii. 11. *Matth.*
xiii. 19. and xxvi. 26.

C H A P.

CHAP. XXXII.

The ARGUMENT.

A Continuation of the same Subject, and a further Description of the lamentable Destruction of Egypt by Nebuchadnezzar: The Prophet illustrating the Dreadfulness of his Fall by a Poetical Description of the Infernal Mansions appointed for Tyrants and Oppressors, where Pharaoh is to have a place allotted for him.

Ver. 2. **T**AKE *up a Lamentation for Pharaoh.*] See the Note on Chap. xxii. 2.

Ibid. *Thou art like a young Lion of the Nations.*] Thou art like a Beast of Prey devouring far and near: See Chap. xix. 3, 6. xxxviii. 13.

Ibid. *Thou art as a Whale in the Seas.*] By the Word *Tannim* we may fitly understand a

Cro-

Chapter Crocodile, as hath been obferved upon Chapter
XXXII. xxix. 3. and the Defcription that follows of this,
Creature, agrees very well to a Crocodile, but
can't be applied to a Whale.

 Ibid. *And thou cameft forth with thy Rivers,
and troubledft the Waters with thy Feet,* &c.] Or,
thou rufhedft forth thro' thy Streams, and troubledft, &c. *i. e.* thou waft the Occafion of great
Commotions and Difturbances to all thy Neighbours: Compare Chap. xxxiv. 18.

Ver. 3.
 Ver. 3. *I will therefore fpread my Net over
thee,* &c.] I will bring thine Enemies upon
thee, who fhall encompafs thee, and Mafter
thee, as a Wild Beaft or Monftrous Fifh that is
taken in a Net: See Chap. xii. 14.

Ver. 4.
 Ver. 4. *Then I will leave thee upon the Land,
and caft thee forth upon the open Field,* &c.]
Thine Armies fhall fall in the open Field, and
become a Prey to Wild Beafts and ravenous
Birds. Compare Chap. xxix. 5.

Ver. 5.
 Ver. 5. *I will lay thy Flefh upon the Mountains, and fill the Vallies with thy height.*] The
vaft Bulk of thine Armies when they are flain,
fhall fill both Mountains and Vallies. See Chap.
xxxi. 12.

Ver. 6.
 Ver. 6. *I will alfo water with thy Blood the
Land wherein thou fwimeft.*] The Land fhall
be foaked with thy Blood wherein thou bareft
Rule, juft as in the Waters the great Fifh have
an abfolute Power over the leffer Fry.

 Ibid. *Even to the Mountains.*] The Mountains fhall be wet with it, as well as the lower
Grounds, Ver. 5. Compare *Ifa.* xxxiv. 3.

          Ver.

Ver. 7, 8. *I will cover the Heavens, and make* Chapter
the Stars thereof dark, &c.] These Metaphors XXXII.
denote the downfal of States and Governments,
Kings and Rulers, being figuratively expressed Ver. 7, 8.
by the Sun, Moon and Stars. Compare *Isa.* xiii.
10. xxxiv. 4. *Joel* ii. 31. *Revel.* vi. 12, 13, 14.
God's Judgments upon particular Countries being Earnests of a General Judgment, they are
described in such Terms as if the whole Frame
of Nature were dissolved.

Ibid. *And set Darkness upon thy Land.*] Every Thing shall look Dark and Dismal. See
Chap. xxx. 3.

Ver. 9. *And I will vex the Hearts of many* Ver. 9.
*People, when I shall bring thy Destruction among
the Nations,* &c.] When thy Exiles shall be
dispersed into foreign Countries, (See Chap.
xxix. 12.) and relate the Miserable Circumstances of thy Destruction, it shall cause Grief and
Consternation in all that hear it. See the following Verse.

Ver. 10. *Yea, I will make many People ama-* Ver. 10.
zed at thee, &c.] See Chap. xxvi. 16. xxvii.
35. xxx. 9.

Ver. 12. *The terrible of the Nations.*] See Ver. 12.
Chap. xxviii. 7.

Ver. 13. *I will also destroy the Beasts there-* Ver. 13.
of from beside the great Waters.] Or, *That
they be no more beside the Great Waters,* as *Noldius* translates the Phrase, *p.* 635. The Horses
shall be consumed in the War, and the other
Cattle that used to feed in the Meadows by the
side of the *Nile,* (See *Gen.* xli. 2.) shall be destroyed

Chapter ſtroyed or drove away as a Prey. See Chap. XXXII. xxix. 8, 11.

Ibid. and Ver. 14. *Neither ſhall the Foot of Man trouble them any more; nor the Hoofs of Beaſts*, &c.] Here is a Tranſition from a proper Senſe to a Metaphorical one : The Prophet in the ſecond Verſe compared the Diſturbances the *Egyptians* gave their Neighbours to troubling and fouling of Waters ; in alluſion to which Metaphor he ſaith here ; that when *Egypt* is made deſolate, and the Number both of Men and Beaſts diminiſhed by their Wars and Confuſions, then their Neighbours will enjoy ſuch quietneſs, as a River does that ſmoothly glides along, and never hath its Streams fouled or diſturbed.

Ver. 16. Ver. 16. *This is the Lamentation wherewith they ſhall lament her.*] This is the Subſtance of a Lamentation which may be properly uſed to bewail the Calamities of *Egypt.* See Ver. 2.

Ibid. *The Daughters of the Nations ſhall lament her.*] *i. e.* The People of the Neighbouring Countries : So the *Daughter of Sion* and of *Babylon* ſignifies the Inhabitants of thoſe Cities. The Expreſſion alludes to the Mourning Women whoſe Profeſſion it was to lament at Funerals. See the Note on *Jer.* ix. 17.

Ver. 17. Ver. 17. *In the Fifteenth Day of the Month.*] Of the Twelfth Month, See Ver. 1. the LXX underſtand it of the Firſt Month, as that indefinite Expreſſion is probably underſtood Chap. xxvi. 1.

Ver.

Ver. 18. *Wail for the multitude of Egypt.*]
See Ver. 2. and 16.

Ibid. *And caſt them down, even her, and the*
Daughters of the famous Nations.] The Prophets are ſaid to do things, when they declare God's purpoſe of doing them : See Chap. xliii. 3. where *Ezekiel* ſaith *he was ſent to deſtroy the City, i. e.* to foretel its Deſtruction. In the ſame Senſe we are to underſtand the Expreſſion here, of caſting down *Egypt, i. e.* foretelling its Ruin, together with God's Judgments upon other Famous Kingdoms in that part of the World, which are reckoned up in the following Verſes, and called here the *Daughters of the Nations :* concerning which Expreſſion See the Note on Ver. 16.

Ibid. *Unto the nether parts of the Earth, with them that go down to the Pit.*] The Expreſſions denote utter Deſtruction, and are parallel to thoſe elſewhere uſed of being brought down to Hell, to the Grave, or into Silence. Compare Chap. xxxi. 14. *Iſa.* xiv. 15.

Ver. 19. *Whom doſt thou paſs in Beauty? go*
down and be thou laid with the Uncircumciſed.] What Reaſon haſt thou now to prefer thy ſelf before others ? ſince thou ſhalt undergo the ſame Fate with the worſt of them. See the Note on Chap. xxviii. 10.

Ver. 20. *They are fallen in the midſt of them*
that are ſlain by the Sword.] They do not *Die the common Death of all Men,* as *Moſes* ſpeaks, *Numb.* xvi. 29. but are cut off by an extraordinary Judgment from the Hand of God himſelf.

M m   Ibid.

Ibid. *Draw her and all her Multitudes.*]
Carry her and her People away to the Grave,
like so many Carcasses. which are buried without any Solemnity. The Words are spoken to
the *Babylonians*, the Executioners of God's Judgments upon *Egypt*.

Ver. 21. Ver. 21. *The strong among the mighty shall
speak to him out of the midst of Hell, with them
that help him.*] Here follows a Poetical Description of the Infernal Regions, where the Ghosts
of deceased Tyrants with their Subjects are represented as coming to meet the King of *Egypt*
and his Auxiliaries, See Chap. xxx. 8. upon
their Arrival to the same Place. *Hell* signifies
here the State of the Dead. Compare Chap.
xxxi, 16; 17. *Isa.* xiv. 9, &c. and see the Notes
there.

Ibid. *They are gone down,* &c.] These War-
riors famous in their Time for their Exploits
have undergone the same Fate with other Men
of Blood, and are gone down to the Grave by
violent Deaths. See Ver. 19.

Ver. 22. Ver. 22. *Asshur is there and all her Company.*]
The *Assyrians* both King and People, whose
Destruction is represented in the foregoing
Chapter.

Ibid. *His Graves are about him.*] The *E-
gyptians* lie buried in the same Place with them.
The Masculine and Feminine Genders are promiscuously used in the following Verses. The
Masculine referring to the Prince whose Subjects the Deceased were; the Feminine to the
Nation or Country to which they belonged.

Ver.

Ver. 23. *Whose Graves are set in the sides* Chapter *of the Pit.*] Compare Chap. xxvi. 20. *Isa.* XXXII. xiv. 15.

Ibid. *And her Company round about her Grave.*] Like lesser Graves placed round the Monument of a Person of great Quality : or the Words may import that Death has made them all equal. Compare Ver. 24, 25.

Ibid. *All of them slain,* &c.] See Ver. 20.

Ibid. *Which caused terror in the Land of the Living.*] Tho' they were a Terrour while they were alive to their Neighbours. See Chap. xxvi. 17.

Ver. 24. *There is Elam and all her Multitude.*] Ver. 24. Which was conquered by *Nebuchadnezzar.* See *Jer.* xlix. 34. and the Notes there.

Ibid. *Yet have they born their Shame with them that go down into the Pit.*] They have been shamefully subdued and lost their Lives and Glory together, as *Asshur* did before them. Ver. 22.

Ver. 25. *They have set her a Bed in the midst* Ver. 25. *of the Slain,* &c.] *Elam* and her People have a Place among the deceased Princes and Potentates. The Word Bed is used for the Grave, *Isa.* lvii. 2. and may perhaps in both Places allude to the costly Monuments or Sepulchres which used to be erected for Persons of Great Quality. *Mittah* a Word of the same Sense is used for a Bier or Coffin, 2 *Sam.* iii. 31.

Ibid. *Her Graves are round about him.*] About those of the King of *Egypt,* and his People.

Ver.

Chapter
XXXII.
〰〰
Ver. 26.

Ver. 26. *There is Meſhech and Tubal and all her Multitude.*] Who are threatned by God with a terrible Deſtruction. See Chap. xxxviii. 2, 3, &c. But they ſeem to be mentioned here by way of *Prolepſis* or Anticipation, as the Criticks call it; for the Deſtruction threatned to *Meſhech* and *Tubal* was not to come to paſs till ſeveral Ages after this Prophecy againſt *Egypt* was fulfilled, as may be gathered from ſeveral Expreſſions in that Prophecy. So the Country of *Goſhen* is called the *Land of Rameſes, Gen.* xlvii. 11. which yet had that Name from the City *Rameſes* built in after times by the *Iſraelites.* See *Exod.* i. 11. By the ſame Figure *Horeb* is called the *Mountain of God, Exod.* iii. 1. Concerning *Meſhech* and *Tubal* See the Note on Chap. xxvii. 13.

Ver. 27.

Ver. 27. *And they ſhall not lie with the mighty that are fallen of the uncircumciſed.*] They ſhall not lie among thoſe Heathen Heroes who died a Natural Death, and are laid in their Graves with Pomp and Magnificence. Compare this Verſe with *Iſa.* xiv. 18, 19.

Ibid. *Which are gone down to Hell,* [or the Grave; See Ver. 21.] *with their Weapons of War, and they have laid their Swords under their Heads.*] Who were carried to their Graves in State, and had their Atchievements and other Enſigns of Honour affixed to their Monuments for perpetuating their Memory. It has been the Cuſtom of all Ages to adorn the Sepulchres of Heroes with their Swords and otheir

other Trophies of War. See 1 *Macc.* xiii. 19. So
Virgil defcribes *Mifenus* his Tomb, *Æn.* 6.

Ingenti mole Sepulchrum Imponit, fuáque
arma viro.

Ibid. *But their iniquity fhall be upon their*
Bones, &c.] Their Death fhall carry in it plain
Tokens of their Sins, and of God's Vengeance
perfuing them for their Cruelty.

Ver. 28. *Yea thou fhalt be broken in the midft*
of the Uncircumcifed, &c.] See Ver. 19.

Ver. 28.

Ver. 29. *There is Edom, her Kings and all*
her Princes, &c.] Of whofe Deftruction *Eze-*
kiel Prophefied, Chap. xxv. 12.

Ver. 29.

Ver. 30. *There be the Princes of the North*
all of them, and the Zidonians.] By the *Princes*
of the North, may probably be underftood the
Tyrians and their Allies, (See Chap. xxvi. 16.)
joyned here with the *Sidonians* their near Neighbours, as they are put together in this Prophecy,
Chap. xxviii. as fharers in the fame Deftruction.
Some by the Princes of the North underftand
Mefheck, Tubal and other Northern Nations.
See Cha. xxxviii. 6, 15. xxxix. 2. whofe Deftruction is foretold in thofe Chapters.

Ver. 30.

Ver. 31. *Pharaoh fhall fee them, and fhall be*
comforted over his Multitude.] As it affords
fome relief to calamitous Perfons to fee others
in the fame condition with themfelves. See
Chap. xxxi. 16.

Ver. 31.

Ver. 32. *For I have caufed my Terror in the*
Land of the living, &c. As thefe Kings and Nations

Ver. 32.

Chapter
XXXII. tions have bin a terror to the World whilst they were in it, Ver. 24, *&c.* so I will be now a terror to them: And especially to *Pharaoh* and his People, in making them a remarkable Example of my Vengeance.

C H A P.

CHAP. XXXIII.

The ARGUMENT.

The Duty of a Prophet in warning a People of their Sins, is exemplified by that of a Watchman; then follows an earnest Exhortation to Repentance, upon Assurance that God will accept it, being for the most part a Repetition of what was said before in the xviiith Chapter. Upon the News being brought to the Prophet that Jerusalem was destroyed by the Chaldeans, he foretels the utter desolation of Judea, to check the vain Confidence of those who still tarried in it, and withal reproves the Hypocrisy of those Jews who were of the Captivity.

Ver. 2. **W**Hen I bring a Sword upon a Ver. 2. Land.] Bring an Enemy against a Land with armed Force. See Chap. xiv. 17.

Ibid. *If the People of the Land take a Man of their Coasts:*] Or, *From among*

Chapter *among them*, to which Senſe the Word *Miktſe*
XXXIII. is tranſlated *Gen.* xlvii. 2.

〰〰

Ibid. *And ſet him for a Watchman.*] Such
Watchmen were placed upon the Turrets of
their City Walls, to give Notice of the Enemies
Approach. See 2 *Sam.* xviii. 24, 25. 2 *Kings*
ix. 17. *Iſa.* xxi. 8.

Ver. 3. Ver. 3. *If when he ſee the Sword come upon
the Land.*] When he ſpies the Enemy march-
ing againſt it. See Ver. 2.

Ver. 4. Ver. 4. *His Blood ſhall be upon his own
Head.*] His Deſtruction is owing to himſelf.
See Chap. xviii. 13. *Acts* xviii. 6.

Ver. 5. Ver. 5. *But he that taketh warning ſhall deliver his Soul.*] Shall ſave his Life from the Danger that threatens it. In like manner he that
takes Warning by the Prophet's Admonition
ſhall preſerve himſelf from the Judgments
threatned againſt Sinners. See Ver. 10.

Ver. 6. Ver. 6. *He ſhall die in his Iniquity,* &c.] See
Chap. iii. 18.

Ver. 7, 8, 9. Ver. 7, 8, 9. *I have ſet thee a Watchman to
the Houſe of Iſrael,* &c.] See Chap. iii. 17,
18, 19.

Ver. 10. Ver. 10. *If our Tranſgreſſions be upon us, and
we pine away in them, how ſhall we then live?*]
Thou haſt threatned that we ſhall *pine away
in our Sins*, Chap. xxiv. 23. How then can the
Promiſes of Life belong to us? The Words of
Perſons deſpairing of Gods Mercy, and from
thence taking Encouragement to go on in their
Sins. See a like Inſtance *Jer.* ii. 25.

Ver. 11. Ver. 11. *Why will ye die O Houſe of Iſrael?*]
See the Note on Chap. xviii. 4.

Ver.

˙Ver. 12, 13. *The Righteousness of the righte-*
ous shall not deliver him in the Day of his Transf-
gression, &c.] See the Note upon Chapter
xviii. 26, 27.

Ver. 13. *If he trust to his own Righteousness.*] Ver. 13.
If he rely upon the Good Works he hath done,
and think the worth of them will overballance
the Guilt of his Evil Deeds. This seems to be
the Sense of the later Jews, who lay this down
for a certain Rule in their *Mishna,* That *all Israel*
hath a Share in the World to come.

Ver. 15. *If the Wicked restore the Pledge.*] Ver. 15.
See Chap. xviii. 7.

Ibid. *Give again that he hath robbed.*] It is
a necessary Condition of obtaining Pardon, that
Men make Restitution of what they have unjustly gotten from others. The Law was express
to this Purpose, *Levit.* vi. 5. where the Offender is required to add a *Fifth Part* to the Principal, and *give it to him to whom it appertaineth;*
to the same purpose is that received Rule among
the Christian Casuists taken from St. *Augustin,*
Epist. 54. *Non dimittitur Peccatum, nisi resti-*
tuatur Ablatum. The Sin is not forgiven, unless
what is taken away be restored.

Ibid. *Walk in the Statutes of Life.*] See the
Note on Chap. xx. 11.

Ver. 16. *None of the Sins that he hath com-* Ver. 16.
mitted shall be mentioned unto him.] See the Note
on Chap. xviii. 22.

Ver. 21. *In the Twelfth Year of our Captivity,* Ver. 21.
&c.] The News of the taking and burning of
Jerusalem was brought to that Part of the *Ba-*
N n   *bylonish*

Chapter
XXXIII.
bylonish Dominions where the Jewish Captives
were, in fomething above a Year and Four
Months after this Calamity happened. See *Jer.*
lii. 12.

Ver. 22.
Ver. 22. *Now the Hand of the* LORD *was
upon me in the Evening.*] I felt a fenfible im-
pulfe of the Prophetical Spirit. See Chap. i. 3.

Ibid. *And had opened my Mouth until he
came to me in the Morning,* &c.] God had given me Commiffion to fpeak in his Name unto
the People, which I had not done before near
the Space of three Years. Compare Chap. xxiv.
1. And the Deftruction of the City which I had
fo often foretold being now brought to pafs
(which at that time you would not believe, See
Chap. xi. 3. xii. 22.) gave an indifputable Authority and Credit to my Words. See the Note
on Chap. xxiv. 27.

Ver. 24.
Ver. 24. *They that inhabit thofe waftes of the
Land of Ifrael.*] They that are left behind in the
Land that is now wafted with Fire and Sword:
See Ver. 27. and Chap. xxxvi. 4.

Ibid. *Abraham was one, and he inherited the
Land.*] If *Abraham* being but a fingle Perfon,
with his Family had the whole Country of *Judea*
given to him, See *Gen.* xiii. 15. there is much
greater reafon to conclude that God will preferve
the poffeffion of it to us, who are a numerous
part of *Abraham*'s Pofterity. Thefe Men
fpake after the Vain manner of the Jews, who
fondly prefume that they have a right in all the
Promifes made to *Abraham:* See *Matth.* iii. 8.
Joh. viii. 33. *Rom.* ix. 7. The Title of *One* is
elfe-

elſewhere given to *Abraham*, as being ſingled
out from the reſt of his Family to be the Original
or Head of the Jewiſh Nation: See *Iſa.* li. 2.
Malach. ii. 15. *Heb.* xi. 12.

Ver. 25. *Ye eat with the Blood.*] Which was
forbidden ſeveral times in the Law, as being
a Rite the Heathens uſed in the Sacrifices they
offered to their Idols (whoſe worſhip is reproved
in the very next words) as Dr. *Spencer* proves at
large *Lib.* 2. *de Legib. Hebraic.* c- 11. who
brings many Arguments to ſhew that the Hebrew Phraſe, *Nal Hadam,* ſhould be tranſlated,
Near the Blood; in alluſion to the Idolatrous
Rite of pouring the Blood of the ſlain Beaſt into
a Veſſel or Pit, and then eating part of the Sacrifice juſt by it.

Ibid. *And lift up your Eyes towards your
Idols.*] See Chap. xviii. 6.

Ibid. *And ſhed Blood.*] See Chap. ix. 9.
xxii. 6, 9.

Ver. 26. *Ye ſtand upon your Sword.*] You
make your *Strength the Law of Juſtice,* according to the Character given of Ungodly
Men, *Wiſd.* ii. 11. Dr. *Spencer* in the forecited
Place thinks that the Expreſſion alludes to a
Cuſtom of the Heathens, who put the Blood of
their Sacrifices into a Veſſel or Pit, in order to
call up and conſult Evil Spirits, and then ſtood
with their Swords drawn to keep the *Dæmons*
off from doing them any harm.

Ibid. *Ye defile every one his Neighbour's Wife.*]
See ibid. Ver. 6. xxii. 11.

Ver.

Chapter
XXXIII.

Ver. 27.

Ver. 27. *They that are in the Waftes;* (See Ver. 24.) *fhall fall by the Sword, &c.*] The Three Judgments here mentioned, together with Famine, are often threatened as the laft and finifhing Strokes of God's Vengeance upon the Jewifh Nation. See Chap. v. 12, 17. vii. 12. xiv. 21. *Jer.* xv. 3.

Ibid. *And they that be in the Forts and in the Caves, fhall die of the Peftilence.*] Comp. *Judg.* vi 2. The Caves here mentioned were a fort of ftrong Holds formed by Nature in the Rocks, or cut out under the Tops of Mountains: They were fo large that Men might fecure themfelves, their Families and their Goods in them. So *David* is faid to *abide in ftrong Holds, and remain in a Mountain in the Wildernefs of Ziph,* 1 *Sam.* xxiii. 14. Such was the Cave of *Adullam,* where *David* had his Refidence for fome time, and was there reforted to by his Relations, 1 *Sam.* xxii. 1. and at another time by his principal Officers: 2 *Sam.* xxiii. 15.

Ver. 28.

Ver. 28. *For I will lay the Land moft defolate.*] See *Jer.* xliv. 2, 6, 22. and Chap. xxxvi. 34, 35. of this Prophecy.

Ibid. *The Pomp of her Strength fhall ceafe.*] All that Riches and Magnificence wherein they pleafed themfelves, as that which gave them Strength and Reputation in the Eyes of the World. See Chap. vii. 24. Or the Phrafe may denote the Beauty and Glory of the Temple, which they looked upon as their chiefeft Strength and Protection: See Chap. xiv. 21.

Ibid. *And the Mountains of Ifrael fhall be defolate.*] See Chap. vi. 2.   Ver.

Ver. 29. *Then shall they know that I am the*
LORD, &c.] See Chap. vi. 7.

Ver. 30. *The Children of thy People* (those of
the Captivity) *are still talking against thee,*
&c.] Or rather, *Of thee,* as the LXX rightly
render it ; *for with their Mouth they shewed
much love,* as it follows in the next Verse.

Ibid. *By the Walls, and in the Doors of their
Houses.*] Both in their publick Places of Con-
course, and in their private Meetings.

Ibid. *Come I pray you, and hear what is the
Word that cometh forth from the* LORD.] These
were such as *drew nigh to God with their
Mouths, but their Hearts were far from him ;*
as *Isaiah* describes their Hypocrisie, Chapter
xxix. 13.

Ver. 31. *They come unto thee as the People*
cometh.] Or as Disciples flock to their Teachers ;
So the *Chaldee* Paraphrase explains it.

Ibid. *And they sit before thee as my People.*]
See the Note on Chap viii. 1.

Ibid. *For with their Mouth they shew much
Love.*] *They make Loves,* or *Jests,* as our
Margin reads out of the *Hebrew* ; which some
Interpreters understand, as if they ridiculed the
Prophets Words, or turned them into Burlesque ;
so the *Vulgar Latin* renders it, *In canticum oris
sui vertunt.* But by comparing this with the
following Verse, where the same Word *Naga-
bim* is spoken of a Song or musical Tune, we
may rather understand the Phrase to this Sense,
that they were delighted with the Prophet's
Harmonious Voice, or taking Eloquence, but
would

Chapter would not make the proper ufe of what he
XXXIII. faid for the correcting their evil Manners.

Ver. 32.   Ver. 32. *And lo, thou art to them as a very
lovely Song,* &c.] They come to hear thee for
their Entertainment, not for their Edification,
as many go to hear Famed and Eloquent Preachers. St. *Auguftin* tells us that he himfelf
was fuch an Auditor of St. *Ambrofe*, before he
was converted: *Confeff. l.* 5. *c.* 13. *Studiofe au-
diebam difputantem in populo, non attentione
qua debui, fed tanquam explorator facundiæ
ejus, utrum conveniret famæ fuæ. -----Verbis ejus
fufpendebar intentus, rerum autem incuriofus &
contemptor aftabam.* " I heard him diligently
" when he difcourfed in the Congregation, but
" not with that Application of Mind which I
" ought to have done; but I came rather out of
" Curiofity to know whether his Eloquence
" was anfwerable to that Opinion the World
" had of him. I was very attentive to his
" Style, and charmed with the fweetnefs of
" his Delivery, but had little Value or Con-
" cern for the Subjects he treated of.

Ver. 33.   Ver. 33. *And when this comes to pafs, lo it
will come,* &c.] Or rather, *lo it is come*; for
fo the fame Phrafe is tranflated, Chap. vi. 2, 6,
10. the Verb being in the Prefent Tenfe, When
you fee my Prophecies concerning the Deftruction of *Jerufalem*, actually brought to pafs, as it
appears they are at this time. See Ver. 21. then
you will be convinced of the Truth of my Mif-
fion, and of your own inexcufable Crime in de-
fpifing my Predictions. See Chap. xxiv. 27.

C H A P.

C H A P. XXXIV.

The ARGUMENT.

God reproves the Ill Conduct of the Governours of the Jewish Nation both Civil and Ecclesiastical: And promises a General Restoration of his People, and their Happy Condition under the Government of the MESSIAS *their King.*

Ver. 2. P*Rophesy against the Shepherds of Israel.*] The Word *Shepherd* in the Prophetical Writings comprehends both Civil and Ecclesiastical Governours. See the Notes upon *Isa.* lvi. 11. *Jerem.* ii. 8. xxiii. 1. Princes being called Shepherds of their People as well as those who have the immedi-

Chapter
XXXIV.

immediate Care of their Souls. See *Pfal.* lxxviii. 71, 72. To the fame Senfe *Homer* calls *Aga-memnon,* Ποιμένα λαῶν, *the Shepherd of the People.* And as the Threatnings here denounced extend to all forts of Governors, fo the feveral Sins of the Princes, Priefts and Prophets are re-proved Chap. xxii. 25, &c. Compare likewife Chap. xlv. 8, 9.

Ibid. *Wo to the Shepherds of Ifrael that feed themfelves.*] That regard their own Profit and Advantage, not the Good of the People com-mitted to their Charge. *Plato* in the firft Book of his *Commonwealth,* defcribing the Office of a Magiftrate, faith, " He fhould look upon him-" felf as fuftaining the Office of a Shepherd, " that makes it his chief Bufinefs to take Care " of his Flock; not as if *he were going to a* " *Feaft* to fill himfelf and fatiate his Appetite, " or to a Market to make what Gain he can to " himfelf." *Eufebius* in his 12th *Book De Præ-paratione Evangelica,* Chap. 44. hath tranfcri-bed the whole Paffage, as an exact Parallel to this place of *Ezekiel.*

Ver. 3.

Ver. 3. *Te eat the Fat.*] Or *the Milk,* as the LXX render it. The *Hebrew* Words *Halab, Milk,* and *Heleb, Fat,* differ only in their Points, fo that the ancient Verfions take them promifcuoufly one for the other. See Chapter xxv. 4.

Ibid. *Te kill them that are fed.*] Them that are Fat ye defign for the Slaughter, wherewith to feed your felves: See *Zech.* x. 5. *i. e.* they took away the Lives of the Wealthy and Subftantial, that

that they might enrich themfelves with their
Eftates. See Chap x.ii. 25, 27.

Ver. 4. *The Difeafed have ye not ftrengthen*
ed, &c.] Ye have not applied proper Remedies
to the Wants and Neceffities of the People committed to your Charge: The Magiftrates have
not took care to relieve the Needy, and defend
the Oppreffed. The Priefts and the Prophets
have not been diligent in giving the People proper Inftructions, in reducing thofe that are in
Error, or in comforting the Difconfolate.

on Ibid. *Neither have ye bound up that which
was broken.*] Ye have not given Eafe to the
Afflicted and Miferable. A Metaphor taken
from Surgeons binding up Wounds. Compare
Ifa. lxii. 1.

Ibid. *Neither have ye brought again that
which was driven away, &c.*] Or, *which was
gon aftray,* as the Word *Niddakuh* is tranflated,
Deut. xxii. 1. Ye have not fought by good Inftructions to reduce thofe that have been feduced
into Error; or to reclaim thofe that are ready to
be loft and perifh in their Sins. Compare *Matt.*
ix. 36. xviii. 11.

Ibid. *But with force and cruelty have ye ruled
them.*] You have tried to reduce them to their
Duty by the rough Methods of Cruelty and
Compulfion, not by the gentle way of Reafon
and Argument. In like manner the Methods
of Inftruction and good Example are particularly recommended to the Paftors of the Chriftian Church, 1 *Pet.* v. 3. 2 *Tim.* ii. 24, 25.

Ver.

Chapter
XXXIV.
〰
Ver. 5.

Ver. 5. *And they were scattered abroad, because there is no Shepherd,* &c.] By Reason of these Neglects of the Governors, the whole Frame of the Government is dissolved, and my People are scattered here and there : Some are fled for Refuge into Foreign Countries. See *Jerem.* xl. 11. Others are carried Captives by their Enemies, who as so many Beasts of Prey have spoiled and devoured them. Compare *Jer.* xii. 9. *Isa.* lvi. 9.

Ver. 6.

Ver. 6. *My Sheep wander'd thro' all the Mountains,* &c.] As Sheep when there is no body to look after them, wander from one Mountain and Hill to another ; so my People have been forced to leave their Habitations, and fly to any Place where they might hope for Protection. Compare Chap. vii. 16. and see the Note upon *Jerem.* xiii. 16.

Ibid. *And none did seek or search after them.*] Their Rulers took no Care of my People while they had Power and Authority ; and now I have displaced them for their Misdemeanours, and there is no Body left whose Office it is to take any further Care of my People. See Ver. 10.

Ver. 10.

Ver. 10. *I will require my Flock at their Hands, and cause them to cease from feeding the Flock.*] I will require a severe Account of their Kings and Princes, their Priests and Prophets, of the Damage my People have sustained through their Ill Management : and I will deprive them of that Honour and Preheminence which they have made such Ill Use of, as I have already displaced *Zedekiah,* and the Princes,

Priests,

Priefts, and others that were in Authority under him.

Ver. 12. *So will I feek out my Sheep, and de-*
liver them out of all places, where they have
been fcattered in the cloudy and dark Day.] I will
bring them Home from their feveral Difperfions, whither they have been driven in the
dark and difmal time of the deftruction of their
Country, and their own Captivity. Compare
Chap. xxx. 3.

Ver. 13. *And I will bring them out from the*
People, &c.] This Prophefie may in fome degree have been fulfilled in the Return of the
Jews from the *Babylonifh* Captivity : But feems
ftill to look further, even to the General Reftoration of the whole Nation? which moft of the
Prophets fortel fhall come to pafs in the latter
Days : Compare Chap. xi. 17. xx. 41. xxviii. 25.
xxxvi. 24. xxxvii. 21. xxxviii. 8. xxxix. 27.

Ver. 14. *Upon the high Mountains of Ifrael.*]
See Chap. vi. 2.

Ibid. *There fhall they lie in a good fold.* &c.]
The Expreffions denote Plenty and Security.
Compare *Ifa.* lxv. 10. *Jerem.* xxxiii. 12. *Hof.*
ii. 18. *Zeph.* iii. 13.

Ver. 16. *I will feek that which is loft,* &c.]
The *Meffias,* whom I will fet over them, (See
Ver. 23.) fhall faithfully difcharge all the Offi-
ces of a Shepherd toward them, which their
former Paftors have neglected. Ver. 4. Comp.
Ifa. xl. 11. lxi. 1. *Matth.* xv. 24. xviii. 11.
John x. 11.

Ver.

Chapter
XXXIV.

Ibid. *But I will deſtroy the fat and the ſtrong.*] Thoſe that oppreſs and domineer over the Weak. See Ver. 20, 21. Comp. Chap. xxxix. 18. *Amos* iv. 1.

Ibid. *I will feed them with Judgment.*] Or *with Diſcretion: i. e.* I will deal with each of them according to their Deſerts, and make a Diſtinction between the Fat and Lean Cattle. See Ver. 18, 20.

Ver. 17.

Ver. 17. *Between Cattle and Cattle, between the Rams and the He-Goats.*] The *Hebrew* runs thus, *Between the ſmall Cattle, and the Cattle of Rams and He-Goats*; between the Weak and the Strong Cattle, *i. e.* between the Rich and the Poor, as the *Chaldee* Paraphraſe explains the Senſe, upon Verſe 20.

Ver. 18.

Ver. 18. Seemeth it *a ſmall thing unto you, to have eaten up the good Paſture,* &c.] This Reproof may fitly be applied to thoſe great Perſons who take no Care that the Poor may enjoy the Benefit of their Superfluities; but rather let them be thrown away and periſh, than they will be at the trouble of ſeeing them diſpoſed of for the good of thoſe that Want.

Ver. 21.

Ver. 2 . *Becauſe ye have thruſt with ſide, and ſhoulder,* &c.] In purſuance of this Compariſon the Oppreſſors of the Weak are commonly ſtyled in Scripture by the Names of Oxen, Bullocks, Rams and He-goats. See *Pſalm* xxii. 12. lxviii. 31. *Dan.* viii. 3, 5.

Ver. 23.

Ver. 23. *And I will ſet up one Shepherd over them,——even my Servant David.*] The *Meſſias* is often deſcribed under the Character of a Shep-

Shepherd both in the Old and New Teſtament. Chapter
See the Note on Ver. 16. And the Title may be XXXIV.
applied to him with reſpect to his Office of King,
as well as that of Prieſt and Prophet : See the
Note on Ver. 2. He is elſewhere ſtyled by the
Name of *David,* as being the Perſon in whom
all the Promiſes made to *David,* were fulfilled.
See *Iſa.* lv. 3, 4. *Jerem.* xxx. 9. *Hoſ.* iii. 5.

Ibid. *He ſhall feed them, and he ſhall be their
Shepherd.*] This Propheſy was remarkably fulfilled, when CHRIST by the Preaching of the
Goſpel *gathered in one the Children of God which
were ſcattered abroad, Joh.* xi. 52. *Eph.* i. 10.
among whom were many *of the Loſt Sheep of
the Houſe of Iſrael, Matt.* x. 6. But it will receive a farther Completion at the general Converſion of the *Jews,* when *the Time* will *come
that they ſhall ſay, Bleſſed is he that cometh in
the Name of the* LORD, *Matth.* xxiii. 37. And
this ſignal Event will uſher in or complete the
Fulneſs of the Gentiles. See *Rom.* xi. 12, 15,
25, 32.

Ver. 24. *And I the* LORD *will be their God.*] Ver. 24.
I will renew my Covenant with them, and receive them again into my Protection. See Ver.
30. Chap. xxxvii. 27. *Levit.* xvi. 12. and the
Notes upon *Jerem.* xxx. 22.

Ibid. *And my Servant David a Prince
among them.*] See the Note on Chap. xxxvii.
22.

Ver. 25. *And I will make with them a Cove-* Ver. 25.
nant of Peace.] As I will be at Peace with
them, ſo I will give them the Bleſſing of outward

Chapter
XXXIV.
ward Peace, and will protect them from the Annoyance of all their Enemies, from Perfecution and outward Violence. See *Jerem.* xxiii. 6.

Ibid. *And will caufe the evil Beafts to ceafe out of the Land.*] This may be meant of Freedom from Perfecution by Infidels and Strangers. Compare Ver. 28. fuch a Security is elfewhere expreffed by *making a Covenant for them with the Beafts of the Field :* See *Hof.* ii. 18. *Job* v. 23. *Ifa.* xxxv. 9. *Levit.* xxvi. 6. The Words are likewife capable of a Literal Interpretation, importing that as God had threatned that after the Defolation of the Land, wild Beafts fhould overrun it, and devour the few Inhabitants that were left, See Chap. v. 17. xxxiii. 27. So upon the repeopling of the Country, thofe Ravagers fhould forfake it.

Ver. 26.
Ver. 26. *And I will make them, and the Places round about my Hill, a Bleffing.*] I will there give remarkable Inftances of my Favour, and the Happinefs which accompanies it. See *Gen.* xii. 2. *Ifa.* xix. 24. *Zech.* viii. 13. God's Hill is the fame with his *Holy Mountain*, Chap. xx. 40.

Ibid. *And there fhall be fhowers of Bleffing.*] Such as fhall produce all forts of Plenty. Compare *Malach.* iii. 10.

Ver. 27.
Ver. 27. *And the Tree of the Field fhall yield her Fruit*, &c.] The fpiritual Bleffings of the Gofpel are fometimes defcribed under the Emblems of Fruitfulnefs and Plenty. See the
Notes

Notes on *Ifa.* iv. 2. xxxv. 2. lxv. 10. *Jerem.* Chapter
xxxi. 12. XXXIV.

Ibid. *When I have broken the Bands of their* ⌇⌇⌇
Yoke.] The fame Expreffion which is ufed
concerning the Deliverance of *Ifrael* out of
Egypt: *Levit.* xxvi. 13. *Jerem.* ii. 20. Their
Final Reftoration being reprefented as the Greater Deliverance of the Two. See *Jerem.* xxiii.
7, 8.

Ibid. *And delivered them out of the Hand
of thofe that ferved themfelves of them.*] See
Jerem. xxv. 14.

Ver. 28. *And they fhall no more be a Prey to* Ver. 28.
*the Heathen, neither fhall the Beafts of the Land
devour them.*] See Ver. 25.

Ibid. *And they fhall dwell fafely,* &c.] See
the Note on *Jerem.* xxiii. 6.

Ver. 29. *And I will raife them up a Plant of* Ver. 29.
Renown.] The *Meffias* is often defcribed under
the Name of the *Branch*; and the *Rod* or *Shoot*
growing of the Stem of *Jeffe.* See *Ifa.* iv. 2. xi.
liii. 2. *Jerem.* xxiii. 5. *Zech.* iii. 8. vi. 12.

Ibid. *And they fhall be no more confumed with
Hunger in the Land.*] But fhall be bleffed with
Plenty of all Things: See Ver. 26, 27. and
Chap. xxxvi. 29.

Ibid. *Neither bear the Shame of the Heathen
any more.*] By whom they were reproached,
as if their God had caft them off. See Chap.
xxxvi. 3, 6, 15.

Ver. 30. *Then fhall they know that I the* Ver. 30.
LORD *their God am with them,* &c.] See
Ver. 24.

Ver.

Chapter XXXIV.

Ver. 31.

Ver. 31. *And ye, my Flock, the Flock of my Pasture, are Men.*] These Words at the Conclusion of the Chapter, explain the Metaphor which runs through the whole : that what was said of a Flock and its Shepherds, is to be understood of Men and their Governours ; and especially of God's People whom he takes Care of, as a Shepherd does of his Flock. See Chap. xxxvi. 38. *Psal.* lxxxi. 2.

CHAP.

CHAP. XXXV.

The ARGUMENT.

*The Prophet renews his former Denunciations
of Judgments upon the* Edomites, *See Chap.*
xxv. 12. *as a juſt Puniſhment for their Inſult-
ing over the Calamities of the Jews.*

Ver. 2. ET thy Face againſt Mount Ver. 2.
Seir.] See Chap. vi. 2.
Mount *Seir* is the ſame
with *Idumea.* See *Deut.*
ii. 5.
    Ver. 4. *I will lay thy* Ver. 4.
Cities Waſte, &c.] See Ver. 9.
    Ver. 5. *Becauſe thou haſt had a perpetual* Ver. 5.
hatred, &c.] See the Note on Chap. xxv. 12.
    Ibid. *In the time that their Iniquity had an
End.*] When their Iniquity received its juſt
Doom. See Chap. vii. 6. xxi. 25, 29.
    Ver. 6. *Sith thou haſt not hated Blood, even* Ver. 6.
Blood ſhall purſue thee.] Since thou haſt loved

P p   Cruelty,

Chapter
XXXV.
Cruelty, and took delight in shedding Blood; Vengeance shall pursue thee, and thou shalt fall into the Hands of those that will be as eager to shed thine. The Phrase, *Thou haft not hated Blood*, is spoken by the Figure called *Litotes* by the Rhetoricians, when the Words imply more than they express. See the Note on *Jerem.* vii. 31.

Ver. 7.

Ver. 7. *And cut off from it him that passeth out, and him that returneth.*] No Travellers shall go forward or backward in it with Safety. See Chap. xxix. 11. Compare *Judg.* v. 6. 2 *Chro.* xv. 5.

Ver. 8.

Ver. 8. *And I will fill his Mountains with his slain Men,* &c.] Every part of the Country shall be filled with the Carcases of those that are Slain. Compare Chap. xxxii. 4, 5.

Ver. 9.

Ver. 9. *And I will make thee perpetual Desolations,* &c.] See Chap. xxv. 13. *Jerem.* xlix. 17, 18. *Malach.* i. 3. Dr. *Prideaux, Script. Hist. Par.* 2. *p.* 299. informs us that the *Nabatheans* having driven the *Edomites* out of their Ancient Habitations in the time of the *Babylonish* Captivity, they settled themselves in the Southern part of *Judea,* where they were afterward conquered by *Hyrcanus,* and obliged to embrace the Jewish Religion, and so became at length incorporated with that Nation. See *ibid. p.* 307.

Ver. 10.

Ver. 10. *These two Nations, and those two Countries shall be mine.*] They settled themselves in part of the Country, and hoped to have got Possession of the whole in time. See the

the Note upon the foregoing Verſe. The *Am-* Chapter
monites had the ſame Deſign, as appears from XXXV.
Jerem. xlix. 1.

Ibid. *Whereas the* LORD *was there.*] They
did not believe that God had placed his Name
there, had choſen it for a place of his peculiar
Reſidence, and would never quite relinquiſh
his Property in it. See Chap. xlviii. 35.

Ver. 11. *And I will make my ſelf known* Ver. 11.
among them, when I have judged thee.] I will
make my People ſee that I have not quite caſt
them off, by my avenging their Quarrel upon
thee.

Ver. 12. *And thou ſhalt know that I am the* Ver. 12.
LORD.] See Chap. vi. 7.

Ibid. *They are laid deſolate,* &c.] See the
Note on Ver. 10.

Ver. 13. *Thus with your Mouth ye have* Ver. 13.
boaſted againſt me.] As if I were not able to
make good my Promiſes toward the *Jews,* or
to aſſert my Right in *Judea.* See Ver. 10.

Ver. 14. *When the whole Earth rejoiceth, I* Ver. 14.
will make thee deſolate.] When I ſhall reſtore
other Countries, conquered by the King of *Ba-*
bylon, to their former Poſterity, thou ſhalt ſtill
lie waſte and deſolate. The *Edomites* never recovered their Country, after the *Nabatheans*
had expelled them out of it. See Dr. *Prideaux,*
in the Place above cited.

Ver. 15. *Thou ſhalt be deſolate----all Idumea.*] Ver. 15.
The Expreſſion is like that of *Iſaiah, Whole Pa-*
leſtina, Iſa. xiv. 29. *i. e.* all the ſeveral Tribes
and Diviſions of it.

CHAP.

CHAP. XXXVI.

The ARGUMENT.

*This and the following Chapter contain a Pre-
diction of the general Restoration both of Ifrael and Judah, a Subject often spoken of by
this Prophet : of which the Return of the
Two Tribes from Babylon may be thought an
Earnest.*

Ver. 1.

Ver. 2.

Ver. 1. *Rophesy unto the Mountains of Israel.*] See the
following Verse.

Ver. 2. *Because the
Enemy hath said against
you, even the ancient
high Places are ours in Possession.*] The *Idumeans* have made their Boasts, (see Ver. 5. and
Chap. xxxv. 10.) that they should become Masters

sters of the Mountainous Parts of *Judea*, where Chapter
the Ancient Fortresses were placed which com- XXXVI.
manded all the rest of the Country. To the
same Sense we are to understand the Expression
of *Treading upon the high Places of the Earth,*
Deut. xxxii. 13. *i. e.* taking Possession of the
Fortresses or Passes which command the rest of
the Country.

Ver. 3. *And ye are taken up in the Lips of* Ver. 3.
Talkers, and are the Infamy of the Heathen.]
Your Calamities have made you become a Pro-
verb, a By-Word and a Reproach among the
Heathen round about you, according to the
Threatnings of the Prophets denounced against
you. See *Deut.* xxviii. 37. 1 *Kings* ix. 7, 8.
Jerem. xviii. 16., *Lam.* ii. 15. *Dan.* ix. 16. *Psal.*
lxxix. 4.

Ver. 4. *Which became a Prey to the Residue* Ver. 4.
of the Heathen that are round about you.] To
these Heathen that are left, after the General
Desolations threatned upon the Neighbouring
Countries, *Moab, Edom, Ammon,* &c. Compare Ver. 36. and *Jerem.* xxv. 20. xlvii. 4.

Ver. 5. *Surely in the Fire of my Jealousy*] In Ver. 5.
that fervent Zeal and Concern that I have for my
own Honour, which is blasphemed among the
Heathen. See Chap. xxxv. 12, 13. Compare
Chap. xxxviii. 19. xxxix. 25.

Ibid. *Against the Residue of the Heathen----*
which have appointed my Land into their Pos-
session.] See the Note on Chap. xxxv. 12.

Ver. 6. *Because ye have born the Shame of* Ver. 6.
the Heathen.] See Chap. xxxiv. 29. xxxv. 12, 13.

Ver.

Chapter
XXXVI.   Ver. 7. *I have lifted up my Hand.*] I have so-
lemnly Sworn : See Chap. xx. 5, &c.

Ver. 7.
Ver. 8.   Ver. 8. *Yield your Fruit to my People of Israel,
for they are at Hand to come.*] This may have
an immediate Aspect upon the *Jews* Return
from *Babylon*, when they were restored to the
Possession of their own Country. If we suppose the Words to relate to the General Restoration of the Nation, the longest Distance of time
that the Things of this World can extend to,
is but as a Moment in respect of Eternity.
Compare *Heb.* x. 37. *Philip.* iv. 5.

Ver. 10.   Ver. 10. *And the Wastes shall be builded.*]
Compare Ver. 33. This may likewise have
been in some Measure fulfilled at their Return
from *Babylon.* Compare *Isa.* lviii. 12. lxi. 4.

Ver. 11.   Ver. 11. *And I will multiply upon you Man
and Beast.*] As God in his Judgments threatens to cut off Man and Beast from a Land ;
See Chap. xiv. 17. So here he promises to re-
plenish it with both. Compare *Jerem.* xxxi. 27.
xxxiii. 12.

Ibid. *And will do better unto you than at
your Beginnings.*] In bestowing upon you the
Blessings of the Gospel : the Promises of which
were made first to the *Jews* and to their Children: *Act.* ii. 39. The Words may likewise imply
that God would give them a more lasting and
secure Possession of their Land than ever they
had before. See the following Verses.

Ver. 12.   Ver. 12. *Yea, I will cause Men to walk upon
you.*] O Mountains, or Land of *Israel*, Ver. 8.

Ver.

Ver. 13. *Thou Land devourest up Men, and* Chapter
hast bereaved thy Nations.] The Neighbouring XXXVI.
People raised this Ill Character upon the Land of
Judea, because of the severe Judgments of the Ver. 13.
Sword, Famine and Pestilence, which had destroyed the greatest part of the Inhabitants.
The Expression alludes to that Evil Report
which the Spies brought upon it, *Numb.* xiii. 32.
that it was *a Land that did eat up its Inhabitants :* as if the Air had been unwholsome, or
the Country always afflicted by some Judgment
from Heaven.

Ver. 14. *Therefore thou shalt devour Men no* Ver. 14.
more, &c.] Thou shalt be free from the Strokes
of Heaven, and from the Annoyance of Enemies
on Earth.

Ver. 15. *Neither will I cause Men to hear in* Ver. 15.
thee the Shame of the Heathen any more, &c.]
See Ver. 6. and Chapter xxxiv. 29.

Ibid. *Neither shalt thou cause thy Nations to
fall any more.*] The *Chaldee* and some other ancient Versions translate the Words, *Neither shalt
thou bereave thy People* [or Nations] *any more :*
as if the Word in the Original were *Shaccal*, the
same which is used in the Sense of *bereaving* in
the foregoing Verses : whereas here the present
Copies read *Cashal*, which signifies to *Fall*. But
it hath been before observed, that Words in the
Hebrew which are near in Sound, often have an
Affinity in their Signification. See the Note upon Chap. xxvii 15.

Ver. 17. *Their Way was before me, as the* Ver. 17.
Uncleanness of a removed Woman.] As such a
Person

Person was under a legal Pollution, and forbidden to come within the Courts of the Temple, or attend upon God's Worship there: So the Defilements the Jews had contracted by their Idolatries, and other heinous Sins, rendered them unqualified to be my People, or to offer up any religious Service to me.

Ver. 18.   Ver. 18. *Wherefore I poured my Fury upon them for the Blood they had shed upon the Land, and for their Idols,* &c.] Murder and Idolatry, two Sins of the first Magnitude, are often joined together in the Catalogue of National Sins recited in this Prophecy: meaning particularly, the Blood of their Children, which they offered to their Idols. See Chap. xvi. 36, 38. xxiii. 37.

Ver. 19.   Ver. 19. *And I scattered them among the Heathen,* &c.] See Chap. v. 12.

Ver. 20.   Ver. 20. *And when they entred unto the Heathen---they profaned my holy Name, when they said unto them,* &c.] Or, *When it was said unto them;* Verbs of the third Person being often taken impersonally. By their evil Practices they brought a Scandal upon my Name, and gave Occasion to the Heathen to say, See what profligate Wretches these are who call themselves by the Name of God's People, whom he hath justly expelled out of their Country which he had given them. The *Chaldee Paraphrast* understands the Words to this Sense, " If these " are God's People, why does he suffer them to " be turned out of the Land which he made the " Place of his own especial Residence? Why " does he not continue to protect them?" But
the

the former Senfe agrees better with the Scope Chapter of the Text, and with St. *Paul*'s Application of it XXXVI. to the Jews of his own Time, *Rom.* ii. 24. and ⌣⌣⌣
with what follows, Ver. 31.

Ver. 21. *But I had Pity for my Holy Name,* Ver. 21.
&c.] *I wrought for my Name's Sake, that it fhould not be polluted among the Heathen,* as the Prophet fpeaks, Chap. xx. 9.

Ver. 22. *I do not this for your fakes, O Houfe* Ver. 22.
of Ifrael.] The Promifes I make in your Favour in the following Verfes, are not owing to any Defert of yours, but purely to vindicate my own Honour. See Ver. 32. and Compare *Deut.* ix 5. *Pfal.* cvi. 8.

Ver. 23. *And I will fanctifie my great Name* Ver. 23.
which was profaned among the Heathen, &c.]
I will give illuftrious Proofs of my Power and Goodnefs, and vindicate my Honour from the Reproaches with which it has been blafphemed among the Heathen, upon the Occafion of your evil Doings.

Ibid. *And the Heathen fhall know that I am the* LORD.] The Return of the Jews from the *Babylonifh* Captivity, was taken Notice of by the Heathens, as a fignal Inftance of God's Providence toward them, See *Pfal.* cxxvi. 2. and their General Converfion will be a much more remarkable Proof of my fulfiling the Promifes made to their Fathers, fo that the Heathens themfelves will be forced to take notice of it. See Chap. xxxvii. 28. It will be an effectual Argument to convince Infidels that your Nation and the reft of the true *Ifraelites* are the only

Q q   Church

Chapter
XXXVI.
〰〰

Church of God, and Profeſſors of his Truth. See *Zech.* viii. 23.

Ibid. *When I ſhall be ſanctified in you before your Eyes.*] When I ſhall *Sanctify my Name,* as it is expreſſed in the former part of the Verſe, and make my Power and Goodneſs known to the World. See the Notes on Chap. xx. 41. xxviii. 22.

Ver. 24.

Ver. 24. *And I will take you out from among the Heathen,* &c.] See Chap. xxxiv. 13. xxxvii. 21. xxxix. 25.

Ver. 25.

Ver. 25. *And I will ſprinkle clean Water upon you, and ye ſhall be clean.*] The Expreſſion alludes to thoſe legal Purifications which were made by ſprinkling Water upon the unclean Perſon, See *Numb.* viii. 7. xix. 13. and denotes the Sacrament of Baptiſm, by which true Believers are cleanſed from their former Sins, and inwardly ſanctified. See *Acts* ii. 38. xxii. 16. *Titus* iii. 5. and Compare *Jerem.* xxxiii. 8. St. *Paul* may probably allude to this Text, when he exhorts the *Hebrew* Converts to *draw nigh* to God, *having their Hearts ſprinkled from an evil Conſcience, and their Bodies waſhed with pure Water,* Heb. x. 22.

Ibid. *From all your Filthineſs, and from your Idols will I cleanſe you.*] When the Prophets foretel the General Converſion of the *Jews,* they uſually mention their Deteſtation of their former Idolatries, as a neceſſary Preparation toward it. See *Iſa.* i. 29. xvii. 7, 8. *Jerem.* iii. 22, 23, &c. *Zech.* xiii. 1, 2. Some account of this Circumſtance of their Converſion hath been

given

given in the Note upon *Ifa.* lxv. 7. and upon the Chapter forementioned Chapter of *Jeremiah.* XXXVI.

Ver. 26, 27. *A New Heart alfo will I give* Ver.26,27 *you,* &c.] See Chap. xi. 19. This Promife will be fulfilled, when the Heart of this People fhall *turn to the* LORD, *and the Veil fhall be taken from it,* as St. *Paul* informs us, 2 *Cor.* iii. 16. Compare *Jerem.* xxxi. 33, 34.

Ver. 28. *And ye fhall dwell in the Land that* Ver. 28. *I gave to your Fathers.*] See Chap. xxviii. 25.

Ibid. *And ye fhall be my People,* &c.] See Chap. xi. 20.

Ver. 29. *I will alfo fave you from all your un-* Ver. 29. *cleanneffes.*] I will take away the Guilt of them, and deliver you from the Punifhments due to them. See *Matth.* i. 21.

Ibid. and Ver. 30. *And I will call for the* Ver. 30. *Corn and will increafe it,* &c.] See the Notes upon Chap. xxxiv. 27, 29.

Ver. 31. *Then fhall ye remember your own Evil* Ver. 31. *Ways.*] See the Note upon Chap. xvi. 61.

Ibid. *And fhall loath your felves in your own Sight,* &c.] See Chap. vi. 9.

Ver. 32. *Not for your Sakes do I this------be it* Ver. 32. *known unto you,* &c.] The Prophet repeats what he faid Ver. 22. on purpofe to check all vain Prefumption in the *Jews,* and confidence of their own intrinfick Worth or Merit : A Fault they have been very prone to in all Ages.

Ver. 33. *I will caufe you to dwell in the Ci-* Ver. 33. *ties, and the Waftes fhall be builded.*] See Ver. 10.

Chapter   Ver. 34. *Whereas it lay desolate in the sight*
XXXVI. *of all that passed by it.*] As *Moses* had threat-
         ned, *Deut.* xxix. 23---28.

Ver. 34.   Ver. 35. *This Land that was desolate is be-*
Ver. 35. *come like the Garden of Eden.*] See Chap. xxviii.
            13. *Isa.* li. 3.

Ver. 36.   Ver. 36. *The Heathen that are left round*
about you, shall know that I the LORD *build the*
ruined Places, &c.] The Heathen Nations
that are near you, (See Ver. 4.) shall be convinced that the restoring the *Jews* to their former
State must be the immediate Hand of God,
who will certainly in due time fulfil what is here
foretold. See Chap. xxxvii. 14.

Ver. 37.   Ver. 37. *I will yet for this be enquired of by*
the House of Israel, to do it for them.] God in
his Anger tells the *Jews*, that he *will not be*
enquired of by them. Chap. xiv. 3. xx. 3, 31. intimating that during their Continuance in Idolatry and other Wickedness, they ought not to
address themselves to him, nor expect any Favourable Answer to their Requests : But now
upon their Repentance and Reconciliation, he
tells them that he *will be enquired of by them,* i.
e. he will dispose their Hearts to apply themselves to him by Prayer, and will answer the
Petitions they make to him for the fulfilling
these his Promises. See *Psal.* x. 17. And Compare *Jerem.* xxix. 13.

Ver. 38.   Ver. 38. *As the Holy Flock, as the Flock of*
Jerusalem in her Solemn Feasts.] The Sheep and
Lambs designed for the Sacrifices which were
offered at the three solemn Feasts, were both
                                          very

very numerous, and likewife of the beft in their
Kind. The Epithet of *Holy, and moft Holy* is
often applied to Sacrifices in the Levitical Law,
as being wholly dedicated to God, and fet apart
for his Worfhip. See *Levit.* vi. 25, 29. *Numb.*
xviii. 9.

Ibid. *So fhall the wafte Cities be filled with
Flocks of Men.*] See Chap. xxxiv. 31.

Chapter
XXXVI.

C H A P.

CHAP. XXXVII.

The ARGUMENT.

Under the Figure of a Refurrection of dry Bones
is foretold the General Reftoration of the
Jews from their feveral Difperfions: and by
the joining of two Sticks is reprefented the
Uniting of Ifrael *and* Judah *into One King-*
dom.

Ver. 1. Ver. 1. 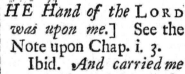 *HE* *Hand of the* LORD
was upon me.] See the
Note upon Chap. i. 3.
            Ibid. *And carried me*
out in the Spirit of the
LORD.] Or, *By the Spi-*
rit of the LORD. Compare Chap. iii. 14. viii.
3. xi. 24. This was performed either by a
                                                local

local Tranſlation of the Prophet, or elſe by way Chapter of Viſion and lively Repreſentation. See the XXXVII. Note upon Chap. viii. 3.

Ver. 3. *O Lord* God, *thou knoweſt.*] This Ver. 3. is only an Act of thy Power and good Pleaſure. Raiſing the Dead to Life again is peculiarly a-ſcribed to God, as being properly the Work of Omnipotence, and a ſort of New Creation. See *Deut.* xxxii. 39. *1 Sam.* ii. 6. *Joh.* v. 21. *Rom.* iv. 17. *2 Cor.* i. 9.

Ver. 4. *O ye dry Bones, hear ye the Word of* Ver. 4. *the* Lord.] A Prophetical and Lively Repre-ſentation of that Voice of the Son of God, which *all that are in the Graves ſhall hear* at the laſt Day, *and ſhall come forth out of them, Joh.* v. 28, 29.

Ver. 5. *Behold, I will cauſe Breath to enter* Ver. 5. *into you.*] The *Breath of Life,* as it is expreſ-ſed, *Gen.* ii. 7. Compare *Pſalm* civ. 30.

Ver. 7. *And as I propheſied, there was a* Ver. 7. *Noiſe, and behold a Shaking.*] Such a Noiſe, or Commotion, as we may ſuppoſe the Bones of an Human Body would make upon their meeting together again, after having been ſevered one from another.

Ver. 9. *Propheſy unto the Wind.*] Or rather, Ver. 9. *To the Breath,* meaning that vital Principle which unites Body and Soul together, and is mentioned as diſtinct from the Four Winds in the following Words.

Ibid. *Come from the Four Winds, O Breath.*] The Words figuratively repreſent the Reſtorati-on of the Jewiſh Nation from the ſeveral Coun-tries

Chapter tries whither they were difperfed over the
XXXVII. World, expreffed by their being *fcattered to-*
ward all Winds, Chap. v. 10. xii. 14. xvii. 21.

Ver. 10.   Ver. 10. *An exceeding great Army.*] To
fignify the great Numbers they will amount to,
when they return from their feveral Difperfions,
and unite into one Body.   They are elfewhere
ftyled *a Remnant,* but that is in comparifon of
the whole Nation.   See the Notes upon *Ifa.* iv.
2. x. 22. xxvii. 12, 13.

Ver. 11.   Ver. 11 *Thefe Bones are the whole Houfe of
Ifrael.*]   They reprefent the forlorn and defpe-
rate Condition to which the whole Nation is
reduced.

Ver. 12.   Ver. 12. *I will open your Graves, and caufe
you to come out of your Graves.*]   I will reunite
you into one Body or Nation, who now lie fcattered and difperfed as the Bones in a Charnel
Houfe.   Compare Ver. 21.   In their State of
Difperfion and Captivity they are called the
Dead Ifraelites in *Baruch,* Chap. iii. 4. and
their Reftoration is defcribed as a Refurrection
by *Ifaiah,* Chap. xxvi. 19. at which time *their
Bones* are faid to *flourifh,* or to be reftored to
their former Strength and Vigour, in the fame
Prophet, Chap. lxvi. 14.   In like manner St.
Paul expreffes their Converfion, and the Gene-
ral Reftoration which fhall accompany it, by
Life from the Dead, Rom. xi. 15.

Ibid. *And bring you into the Land of Ifrael.*]
See Ver. 25. and the Note upon Chap. xxviii.
25.

Ver.

Ver. 14. *And shall put my Spirit in you, and* Chapter
ye shall live.] That Principle of Life expressed XXXVII.
by *Breath* or Spirit, Ver. 9. Not excluding that
New Spirit of Grace, which God will at that Ver. 14.
time plentifully bestow upon them. See Chap.
xi. 19. xxxvi. 26, 27. The Principle of Grace is
often spoken of as a Higher Principle of Life,
and the Earnest of our heavenly Happiness.
See *Rom.* viii. 11. 1 *Cor.* vi. 17. xv. 45.

Ver. 16. *Take thee one Stick, and write upon* Ver. 16.
it, &c.] *i. e.* one Rod; the Expression alludes
to *Numb.* xvii. 2. where *Moses* is commanded to
take twelve Rods, one for each Tribe, and to
write the Name of the Tribe upon the Rod.

Ibid. *For Judah, and the Children of Israel*
his Companions.] Not only the Tribe of *Ben-*
jamin, but many of the other Tribes joined
themselves to the Tribe of *Judah,* and kept close
to the Law of God, and the worship of his
Temple. See 2 *Chron.* xi. 12—16. xv. 9. xxx.
11, 18.

Ibid. *For Joseph the Stick of Ephraim, and*
for all the House of Israel his Companions.] Upon *Reuben*'s forfeiting his Birth-right, that Privilege was conferred upon the Sons of *Joseph,* of
whom *Ephraim* had the Precedence. See 1 *Chron.*
v. 1. *Gen.* xlviii. 20. which made him reckoned the Head of Ten Tribes: *Samaria* the Seat
of that Kingdom, being likewise situate in the
Tribe of *Ephraim:* Upon these Accounts the
Name of *Ephraim* signifies in the Prophets the
whole Kingdom of *Israel,* as distinct from that
of *Judah:* and particularly in the Prophet *Ho-*
sea,

R r

Chapter *sea,* Chap. v. 3, 5, &c. See likewise *Jerem.* xxxi.
XXXVII. 6, 18.

Ver. 17.

Ver. 17. *And join them one to another into
one Stick.*] A Rod or Scepter is an Emblem of
Power; See *Psal.* cx. 2. so the joining these two
Rods or Sticks together denotes uniting the two
Kingdoms under one Prince or Governour : See
Ver. 22.

Ver. 18.

Ver. 18. *Wilt thou not shew us what thou
meanest by these?*] Ezekiel foretold many
Things by Signs, and the *Jews* were very in-
quisitive into the meaning of them; tho' sometimes their Curiosity proceeded rather from a
secret Contempt of the Prophet and his Predictions, than a real Desire of Information. See
Chap. xii. 9. xvii. 12. xx. 49. xxiv. 19.

Ver. 19.

Ver. 19. *Which is in the Hand of Ephraim.*]
Of which he is the Head : See Ver. 16.

Ibid. *They shall be one in my Hand.*] I will
make them one Nation, and appoint one King
to rule over them, the *Messias.* See Ver. 22.

Ver. 20.

Ver. 20. *And the Sticks whereon thou wri-
test shall be in thine Hand before their Eyes.*]
Thou shalt place the Sticks or Rods thus joined
together before their Eyes, as a visible Token
or Pledge of the Truth of what I enjoin thee to
speak to them in the following Words.

Ver. 21.

Ver. 21. *I will take the Children of Israel
from among the Heathen,* &c.] See Chap. xx.
34. xxxiv. 13. xxxvi. 24. xxxix. 25.

Ver. 22.

Ver. 22. *And I will make them one Nation.*]
They shall not be divided any more into separate Kingdoms : the Consequence of which was
their

their setting up separate Ways of Worship, and *Chapter*
espousing separate Interests. Compare *Isa.* xi. XXXVII.
13. It has been already observed, that the Prophesies which foretel of the General Restoration
of the *Jews*, join *Judah* and *Israel* together, as
equal Sharers in that Blessing.

Ibid. *And one King shall be King to them all.*]
The *Messias*, who is that one Shepherd and
Prince that shall rule over them all, as one Nation: See Chapter xxxiv. 23, 24. compared
with *Luke* i. 32, 33. The *Messias* is described as
King of the *Jews* in most of the Prophesies of
the Old Testament, beginning with that of
Gen. xlix. 10. concerning *Shiloh*. From *David*'s time he is commonly spoken of as the Person in whom the promises relating to the Perpetuity of *David*'s Kingdom were to be accomplished. This was a Truth unanimously owned by the *Jews* ; See *Joh.* i. 49. to which our
Saviour bore Testimony before *Pontius Pilate*,
when the Question being put to him, *Art thou
a King?* he made Answer, *Thou sayest* [the
Truth] *for I am a King:* Thus those Words
should be translated, for St. *Paul* alluding to them,
calls them *a good Confession*, 1 *Tim.* vi. 13. The
same Truth *Pontius Pilate* himself asserted in
that Inscription which he providentially ordered to be written upon the Cross: See *Joh.* xix.
19-22. so that the chief Priests impiously re-
nounced their own avowed Principles, when
they told *Pilate*, That *they had no King but Cæ-
sar*, Ibid. Ver. 15.

Chapter
XXXVII.

Ver. 23.

Ver. 23. *Neither shall they defile themselves any more with their Idols.*] See the Note upon Chap. xxxvi. 25.

Ibid. *Nor with their detestable things.*] Or, *Abominations,* as the Word *Shikkuts* is elsewhere translated, and commonly applied to Idols. See Chap. xx. 7. 2 *Kings* xxiii. 13. *Dan.* ix. 27.

Ibid. *Nor with any of their Transgressions.*] This Expression comprehends in it, their being touched with an hearty Compunction for their great Sin of rejecting and crucifying the *Messias,* their King and Saviour. See *Zech.* xii. 10.

Ibid. *And will save them out of all their dwelling Places wherein they have sinned, and will cleanse them.*] See Chap. xxxvi. 20, 25, 28.

Ver. 24.

Ver. 24. *And David my Servant shall be King over them,* &c.] See Chap. xxxiv. 23.

Ibid. *They shall also walk in my Judgments,* &c.] See Chap. xxxvi. 27.

Ver. 25.

Ver. 25. *And they shall dwell in the Land that I have given to Jacob my Servant.*] A Promise often repeated in this Prophecy: See Ver. 12, 21. and the Note on Chap. xxviii. 25.

Ver. 26.

Ver. 26. *Moreover I will make a Covenant of Peace with them,* &c.] See Chap. xxxiv. 25. The Words may likewise be understood in a spiritual Sense, That God will be reconciled to them through Christ, and admit them into that Covenant of Peace, of which he is the Mediator; and therefore is called *our Peace, Eph.* ii. 14. And then the following Words, *It shall be an everlasting Covenant with them,* may fitly be explained of the Gospel, being such a Covenant as shall

never

never be abolished, or give way to any new Dif- Chapter
penfation. Compare *Ifa.* lv. 3. *Jerem.* xxxii. 40. XXXVII.
Ibid. and Ver. 27. *And will set my Sanctuary*
in the midst of them for evermore. My Taberna-
cle also shall be with them.] God's placing first
his Tabernacle, and then his Temple among the
Jews, was a Pledge and Token of his Prefence
among them, and Protection over them. See
Levit. xxvi. 11, 12. and the Note upon Chap.
xi. 16. of this Prophecy. And here he promifes
new and more valuable Tokens of his Prefence
among them, by the Graces of his Holy Spirit,
and the Efficacy of his Word and Sacraments.
Compare 2 *Cor.* vi. 16. and perhaps will vouch-
fafe them fome extraordinary Appearance of the
Divine Majefty. See Chap. xliii. 4, 5, 7. *Zech.*
ii. 5.

Ibid. *Yea, I will be their God,* &c.] See Chap.
xi. 20.

Ver. 28. *And the Heathen shall know that* Ver. 28.
I the Lord *do sanctify Israel.*] The Converfion
of the Jewifh Nation and their being reftored
to their former State of Favour and Acceptance
with God, will be a Work of Providence taken
Notice of by the Heathens themfelves, who fhall
join themfelves to the Jews, as the Church of
God and Temple of Truth. See Chap. xxxvi.
23.

C H A P.

C H A P. XXXVIII.

The ARGUMENT.

*The Prophecy contained in this and the following
Chapter concerning* Iſrael's *Victory over* Gog
and Magog, *without queſtion relates to the
latter Ages of the World, when the whole
Houſe of* Iſrael *ſhall return into their own
Land,* Chap. xxxix. 25, 26. *And the Expreſſions we meet with in this Chapter,* Ver. 8,
and 16. *that this ſhould come to paſs in the
latter Days, and after many Days, or a conſiderable number of Years, and that* God *had of
old Propheſied concerning this Tranſaction:
Theſe and other Circumſtances of this Prophecy
are a Proof that the Event was to happen a
great while after the ſeveral Predictions of
the Prophets concerning it. So that this muſt
be lookt upon as one of thoſe Obſcure Prophecies of Scripture, the fulfilling whereof will
beſt explain their Meaning.*

Ver. 2.

Ver. 2.  ET thy Face, (see Chapter Chapter
vi. 2.) *againſt Gog, the* XXXVIII.
Land of Magog.] Or, of Ver. 2.
the Land of Magog. Ma-
gog was the Son of *Ja-*
phet, Gen. x. 2. from
whence the *Scythians* are generally ſuppoſed to
be derived. The *Mogul Tartars,* a People of
the *Scythian* Race, are ſtill called ſo by the *A-*
rabian Writers, as Dr. *Hyde* informs us, in his
Epiſtle *De Menſuris Sinenſibus.* By *Gog* and
Magog may moſt probably here be meant the
Turks, who were originally Natives of *Tartary,*
called *Turcheſtan* by the Eaſtern Writers : and
whoſe Language is derived from that of the *Tar-*
tars. The Land of *Canaan* hath been for ſeveral Years in the Poſſeſſion of the *Turks* ; ſeveral
Texts in *Ezekiel* foretel the *Jews* Settlement in
that Country again ; and ſome of the Expreſſions in this and the following Chapter intimate,
that the People called here by the Name of *Gog,*
and their Allies, will attempt to recover it again
out of the Hands of the *Jews,* its rightful
Owners : This may probably occaſion the War
and Victory here ſpoken of. But this is what
cannot be poſitively affirmed ; only thus much
one may venture to ſay, That ſince the whole
Strength of *Europe* was ſo unſucceſsful in their
Attempts to recover that Land out of the Hands
of the Infidels in the Holy War, it looks as if
God had reſerved that Work to ſome further time
of

Chapter
XXXVIII.
〰〰

of his own Appointment, when that Country
fhould be the Scene of fome extraordinary Event
of Providence. We may further obferve, that the
Second Woe, mentioned *Revel.* ix. 12. xi. 14. is
by many Learned Men underftood of the *Tur-*
kifh Empire; and in Confequence of that Interpretation, the putting an End to that Tyranny
will be an Introduction to fome extraordinary
Changes in the Chriftian part of the World.

Ibid. *The chief Prince of Mefhech and Tubal.*]
The King or Head of all thofe Northern Nations
which lie upon the *Euxin* Sea. See the Notes
upon Chap. xxvii. 13. The *Turk* is called *the*
King of the North in *Daniel,* Chap. xi. 40. as
feveral Commentators interpret that Place. The
LXX Interpreters take the Word *Rofh,* commonly tranflated *Chief,* for a proper Name, fo
they render the Sentence thus, *The Prince of*
Rofh, Mefhech and Tubal. Rofh taken as a Proper Name, fignifies thofe Inhabitants of *Scythia,*
from whence the *Ruffians* derive their Name
and Original.

Ver. 4.

Ver. 4. *And I will turn thee back, and put*
Hooks into thy Chaws.] I will difappoint all
thy Defigns, and turn thee about as eafily as a
Fifherman mafters a great Fifh, when he hath
once faftened the Hook into his Jaws. See
Chap. xxix. 4.

Ibid. *And I will bring thee forth, and all*
thine Army, &c.] The Senfe would be plainer
if the Words were thus tranflated, *After I have*
brought thee forth, &c. In which Senfe the Co-
pulative *Vau,* is fometimes ufed. See *Noldius*
Concordance, p. 291.

Ibid.

Ibid. *Horses and Horsemen.*] See Ver. 15.

Ver. 5. *Persia, Ethiopia, and Libya with them.*]
Their Allies *Ethiopia* and *Libya* are called *Cush*
and *Phut* in the *Hebrew*, and are joined together as Allies, Chap. xxx. 5. See the Note there.
Persians are joined in like manner with *Afri-*
cans; Chap. xxvii. 10.

Ibid. *All of them with Shield and Helmet.*]
So the *Libyans*, or People of *Phut* are described,
Jerem. xlvi. 9. as *Handling the Shield*, i. e. being remarkable for their great and large Shields,
as *Xenophon* relates of them, *Cyripæd. lib. 6.*

Ver. 6. *Gomer and all his Bands, the House*
of Togarmah of the North Quarters.] *Gomer* is
joined with *Magog*, *Gen.* x. 2. and probably fignifies *Galatia*, *Phrygia* and *Bithynia*, which
with *Cappadocia* denoted by *Togarmah*, comprehends all the Northern Parts of *Asia Minor*,
which border upon the *Euxin* Sea. See the meaning of *Togarmah* explained in the Note upon
Chap. xxvii. 14.

Ibid. *And many People with thee.*] Those of
Cilicia, *Pamphylia*, and other Nations inhabi-
ting *Asia Minor*.

Ver. 7. *Be thou prepared----thou and all thy*
Company that are assembled with thee.] The
Prophet *Ironically* encourages *Gog* to make all
Warlike Preparations and muster all his Forces
together, that God may gain the greater Ho-
nour by their signal Defeat. See Ver. 16. and
Compare *Jerem.* xlvi. 2, 3, 14. li. 12.

Ibid. *And be thou a Guard unto them.*] Let
them rely upon thy Prowess and Conduct as
their Leader.

S f   Ver.

Ver. 8. *After many Days thou ſhalt be viſited*, &c.] This Judgment ſhall be inflicted, by God upon thee, (Compare *Iſa.* xxix. 6.) after a Succeſſion of many Generations : *in the latter Years*, or *Days*, as it follows here and Ver. 16. *i. e.* toward the end of the World, Compare *Dan.* viii. 26. Particularly the Expreſſion of *Latter Days*, or Years is uſed to denote the Times of the General Reſtoration of the Jewiſh Nation. See *Deut.* iv. 30. *Jerem.* xxx. 24. *Hoſ.* iii. 5.

Ibid. *Thou ſhalt come into the Land that is brought back from the Sword.*] The Land is put for the People of the Land, who are ſaid to be *brought back from the Sword*, as they are elſewhere ſtyled a *Remnant, i. e.* thoſe that ſhould ſurvive after the Hardſhips they had ſuffered in their ſeveral Diſperſions, and the Judgments that ſhould fall upon the Diſobedient in their Return Home : See the Notes upon Chap. xx. 34---38. and upon *Iſa.* iv. 2. And perhaps thoſe Words of *Jeremiah*, Chap. xxxi. 2. may be beſt explained to this Senſe, *The People that were left of the Sword, found Grace in the Wilderneſs.* The whole Chapter relates to the General Converſion and Reſtoration of the Jews, and the Prophet ſpeaks in that Verſe of the Favours God would ſhew to thoſe that ſhould eſcape the ſevere Judgments that ſhould deſtroy the Diſobedient in their Paſſage home to their own Country, called the *Deſert* or *Wilderneſs* by *Iſaiah*, Chap. xl. 3. and by *Ezekiel the Wilderneſs.*

derneſs of the People, or Nations, Chap. **xx**. 35. Chapter
See the Notes upon that Place. XXXVIII.

Ibid. *And gathered out of many People.*] See
the Note upon Chap. xxxiv. 13.

Ibid. *Againſt the Mountains of Iſrael*, [See
Chap. xxxvi. 1, 4.] *which have been always
waſte.*] Or rather, *altogether waſte*, as the LXX
rightly tranſlate it.

Ibid. *But it is brought forth out of the Nations, and they ſhall dwell ſafely all of them.*] Or,
And they have dwelt ſafely all of them; the *future Tenſe* being often put for the *Preter perfeEt*.
The Senſe is, that after the Return of the People of *Iſrael* into their own Country, and their
having lived there for ſome time in Peace and
Safety, this Enemy will think to take Advantage of their Security, and fall upon them unex-
peEtedly. Compare Ver. 11.

Ver. 9. *Thou ſhalt aſcend and come like a* Ver. 9.
Storm.] A Compariſon elſewhere made uſe of
to expreſs the Devaſtations which attend a deſtroying Army. See Chap. xiii. 11. *Iſa.* xxviii. 2.

Ibid. *Thou ſhalt be like a Cloud to cover the
Land.*] Thou ſhalt overſpread the Land like a
Dark Cloud which makes every thing look Melancholy and Diſmal. See Chap. xxx. 3. *Jerem.*
iv. 13.

Ver. 11. *I will go to the Land of unwalled* Ver. 11.
Villages, &c.] A Deſcription of a People that
live ſecurely without any apprehenſion of Danger. Compare *Jerem.* xlix. 31.

Ibid. *To them that are at reſt and dwell ſafely.*] According to the Promiſe often repeated in

the

the Prophets, that *In thofe Days Ifrael fhould dwell fafely, and none fhould make them afraid.* See Chap. xxxiv. 28. *Jerem.* xxiii. 6. and the Note there.

Ver. 12.

Ver. 12. *To turn thine Hand upon the defolate Places* that are now *inhabited.*] *Judea* is defcribed as a Country that lay defolate before the Jews return into it. See Chap. xxxvi. 34, 35. After it had been for fome time reinhabited, *Gog* and his Affociates defigned to fall upon it with all their Forces ; in that Senfe *to turn the Hand,* is taken. *Ifa.* i. 25. See the Note there.

Ibid. *That dwell in the midft of the Land.*] *In the Navel of the Land,* as the *Hebrew* reads, *i. e.* in *Jerufalem,* becaufe that ftood in the middle of the Holy Land, and likewife was fituate upon a rifing Ground, which the *Hebrew* Metaphorically expreffes by the *Navel.* See *Judg.* ix. 37.

Ver. 13.

Ver. 13. *Sheba and Dedan, and the Merchants of Tarfhifh---fhall fay unto thee, Art thou come to take a fpoil?*] Thefe were People that dealt much in Trade : the two former dwelling in the Eaft, the latter often failing from the *Spanifh* Coafts into the Eaftern Parts ; they are mentioned Chap. xxvii. 12, 15, 20, 22. as having Commerce with *Tyre,* which bordered upon *Judea.* Thofe Merchants affoon as they heard of this intended Invafion, came into *Gog*'s Camp as to a Market, to buy both Perfons and Goods which fhould come into the Conqueror's Power. See the Note upon Chap. xxvi. 2.

Ibid.

Ibid. *With all the young Lions thereof.*] The Chapter *Targum* underſtands it of their Kings, *i. e.* their chief Merchants who are deſcribed as ſo many Princes, *Iſa.* xxiii. 8. and are called *Lions* becauſe of the Injuſtice and Oppreſſion they too commonly practiſed in their Commerce. See Chap. xxviii. 16. But the LXX tranſlate the Word *Kephirim,* Towns or Villages, in which Senſe it is taken *Nehem.* vi. 2. and in other Places.

Ver. 14. *In that Day.*] At that remarkable time, when God ſhall bring again the Captivity of *Iſrael* and *Judah,* ſo often ſpoken of by the Prophets. See the Note upon *Iſa.* iv. 2.

Ibid. *When my People Iſrael dwelleth ſafely, ſhalt not thou know it?* &c.] Aſſoon as the News of their being ſettled in their own Country comes to thy Knowledge, thou wilt certainly make Prepartions to Invade them.

Ver. 15. *And thou ſhalt come from thy Place out of the North Parts.*] See Ver 6.

Ibid. *Thou and many People with thee, all of them riding upon Horſes,* &c.] The Character here given of this People, may properly be applied to the *Turks,* the chief Strength of whoſe Armies conſiſts in their Cavalry, and the great Numbers of them which they bring into the Field, as the Writers of the *Turkiſh* Hiſtory obſerve. Compare *Revel.* ix. 16. which Place ſeveral Interpreters expound of the *Turks.* We may not improbably apply thoſe Words of the Prophet *Zechariah* to the Event here ſpoken of, Chap. xii. 4. *I will ſmite every Horſe with Aſto-*

niſhment,

Chapter
XXXVIII.

~~~~~
Ver. 16.

Ver. 17.

nishment, aud his Rider with Madness, and will open mine Eyes upon the House of Judah.

Ver. 16. *As a Cloud to cover the Land.*] See Ver. 9.

Ibid. *That the Heathen may know me, &c.*] This signal Victory over *Gog* and his Associates, shall be a Means of bringing Infidels to give Glory unto me. Compare Chap. xxxix. 21. and see the Note upon Chap. xxxvi. 23.

Ver. 17. *Art thou he?*] The Words would be more significant, if they were translated, *Art thou not he?* a Sense which *He* the Particle of Interrogation often imports. See the Note upon Chap. xx. 4.

Ibid. *Of whom I have spoken in old Time by my Servants the Prophets, who have prophesied in those Days, many Years?*] Or, And *Years.* The Prophet is speaking here of some terrible Enemy to God's People, who shall be subdued by the immediate Hand of Heaven, which Victory should make way for glorious Times of Peace and Prosperity. This Enemy is said to be foretold *of old by the Prophets,* and is therefore probably described under the Names of such Nations as were the chief Enemies to the Jews in the particular Times of each Prophet. Such we may suppose the *Assyrian* to be, spoken of by *Isaiah,* Chap. xiv. 24, 25. and by *Micah,* Chap. v. 5. The same Enemy may probably be intended under the Figure of *Tyre,* See the Note on Chap. xxviii. 24. of *Egypt,* See the Note upon Chap. xxix. 21. and compare *Isa.* xi. 15. with *Zech.* x. 11. of *Moab,* See *Isa.* xxv. 10. of *Edom,*

See

See *Ifa*. xxxiv. 6. lxiii. 1. *Joel* iii. 20. *Obad*. Ver. Chapter
18, 19. and under the Name of *Leviathan*, *Ifa*. XXXVIII.
xxvii. 1. To thefe we may add thofe Prophe-
cies which fpeak of fome great and general Deftruction of God's Enemies before the Day of
Judgment, or Confummation of all things. Such
are *Pfalm* cx. 5, 6. *Ifa*. xxvi. 20, 21. xxxiv. 1,&c.
lxvi. 16. *Jerem*. xxx. 7, 10. *Joel* iii. 9, 14. *Obad*.
Ver. 15, &c. *Zech*. xii. 1. xiv. 1, &c. *Zechariah*
lived indeed after *Ezekiel*'s Time, but a great
while before the fulfilling of this Prophecy. The
Expreffions here ufed, *of old time*, and *which
prophefied in thofe Days* [and] *Years*, plainly imply that there was to be a Succeffion of many
Ages between the publifhing thofe Prophecies and
this Event foretold by them : and therefore feem to
look beyond the Times of *Antiochus Epiphanes*,
to which fome Expofitors apply this Place of
Ezekiel. See the Note upon Chap. xxxix. 9.

Ver. 18. *My Fury fhall come up in my Face.*] Ver. 18.
An Expreffion taken from human Paffions,
which caufe the Blood to fly up into the Face.
So *Ifaiah* defcribes Almighty God as *Burning
with Anger, his Lips* being *full of Indignation,
and his Tongue as a confuming Fire*, Chap. xxx.
27. See the Note upon that Place.

Ver. 19. *For in the Jealoufy and in the Fire of* Ver. 19.
my Wrath have I fpoken.] See Chap. xxxvi. 5.
xxxix. 25.

Ibid. *Surely in that Day there fhall be a great
fhaking in the Land of Ifrael.*] Great Changes
and Alterations in Kingdoms and Governments
are expreffed in Scripture by *fhaking of Heaven
and*

and Earth, the Sea and the dry Land. See *Haggai* ii. 6, 7, 21, 22. *Heb.* xii. 26. and by Earthquakes, *Revel.* vi. 12. xi. 13. xvi. 8.

Ver. 20.

Ver. 20. *So that the Fishes of the Sea, and the Fowls of Heaven,* &c.] Every part of the Creation shall bear its Share of this Calamity, as if there were a Convulsion of the whole Frame of Nature. Compare *Jerem.* iv. 24, &c. *Hof.* iv. 3. The Prophets often describe God's Judgments upon particular Countries or Persons, as if it were a Dissolution of the whole World, because his particular Judgments are an Earnest of the general Judgment. See the Notes upon *Isa.* xiii. 10.

Ibid. *And the Mountains shall be thrown down,* &c.] These Expressions may probably be meant of Walls, Towers, and other Fortifications, which are dismantled and demolished in the time of War. Compare *Jerem.* li. 25.

Ver. 21.

Ver. 21. *I will call for a Sword against him.*] I will appoint a Sword to destroy him : Compare Chap. xiv. 17. God's Decrees are expressed by his speaking the Word, and giving out his Command. So he is said to *call for a Dearth upon the Land of Canaan. Psalm* cv. 16.

Ibid. *Throughout all my Mountains.*] See Ver. 8.

Ibid. *Every Man's Sword shall be against his Brother.*] God often destroys his Enemies by intestine Quarrels among themselves, and making them Executioners of his Judgments upon each other. See 2 *Chron.* xx. 23. *Judg.* vii. 22. 1 *Sam.* xiv. 20.

Ver.

Ver. 22. *I will plead against him with Pesti-* Chapter
lence and with Blood.] Or, *I will plead with* XXXVIII.
him. See Chap. xx. 35. God pleads with Men
by his Judgments, which are a manifest Token Ver. 22.
of the Vengeance due to their Sins. See *Isa.*
lxvi. 16. *Jerem.* xxv. 31. Pestilence is joined
with Blood here, as it is Chap. v. 17. xiv. 19.
xxviii. 23.

Ibid. *And will rain upon him and his Bands*
---an overflowing Rain, and great Hail-stones,
Fire and Brimstone.] God shall as plainly shew
himself in the Destruction of these his Enemies,
as when he consumed *Sodom* and *Gomorrah* by
Fire and Brimstone from Heaven, *Gen.* xix. 24.
and discomfited the Armies of the *Canaanites*
and *Philistines* by Tempests of Thunder and
Hail. See *Josh.* x. 10. 1 *Sam.* vii. 10. Compare
Psal. xi. 6. *Isa.* xxix. 6. xxx. 30. and see Chap.
xiii. 11. of this Prophecy.

Ver. 23. *Thus will I magnify my self, and sancti-*
fy my self, &c.] Compare Ver. 16. and see the
Note upon Chap. xxxvi. 23.

Tt CHAP.

C H A P. XXXIX.

See the ARGUMENT of the foregoing Chapter.

Ver. 1.

Ver. 1.  *Gog, the chief Prince of Meſhech and Tubal.*] See Chap. xxxviii. 2.

Ver. 2. *And I will turn thee back.*] See ib. Ver. 4.

Ibid. *And leave but a sixth part of thee.*] So the Word *Shiſſha,* or *Shiſſah,* as it is read with a different Termination, ſignifies Chap. xlv. 13. Others render it, *I will ſtrike thee with Six Plagues,* viz. Thoſe mentioned Chap. xxxviii. 22.

Ibid. *And I will cauſe thee to come up from the North Parts,* &c.] The Words may be better tranſlated, *After I have cauſed thee to come up from the North Parts, and have brought*
                                        thee

thee upon the Mountains of Ifrael. See a like
Conftruction, Chap. xxxviii. 4.

Ver. 3. *And I will fmite thy Bow out of thy
Left Hand, &c.*] There fhall be no might in
thy Hand, as *Mofes* threatens the *Ifraelites,
Deut.* xxviii. 32. Thou fhalt not be able to ufe
thy Weapons to any purpofe.

Ver. 3.

Ver. 4. *I will give thee to the ravenous Birds
of every fort, &c.*] See Verfe 17. Chapter
xxxiii. 27.

Ver. 4.

Ver. 6. *And I will fend a Fire on Magog.*]
I will confume him by Fire and Brimftone out
of Heaven. See Chap. xxxviii. 22. *Fire* doth
likewife fignify the fierceft of God's Judgments.
See the Note upon Chap. xxx. 8.

Ver. 6.

Ibid. *And among them that dwell carelefly in
the Ifles.*] The Inhabitants of the Sea-Coaft
which dwell fecurely, and think no harm can
come upon them. The Expreffion relates to the
Merchants of Tarfhifh, and others mentioned
Chap. xxxviii. 13. All Countries lying upon the
Sea-Coaft are called *Iflands* in the *Hebrew* Language.

Ver. 7. *So will I make my holy Name known
in the midft of my People Ifrael.*] See Ver. 21.
and Chap. xxxviii. 16, 23.

Ver. 7.

Ibid. *And I will not let them pollute my holy
Name any more.*] The Words in the *Hebrew*
run thus, *I will not pollute my Holy Name any
more,* i. e. I will not fuffer it to be polluted, as
the Verbs Active often fignify only Permiffion.
See the Note upon Chap. xiv. 9. The Senfe is,
I will not fuffer my Name to be difhonoured
any

any more, nor let it be said among the Heathen that I was not able to rescue my People out of the Hand of their Enemies.

Ver. 8. *Behold it is come, and it is done, saith the Lord* GOD.] The time appointed for this Great Destruction is come, and it is the last and finishing Stroke of God's Justice upon the Enemies of his Church and Truth. Compare *Revel.* xvi. 17. xxi. 6.

Ibid. *This is the Day whereof I have spoken.*] *By my Servants the Prophets,* Chap. xxxviii. 17.

Ver. 9. *And they that dwell in the Cities of Israel shall go forth, and shall set on Fire and burn the Weapons,* &c.] In token of an entire Conquest, and that such a lasting Peace should ensue, that there should be no more need of warlike Preparations. Compare *Psal.* xlvi. 9.

Ibid. *Seven Years.*] The burning the Weapons of War must be the Consequent of a complete Victory : So that the *seven Years* here mentioned cannot be meant, as some would understand them, of those terrible Conflicts which the Jews had with *Antiochus Epiphanes,* from the 143d or 145th Year of the *Æra Seleucidarum,* (according to the different Computation of the Beginning of that Persecution. See 1 *Maccab.* i. 20, 29.) to the 151st Year of the same *Æra,* when *Nicanor* was slain : *ibid. c.* vii. 1, 43. Nor is that true which this Opinion supposes, *viz.* that *Nicanor's* Death put an End to the Troubles of the Jews : for after that *there was great Affliction in Israel, the like whereof had not been since the time that a Prophet had not been seen among them,* as the same Writer informs us,

1 *Maccab.*

1 *Maccab.* ix. 27. So that this Passage of *Eze-* Chapter *kiel's* Prophecy must necessarily be expounded XXXIX. of some other Event. ∿

Ver. 10. *So that they shall take no Wood out of* Ver. 10: *the Field,* &c.] The Quantity of these Weapons will afford sufficient Fewel for all that time.

Ibid. *They shall spoil those that spoiled them, and rob those that robbed them.*] The same Measure they dealt to others, shall be measured out to them again. Comp. *Isa.* xiv. 2. xxxiii. 1. *Revel.* xiii. 10. xviii. 6.

Ver. 11. *The Valley of the Passengers on the* Ver. 11. *East side of the Sea.*] i. e. The Sea of *Gennesareth,* as the *Chaldee* Paraphrast explains it. In the *Hebrew* Language all Lakes are called by the Name of *Seas.* The same is called the Eastern Sea, Chap. xlvii. 18. to distinguish it from the *Mediterranean,* called the *Great Sea Westward, Josh.* xxiii. 4. The Valley near this Sea or Lake is called *the Valley of the Passengers,* because it was a great Road by which the Merchants and Traders from *Syria* and other Eastern Countries went into *Egypt.*

Ibid. *And it shall stop the Noses of the Passengers.*] Or, *The Passengers shall stop their Noses:* *viz.* to avoid the Smell of so many Carcasses: The *Transitive* is often taken in a *Passive* or *Impersonal* Sense, as hath been observed upon *Isa.* xliv. 18.

Ver. 13. *Yea, all the People of the Land shall* Ver. 13. *bury them.*] See the Note on the following Verse.

Ibid. *And it shall be to them a Renown, the Day that I shall be glorified.*] Or, *The Day that I* shall

Chapter *ſhall be glorified ſhall be to them* [a Day] *of* Re-
XXXIX. *nown* i.e. a remarkable Day of Joy and Glad-
ness. See Ver. 21, 22.

Ver. 14.   Ver. 14. *And they ſhall ſever out Men of continual Employment paſſing thro' the Land, to bury
with the Paſſengers thoſe that remain upon the
Face of the Earth.*] The latter part of the Sentence may more clearly be tranſlated thus, *even
Buriers with the Paſſengers,* [to bury] *thoſe that
remain,* &c. For the Paſſengers or Searchers are
diſtinguiſhed from thoſe whoſe Office it is to bury the Dead, in the following Verſe.

     Ibid. *After the end of ſeven Months ſhall they
ſearch.*] All the People ſhall be employed ſeven
Months, in burying the Dead, Ver. 13. and after
they are ended, particular Perſons appointed for
that purpoſe, ſhall make a clear Riddance.

Ver. 15.   Ver. 15. *Then he ſhall ſet up a Sign by it.*] A
Stone, or ſome other Mark of Diſtinction, that
Men may avoid paſſing over them. See the *Ex-
cerpta* out of Dr. *Pocock's Miſcellany Notes,* in
the *Synopſis* upon *Luke* xi. 44.

Ver. 17.   Ver. 17. *Speak to every feathered Fowl, and to
every Beaſt of the Field,* &c.] It was the Cuſtom
for Perſons that offered Sacrifice to invite their
Friends to the Feaſt that was made of the Remainder. See *Gen.* xxxiv. 54. 1 *Sam.* ix. 13. So
here the Prophet by God's Command, invites the
Beaſts and Fowls to partake of the Sacrifice of his
Enemies ſlain.

     Ibid. *Gather your ſelves to my Sacrifice, that I
do ſacrifice for you.*] The Slaughter of God's Enemies is called a *Sacrifice,* becauſe it is offered up
as

as an Atonement to the Divine Justice. Comp. Chapter this Verse with *Isa.* xxxiv. 6. *Zeph.* i. 7. *Rev.* XXXIX. xix. 17.

Ibid. *Upon the Mountains of Israel.*] Where this great Army was to be destroyed: See Ver. 4.

Ver. 18. *Of Rams, of Lambs, of Goats, of Bul-* Ver. 18. *locks.*] Of all Ranks and Kinds, who shall be brought like Beasts to the Slaughter. Comp. *Psal.* lxviii. 31. *Isa.* xxxiv. 6. *Jerem.* l. 27. li. 40.

Ibid. *All of them Fatlings of Basan.*] See *Deut.* xxxii. 14.

Ver. 19. *And drink Blood till ye be drunken.*] Ver. 19. Or be *filled,* or satiated: for so the *Hebrew Ravah* usually signifies. See *Cantic.* v. 1. *Hag.* i. 6. *Jerem.* xxxi. 14, 25. and the *Greek* Verb Μεθυω is taken in the same Sense, *John* ii. 10. and so I conceive it should be understood 1 *Cor.* xi. 21. where the Apostle reproving the Abuse of their Love Feasts, saith, *One is hungry, and another drinks,* or fills himself *to the full.*

Ver. 20. *Thus shall ye be filled at my Table.*] Ver. 20. The Feast made upon the Peace-Offerings or Sacrifices of Thanksgiving, is properly called *the Table of the Lord.* See *Malach.* i. 12. From whence the Expression is applied to the Feast of the Lord's Supper, 1 *Cor.* x. 21.

Ver. 21. *And I will set my Glory among the* Ver. 21. *Heathen,* &c.] See Chap. xxxviii. 16, 23.

Ver. 22. *So the House of Israel shall know that* Ver. 22. *I am the* LORD *their God,* &c.] Both by my Acts of Mercy in returning their Captivity: See Ver. 28, 29. and by my Judgments executed upon their Enemies.

Ver.

Chapter **Ver. 23, 24.** *And the Heathen shall know that*
XXXIX. *the House of Israel went into Captivity for their*
〰〰 *Iniquity, &c.*] They were not carried away by
Ver. 23. their Enemies because I wanted Power to rescue
them, but as a just Punishment of their Sins. See
Chap. xxxvi. 18, 19, 20.

Ver. 25. **Ver. 25.** *Now will I bring again the Capti-*
vity of Jacob.] See Chap. xxxiv. 13. xxxvi. 24.
xxxvii. 21.

Ibid. *And have mercy upon the whole House*
of Israel.] See Chap. xx. 40.

Ver. 26. **Ver. 26.** *After that they have born their*
Shame, and all their Trespasses, &c.] The Shame
and Reproach due to their Sins: See *Dan.* ix.
16.

Ibid. *When they dwelt safely in their Land,*
and none made them afraid.] By their Sins abu-
sing those gracious Promises of Peace and Safety
which I had given them : See *Levit.* xxvi. 5, 6.

Ver. 27. **Ver. 27.** *And am sanctified in them in the*
sight of many Nations.] See Chap. xxxvi. 23.

Ver. 28. **Ver. 28.** *Then shall they know that I am the*
LORD *their God.*] See Ver. 22. Chap. xxxiv. 30.

Ver. 29. **Ver. 29.** *Neither will I hide my Face any more*
from them.] I will never withdraw my Favour
or Protection from them. See *Isa.* liv. 8.

Ibid. *For I have poured out my Spirit upon the*
House of Israel.] There will be a new Effusion
of God's Spirit upon the Jews in order to their
Conversion: See *Isa.* lix. 20, 21. a place applied
by St. *Paul* to this very Purpose, *Rom.* xi. 26,
27. Compare likewise *Zech.* xii. 10. and Chap.
xi. 19. xxxvi. 27. of this Prophecy.

C H A P. XL. Fol. 343.

Vestigium TEMPLI HIEROSOLYMITANI, juxta mentem *VILLALPANDI*, & universarum illius Porticuum à *SOLOMONE* constructarum; ad primarium Exemplar olim à Deo inventore *DAVIDI* traditum & ab Angelo postea, *EZEKIELE* prospectante, commensuratum.

OCCIDENS

MERIDIES

SEPTENTRIO

ORIENS

Area atrij exterioris Spectans Africum.

Area atrij exterioris Spectans Caurum.

Area atrij exterioris Spectans Austrum.

Area atrij exterioris Spectans Septentrionē.

Atrium internum Leviticum.

Altare holocaustorum.

Area atrij exterioris Spectans Rurū.

Area atrij exterioris Spectans Orientem.

Area atrij exterioris Spectans Aquilonem.

CHAP. XL.

The General ARGUMENT to the following Chapter.

GOD *having forsaken the City and Temple of*
Jerusalem, *and given them up to Destruction, for
the Idolatries and other Sins committed there;
in this and the following Chapters, he sheweth
to the Prophet in Vision, the Model or Plan of
another Temple, of the same Dimensions with
that built by* Solomon; *as* Villalpandus, *and
other learned Men, with great Probality suppose.* David *had the Pattern of that Temple,
which* Solomon *was to build reveal'd to him
by God: See* 1 Ch. xxviii. 11, 19. *as* Moses *had
the Model of the Tabernacle represented to him
by a Vision, while he was in the Mount,* Ex. xxv.
40. *And here the Plan of* Solomon's *Temple is
again discovered to* Ezekiel, *who foretelling the
Destruction of this Temple by the* Chaldeans,
shews how highly it was valued by the Jews, *when
he calls it,* The Excellency of their Strength,
and the Desire of their Eyes, Chap. xxiv. 21.

They

A COMMENTARY

*They looked upon it as the Honour, Glory, and
Safeguard of their Nation. This lying in Ruins
at the Time of this Vision, the Jews had need
of being comforted, instructed, and humbled upon that Occasion; they would not have cared for
the Thoughts of returning Home, were there
no Promise made of restoring the Temple, as
well as their Commonwealth; the Temple being
the Pledge of God's Presence among them. Moses
his Ritual Law would soon have been adapted
to the Manners of the Gentiles, where they lived,
if the Expectations of a new Temple, to which
most of its Rites were fitted, had not restrained
their Propensity to Idolatry; and they would
have been dispirited beyond measure, as they were
afterward, upon Sight of their second Temple,
if the Prophet had plainly foretold, that their
new Temple should fall short of the Glory of the
old one: They were therefore to be incouraged
to the Observation of their Law, with the
Hopes of returning to rebuild their Temple, which
should be finished after the Plan of that of Solomon.*

*We cannot suppose any exact Model of Solomon's
Temple remaining, which might be transmitted
to those that returned from the Captivity; for
it was above seventy Years from the Destruction
of the first Temple to the Finishing the second,
in the sixth Year of Darius, Ezr. vi. 15. During which Interval, the ancient Priests must
be all dead; and those that were younger could
have but confused and very imperfect Ideas of
it. To direct them therefore in the Dimensions,
Parts, Order, and Rules of their new Temple,*

is

is one *Reason*, why Ezekiel *is so particular in the Description of the Old. And no doubt but* Zerobabal's *Temple was accordingly conformable to that of* Solomon, *in Figure, Disposition of Parts, and Order of the whole Fabrick and Service: If in State or Magnificence there was some Variety; that is to be imputed to the Necessity of their Circumstances, and doth not imply any essential Alteration.*

However *the Building being found inferior to the Model here prescribed, the first Discovery of which was a sensible Mortification to the ancient Men that had seen the first Temple,* Ezr. iii. 12. *It was natural for the* Jews *of former Ages, that studied the Style of Prophecy, to conclude, as many of the* Jewish *Writers of later Times, have done, that* Ezekiel's *Temple had a further View, and the chief Intent and Design of it was that to be fulfilled under the* Messias. *Whatever was August and Illustrious in the Prophetick Figures, and not literally fulfilled in or near their own Times, those Things were justly thought to belong to the Days of the* Messias; *But as for minuter Circumstances, there is no more Necessity of giving them a Place in the spiritual Application of a Prophecy, than in the Explication of a Parable. The Temple, and the Temple Worship, was a proper Figure of* Christ's *Church, and of the Spiritual Worship to be instituted by Him: And the Notions of the* Jews *were to be raised by Degrees to a further and higher Meaning, hereafter to be compleated, without destroying their Obligations to the Statutes and Ordinances God enjoined for the present.*

Y y 2

There

There was the more reason for Ezekiel's *keeping
to the Figure of* Solomon's *Temple, in speaking of the times of the* Messias; *because* Solomon *was a Type of the* Messias, *chiefly in this
respect, that he was to* Build *an House for the*
Name *and Worship of God, according to* Nathan's *Prophecy concerning him, 2* Sam. vii. 13,
14. *several Parts of which Prophecy are applied to Christ in the New-Testament : See* Heb.
i. 5, Luke i. 32. *this Exposition of that Place
receives a further Confirmation from hence, that
other Prophets foretel the same thing concerning the* Messias. *Beside those Passages in* Ezekiel, *which are under our present Consideration,*
Zechary *after him Prophesied that the* Man
whose Name is the B R A N C H shall build the
Temple of the L O R D, and bear the Glory,
and sit and rule upon his Throne, and shall be
a Priest upon his Throne, and the Counsel of
Peace shall be between them both; *i. e. between the Kingdom and the Priesthood; the
same Person shall be both King and Priest, and
his Offices shall not interfere with, or obstruct
each other.* Zech. vi. 12, 13.

The New-Testament copies the style of the Old;
St. Paul *in his Epistles calls the Christian Church
by the Name of the* House *or* Temple of God,
see 1 Cor. iii. 16. 2 Cor. vi. 16. Eph. ii. 20, &c.
1 Tim. iii. 15. Heb. iii. 6. *In pursuance of the
same Metaphor he tells us that* Antichrist shall
sit in the Temple of God, *meaning the Christian
Church,* 2 Thess. ii. 4. *And* St. John *in the*
Revelation *not only describes the heavenly Sanctuary by Representations taken from the* Jewish
Temple

Temple (a), *but likewise transcribes several of Ezekiel's Expressions* (b); *and borrows his Allusions from the state of the Temple as it was built by* Solomon, *not as it stood in our Saviour's time; as if the former had a more immediate reference to the times of the Gospel.* Thus Revel. iv. 1. &c. *the Throne of God is represented like that over the Ark, where the Shekinah, or Divine Glory sate, encompassed with* Four Cherubims [*See the Note upon Verse 6th of the following Chapter*] *and with the Seats of four and twenty Elders, alluding to the Heads of so many Priestly Courses. And* before the *Throne is placed a Sea of Glass,* like unto Chrystal, *resembling the famous Molten Sea of* Solomon. *All these Ornaments were proper to the first Temple, as it was finish'd by* Solomon, *whereas in the second Temple there was no proper Ark, no Throne encompassed by Cherubims, no visible Glory, no Molten Sea; and but four of the four and twenty Courses of the Priests returned from* Babylon: *See* Ezra ii. 36, 39. *Upon the whole we may conclude, that the general Scope of* Ezekiel's *Temple is, by giving a Promise of restoring* Solomon's, *to preserve the* Jews *from defiling themselves with Idolatry during their Captivity; and when the time of that should be expired, to encourage them to go Home, and rebuild their Temple, and observe the Laws and Ordinances prescrib'd by* Moses, *for performing God's Worship there, which yet was never*

(a) Revel. xi. 19. xiv. 17. xv. 5, 8.
(b) Revel. iv. 2, 3, 6. xi. 1, 2. xxi. 12. &c. xxii. 1, 2.

Chapter
XI..

to be equal to Solomon's *in every respect ; before the* Messias *should come, who should supply its Defficiencies, and whose Church should resemble* Solomon's *Temple in Semmetry and Beauty, in Firmness and Duration, in a regular, orderly and decent Worship of the true God, and in the manifestation of the divine Presence, at first by the miraculous Gifts of the Holy Ghost, and ever since by the inward Assistances, Comforts and Protection of the same Spirit.*

T H E XLth Chapter contains a Description of the two outward Courts, with the Chambers thereto belonging, together with the Porch of the Temple.

Ver. 1.

Ver. 1.

N the five and twentieth Year of our Captivity.]See the Note upon Chap. i. 2.
Ibid. *In the beginning of the Year, in the tenth Day of the Month,*] i. e.
The first Month called here the *Beginning of the Year*, which in the Ecclesiastical Computation was the Month *Nisan*. The word Month likewise taken indifinitely, signifies the first Month, Chap. xxvi. 1.

Ibid. *In the fourteenth Year after that the City was smitten.*] *Zedekiah's* Reign commenced from *Jehoiakin's* Captivity, in the xi*th* Year of whose Reign the City was destroyed, *Jerem.* lii. 5, 6. So the fourteenth Year after the Destruction of the City must be co-incident with the xxv*th* of *Jehoiakin's* Captivity.

Ibid.

Ibid. *The hand of the LORD was upon* Chapter
me.] See Chap. i. 3.   XL.

Ver: 2. *In the Visions of God brought he me*
into the Land of Israel.] See the Note on Chap. Ver. 2.
viii. 3.

Ibid. *And set me upon a very high Mountain.*]
The Expression points out Mount *Moriah*, where-
on the Temple was built, which is here called
a *very high Mountain*; becaufe it reprefents the
Seat of the Chriftian Church, foretold by the
Prophets that it fhould be *eftablished upon the*
top of the Mountains: See *Ifa.* ii. 1. *Micah.* iv. 1.
Compared with *Revel.* xxi. 10.

Ibid. *By which was a Frame of a City on the*
South.] Mount *Moriah* lay Southward of the
Hill of *Sion*, or the City of *David*, tho' both
of them lay Northward in refpect of the lower
Part of the City, which from the times of *Solo-*
mon was moft commonly call'd by the Name
of *Jerufalem:* See *Pfal.* xlviii. 2. *Ifa.* xiv. 13.
and Dr. *Lightfoot's Geographical Defcription of*
Jerufalem, Ch. xxii. So the words defcribe the
fituation of the Temple on the South Side of
Mount *Sion*; which with all its Courts, Buildings, and Walls encompaffing the Courts, and
the whole Area, or holy Mountain, fee Chap.
xlii. 20. refembled a City for bignefs. So *Ta-*
citus lib. 5. *Hift.* defcribes the Temple as built
like a Citadel for Strength and Largenefs.

Or we may fuppofe that the Prophet being
brought by the Spirit from *Chaldea* into the
Land of *Ifrael*, which lay Southward of *Baby-*
lon, fee Chap. i. 4. might fee placed juft before
his Eyes a Reprefentation of the City and Temple,

Chapter ple, ſtanding upon an Eminence, both in reſpect
XL. of their natural Situation, and that the Prophet
might take a better View of them: For it appears
from Chap. xlviii. 15, &c. that he had a View
of the Holy City which was to be reſtored, as
well as of the Temple.

Ver. 3.   Ver. 3. *Behold there was a Man, whoſe appea-*
rance was like the appearance of Braſs.] or bur-
niſhed or poliſhed Braſs, as we read Chap. i. 7.
and *Dan.* x. 6. that is, of a bright or flaming Colour.   This ſeems to be an inferior Angel; becauſe he is diſtinguiſhed from the Divine Glory,
or the *Logos* appearing in the *Shekinah,* Chap.
xliii. 6. comp. Chap. ix. 3.

Ibid. *With a Line of Flax in his Hand; and*
a meaſuring Reed.]   The uſe of the Line was to
meaſure the Land of *Iſrael,* and of the Reed to
take the Dimenſions of the Buidings in and about
the Temple: as alſo to ſet out ſeveral Portions of
Land belonging to the Sanctuary and City, to the
Prince and People.   See Chap. xlv. 1, &c, xlvii.
3. &c.

Ibid. *And he ſtood in the Gate.*] Probably the
North Gate, being the firſt Entrance the Prophet may be ſuppoſed to have arrived to, as he
came from *Chaldea,* which lay Northward of
Judea: See the Note upon Ver. 2.

Ver. 4.   Ver. 4. *Son of Man.*] See the Note upon
Chap. ii. 1.

Ibid. *Behold with thine Eyes, ------ declare all*
thou ſeeſt to the Houſe of Iſrael.] Comp. Chap.
xliii. 10. xliv. 5. The Temple now repreſented
was partly deſigned to aſſure the People that their
Temple ſhould be reſtored; and to ſerve them as
a Model

a Model by which they should rebuild it, at their Return from Captivity. The *Jewish* Writers do confirm this Opinion, when they tell us, " That " the Children of the Captivity who returned " from *Babylon*, followed the Platform of that " Temple which *Ezekiel* described, as far as their " Circumstances would allow." See *Dr. Light-foot's Description of the Temple*, Chap. x.

Ver. 5. *And behold a Wall on the outside of the House round about.*] A Wall went round the whole Compass or Square of the Holy Mountain whereon the Temple was situate, to separate the Holy Ground from that which was Prophane: See Chap. xlii. 20.

Ibid. *And in the Man's Hand a measuring Reed of six Cubits long, by the Cubit, and a Hand-breadth.*] The Prophet explains what sort of Cubit he means in the following Delineation of the Temple, *viz.* such a one as consists of six Hand-breadths, or one Hand-breadth over the Cubit used in *Chaldea*, where he now lived. Comp. Chap. xli. 8. xliii. 13. This is the Measure of a Scripture Cubit, generally agreed to be equivalent to eighteen Inches, or a Foot and a half of our Measure: See *Bp Cumberland of Scripture Weights and Measures*, p. 36, &c.

Ibid. *So he measured the breadth of the Building one Reed, and the height one Reed.*] The Breadth or Thickness of the Wall was equal the Height of It.

Ver. 6. *Then he came unto the Gate which looketh toward the East.*] The Temple being placed toward the West Part of the Holy Mountain, as the Sanctuary was at the West End of the

Z z Temple,

Temple, (fee the Note upon Chap. viii. 16.) this was the firſt Gate that led to it. This Gate opened into the firſt Court, or the Court of the People, fee Ver. 19. and is called the *Kings Gate*, 1 *Chron.* ix. 18. as being built by King *Solomon.*

Ibid. *And went up the Stairs thereof.*] Which confifted of feven Steps, as the *Septuagint* exprefly mentioned, comp. Ver. 22. 26.

Ibid. *And meaſured the* [one] *Threſhold of the Gate which was one Reed broad, and the other Threſhold,*&c.] He went up the Stairs that he might more eafily meafure the upper Lintel, as well as the lower Threfhold. The word *Saph* tranflated Threfhold, fignifies the Lintel upper Part of the Door-Cafe, as well as the Threfhold properly, fo called, or lower Part of it. The Plural *Sippim,* comprehends both, fee Chap. xli. 16. *Iſa.* vi. 4. and the *Septuagint* tranflate it there ∽πέρθυϱον, the *Lintel.* Some underftand the word here of the two Side-pofts, in which fenfe it is ufed *Amos* ix. i.

Ver. 7. *And every little Chamber was one Reed long, and one Reed broad,* &c.] Along the Wall of the Porch were Chambers, three on each Side, Ver. 10. Thefe the Angel meafured, and they were of equal Dimenfions, each one Reed fquare, with a Paffage of five Cubits breadth between them.

Ibid. *And the Threſhold of the Gate by the Porch of the Gate within, was one Reed.*] The inward Threfhold at the furtlier End of the Porch looking into the firft Court, was of the fame Size with the outward one; Ver. 6. comp. Ver. 15.

Ver.

Ver. 8. *He measured also the Porch of the Gate* Chapter
within, one Reed.] Or, *He even measured,* &c. XL.
for the words seem to be a Repetition of what
was said in the latter Part of the seventh Verse; Ver. 8.
so the *Vulgar Latin* understood it, and therefore
omit the whole Verse; and the *Septuagint* in the
Alexandrian Copy published by Dr. *Grabe,* join
the two Verses in sense together: See the like
Repetitions, Ver. 11, 12 and 16. and Chap. xli. 11.

Ver. 9. *Then measured he the Porch of the Gate* Ver. 9.
eight Cubits, &c.] This was a Portico beyond the
little Chambers, which looked *inward,* i. e. into
the first Court ; it was eight Cubits wide, and the
two side Posts were two Cubits thick, which made
up the ten Cubits mentioned ver. 11. The word
Ael translated Post, is the same in sense with *Me-*
zuzah, Chap. xlv. 19. which properly signifies
the side Post that supports the Lintel: See *Exod.*
xii. 22.

Ver. 10. *And the little Chambers of the Gate* Ver. 10.
Eastward, &c.] Or, The little Chambers of the
Eastern Gate, which he has been hitherto describing; and the Form of which is here repeated.
These Rooms were for the use of the Porters,
that took Care of the several Gates that led to
the Temple, See 1 *Chron.* ix. 18; 23, 24. xxvi. 12,
13. 18.

Ibid. *And the Posts had one measure on this*
side, and on that side.] The side Posts or Fronts
of the Doors belonging to each row of Chambers were of the same size.

Ver. 11. *And he measured the breadth of the* Ver. 11.
entry of the Gate ten Cubits.] See ver. 9.

Z z 2 Ibid.

Ibid. *And the length of the Gate thirteen Cubits.*] By the *Length* of the Gate *Villalpandus*
underftands the Height, which he fuppofes to have
been two Reeds, or twelve Cubits and a half
high; for he reckons every Reed to confift of
fix ordinary Cubits, and a fourth Part over, which
in the common Computation of full Numbers for
Fractions, may be called thirteen Cubits. *Bern.
L'Amy* in his Book *de Tabernaculo Fœderis*, explains the Expreffion of the Breadth of the Walls
on each fide of the Gate, which he fuppofes to be
fix Cubits and an Half. And fo the feventy Interpreters may be thought to underftand the words,
who tranflate the *Hebrew Oreb* by Εὖρ⊙., Breadth.

Ver. 12.

Ver. 12. *The Place alfo before the Chambers
was one Cubit* on this fide, *and ------ on that fide.*]
There was a Border, or a Rail which enclofed a
Cubit's fpace before each Chamber.

Ibid. *And the little Chambers were fix Cubits
on this fide, &c.*] See ver. 7.

Ver. 13.

Ver. 13. *He meafured then the Gate from the
roof of one little Chamber, to the roof of another;
the breadth was five and twenty Cubits.*] Mea-
furing the Arch of the Gate from North to South,
it was in breadth five and twenty Cubits; which
L'Amy thus computes, the Breadth of the Gate
ten Cubits, the Breadth of both the fide Walls
thirteen Cubits, and two Cubits for the Space or
Border on each fide of the Chambers; ver. 12.

Ibid. *Door againft Door.*] The Door on each
Chamber exactly anfwered the Door on the op-
pofite fide.

Ver. 14.

Ver. 14. *He made alfo Pofts of threefcore Cubits.*] The Angel defcribed or made a Delineation

tion of the Heighth of the Columns or Pillars, which were to support the Rooms or Stories over the Arch of the Gate, and these were in Heighth sixty Cubits; the whole Building being divided into three Stories, like those described Chap. xlii. 6. The Heighth of each Story is thus computed by *Villalpandus Part 2. lib. 5. Cap. 16.* That the Pillars of the lower Story were twenty Cubits high; those of the second, fifteen; and the uppermost, twelve; the Remainder being allowed for the Floors and the Roof. The Word *Posts* in this Verse signifies Pillars, comp. Chap. xlii. 6.

Ibid. *Even unto the Posts of the Court round about the gate.*] *Villalpandus* and several Interpreters suppose there is an *Ellipsis* in the Words, which they thus supply; And *there was one measure* to the Pillars of the Court, *and* of the Gate round about; which makes the Sense run plain and easy, comp. Chap. xli. 9. where there is the same *Ellipsis.*

Ver. 15.

Ver. 15. *And from the face of the gate of the Entrance unto the face of the inner Gate, were fifty Cubits.*] The whole length of the Porch, from the outward Front (comp. Chap. xli. 21. 25.) unto the inner Side, which looks into the first Court, ver. 17, was fifty Cubits; which may be thus computed; twelve Cubits for the Thickness of the Wall at each End, ver. 6. eighteen for the three Chambers on each Side, ver. 7. and ten Cubits for the Spaces between the Chambers; allowing the same Space between the Chambers on each Side, and the two Walls. Ibid. *Villalpandus* observes the just Proportion between the breadth and length of the Gate, the length being double to the breadth, ver.

ver. 13. The fame, he tells us, was obſerved between the Breadth of the Cloyſters of the outward Court, which was fifty Cubits, and the Contents of the whole *Area*, which was an Hundred. See the Note on ver. 18.

Ver. 16.

Ver. 16. *And there were narrow windows to the little Chambers, and to their poſts within the Gate round about.*] Every one of theſe little Chambers, ver. 7. had a narrow Window to it toward the Inſide of the Gate, where the Paſſage was; and ſo there was over the ſide Poſts or Fronts, placed at the Entrance of every Chamber. By *narrow* or cloſed *Windows*, ſome underſtand Windows with Lattice-Work, to let in the Light. But the Phraſe ſeems equivalent to that which is more fully expreſſed 1 *Kings* vi. 4. by *open and narrow Windows*; i. e. as the Margin of our Bibles doth very well explain it; *broad within* [to diſperſe the Light] and *narrow without*.

Ibid. *And likewiſe the Arches.*] By Windows to the Arches. *Villalpandus* underſtands the Stone itſelf wrought into Figures of Net-work, and made in the ſhape of a Lattice. The Word tranſlated *Arches* doth likewiſe ſignify a Porch, or Entrance, and ſo the *vulgar Latin* tranſlates it; and then the Senſe is, that there were Windows over every Door; Compare ver. 31 and 34, with ver. 37; where the ſame Senſe is expreſſed in the two former Verſes; by *Arches, Aelamo* in the *Hebrew*, and in the latter, by *Poſts*, or Fronts, *Aelau*.

Ibid. *And the windows were round about inward.*] A Repetition of what was ſaid in the former Part of the Verſe, ſee ver. 10.

Ibid.

Ibid. *And upon each post were Palm-trees.*] A
Palm-tree was carved upon the Chapiter of each
side Post, or Front, see ver. 26.

Ver. 17. *Then brought he me into the outward
Court.*] There were two Courts belonging to *Solomon's* Temple; the outward for the People, the
inward for the Priests. It is probable, that *Solomon*
built only the inner Court, see 1 *Kings* vi. 36.
compared with Chap. viii. 64; and that the outer
Court was built after his Time, whereupon it is
called the *new Court*, 2 *Chron.* xx. 5. After which
Time there is particular mention of the *two Courts
of the House of the LORD*, 2 *Kings* xxi. 5.
A third Court, called the *Court of the Gentiles*,
was afterwards added by *Herod*, when he rebuilt
the Temple.

The *Great Court*, mentioned 2 *Chron.* iv. 9. as
distinct from the Court of the Priests, Dr. *Lightfoot* explains of the Holy Mountain, or Area, where
the Temple stood, which *Solomon* enclosed with
a Wall, and separated it from common Ground:
so that Text 1 *Kings* vii. 12. *The Great Court
round about was with three rows of hewed Stones,
&c.* is to be understood only of this Enclosure,
according to his Opinion. See his *Description of
the Temple*, Chap. 10, and 18.

Ibid. *And lo, there were Chambers and a Pavement made for the Court round about.*] These
Chambers were over the Cloyster, and supported
by it, see v. 14, and Chap. xlii. 8. They might be
for the use of the Priests, and likewise to be Store-
houses for Tithes and Offerings, see 1 *Chron.*
xxviii. 12.

Ibid.

Ibid. *Thirty Chambers were upon the Pavement.*]
The Number of them *Villalpandus* thus divides:
Toward the Eaſt and Weſt, ſeven on a Side, an-
ſwering one another; on the North and South
Sides, eight a-piece, abating one Chamber, both
on the Eaſt and Weſt Side, for the Thickneſs of
the Walls or Arches, which ſupported thoſe two
Gates, which he ſuppoſes to be higher than the
North and South Gates.

Ver. 18. *And the Pavement by the Side of the
Gates, over-againſt* [or equal to] *the length of the
Gates, was the lower Pavement.*] The Breadth
of this Pavement, that lay on the Side of the Gate,
was equal to the Length of the whole Porch or
Gate, which was fifty Cubits, ver. 15. This will
plainly appear, if we conſider, that the Area of
the outward Court contained an hundred Cubits,
ver. 19: So the Portico's, or Cloyſters, cutting the
Area in right Angels, by the Gate placed in the
middle of the Court, the Pavement belonging to
each Side of the Gate, or Cloyſter, muſt be juſt half
that Dimenſion, *viz.* fifty Cubits. The Word Gates
in the plural Number, ſeems to be uſed for the ſin-
gular, as it implies the whole Building conſiſting
of upper Rooms, as well as the lower Paſſage:
See the Note upon ver. 14. The Word *Leümmah*,
which our tranſlation renders *over-againſt*, often
ſignifies Equal, anſwerable, or the ſame Proportion. See *Notidius*, p. 525. and ſo it is uſed Chap. i.
20. iii. 8. xlv. 7. xlviii. 13. *&c.* This was called
the lower Pavement, in reſpect of the ſeveral A-
ſcents which were ſtill to go up, the nearer you
came to the Temple. See Dr. *Lightfoot's Deſcription of the Temple*, Chap. 20. *Villalpandus* explain

plains the lower Pavement by Way of Diſtinction
to the upper Rooms, or Chambers, placed over
them, for the uſe of the Prieſts, or as Store-rooms
for the Service of the Temple.

Ver. 19. *Then he meaſured the Breadth from*
the fore-Front of the lower Gate unto the fore-
Front of the inner Gate without, an hundred Cu-
bits eaſtward.] That is, unto the hither Side of the
Gate which faced the inner Court. He meaſured
the whole Space of Ground between the Weſt
Front of the lower Gate, to the Front of the upper Gate, which leads into the Eaſtern inner Court,
and found it an hundred Cubits; the ſame was the
Space between the South Front and North Front:
ſo the Court was exactly ſquare. See ver. 23, 27.
47. The Expreſſion is Elliptical; as if he had ſaid,
there were an hundred Cubits from Weſt to Eaſt,
and from North to South. There were two Gates
belonged to the Porch, or Paſſage, that led to the
inner Court; the firſt was Eaſtward looking toward the outer Court, which is here meant; the
other looked Weſtward into the inner Court. The
Gate at the Eaſt End of the outer Court is called the
lower Gate, for the ſame Reaſon as the Pavement is
called the lower Pavement; ver. 18; becauſe there
was ſtill an Aſcent, as you went from one Court to
the other. The Expreſſion of the *inner Gate, with-*
out, is explained in the Note upon Chap. xlvi. 2.

Ibid. *North-ward.*] The *Septuagint* join this word
to the following Verſe, and render the Sentence
thus; *And he brought me to the North, and behold*
the Gate looking to the North in the outer Court.

Villalpandus explains the 19th Verſe to this
Senſe; That the outward Court conſiſted of ſeven

Squares,

Chapter
XL.

Squares, an hundred Cubits each; the firſt placed
directly before the Court of the Prieſts, and of the
ſame Dimenſions with it; the others extended on
the North and South Sides of the outer Court, and
likewiſe commenſurate with the Sides both of the
inner Court and of the Temple, each of which contained 100 Cubits. By which Deſcription it muſt
contain a Square of 300 Cubits on the Eaſt Part,
and 200 Cubits both on the North and South Side.
Conſult *Villalpandus's Delineation of the Temple.*

Ver. 20.

Ver. 20, 21. '*And the Gate of the outward
Court that looketh toward the North.----And the
little Chambers thereof,* &c.] The whole Model
was the ſame with that of the Eaſt Gate: See Ver.
9, 10, 13, 15, 16.

Ver. 22.

Ver. 22. *And they went up into it by ſeven
Steps.*] See Ver. 6.

Ibid. *And the Arches thereof were before them.*]
Or at the Entrance of them. The *Septuagint* render the Word *liphni,* before them, as if it meant
the ſame with *el penimith,* within, or inward,
Chap. xlii. 4. This Senſe is followed by moſt Ex-
poſitors, to denote that the Arches were within,
or at the Top of the Stairs; but the Phraſe may
probably mean the ſame with *Nal Penehem,* ſuitable to them; *i. e.* to thoſe of the Eaſt Gate. See
the following Note.

Ver. 23.

Ver. 23. *And the Gate of the inner Court was
over-againſt the Gate toward the North and toward the Eaſt.*] The Word might be tranſlated
more plainly thus; *And the Gate of the inner Court
was proportionable,* or anſwerable, *to the Gate that
was toward the North and toward the Eaſt.* The
Expreſſion is Elliptical, as that of ver. 19. and the
full

full Import of it is, That the North Gate of the inner Court did exactly anſwer this North Gate of the outer Court, deſcribed ver. 20, 22. And in like manner, the Eaſt Gate of the inner Court anſwered the Eaſt Gate of the outward Court. The Word *Neged*, tranſlated *over-againſt*, ſignifies here ſuitable, or proportionable; in which Senſe it is uſed Chap. xli. 16. and *Gen.* ii. 18. *I will make him an Help*, *Kenegdho*, *ſuitable to him*: So an equivalent Expreſſion, *Nal Penehem*, *before them*, is uſed in deſcribing the Houſe which *Solomon* built, 1 *Kings* vii. 6. where our Margin expreſſes the Senſe very properly, *The Porch was according to them*; i. e. anſwerable to them, or of the ſame Proportion with them. See the Note upon Chap. xli. 4. So the *Greek* Propoſition Καθέναντι may moſt properly be underſtood, Rom. iv. 17. Καθέναντι ὃ ἐπίς-δυσε Θεῦ, not *before*, but *like unto him whom he believed*, even *God*; to this Senſe: That *Abraham* is a Father of many Nations, in like manner as the God in whom he believed, is the Father of *Gentiles* as well as *Jews*; as it is ſaid in the foregoing Chapter, ver. 29.

Ver. 24, 25, 26. *After that he brought me to-ward the South*, &c.] The 23d Verſe is to be read in a *Parentheſis*, where the Prophet having ſhewed the exact Correſpondence between the Gates of both Courts, he proceeds in the three following Verſes to deſcribe the South Gate of the outer Court, by the ſame Dimenſions he had before given of the Eaſt and North Gate. He takes no Notice of the Weſtern Gate of the outer Court, becauſe it joined to the Eaſtern Gate of the inner Court, which he deſcribes ver. 32.

Ver. 24,
25, 26.

A a a 2

Ver.

Chapter
XL.

Ver. 27. *And there was a Gate in the inner Court toward the South.*] The South Gate in the inner Court was exactly parallel to the South Gate in the outer. See ver. 23.

Ibid. *And he measured from Gate to Gate an hundred Cubits.*] See ver. 19, 23, 47.

V. 27, 28.

Ver. 27, 28. *And there was a Gate in the inner Court toward the South. ----- And he brought me to the inner Court by the South Gate.*] *Villalpandus*, and those of his Opinion, who maintain that the outer Court inclosed the inner on the East, North and South Sides, explain these Words to this Sense; That the Prophet was conducted from the South Gate of the outer Court, ver. 24. to the South Gate of the inner Court; which was over-against it, and so into the inner Court itself.

V. 28, 29.

Ver. 28, 29. *And he brought me to the inner Court toward the South,* &c.] After he had measured the inner Court, he took the Dimensions of the South Gate itself, and the Chambers thereto belonging, and found them of the same Dimensions with the former.

Ver. 30.

Ver. 30. *And the Arches round about were five and twenty Cubits long, and five Cubits broad.*] Length is here taken for Height, as before, ver. 11. The Words express the Dimensions of those Arches, which were between the several little Chambers, between each of which there was the Space of five Cubits, ver. 7.

Ver. 31.

Ver. 31. *And the Arches thereof were toward the outer Court.*] or *were like* [those of] *the outer Court*; for the Preposition *El* is sometimes taken in this Sense, see *Noldius*, p. 63. If we understand it according to the common Interpretation, that
the

the Arches or Fronts (fee the Note on ver. 16.)
of the inner Court looked toward the outer, it is
a Confirmation of *Villalpandus's* Opinion, that the
outer Court furrounded the inner. See the Note
upon ver. 19.

Ibid. *And the going up to it had eight Steps.*]
Whereas in the outer Court the Afcent had but
feven; ver. 22, 26. The fifteen *Pfalms* from the
cxx*th* forward, called *Songs of Degrees*, or Afcents,
are fuppofed to have been fung upon fome of thefe
Steps, or Afcents.

Ver. 32 to 37. *And he brought me into the inner* Ver. 32.
Court toward the Eaft, &c. ------ *And he brought*
me to the North Gate, &c.] The Eaft and North
Gate had the fame Dimenfions with the South
Gate, defcribed ver. 28, 29, 31.

Ver. 34. *And the Arches thereof.*] What is ex- Ver. 34.
preffed here by *Arches*, is fignified by *Pofts*, or
Fronts, ver. 37. See the Notes upon ver. 10, and 16.

Ver. 38. *And the Chambers and the Entries* Ver. 38.
thereof were by the Pofts of the Gates, when they
wafhed the Burnt-Offering.] The Chambers mentioned ver. 36. were near the Entrance of the North
Gate, where they wafhed the Legs and Entrails of
the Burnt-Offering, and marble Tables were placed there for that Purpofe; fee Dr. *Lightfoot of*
the Temple, Chap. 35. According to this Expofi-
tion the Word *Gates* ftands for the fingular Number, as ver. 18. But that learned Author obferves
in the fame Chapter, that they wafhed the Sacrifices on the South Side of the Court of the Priefts,
as well as on the North Side, when the Sacrifices
were more numerous than the North Side could
well contain; fo he underftands the Word Gates

as

Chapter as comprehending both North and South Gate;
XL.   and confirms this Interpretation from the placing
       of the Lavers, which were defigned for that Ufe,
       and were fet five on the right Side of the Houfe,
       and five on the left, 1 *Kings* vii. 39.

V. 39, 40.   Ver. 39, 40. *In the Porch of the Gate were*
two Tables on this fide, and two Tables on that
fide, &c.]   Thofe Expofitors, who be the word
Gates in the foregoing Verfe underftand both the
North and South Gates, render the fenfe of thefe
two Verfes perfpicuoufly thus: *In the Porch of*
one *Gate,* (viz. that on the South) *were two Ta-*
bles on this fide, and two Tables on that fide, &c.
And at the outer fide of the Step of the entry of
the North Gate were two Tables; which Interpretation agrees very well with what follows,
Ver. 41. *Four Tables were on this fide, and four*
Tables on that fide.   But they that underftand
thefe Verfes to be only a Defcription of the North
Gate, (on which fide of the Altar the Sacrifices
were commonly killed) fuppofe that two Tables
were on each fide, as you came into the Porch of
that Gate, and two on each fide of the inner part
of the Gate that looked toward the Altar.

Ver. 39.   Ver. 39. *The fin Offering, and the Trefpafs-*
Offering.]   It is no eafy matter to afcertain the
Difference between a Sin-offering and a Trefpafs-
offering.   Dr. *Outram l. de Sacrificiis,* is of Opinion that a Trefpafs-offering implied an Injury
done to another, as well a Breach of God's Law.
Dr. *Lightfoot* hath accurately related the Senfe
of the *Jewifh* Writers upon this Subject, in his
Temple Service, Chap. viii. fect. 2, 3.

                                    Ver.

Ver. 43. *Within were Hooks an Hand broad* Chapter
faftened round about.] Within the Gate or En- XL.
trance on the North fide of the Inner Court, were
Iron Hooks for the hanging up the Beafts that Ver. 43.
were to be facrificed, in order to the flaying off
their Skins. See Dr. *Lightfoot's Defcription of
the Temple,* Chap. xxxv.

Ibid. *And upon the Tables was the Flefh of
the Offering.*] or, they laid *the Flefh of the Offering.* Upon thofe Marble Tables the Priefts
laid the Flefh of the flain Beafts, and there cut
it in Pieces, and fitted it for laying upon the Altar. See *Levit.* i. 6.

Ver. 44. *And without the inner Gate were the* Ver. 44.
Chambers of the Singers in the inner Court.] On
the further Side of the inner Gate, as you come
into the inner Court, (comp. Ver. 40.) were the
Chambers of the Singers, who conftantly attended upon the Service of the Temple. See 1 *Chron.*
vi. 31, 32.

Ibid. *Which was on the fide of the North-gate,
and their profpect was toward the South.*] Thefe
Chambers were placed at the North Eaft Corner
of the inner Court, and fo had their Profpect toward the South.

Ibid. *One at the fide of the Eaft Gate, having
the Profpect toward the South.*] They had likewife Chambers on the South Eaft Corner of that
Court which had their Profpect toward the
North.

The Copies which the *Septuagint* followed,
read this Verfe to a clearer and better Senfe
thus: *And he brought me into the Inner Court,
and behold, there were two Chambers; one on*
                                                    the

the side of the North Gate, looking toward the South; and the other on the side of the South Gate, looking toward the North.

Ver. 45.

Ver. 45. *This Chamber whose Prospect is toward the South, is for the Priests, &c.*] The word *Chamber* may stand for Chambers in the Plural, (as *Side-Chamber* doth, Chap. xli. 5, 9.) and signify a Row of Buildings on the North side of the inner Court, distinct from the Chambers of the Singers, Ver. 44. and designed for the use the Priests who were in constant Attendance, according to their Courses, upon the Service of the Temple. See *Numb.* xviii. 5. 1 *Chron.* vi. 49. 2 *Chron.* xiii. 11.

Ibid. *The Keepers of the Charge of the House.*] They took care of the holy Vessels, and kept constant Watch and Ward (as the word *Mishmereth* properly signifies) about the Temple. See 1 *Chron.* ix. 23. *Ps.* cxxxiv. 1. The word Priests may include *Levites* under it, as *Levites* elsewhere comprehends Priests. See Chap. xliv. 10. xlviii. 11.

Ver. 46.

Ver. 46. *And the Chamber whose Prospect is toward the North, is for the Priests and Keepers of the Charge of the Altar.*] Another Row of Chambers on the South side of the inner Court is for the descendants of the Family of *Aaron,* whose Office it is to attend upon the Service of the Altar, and keep the Fire burning thereon perpetually, *Levit.* vi. 12, 13.

Ibid. *These are the Sons of Zadok among the Sons of Levi.*] To the eldest House of the Sons of *Aaron* the High Priesthood belonged; so that Office of right belonged to *Zadok,* though the
Family

mily of *Ithamar* ufurped it for fome time, from
Eli who was High Prieft in *Samuel's* time, to
Abiathar, whom *Solomon* difpoffeffed and reftored
the High Priefthood to the right Line, by pla-
cing *Zadok* in his room, 1 *Kings* ii. 27, 35. The
Family of *Zadok* is only taken notice of in this
Vifion, it may be for this reafon, becaufe they
kept clofe to the Worfhip of God ; when the
Priefts of *Ithamar's* Line forfook it, and fell into
Idolatry. See Chap. xliv. 15. And the eldeft
Son of *Zadok's* Family having an unqueftionable
Title to the High Priefthood, See *Numb.* xxv. 13.
upon that Account was an eminent Type of the
Meffias the Eternal High Prieft. See *Numb.* xxxv.
25, 28.

Ver. 47. *And he meafured the Court an hun-*
dred Cubits long, and an hundred Cubits broad,
four fquare.] The inner Court was of the fame
Dimenfions with the outer : See Ver. 19, 23,
27.

Ibid. *And the Altar* that was *before the Houfe.*]
Or, rather, *and the Altar* was *before the Houfe ;*
i. e. ftood in the inner Court juft before the Porch
that opened into the Temple. The Altar was
now meafured, the Meafure of it being defcribed
afterwards, Chap. xliii. 13, *&c.*

Ver. 48. *And meafured each Poft of the Porch,*
five Cubits on this fide, and five Cubits on that
fide.] By the Pofts are meant the fide Pofts or
Columns on each fide of the Door or Entrance,
fee Ver. 9. thefe were meafured to be five Cubits
thick both on the North and South fides.

Ibid. *And the breadth of the Gate was three*
Cubits on this fide, and three Cubits on that fide.]

B b b   By

Chapter
XL.

By the Breadth of the Gate *Villalpandus* understands the space of the Wall on each side, from
the Entrance it self to the two Corners; com. Ch.
xli. 3. which supposing with the Text here to take
up six Cubits, and the Entrance of the Porch to
be 14 Cubits, both those Dimensions make up the
length of the Porch to be twenty Cubits from
North to South, according to the Measure set down
in the following Verse. This Interpretation is
countenanced by the *Septuagint*, who translate
the latter Part of the Verse thus: *And the breadth
of the Gate fourteen Cubits, and the sides of the
Gate of the Porch, three Cubits on this side, and
three Cubits on that side.*

Ver. 49.

Ver. 49. *The length of the Porch was twenty
Cubits.*] The same Length with the Porch of
Solomon's Temple, 1 *Kings* vi. 3. which being
there said to be of the same Measure with the
Breadth of the House, must be understood of its
Dimensions from North to South.

Ibid. *And the breadth eleven Cubits.*] The
Porch in *Solomon's* Temple was but *Ten* Cubits in
Breadth, 1 *Kings* vi. 3. the Length of such Buildings being commonly double to the Breadth:
See Ver. 13, 15, 21, 25, 33 and 36th of this Chap.
and Chap. xli. 2. Some Copies of the lxx read *Ten
Cubits*; and *L'Amy* conjectures that was the Ancient Reading in the *Hebrew*. St. *Jerom* upon
the Place suspects there might be a Mistake in the
Hebrew Copy, tho' the Emendation he offers doth
not at all render the Sense clearer.

Villalpandus supposes the Breadth of the Porch
to be Ten Cubits and an half, (see the Note on
Ver.

Ver. 11.) which putting an entire Number in the room of a Fraction, may be accounted Eleven.

Chapter XL.

Ibid. And he brought me *by the Steps whereby they went up to it.*] The Ascent was by eight Steps according to the *Vulgar Latin*; the same Number which belong'd to the several Entrances into the inner Court; see ver. 31, 34, 37. The Copies of the lxx read *Ten Steps.*

Ibid. And there were Pillars by the Posts.] By the side Posts of the Door or Entrance, see Ver. 48. like those erected in *Solomon's* Temple called *Jachin* and *Boaz*, 1 *Kings* vii. 21. which were set up *before the Temple*, as it is expressed 2 *Chron.* iii. 17.

CHAP. XLI.

The ARGUMENT.

This Chapter contains a Description of the Measures, Parts, Chambers, and Ornaments of the Temple it self.

Ver. 1.   Ver. 1.

Fterwards he brought me to the Temple, and measured the Posts six Cubits broad on one side, and six Cubits broad on the other side, which was the breadth of the Tabernacle.] By the Posts are meant the Peers or Door-Cases on each side of the Entrance, see Chap. xl. 9, 48. These were six Cubits thick on the North and South sides. *Rochob* translated *Breadth*, sometimes signifies Thickness; see Ver. 9. and 12, of this Chapter, and Chapter xl. 5. the same Thickness had the upper Lintel over the Door; for so *Villalpandus* rightly explains the *Hebrew* word *Ohel*, which we render Tabernacle. That word sometimes signifies a *Covering*, and so it is render'd by our Translators, *Exod.* xxvi. 7. and is to be understood in
the

the fame Senfe, *Exod.* xxxvi. 14. where our
Englifh reads, *For a Tent over the Tabernacle,*
but it fhould be tranflated, *For a Covering over
the Tabernacle;* to which fenfe the lxx tranflate
it in both Places. In this Signification it may
not be unfitly applied to the upper Lintel, which
is a kind of Covering to the Door, and thus it is
generally underftood by the *Rabbins* upon this
Place.

Chapter
XLI.

Ver. 2. *And the breadth of the Door was ten
Cubits. and the fides of the Door were five Cubits on this fide, and five Cubits on the other
fide.*] The Entrance itfelf being ten Cubits
broad, and the Wall on each fide five Cubits,
makes the Breadth of the Houfe it felf to be juft
twenty Cubits, as it is expreffed in the latter part
of the Verfe, which was the fame in *Solomons*'s
Temple, 1 *Kings* vi. 2.

Ver. 2.

Ibid. *And he meafured the length thereof forty
Cubits.*] The Length of the firft Sanctuary, as
diftinct from the inward, or the Holieft of all,
which was twenty Cubits in Length, Ver. 4. and
made the whole Structure fixty Cubits long:
wherein it agreed with *Solomon*'s Temple, 1 *Kings*
vi. 2, 17.

Ver. 3. *Then he went inward, and meafured
the Poft of the door two Cubits,* &c.] From the
outward Sanctuary he went forward toward the
Holieft of all, and meafured the Thicknefs of the
Partition Wall, called the *Vail of the Temple,*
Matth. xxvii. 51. to be two Cubits, the Entrance
itfelf to be fix Cubits, and the Breadth of the
Wall on each fide the Door to be feven Cubits;
comp. Chap. xl. 48. where the *Breadth of the*
Gate

Ver. 3.

Gate is taken in the same Sense; the Breadth of the Wall thus computed making up fourteen Cubits, and being added to the Breadth of the Entrance it self, makes up twenty Cubits, the Breadth of the inner Sanctuary, as it is set down in the following Verse.

Ver. 4.

Ver. 4. *So he measured the length thereof twenty Cubits, and the breadth twenty Cubits.*] It was an exact Cube of the same Dimensions in Length, Breadth and Height: See 1 *Kings* vi. 20.

Ibid. *Before the Temple.*] The words should rather be render'd, *according to the* [Breadth of] *the Temple.* The *Hebrew* word, *El-pené*, before, is promiscuously used with *Nal-pené*, which signifies *of the same size*, or Proportion, see the Note on Chap. xl. 23. and so it is used 2 *Chron.* iii. 8. where the Text speaking of this Subject runs thus in the *Hebrew, He made the most holy House, the length thereof before the face of the Breadth of the House*; where our Translation very properly expresses the same Sense, *According to the Breadth of the House.* In the same Sense the Phrase is used, 1 *Kings* vi. 3. so the Sense here is, that the Breadth of the inner Sanctuary was equal to the Breadth of the outer part of the Temple, which is said to be twenty Cubits, ver. 2.

Ver. 5. *After he measured the Wall of the House six Cubits.*] The Thickness of the Wall from the Foundation the first Story of the Side Chambers; See ver. 8.

Ver. 5.

Ibid. *And the breadth of every Side Chamber four Cubits.*] The Side Chambers upon the lowermost Floor were four Cubits in Breadth, 1 *Kings* vi. 6. Therefore *Villalpandus* understands these Words

Words of the Thickness of the Buttresses which supported those Side Chambers.

Ver. 6. *And the Side Chambers were three, one*
over another.] They were three Stories high; see
1 *Kings* vi. 6.

Ibid. *And thirty in order.*] As in *Solomon*'s Temple, according to *Josephus*'s Description of it, *Antiq. lib.* 8. *C.* 3. *Sect.* 2. and built *round about the
House on every Side*; as it is expressed in the foregoing Verse; to which the Text in the first Book
of *Kings* agrees, Chap. vi. 5. The *Talmudists* increase the Number to eight and thirty, placing fifteen on the North Side, fifteen on the South, and
eight on the West Side of the Temple, see *Cod.
Middoth. C.* 4. The supernumerary Chambers being probably added in latter Times.

Ibid. *And they entred into the Wall which was
for the Side Chambers round about.*] At five Cubits Height from the Ground, the Wall or the
Buttresses which supported these outward Chambers (see ver. 5.) abated of their Thickness one Cubit, and there was a Rest or a Ledge of one Cubits
Breadth, on which the Ends of each Story were
fastened. See 1 *Kings* vi. 6, 10.

Ibid. *But they had not hold in the Wall of the
House.*] They were not fastened into the main
Wall of the House, but rested on the outside of
the Wall were it grew narrower; which is meant
by *Migrehoth*, the *narrowest Rests*, or Rebatements,
which we read 1 *Kings* vi. 6.

Ver. 7. *For there was an enlarging and a wind-*
ing about still upward to the Side Chambers, &c.]
So much of Breadth was added to the Side Chambers, as was taken out of the Thickness of the
Wall;

Wall; fo that the middle Story was one Cubit
larger, and the uppermoft Story two Cubits larger than the lower Rooms. And winding Stairs
which enlarged as the Rooms did, went up between each two Chambers from the Bottom to
the Top; and there were two Doors at the Top
of each Pair of Stairs, one Door opening into one
Room, the other into that overagainft it. See 1
Kings vi. 8. The *Talmudiſts* add, that thefe Winding Stairs were continued from one Side of the
Temple to the other, beginning at the North Eaft
Side, and by thefe they went into the upper Room
which was over the Sanctuary. See *Cod. Middoth.
Cap.* 4 *Sect.* 5.

Ver. 8.   Ver. 8. *I faw alfo the Height of the Houſe round
about.*] By the Houfe is meant thefe Chambers
three Stories high; in which Senfe the Word *Beth,
Houſe,* is ufed ver. 9.

Ibid. *The Foundations of the Side Chambers were
a full Reed of ſix great Cubits.*] By the *Foundations of the Side Chambers, Villalpandus* underftands
thofe Refts or Buttreffes which fupported them,
which were at ſix Cubits Diftance from each other.
Bernard L'Amy fuppofes this Verfe to contain a
Defcription of the fecond Story of thefe Side Chambers, which were ſix Cubits broad, being one Cubit wider than the lower Rooms; fee the Note
on ver. 7. Concerning the Size of thefe Cubits, fee
the Note upon Chap. XL. 5. They are called *great
Cubits,* becaufe they are larger than the Cubit ufed
in *Chaldea,* as was there obferved.

Ver. 9.   Ver. 9 *The Thickneſs of the Wall that was for
the Side Chamber without, was five Cubits.*] This
is to be underftood, not of the Wall of the Temple,

ple, which was fix Cubits thick, ver. 5. but of
the outward Wall that enclofed thefe fide Chambers. *Side Chamber* in the fingular Number is
ufed for the Plural, as in ver. 5. and Chap. xlii. 1.
So *Door* is ufed for Doors, ver. xvi. 20. *Poft*
for *Pofts*, ver. 21. *Chamber*, Chap. xlii. 1. for
Chambers, ver. 4.

Ibid. *And that which was left,* [or the void
Space] *was the place of the fide Chambers that
were within*] or, *that belonged to the Houfe,* or
Temple. This void Space was of the fame Meafure, *viz.* Five Cubits, comp. ver. 11. So the Senfe
is fupplied by *Villalpandus* and *Noldius,* N. 889.
comp. Chap. xl. 14. The fpace of Five Cubits
was allowed for the lower Chambers, tho' the
upper Stories were wider, by Reafon of the Re-
batement of the Wall: See ver. 7. and 1 *Kings*
vi. 6. Others underftand this fpace of five Cubits to be allowed for a Walk before the Chambers, or a Paffage from one Chamber to another, fee ver. 11.

Ver. 10. *And between the Chambers was the
widenefs of twenty Cubits round about the
Houfe.*] The Chambers called *Lefhacoth* in
the *Hebrew,* are to be diftinguifhed from the
fide Chambers mentioned in the foregoing Verfes; they mean probably the Chambers of the
inner Court defcribed Chap. xl. 44, 45. Between
thefe and the Temple was left a Space of 20 Cubits.
The Temple ftood in an Area of an hundred Cubits fquare, ver. 14. and was feventy Cubits wide,
ver. 12. to which adding the five Cubits on either Side mentioned ver. 9. and the twenty Cu-

C c c   bits

Chapter bits in this Verſe, makes up juſt an hundred
XLI. Cubits.

Ver. 11. Ver. 11. *And the doors of the ſide Chambers were toward the place that was left, &c.*] or, *toward the void Space:* The Doors of the lower Rooms opened into this void Space before the Chambers, ver. 9. Or it may be underſtood of the two Doors on the North and South ſide, which opened on the top of the Stair-caſe into the upper Rooms, ſee ver. 7.

Ibid. *And the breadth of the place that was left was five Cubits round about.*] See ver. 9.

Ver. 12. Ver. 12. *Now the Building that was before the ſeparate Place, at the end toward the Weſt, was ſeventy Cubits broad.*] *Bernard L'amy* ſeems to give the cleareſt Account of this difficult Place, *lib.* 6. c. 11. n. 2. He underſtands this word *Binian* tranſlated *Building,* of a Wall or Incloſure, as it is uſed Chap. xl. 5. which ran along the outſide of the Prieſt's Court, commenſurate with the Breadth of the Weſtern ſide of the Temple, which was ſeventy Cubits from North to South; and extended in Length from Eaſt to Weſt ninety Cubits; ten Cubits ſhorter than the whole Area itſelf, (ſee the following Verſe) and incloſing a void Space of five Cubits Breadth, which lay between the ſide Chambers and the Incloſure; ſo he explains thoſe Words, *the Wall of the Building was five Cubits thick round about;* comp. Chap. xlii. 10. which void Space he underſtands by *the ſeparate place* in this Verſe, and *the place which was left,* ver. 11.

Ibid. *Seventy Cubits broad.*] This was the Breadth of the Temple at the Weſt End, and

the

the Buildings adjoining to it, which the above-mention'd Author thus computes: The Breadth of the Oracle twenty Cubits, the thickness of the side Walls, six Cubits on each side; the side Chambers six Cubits on each side, (see the Note upon Verse 8.) Thickness of the out-Walls of those Chambers five Cubits on each side; a Walk or Gallery of five Cubits before those Chambers, (see the Note on Verse 9.) and the utmost Wall enclosing the whole Building, five Cubits. Those that differ from him as to some of those particulars, make up the Sum of seventy Cubits, by making an Allowance for the Stairs, and for Conveyances to carry off the Water.

Ver. 13. *So he measured the House an hundred Cubits long, and the separate place, &c.*] The whole Temple, with the Porch and Walls, was in Length an hundred Cubits from East to West, which may be thus computed: The Thickness of the Wall of the East Porch five Cubits; the Passage thro' the Porch, eleven Cubits; the Wall between the Porch and the Temple, six Cubits; the outward Sanctuary, forty Cubits; the Partition Wall two Cubits; the Holiest of all, twenty Cubits; the Thickness of the West Wall, six Cubits; the side Chambers at the West End of the Holy Place, five Cubits, and outer Wall of those Chambers, five Cubits.

Ver. 14. *Also the breadth of the face of the House, and of the separate place toward the East, an hundred Cubits.*] The whole Front of the House Eastward was an hundred Cubits, which some Expositors thus compute: The Breadth of the Temple, twenty Cubits; the Thickness of

the

Chapter
XLI.
~~~

the outward Walls, twelve Cubits; the side
Chambers, eight Cubits; (of these Dimensions
they explain the latter Part of the 5th Verse of
this Chapter) the Walls of those Chambers, five
Cubits on each side; the Breadth of the void
space, five Cubits on each side, and the twenty
Cubits round about the House, ver. 10. Others
compute the Sum a different way, by making
different Allowances for the outward Buildings,
and the several Passages from one part of the
Temple to the other.

Ver. 15.

Ver. 15. *And he measured the length of the
Building over against the separate Place, which
was behind it.*] *Noldius* translates this Sentence
more clearly, thus: *And he measured the length
of the Building which was before the separate
place,* [and] *that which was behind it,* or opposite to it; by which he understands the North
and South Porch; the East and West sides having been measured before, ver. 12, 14. see his
Concordance, p. 104. The Phrase *El pené,* translated here *Over-against,* is rendered *Before,* in
our *English* Version, Chap. xliv. 4.

Ibid. *And the galleries thereof on one side, and
on the other side, an hundred Cubits; with* [or
and] *the inner Temple, and the porches thereof.*]
As the Temple, and the Area wherein it stood,
made a Square of an hundred Cubits; so the
Courts and Buildings thereto belonging, were of
the same Dimensions; see Chap. xl. 19, 47.

By the *Galleries* are meant the side Chambers described Verse 6, 7. Compare the following Verse.

Ibid.

Ibid. *With the inner Temple.*] Called the inner House, ver. 17. and Chap. xlii. 15. to diſtinguiſh it from the Courts and Buildings which were about it.

Ver. 16. *The door poſts, and the narrow Windows, and the galleries round about in their three ſtories.*] He meaſured likewiſe the thickneſs of the Walls on each ſide of the Porch; ſee Chap. xl. 48. and the thickneſs of the Door-caſes, at the Entrance into the Temple, Chap. xli. 1. as alſo, the narrow Windows belonging to the three Stories of Chambers, which were placed on the outſide of the Temple: See Ver. 6. and Chap. xl. 16.

Ibid. *Over-againſt the Door cieled with Wood round about.*] Or, *Anſwerable* to which was *the Door cieled with Wood.* The Doors of the little Chambers exactly anſwered one another, as thoſe belonging to the Porch did, Chap. xl. 13. The word *Neged, Over-againſt,* ſignifies likewiſe, *Anſwerable* or Proportionable: See the Note on Chap. xl. 23.

Door ſignifies every Door, ſee the Note upon Verſe 9.

Ibid. *And from the Ground up to the Windows.*] He meaſured from the Ground up to the Windows of the Temple, which were placed above the ſide Chambers.

Ibid. *And the Windows were covered.*] Either becauſe the ſide Chambers jetting out beyond the main Wall of the Temple, hindred their being ſeen in the inner Court: or elſe they were cover'd on the inſide with Curtains drawn before them.

Ver.

Chapter
XLI.

Ver. 17.

Ver. 17. *To that above the door, even to the inner house, and without, &c.*] This Verse may best be explained by joining it to what went before, to this Sense: That the Windows were made in exact Proportion, both over the Porch and through every Part of the Temple, and the Buildings adjoining to it. The *inner House* may mean only the first or outward Sanctuary in this Verse, as it is distinguished from the Porch and outer Buildings, expressed by the word *without;* comp. ver. 15. For it is generally supposed that there were no Windows in the inner Sanctuary. But *Villalpandus* explains the words, *Even unto the inner House*, in an exclusive Sense, as if he had said, As far as the inner House; and by the *Walls round about*, understands the North and South Walls of the Temple. *Part.* 2. l. 4. c. 34.

Ver. 18.

Ver. 18. *And it was made with Cherubims and with Palm-trees, &c.*] On the inside of the House, the Walls were adorned with carved work of Cherubims and Palm-trees, as *Solomon's* Temple was, 1 *Kings* vi. 29. The Cherubims and Palm-trees were placed alternately, and according to the different way of counting them, you might reckon a Palm-tree placed between two Cherubims, or a Cherubim placed between two Palm-trees.

Ver. 19.

Ibid. Ver. 19. *And every Cherub had two faces; so that the face of a Man was toward the Palm-tree on the one side; and the face of a young Lion toward the Palm-tree on the other side.*] The Cherubims had four Faces or Appearances: See Chap. 1. 10. but only two of these appeared

-appeared in the carved Work; the two other Chapter
Faces, *viz.* that of an Ox and an Eagle being XLI.
fuppofed to be hid in the Plain or Surface of the
Wall.

Ver. 20. *From the Ground up to above the* Ver. 20.
Door.] Up to the Windows, as it is expreffed
ver. 16. up to the Cieling, as the *Septuagint* explain it.

Ver. 21. *The pofts of the Temple were fquared,* Ver. 21.
and the face of the Sanctuary.] i. e. The Entrance into the inner Sanctuary, comp. Chap. xl.
15. The Lintels or Door-poft both of the Temple and inner Sanctuary were not Arched but
fquare, with a flat Beam or upper Lintel, laid upon the top of the fide Pofts, comp. 1 *Kings* vi. 33.
where the Margin tranflates the word *Rebingim*,
Four-fquare.

Ver. 22. *The Altar of Wood was three Cubits* Ver. 22.
high, and the length thereof two Cubits.] The
Septuagint add by way of Explication, *And the*
breadth thereof two Cubits; that it might be Four-
fquare, as *Mofes*'s Altar of Incenfe was, *Exod.*
xxx. 2. The Altar here defcribed is a Cubit higher,
and double the Breadth to that of *Mofes*, which
is fuppofed to be agreeable to the Dimenfions of
the Altar made by *Solomon*, who did not exactly
obferve the Proportions prefcribed to *Mofes*, in
making the Cherubims and the other Furniture of
the Temple: God having given a new Model to
David of all the Parts and Ornaments of the
Temple. See 1 *Chron.* xxviii. 12, 19. This Altar was made of Wood, but overlaid with Gold,
Exod. xxx. 3. and therefore is called the *Golden*
Altar, 1 *Kings* vii. 48. *Revel.* viii. 3.

Ibid.

Ibid. *And the Corners thereof, the length thereof, and the Walls thereof* were *of Wood.*] The
Corners are the same with the *Horns* mentioned
Exod. xxx. 2. being made out of the four Posts
which supported each Corner of the Altar. The
Surface or Top of it is called the *Length*, and
the sides the *Walls.*

Ibid. *This is the Table that is before the
LORD.*] Comp. Chap. xliv. 16. The words
Altar and Table are used promiscuously, as hath
been observed upon Chap. xxiii. 41. Incense was
an Emblem of the Prayers of Saints; see *Psal.*
cxli. 2. *Revel.* viii. 3, 4. which are the Spiritual Sacrifices of those that worship God *in Spirit and in Truth*; see *Hos.* xiv. 2. This Table
or Altar is said to be before the LORD, *i. e.* in
the Place of his peculiar Presence, comp. *Exod.*
xxx. 8. In the same Sense the Burnt-offering is
said to be made *at the Door of the Tabernacle
of the Congregation, before the LORD, i. e.* in
the Place dedicated to his Worship, *Exod.* xxix.
42. and the Lamp is said to *burn before the
LORD*, Chap. xxvii. 21. tho' the Candlestick
stood in the outward Sanctuary.

Ver. 23. *And the Temple and the Sanctuary
had two doors.*] Each of them had a double, or
a folding Door, see 1 *Kings* vi. 31, 34.

Ver. 24. *And the doors had two leaves* apiece.]
The two Doors being exceeding large, that of
the outward Sanctuary Ten Cubits broad, and that
of the inner, six; see ver. 2, 3. and of an Height
proportionable; each of them had two Leaves;
that they might be more easily opened, and each
Leaf

Leaf had a Wicket in it. Compared 1 *Kings*
vi. 34.

Ver. 25. *And* there were *made on them, on
the doors of the Temple, Cherubims and Palm-
trees.*] On the Doors both of the outward and
inward Sanctuary; comp. 1 *Kings* vi. 32, 34.

Ibid. *And* there were *thick planks upon the
face of the porch without.*] There was a Wain-
scot work of Boards faftened to the End of the
great Beams, which came out beyond the Wall
of the Porch: Thefe were laid fo, as to make a
Frize-work over the Entrance into the Eaftern
Porch.

Ver. 26. *And there were narrow windows and*
*Palm-trees on the fides of the Porch, and upon
the fide Chambers of the Houfe.*] Comp.
Chap. xl. 16. Ver. 26.

Ibid. *And thick Plancks.*] The Senfe would
be plainer, if we tranflate it, *And* [upon] *the
thick Planks*; i. e. the Figures of Palm-trees
were carved upon that Wainfcot, which was defcribed in the foregoing Verfe.

CHAP.

CHAP. XLII.

The ARGUMENT.

A Defcription of the Priefts Chambers, and their ufe, and the Dimenfions of the Holy Mountain whereon the Temple ftood.

Ver. 1.   Ver. 1.  *HEN he brought me forth into the outer Court, the way toward the North,* &c.] The Angel now brings the Prophet out of the inner Court by the North Gate, into fome Chamber or Building, which looked toward the South fide of the Temple, and faced the Wall or Inclofure that encompaffed the North fide of the inner Court and Temple, mentioned Chap. xli. 12, 15. Some

fupſuppoſe this to be a Building diſtinct from all the Parts of Temple hitherto deſcribed.

The words of the 7th and 9th Verſes imply, that it was a diſtinct Building from the outer Court.

Ibid. *Into the Chamber that was over-againſt the ſeperate place, and before the building.*] Or, before the ſeparate Place, and before the Building: For the Prepoſition *Neged* is uſed in both Parts of the Sentence. *Chamber* is put for Chambers, ſee ver. 4. and Chap. xli. 9.

Ver. 2. *Before the length of an hundred Cubits* was the *North door, and the breadth was fifty Cubits.*] This North Door faced one of the Cloyſters, whoſe Length was an hundred Cubits, and its Breadth fifty; which was the Proportion of all the Cloyſters; ſee the Note upon Chap. xl. 15. *Noldius* tranſlates the Words to this Senſe, *Unto the place whoſe Length was an hundred Cubits towards the North door.* He ſuppoſes theſe Buildings to be diſtinct from any hitherto deſcribed, and adds, that the *Jews* profeſs their Ignorance, how they were ſituate; becauſe there was nothing in the ſecond Temple that anſwered to them: See his *Concordance*, No. 390.

Ver. 3. *Over-againſt the twenty* Cubits, *which were for,* [or which belonged to] *the inner Court, and over-againſt the Pavement which* was *for* [or belonged to] *the outer Court.*] One ſide of theſe Buildings look'd upon the void Space about the Temple, which contained twenty Cubits, mentioned Chap. xli. 10. and the other ſide was toward the Pavement belonging to the outer Court, deſcribed Chap. xl. 17.

Ibid.

Chapter
XLII.

Ibid. *Was gallery against gallery in three sto-ries.*] Like those mentioned Chap. xli. 16.

Ver. 4.

Ver. 4. *And before the Chambers* was *a walk of ten Cubits inward.*] There was a Walk or Cloyster of ten Cubits Breadth, running along the inside of the Wall, which divided the Buildings into two Rooms, one half of which looked into the outer Court, the other into the Inner, see Chap. xlvi. 19.

Ibid. *A way of one Cubit.*] This some understand of an Entrance at each End of the Cloyster.

Ibid. *And their Doors toward the North.*] See ver. 1, 2.

Ver. 5.

Ver. 5. *Now the upper Chambers were shorter, for the Galleries were higher than those, than the lower, &c.*] The Marginal Reading in the *Hebrew* is to be preferred, the Sense of which is, *For the Galleries did abate of these,* i. e. of the lower and middlemost Parts of the Building; the Reason of which is assign'd in the next Verse.

Ver. 6. *For they* were *in three* Stories, *but had not Pillars, as the Pillars of the Courts,* &c.] The two upper Stories had Balconies standing out of them, the Breadth of which was taken out of the Rooms themselves, and made them so much the Narrower, because the weight of the Balconies was not supported by Pillars, as the Rooms over the Cloysters of the outward Court were, but only by the Wall. This is *L'Amy's* Exposition of the Words.

Ver. 7. *And the Wall that was without-----toward the outer Court, on the forepart of the*
Chambers,

Chambers, the length thereof was fifty Cubits.] The Wall that enclosed these Buildings, was commensurate with the Breadth of one of the Cloysters of the outer Court, which were fifty Cubits Broad? See ver. 2.

Ver. 8. *For the length of the Chambers that* *were in the outer Court was fifty Cubits.*] The Chambers that were built over the Cloysters were in Length fifty Cubits. What is called *Length* here, is expressed by *Breadth*, ver. 2. as that is opposed to the Length of the outer Court, which was an hundred Cubits: See the following Words.

Ibid. *And lo before the Temple were an hundred Cubits.*] The words imply that the Angel conducted the Prophet from these North Chambers, to those on the South side: Ver. 11, 13. so that crossing over that space of Ground, that fronted the East side of the Temple, they took Notice of its Dimensions, which they had before measured and found to be an hundred Cubits; See Chap. xli. 14. The lxx with a small Alteration of the *Hebrew* Text, and reading probably *Hennah* for *Hinneh*, and *Haelle col* for *Häecal* translate the Sentence thus: *The one side was opposite to, or answered the other, and in all were an hundred Cubits;* meaning that the Chambers on the North and South side, contained each of them fifty Cubits.

Ver. 9. *And from under these Chambers was* *the entry on the East side, &c.*] The Entry into these South Chambers was by a pair of Stairs at the East Corner of the outer Court. Compare this Verse with Chap. xlvi. 19. and with the

De-

Chapter
XLII.
Chap. xii.

Description Dr. *Lightfoot* gives of the Stairs that went up into the Chamber about the Temple, Chap. xii. tho' his Description belongs to the Temple as it was in our Saviour's Time.

Ver. 10.

Ver. 10. *The Chambers were in the thickness of the wall of the Court toward the East.*] Or rather, *In the breadth of the Wall.*—— i. e. in the Breadth of Ground which that Wall enclosed; so those words Chap. xli. 12. *The wall of building was five Cubits thick round about,* are explained by some of a Space of Ground five Cubits broad enclosed by that Wall. See the Note there.

Ibid. *Over-against the separate place, and over-against the building.*] Or, *Before the separate place, and before the building:* See ver. 1, 13. The Expressions denote, that these South Chambers had the same Situation, with respect to the Temple, as the North Chambers had, spoken of ver. 1.

Ver. 11.

Ver. 11. *And the way before them was like the appearance of the Chambers that were toward the North.*] Such a Way led to these Chambers, as is described leading to the Chambers on the North side, ver. 4.

Ibid. *as long as they,* and *as broad as they, and their goings out were both according to their Fashions,* &c.] The Proportions of both were the same; and the Windows, Doors and Passages belonging to these, were exactly Uniform with those on the North side.

Ver. 12.

Ver. 12. *And according to the doors of the Chambers that were toward the South.*] The Sense would be plainer if the words were thus tran-

tranflated, *And fuch were the doors of the Cham-* Chapter
bers toward the South, [as thofe toward the XLII.
North.] In which Senfe the Affix *Ke,* is ufed ◡◠◡
in the foregoing Verfe.

Ibid. [There was] *a door in the head of the
way,* &c.] Like that defcribed ver. 9.

Ver. 13. *The North and South Chambers,* Ver. 13.
&c.] Which were defcribed in the foregoing Part of the Chapter. See Verfe 8, 10,
11, 12.

Ibid. *They be holy Chambers, where the Priefts
that approach unto the LORD, fhall eat the
moft holy things.*] The Shew-bread, the remainder of the Meat-offering, Sin-offering, and Trefpafs-offering, and exprefly called the *moft holy
things, Levit.* vi. 14, 17. xxiv. 9. *Numb.*
xviii. 9. and are diftinguifhed from the holy things,
fuch as are the Peace-offerings, Firft-fruits and
Tithes, *Livit.* xxi. 22. Thefe were to be eaten
within the Precincts of the Temple, by the Direction of the fame Laws.

Ibid. *There they fhall lay up the moft holy
things.*] Thefe Rooms were likewife fet apart
for laying up the remainder of the Sacrifices,
'till they were eaten by the Priefts and their Families: See *Levit.* x. 13. xxii. 13.

Concerning the difference between the Sin-
offering, and the Trefpafs-offering, fee the Note
upon Chap. xl. 39.

Verfe 14. *And when the Priefts enter* Ver. 14.
therein.] Within the inner Court. Chapter
xliv. 17.

Ibid

Chapter
XLII.

Ibid. *They ſhall not go out of the Holy-Place into the outward Court ; but there they ſhall lay their Garments wherein they miniſter.*] They ſhall not go into the Court of the People in their Prieſt-ly Veſtments, but ſhall lay them up in ſome of theſe Chambers: The Prieſtly Garments were on-ly to be uſed in the Time of their Miniſtration, as appears from *Exod.* xxix. 43. and is farther con-firmed from this Verſe, and Chap. xliv. 19. *Jo-ſephus* aſſerts the ſame, *De Bello Jud. lib.* vi. *cap.* 15.

The Chriſtian Church followed the Practice of the *Jewiſh,* in this as well in many other Cu-ſtoms: The Teſtimony of St. *Jerom,* in his Com-mentary upon Chap. xliv. 19. of this Prophecy, plainly proves, That the Clergy of that Age wore a diſtinct Habit from the Laity, at the Time of their performing the publick Offices of Religion : *Religio Divina alterum habitum habet in mini-ſterio, alterum in uſu vitaq; communi.* And that this was the Practice of the earlier Ages of the Church, may be probably concluded from the Te-ſtimony of *Polycrates,* a Writer of the next Age to the Apoſtles, who tells us, That St. *John* wore an Ornament upon his Head, reſembling the *Mi-tre* with a Plate upon it, which was worn by the *Jewiſh* High-Prieſt. See *Euſeb. Hiſt. Eccl. lib.* 5. *cap.* 24. And in the next Age, *Pontius,* the Writer of St. *Cyprian's* Life and Martyrdom, acquaints us, that the Biſhop's Seat in the Church uſed to be covered with *White* (*a*) : and it can hardly be ima-

---

(*a*) *Sedile erat fortuito linteo ſtratum, ut & ſub iſtu Paſſionis Epiſ-copatus honore frueretur.*

gined,

gined, there should be a peculiar Dress for the
Bishop's Seat, and none for the Bishop himself.

Chapter
XLII.

Ibid. *And shall approach to those Things that
are for the People.*] The Words should rather be
thus translated, *And shall come into* the Court *belonging to the People*; the outer Court mentioned at the Beginning of the Verse.

Ver. 15. *Now when he had made an End of
measuring the inner House.*] The inner House denotes the Temple, as it is distinguish'd from the
Courts about it. Comp. Chap. xli. 15.

Ver. 15.

Ibid. *He brought me forth to the Gate whose
Prospect is toward the East.*] The Gate that o-
pened into the first Court; see Chap. xl. 6.

Ver. 16. *He measured the East Side with the
measuring Reed, five hundred Reeds, &c.*] This
and the following Verses contain the Measures of
the Holy Mountain, or *Area*, upon which the
Temple stood, which is described to be an exact
Square, consisting of five hundred Reeds in measure on each Side of it. We may observe, that
the *Heavenly Jerusalem* represented to St. *John*,
Revel. xxi. 16. is likewise described as four-square,
that Figure being an Emblem of Solidity. And
Ezekiel's Vision, as well as St. *John*'s, is designed, in its mystical Sense, to represent the Regu-
larity and Strength of *Christ*'s *Church* and Kingdom. Comp. with this Verse Chap. xl. 47. xli.
13, 14. xlv. 2. xlviii. 20.

Ver. 16.

Capellus is of Opinion, that instead of *five hundred Reeds*, we ought to read *five hundred Cubits:* He supposeth the Word *Ammoth, Cubits*,
wanting in the present Reading of the Text, to
have been rejected as spurious by the Correctors

E e e

of

Chapter
XLII. of the *Hebrew* Copies, by reason of its Affinity with *Meoth, an Hundred;* and the Word *Kanim, Reeds,* substituted in its Place. This Emendation he justifies from the Authority of the *Septuagint,* who read *Cubits* both in the 17*th* and 20*th* Verses: Which Reading St. *Jerom* acknowledges to have been in the *Greek* Copies in his Time; he confirms it likewise from the parallel Text, Chap. xlv. 2. which he thinks according to the Rules of Grammar, should be expounded of Cubits. And he farther argues, that the *Jews* themselves formerly understood this Text of Cubits; because they are generally of Opinion, that the Temple stood in an Area or Square, containing five hundred Cubits on every Side; see Dr. *Lightfoot of the Temple,* Chap. 2. Whereas, according to the present Reading, the whole Compass of the Area will amount to three Miles and an half, according to the same Author's Computation; which is more than half the Circuit of the whole City of *Jerusalem* in its most flourishing Condition. See the *Excepta* out of *Capellus's Triplex Delineatio Templi,* in the First Volume of the *Polyglott Bible.*

Whereas the Angel is said to measure the *East Side* of this Square *round about,* and so of the other three Sides; we need not from hence conclude, that the whole Compass of the Ground was measured four Times over; for the Phrase *round about* often signifies, in this Prophecy, only from Side to Side, or from one End to another; see Chap. xl. 14. xli. 16. The Words therefore only import, that the Angel continued measuring from

one

one Side to the other, 'till he had gone over the whole Compaſs of the Area.

Ver. 20. *It had a Wall round about,* &c.] To defend it from being invaded or prophaned, comp. *Revel.* xxi. 17. Such a ſquare Wall as is here deſcribed, ſeems only capable of a myſtical Senſe and Interpretation. See the Note upon ver. 15.

Ibid. *To make a Separation between the Sanctuary and the prophane Place.*] By the *Sanctuary* is here meant the whole Compaſs of Ground, which was the Precincts of the Temple, elſewhere called the *Holy Mountain.* See Chap. xliii. 12. In compariſon of which, *Jeruſalem* itſelf, though upon ſeveral Accounts ſtiled *The Holy City*, was eſteemed but as prophane Ground. See Chap. xlviii. 15.

E e e 2   CHAP.

CHAP. XLIII.

The ARGUMENT.

The Glory of the LORD *is reprefented as Returning to the Temple, where GOD promifes to fix his Refidence, if the People Repent, and Forfake thofe Sins which made Him depart from them. Then the meafures of the Altar, and the Ordinances relating to it are fet down.*

Ver. 1.   Ver. 1. HEN he brought me to the Gate, even the Gate that looketh toward the Eaft.] The Eaftern Gate of the Priefts Court, which was juft before the Temple. Comp. ver. 4. and Chap. xliv. 1. xlvi. 1.

Ver. 2.   Ver. 2. *And behold the Glory of the GOD of Ifrael came from the Way of the Eaft.*] The Word *Behold* is an Expreffion of Joy and Admiration; as if the Prophet had faid, Behold a wonderful and

and joyful Sight! the Glory of that God, who calls himſelf *the GOD of Iſrael,* as chooſing to dwell among them, and to give evident Tokens of his Preſence among them, and protection over them. This Glory which had departed from this Place for ſo long a Time, now returned to it, and fixed its Reſidence there, The Glory of the LORD, when it forſook the Temple, is deſcribed as departing from the Eaſtern Gate of it, Chap. x. 19. Afterward it is repreſented as quite forſaking the City, and removing to a Mountain on the Eaſt Side of the City, Chap. xi. 23. and now it returns by the ſame Way it departed.

Ibid. *And his Voice was like the Noiſe of many Waters.*] Great and Terrible. Comp. Chap. i. 24. *Revel.* i. 15. either to ſignify the Dreadfulneſs of God's Judgments, or the Efficacy of his Commands, who calls Things into Being by ſpeaking the Word.

Ibid. *And the Earth ſhined with his Glory.*] The Rays of his Glory, like the Sun-Beams, enlightned the Earth. Comp. Chap. x. 4. *Iſa.* vi. 3. *Habak.* iii. 4.

Ver. 3. *And it was according to the Viſion which I ſaw when I came to deſtroy the City.*] See Chap. ix. 3, 5. The Prophets are ſaid to do thoſe Things which they foretell ſhall come to paſs. See the Notes upon Chap. xiii. 19. xxiii. 45. and upon *Jeremy* i. 10.

Ver. 4. *And the Glory of the LORD came into the Houſe by the Way of the Gate, whoſe Proſpect is toward the Eaſt.*] See ver. 1, 2. and Chap. xliv. 2.

Ver. 3.

Ver. 4.

Ver.

Chapter
XLIII.

Ver. 5.

Ver. 5. *So the Spirit took me up.*] See Chap. iii.
12, 14. viii. 3. xxxvii. 1. xl. 2.

Ibid. *And he brought me into the inner Court.*]
Carried from the Gate that enters into it, into the
middle of it, juſt before the Temple.

Ibid. *And behold the Glory of the LORD
filled the Houſe.*] That Glory, or Symbol of the
Divine Preſence, which I ſaw coming from the
Eaſt, ver. 13. entered into the Temple, and ſettled there; as it did when it was finiſh'd by *Solomon*, 1 *Kings* viii. 10, 11.

Ver. 6.

Ver. 6. *And I heard him ſpeaking to me out
of the Houſe.* With a great and mighty Voice,
ver. 2.

Ibid. *And the Man ſtood by me.*] See Chap.
xl. 3.

Ver. 7.

Ver. 7. *The Place of my Throne, and the Place
of the Soles of the Feet.*] The Senſe would be
plainer, if the Beginning of the Verſe were thus
rendered, This is *the Place of my Throne,* &c.
The *Cherubims* were God's Throne, from whence
he is ſaid to *dwell* or *ſit between the Cherubims,*
and the Ark was his Footſtool. See *Pſalm* xcix.
1, 5.

Ibid. *Where I will dwell in the midſt of the
Children of Iſrael for ever.*] He means the Promiſe
formerly made with Relation to the Tabernacle
and Temple. See *Pſalm* lxviii. 16. cxxxii. 14.
which is to be underſtood, as thoſe were under
the Condition of their Obedience, ſee ver. 9. and
to be eminently fulfilled in *Chriſt,* in whom all
the Promiſes of the Old Teſtament are to have
their final Accompliſhment. *Zachary* propheſies
of the *Meſſias,* Chap. vi. 13. that he ſhould build
the

the Temple *of the* LORD, and *bear the Glory*; Chapter
i. e. as the spiritual Sense of these Prophecies is XLIII.
explained in the New Testament, He shall build
the *Christian Church*; in him shall *all the Full-*
ness of the Godhead dwell Bodily, and really, not
in Types and Figures. See *Heb.* iii. 3. *Matt.* xvi.
18. *Joh.* i. 14. *Coloss.* ii. 9. To the same Sense
we may explain the Prophecy of *Haggai*, Chap.
ii. 7. *The Glory of the latter House shall be greater*
than that of the former. There was no visible *She-*
kinah, or Glory, appeared in the second Temple,
'till *the* LORD, *whom they expected, came to*
his Temple, Malach. iii. 1. *i. e.* 'till the *Messias*,
who was *the Brightness of his Father's Glory*, appeared there, and made it an illustrious Figure of
that true Church, or Temple of Believers, where
he would continue his Presence for ever. See
2 *Cor.* vi. 16.

Ibid. *And my Holy Name shall the House of*
Israel no more defile by their Whoredom.] By Idolatry, often described in Scripture, and particularly by this Prophet, under the Metaphor of Fornication; see Chap. xvi. and xxiii. The Captivity
had that good Effect upon the *Jews*, that they
scarce ever afterwards relapsed into Idolatry. The
intire Destruction of Idolatry is likewise often
mentioned as a Blessing reserved for the *Latter*
Days, when the *Jews* shall be converted, and
the Fullness of the Gentiles come into the Church.
See the Note upon *Isa.* i. 30.

Ibid. *Nor by the Carcasses of their Kings in*
their high places.] Idols are called *Carcasses*; because they are without Life and Motion, and
likewise upon the Account of their being Hate-

ful

Chapter ful and Loathſome in the ſight of God: See
XLIII. *Levit.* xxvi. 30. *Jer.* xvi. 18. They are called
~~~~~~ the *Carcaſſes of Kings*; becauſe they were ſet up,
and the Worſhip of them encourag'd by the Idolatrous Kings of *Judah*, who erected High-places for that purpoſe near *Jeruſalem*, in the very
ſight and view of the Temple; ſee *2 Kings* xxiii.
13. By this means the Temple itſelf was pro-
fan'd by thoſe that came directly from the Worſhip of Idols, to attend upon God's Service in the
Temple; ſee Chap. xxiii. of this Prophecy, 38,
39.

Ver. 8.   Ver. 8. *In their ſetting up their Threſholds
by my Threſholds*, &c.] Their Kings ſtill advanced to greater Degrees of Idolatry, in ſetting up
Altars and Images for their Idols in the Temple
itſelf, and the Courts before it: See Chap. v.
11. viii. 6, 15. *2 Kings* xvi. 14. xxi. 4, 5, 7.
     Ibid. *And the wall between me and them.*]
The Margin gives a plainer Senſe, *For there was
but a wall between me and them.*

Ver. 9.   Ver. 9. *Now let them put away their Whoredom*, &c.] See the Note upon ver. 7.

Ver. 10.   Ver. 10. 11. *Shew the Houſe to the Houſe of
Iſrael, that they may be aſhamed of their Iniquities*, &c.] The Words, if underſtood as ſpoken to the *Jews* of that Age, imply, that the
Houſe here deſcribed, with the whole Platform
of it, and the Ordinances relating to it, might
be a Model for them to imitate, as far as they
were able, when they ſhould return to their own
Country, and rebuild the Temple. See the general Preface before Chap. xl. The ſame Draught
or Deſcription, when duly conſidered, would be
a proper

a proper Inducement to make them sensible of Chapter
their former Deviations from God's Worship, and XLIII.
touched with deep Remorse for those Sins, which
provoked him to deprive them of the Honour
of his Residence among them, and the Benefit
of his Ordinances: See ver. 7, 8. But we may
probably suppose, that the Words may have a
farther View, and import that the Model of God's
Temple, here set forth, is but a Pattern of Heavenly things, as *Moses*'s was, *Exod.* xxv. 40. and
a Type of that pure Church *built upon the Foun-*
dation of the Apostles and Prophets, Jesus
Christ being the Chief Corner Stone ; which we
may hope God will in due Time every where
Restore.   And in the mean Season, it is the Duty of all good Christians, according to their A-
bilities, to inform themselves and others, what is
the Pattern, Form and Fashion of this true
Church of God, in order to reform all those
Deviations, which have been made from it.

Ibid. *And let them measure the Pattern.*] In
order to build their new Temple by it, when
they shall return from Captivity, as far as their
Abilities will reach: See the general Preface before the xlth Chapter.   For the same purpose
the Prophet is commanded to write it in their
sight, in the following Words.

Ver. 11. *And if they be ashamed.*] Or, *And* Ver. 11.
that they may be ashamed: So the Particle *In*
is often used, see *Noldius*, p. 90.

Ver. 12. *Upon the top of the Mountain.*] Ver. 12.
Whereupon the Temple stood; see Chap. xl. 2.

Chapter
XLII.

Ver. 13.

Ibid. *The whole limit thereof round about shall be most holy.*] See Chap. xlii. 20.

Ver. 13. *The Cubit, is a Cubit and an Hand breadth.*] see Chap. xl. 5.

Ibid. *The bottom shall be a Cubit, and the breadth a Cubit, and the border thereof ---- shall be a Span.*] The *Bottom* signifies the Basis or Foundation; see ver. 14. this shall be a Cubit in Height, and a Cubit over in Breadth; the Parts above the lower Settle being contracted, and growing narrower by the breadth of a Cubit, see the following Verse. This lower Ledge or Settle about the Altar had a Border of the Height of a Span, or half a Cubit, see ver. 17. to keep the Blood that was poured out at the Foot of the Altar, from running upon the Pavement; but it was convey'd away into Holes at the South West Corner of the Altar, and so into a Sink or common Shore under Ground.

Ibid. *And this shall be the higher place of the Altar.*] The *Hebrew* reads, *The back of the Altar*; which imports, that this Basis was the Protuberance of the Altar, or the widest part of it. The *Hebrew* word, *Gab*, signifying any part that sticks out, and is used for the Eye-brows, the Protuberance of an Hill, or such like Eminence.

Ver. 14.

Ver. 14. *And from the Bottom upon the ground even to the lower settle shall be two Cubits.*] The Altar was made narrower as it came nearer to the top; these Narrowings, or In-benchings are called here Settles. The word is *Azarah* in the *Hebrew*, which is elsewhere used for a
Court;

Court; because the Priests trod upon these Settles, as they and the People did in the Courts before the Temple. From the Foundation to the lower of the two Settles here mentioned, the Text saith, was to be two Cubits; which seems to contradict the words in the Verse before, *The bottom shall be a Cubit,* This Difference in Expression Dr. *Lightfoot* thus reconciles, in *his Description of the Temple,* Chap. 34. That the Foundation, as it lay flat upon the Ground, was but a Cubit high; but then there arose a Slope of another Cubits Height, which was thicker than the Compass of the Altar, just above it; So that from the Ground to the top of the Rising was two Cubits. And thus he reconciles the Description here given with that of the *Talmud,* which reckons Five Cubits from the lower Settle to the Higher; whereas the Prophet counts but Four, in the following Words.

Ibid. *And the breadth one Cubit.*] The Breadth of this lower Settle or Border was one Cubit, which made that part of the Altar, which was above it, narrower by a Cubit on every side of the Square, than that part which was nearer the Foundation.

Ibid. *And from the lesser settle, even to the greater settle, shall be four Cubits, and the breadth one Cubit.*] Dr. *Lightfoot* in the same Place assigns this Reason, why the upper Settle is here called the *Greater;* because the upper Settle, tho' it were less in Compass, (being narrower by two Cubits on every side of the Square) yet was larger it Breadth; the lower

Settle rifing with a leaning Slope, as was obferved before, which took up a confiderable part
of its Breadth, and made the Walk upon it not fo
large as that upon the upper.

Ver. 15. *So the Altar fhall be four Cubits.*]
i. e. From the upper Settle, which makes the
Altar ten Cubits high, the fame Height with that
made by *Solomon*, 2 *Chron.* iv. 1. The 14th
Verfe reckons fix Cubits to the upper Settle, and
here are four Cubits added to the top of the
Altar. The Dimenfions of the Altar are the
fame in the *Talmud*, as Dr. *Lightfoot* obferves
in the place above cited ; who further Remarks
out of the *Jewifh* Writers, that within two Cubits of the Top, or the Place where the Hearth
was, there was another Narrowing or Bench,
of a Cubit's Breadth, where the Priefts ftood to
officiate.

The Altar is twice mentioned in this Verfe,
under two different Names, the firft *Harel*, that
is, *the Mountain of God*, being fo called, as
fome *Rabbins* think, in oppofition to the Idolatrous Altars built upon high Places; the fecond
Ariel, that is, *the Lion of God*, having that
Name given to it, becaufe it devoured and confumed the Sacrifices offered upon it. See *Ifa.*
xxix. 1.

Ibid. *And from the Altar and upward fhall be
four horns.*] To be added at each Corner, as
was in *Mofes*'s Altar, *Exod.* xxvii. 2. Thefe
were Squares of a Cubit on each fide, and hol-
low in the middle ; and into thefe Cavities fome
of the Blood of the Sacrifices was put, fee ver.
20.

20. They rofe from the uppermoft Bench, where Chapter the Prieft ftood to Officiate. XLIII.

Ver. 16. *And the Altar* fhall be *twelve* Cubits *long, twelve broad,* &c.] The upper Part of it fhall Ver. 16. be an exact Square, reckoning from the fecond Settle, which is properly called the Altar, and diftinguifhed from the Bottom or Foundation : See *ver.* 15.

Ver. 17. *And the Settle* fhall be *fourteen* Cubits Ver. 17. *long, and fourteen broad.*] This is to be underftood of the lower Settle, which was two Cubits wider than the upper Part of the Altar, as appears by the Defcription already given.

Ibid. *And the Border about it fhall be half a Cubit.*] Or a Span, as it is exprefs'd, *ver.* 13.

Ibid. *And the Bottom thereof fhall be a Cubit about.*] a Cubit wider than the lower Settle. See *ver.* 13.

Ibid. *And his Stairs fhall look toward the Eaft.*] God forbad his Priefts to go up by Steps to his Altar, *Exod.* xx. 26. which is ufually expounded, that he would not have his Altar fet upon a great Afcent, in Imitation of the Heathen High Places; Yet *Solomon*'s Altar was ten Cubits high, 2 *Chron.* iv. 1. Which neceffarily required fome Afcent for the Priefts to go, that they might officiate on the Top of it. And in this Place there is exprefs mention of Stairs to go up to the Altar here defcribed, being of the fame Height with *Solomon*'s. The *Jews* tells us, That fince the Law prohibited Stairs, or Steps, the Afcent to the Altar was by a gentle Rifing, which they call *Kibbefh*, of thirty two Cubits in Length, and fixteen in Breadth; the
Landing-

Landing-Place being upon the upper Bench or Walk, next the Hearth or Top, of which mention hath been already made in the Notes upon *ver.* 16. See Dr. *Lightfoot,* in the forecited Place, and Dr. *Prideaux Connect. of Script. Hist.* *Part I.* where there is a *Draught of the Altar,* and the Ascent to it, which very much helps to explain the Description here given of it.

This Ascent is directed to be placed at the East-Side of the Altar, that they who went up should look toward the West, and upon the Temple, and should turn their Backs to the Rising-Sun, in opposition to the Rites of those Idolaters, who worshipped the Rising-Sun. See the Note upon *Chap.* viii. 16.

Ver. 18.　Ver. 18. *And to sprinkle Blood thereon.*] See *Levit.* i. 5. iii. 8.

Ver. 19.　Ver. 19. *And thou shalt give to the Priests, the Levites, that be of the Seed of* Zadok.] See the Notes on *Chap.* xl. 45. xliv. 15.

Ibid. *A young Bullock for a Sin offering,* &c.] To confecrate the new Altar therewith, and the Persons who were to offer Sacrifice upon it. Comp. *Chap.* xlv. 18, 19, and *Exod.* xxix, 10, 12, and *ver.* 36.

Ver. 20.　Ver. 20. *And upon the four Corners of the Settle.*] The Word *Settle* may signify both the Settles; as the singular Number elsewhere stands for the Plural. See the Note upon *Chap.* xli. 9.

Ver. 21.　Ver. 21. *And he shall burn it.*] Or rather, *It shall be burnt,* as the lxx rightly express the Sense; the Verb Transitive being often used for the Impersonal. See the Note upon *Isa.* xliv. 18.

Ibid.

Ibid. *In the appointed Place of the House without the Sanctuary.*] In some Place appointed for
that Purpose, within the Precincts of the Holy
Mountain. The Temple itself is called the *Inner
House*, Chap. xli. 15. xlii. 15. to distinguish it
from the outward Courts, and Precincts thereof.
The Body of the Bullock, whose Blood was to
sanctify the Altar, was to be *burnt without the
Camp*, by the Order of the Law, *Exod.* xxix.
14.

This was the first Day's Sacrifice, the Ceremony of Consecration being to last seven Days.
See *Ver.* 26.

Ver. 22. *And on the second Day thou shalt of-Ver. 22.
fer a Kid of the Goats without Blemish for a Sin-
Offering.*] This is over and above the Sacrifices of
Consecration, prescribed *Exod.* xxix. 1. Some o-
ther Rites are prescribed in the following Ordinances that differ a little from those ordain'd by
Moses: See the Note upon Chap. xlvi. 4.

Ver. 23. *Thou shalt offer a young Bullock, and Ver. 23.
a Ram out of the Flock.*] Called the *Ram of Consecration, Exod.* xxix. 31. *Levit.* viii. 22. These
Sacrifices were to be repeated every one of the
seven Days of Consecration. See ver. 25.

Ver. 24. *And the Priest; shall cast Salt upon Ver. 24.
them.*] Every Sacrifice was to be salted with Salt.
Levit. ii. 13.

Ver. 26. *Seven Days shall they purge the Altar, Ver. 26.
and purify it.*] Seven Days were appointed for the
performing the Ceremonies of purifying the Altar, and consecrating the Priests. See *Exod.*
xxix. 35. *Levit.* viii. 34.

Ibid.

Chapter XLIII.

Ibid. *And they shall consecrate themselves.*] The Expression in the *Hebrew* is, *They shall fill their Hands*; the Phrase being taken from that Ceremony used in Consecrating a Priest, of filling his Hands with Part of the Sacrifice then offered. See *Exod.* xxix. 24.

Ver. 27.

Ver. 27. *Upon the eighth Day, and so forward.*] See *Levit.* ix. 1.

Ibid. *Your Peace-Offerings.*] The Margin reads, *Thank-Offerings,* because they were Offerings of Thanksgiving for Mercies received.

CHAP.

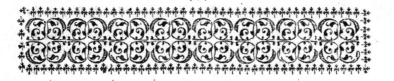

C H A P. XLIV.

The ARGUMENT.

*The Chapter begins with a Description of the Glory of
God returned into the Temple : then follows a Reproof of the People for suffering idolatrous Priests
to profane the Temple by ministring there ; and Ordinances are set down relating to the Deportment of
God's true Priests, and the Maintenance due to
them.*

Ver. 1. HE N *he brought me back the*   Ver. 1.
*way of the Gate of the out-
ward Sanctuary.*] From the
Altar to the Gate belonging
to the Court of the Priests,
that leadeth to the outward
Court of the Temple. Comp. Verse 27, and Chapt.
xlvi. 1. All the Courts were reckoned Holy
Ground, and called sometimes by the Name of
the Temple : See *Joh.* viii. 20. *Act.* xxi. 28.

Ibid. *And it was shut.*] After that the Glory of
the Lord had entered that Way : Chap. xliii. 4. to

G g g   signify

Chapter
XLIV.

⌇⌇⌇

Ver. 2.

Ver. 3.

signify that the Divine Prefence would never forfake the Temple any more.

Ver. 2. *This Gate fhall be fhut, it fhall not be
opened.*] It fhall not ftand open continually, as it
foimerly did, but only at certain Seafons : See
Ver. 3. and Chap. xlvi. 1. and that out of refpect
to the Divine Glory which made its Entrance into
the Temple that Way, where it had now took up
its fixed Refidence : See Chap. xliii. 7. not to depart any more by the Eaft-gate of the Temple, as
it formerly did : See the Note on Chap. the
xliii. 4.

Ibid. *Becaufe the LORD, the God of Ifrael,
hath entered in by it.*] That is, the Glory of the
LORD, as it is expreffed Chap. xliii. 2, 4. The
Glory of God is himfelf, and is often called by
the Name of the LORD, or the God of *Ifrael*:
See *Exod.* xxiv. 10. *Ifa.* vi. 1, 5.

Ver. 3. *It is for the Prince.*] *Solomon* placed his
Seat at the Entrance into the inner Court before
the Altar of the LORD, 2 *Chron.* vi. 13. and here the
Prince feems to have had his Place in after Times,
whenever he came to worfhip at the Temple:
See 2 *Chron.* xxiii. 13. xxxiv. 31. Not far from
which Place, a Seat was placed for the High-
Prieft, as may be gathered from *Eli's* Seat mentioned 1 *Sam.* i. 9. And from whence the
High-Prieft pronounced the Bleffing after the
Service was ended : See *Ecclus.* l. 20., and *Lightfoot, Temple Service,* c. 36. Some underftand
by the Prince, the High-Prieft; which Title does
very properly belong to the *Meffias,* who is
both King and Prieft, and hath the Style of Prince
given him, Chap. xxxiv. 23. But in the Parallel

rallel Place to this, Chapt. xlvi. 2. 3, 8, 9. the Word Prince is oppofed to the People : And other Ordinances are there laid down, which cannot be fitly applied to the *Meffias*. For which Reafon I conceive the Word muft be taken here in its ufual Senfe, to denote the Chief Governors of the *Jews*, fuch, as were *Zerubbabel* and *Nehemiah* after the Captivity.

Ibid *The Prince fhall fit in it to eat Bread before the* LORD.] To eat Part of the Peace-offerings, which are to be provided at his Charge : See Chapt. xlvi. 2. Bread ftands for all fort of Entertainments : See *Gen.* xliii. 31. and particularly for a Religious Feaft made of the Remainder of a Sacrifice, *ibid. c.* xxxi. 54.

Ibid. *He fhall enter by the way of the Porch of that Gate,* &c.] See Chapt. xlvi. 8.

Ver. 4. *Then brought he me the way of the North-gate before the Houfe.*] The Eaft-gate being *fhut,* Ver. 1.

Ibid. *And behold the Glory of the* LORD *filled the Houfe of the* LORD.] There was no Door into the Houfe on that Side, but I could fee the Brightnefs of the Divine Glory fhining through the Windows. See Chapt. xliii. 3, 5.

Ibid. *And I fell upon my Face.*] See Chapt. i. 28.

Ver. 5. *Mark well, and behold with thine Eyes,* &c.] See Chapt. xl. 4. xliii. 2.

Ibid. *Mark well the entering of the Houfe with the going forth of the Sanctuary.*] The Word *Laws* is here to be repeated, to this Senfe, that the Prophet fhould admonifh the People of the Laws relating to the admitting certain Perfons into the Temple or the Courts of it, and fuffer none that

Ver. 4.

Ver. 5.

Chapter are unqualified to attend upon God's Service there:
XLIV. See the following Verses.

Ver. 6. *And* ſay *to the rebellious* [Houſe] *even to*
Ver. 6. *the Houſe of* Iſrael.] See Chapt. ii. 5.

Ib·d. *Let it* ſuffice *you of all your Abominations.*]
Let the Time paſt be ſufficient for you to have
provoked me with your Abominations : See Chapt.
xlv. 9. Comp. 1 *Pet.* iv. 3. We find the ſame
Expreſſion *Numb.* xvi. 3. where our Tranſlation
reads, *ye take too much upon you :* But the Phraſe
may more properly be tranſlated, *Let it* ſuffice *you,*
[to have uſurped an Authority hitherto.]

Ver. 7. Ver. 7. *In that you* have *brought* into my Sanctuary, *Strangers uncircumciſed in Heart,* &c.] In
ſetting up Idols within the Precincts of mine own
Houſe, and appointing idolatrous Prieſts to officiate
there : See Chapt. xliii. 8.

Ibid. *When* ye *offer my Bread, my Fat and my*
Blood.] At the ſame Time that ye offer my Sacrifices upon the Altar. Or the Words may imply
that they ſuffered Heathens to offer at God's
Altar, expreſly againſt the Law, *Levit.* xxii. 27.

By *Bread* may be underſtood, the Meat-Offerings made of Flower which accompanied the other
Sacrifices : Altho' every Thing offered upon the
Altar, is properly called the *Bread of God :* See
the Note upon Chapt. xxiii. 41. The Fat and
Blood of every Sacrifice was peculiarly appropriated
to God : See *Levit.* iii. 16. xvii. 11.

Ibid. *And they have broken my Covenant.*] Idolatry was a direct Breach of that Covenant God
had entered into with the Jews, that he *would*
be their God, and they his People, *Levit.* xxvii. 12.
Upon which Account it is ſo often repreſented un-

der

der the Metaphor of Adultery and Fornication : Being a Breach of that Covenant which is usually described under the Notion of a Marriage Contract : See the Note upon Chap. xvi. 8.

Ver. 8. *And ye have not kept the Charge of my holy Things,* &c.] You have not observed the Laws I gave you, for taking care of the Things relating to my House and Worship; but have appointed such Persons to officiate there, as best suited with your own Inclinations : See the Note upon Chap. xl. 45. Ver. 8.

Ver. 9. *No Stranger shall enter into my Sanctuary.*] To offer any Sacrifice or Oblation there ; See Ver. 7. nor be suffered to go beyond the Precincts appointed for Proselytes. Ver. 9.

Ver. 10. *And the Levites that are gone far from me,* &c.] The same who are called the *Priests, the Levites,* Ver. 15. *i. e.* the Sons of *Levi* who are Priests. Many of these departed from attending upon God's Service, and fell into Idolatry ; first, in the general Apostasy of the Ten Tribes, afterwards under *Ahaz,* and other wicked Kings of *Judah*: See 2 *Kings* xxiii. 9. these shall bear the Punishment due to their Iniquity, and shall be degraded from attending upon the higher Offices belonging to the Priesthood, and thrust down to meaner Services. See Ver. 13. It is not likely that any of those Priests who had been defiled with Idolatry in former Times, lived to see the Restoration of God's worship in the Temple after the Captivity: So the Punishment here allotted to them, either relates to their Posterity: God having particularly threatned to punish the Sin of Idolatry to *the third and fourth Generation, Exod.* xx. 5. Or Ver. 10.

5: Or elfe the Ordinances here prefcribed, are
ftanding Rules that were to be perpetually obferved, whenfoever this Cafe fhould happen.

The Difcipline of the *Chriftian* Church was ftill
more fevere : For whoever of the Clergy had committed Idolatry in the Times of Perfecution, was
for ever deprived of his Funftion; and even for leffer
Crimes they were degraded from an higher to a
lower Station; as the learned Mr. *Bingham*, in his
Eccl. Antiq. Book 17. *Chap.* 3. hath fhewed in feveral
Inftances.

Ver. 11.

Ver. 11. *Having Charge of the Gates of the
Houfe.*] Performing the Office of Porters, an inferior Station belonging to the Levites : See
1 *Chron.* xxvi. 1.

Ibid. *They fhall flay the burnt Offering.*] Kill the
Beafts appointed for the daily Burnt-offering and
other Sacrifices, and flay their Skins, which was
an Office ufually performed by the Levites: See 2
Chron. xxxv. 11.

Ibid. *And they fhall ftand before them.*] They
fhall be Servants to the People, in undergoing the
moft fervile Offices belonging to the Temple;
whereas it is the proper Office of a Prieft, to be
God's immediate Minifter: See *Deut.* x. 8. xvii. 12.

Ver. 12.

Ver. 12. *Becaufe they miniftered to them before
their Idols, and caufed the Houfe of Ifrael to fall into
their Iniquity.*] They led the People into Idolatry,
by giving them an ill Example.

Ibid. *Therefore have I lift up my Hand againft
them.*] I have folemnly fworn that I will Punifh
them for this their Sin: See the Note on Chap.
xx. 6.

Ver. 13.

Ver. 13. *And they shall not come near to me, to do*
the Office of a Priest unto me, &c.] They shall not
offer Sacrifice at my Altar, or come into the Temple, to perform any Part of the priestly Office
there. So *Josiah* discharged the Priests that had
been guilty of Idolatry, from attending upon the
Service of the Altar: 2 *Kings* xxiii. 9.

Ver. 14. *But I will make them Keepers of the*
Charge of the House, for all the Service thereof, &c.]
They shall perform the servile Offices belonging to
my Temple and worship: See 1 *Chron.* xxiii. 28,
32.

Ver. 15. *But the Priests, the Levites.*] The Sons
of *Levi* who are Priests. Comp. *Deut.* xvii. 9.
xviii. 1. xxiv. 8.

Ibid. *The Sons of Zadock.*] See Chap. xl. 46.
xliii. 19.

Ibid. *To offer to me the Fat and the Blood*] See
Ver. 7.

Ver. 16. *They shall enter into my Sanctuary, and*
they shall come near to my Table.] The foregoing Verse
expresses their ministring at the Altar, and offering
Sacrifice there: This denotes Attendance upon
God's Service within the Temple: The principal
Part of which was burning Incense there upon the
Altar placed in the Temple for that purpose:
Which mystically implied the offering up the
Prayers of the People to God. This Altar of In-
cense is called here the Table of the LORD,
as it is Chap. xli. 22. See the Note there.

Ver. 17. *When they shall enter in at the Gates of*
the inner Court.] The Court just before the Temple, where the Altar of Burnt-Offering stood. Ver.
27 of this Chapter.

Ibid.

Chapter   Ibid. The Ephod, Breeches, Miter and Girdle,
XLIV.   which was the Habit of the ordinary Priests, were
all of fine Linnen, contrived for *Glory and Beauty*:
Exod. xxix. 40. Fine Linnen being the Habit of Perfons of the greateft Quality. See the Note upon
Chap. xxvii. 7.

     Ibid. *While they Minifter in the Gates of the inner Court, and within.*] Or *in the Houfe*, or Temple it felf, as *Noldius* tranflates the Word *Bayetha. Num.* 829.

Ver. 18.   Ver. 18. *They fhall not gird themfelves with any thing that caufeth Sweat.*] With a woolen Girdle, which may make them Sweat, during their laborious Services about the Altar, and make their Garments fmell offenfively. But the *Chaldee* Paraphrafe renders it thus: *They fhall not be girt about their Loins, but be girt upon* (or about) *their Heart.* i. e. They fhall not wear Girdles about their middle, or under their Arm Pits, either of which may caufe them to Sweat, but fhall wear them about their Breafts. So St. *John* defcribes our Lord appearing in the Habit of a High Prieft, and *girt about the Paps with a Golden Girdle*, Rev. i. 13.

Ver. 19.   Ver. 19. *And when they go forth into the utter Court, they fhall put off their Garments wherein they miniftered.*] See the Note on Chap. xlii. 14.

     Ibid. *And they fhall not Sanctify the People with their Garments.*] By the Rules of the Law, things immediately dedicated to God's Service, did convey fome Degree of Holinefs to common things that touched them : So the Altar *fanctified the Gift* that was laid upon it : See *Levit.* vi. 27. *Matth.* xxiii. 13. Thus fome fort of Holinefs might be deriv'd to the Garments of the People, by touching
                   thofe

thofe of a Prieft : Which God would have prevented, to keep up an exact Difference between the
Holy and Profane, Ver. 23.

Ver. 20. *Neither fhall they fhave their Heads.*]
This Prefcription is implied in thofe Words of the
Law, Levit. xxi. 5. efpecially according to the
Tranflation of the *Septuagint*, who render the Sen-
tence, *Thou fhalt not fhave thy felf with Baldnefs*
[to make Baldnefs] *upon thy Head for the Dead.*
They indeed underftand it as an Expreffion of
Mourning for the Dead, which agrees with the
Senfe of the Parallel Texts, *Levit.* xix. 27, 28.
Deut. xiv. 1. But the Words in the Original con-
tain a general Prohibition, and confequently include the Times of Mourning as well as other
Seafons. St. *Jerom* upon the Place does with great
Probability fuppofe, that the *Jewifh* Priefts were
forbid to fhave their Heads, thereby to diftinguifh
them from feveral of the Heathen Priefts, particularly the *Egyptian* Priefts of *Ifis* and *Serapis*, who
had their Heads fhaved and uncovered, which were
Funeral Rites, and therefore proper to be ufed in
the Worfhip of the Heathen Gods, who were no
better than dead Men : See *Baruch* vi. 31. Learned
Men have obferved, That many other *Jewifh* Laws
were made, in Oppofition to the Funeral Rites obferved in the Heathen Worfhip.

Ibid. *Nor fuffer their Locks to grow long.*] It is
the Opinion of Dr. *Spencer, Leg. Hebr. lib.* 2. *c.* 25.
and *Schindler*, that this Law is likewife taken out
of the fame Chapter of *Leviticus* at the 10th Verfe ;
where our Tranflation renders the Original, *He
fhall not uncover his Head.* But the *Chaldee* Paraphrafe tranflates the Words, *He fhall not nourifh the*

Hair

Chapter
XLIV.
~~~~~

Hair of his Head: which Senfe feveral Interpreters follow: Letting the Hair grow long and neglected, being a Sign of Mourning, as well as fha-
ving it clofe to the Head.

Ver. 21.

Ver. 21. *Neither fhall any Prieft drink Wine,
when they enter into the inner Court.*] During the
Time of their Miniftration: See Ver. 17. This
Law is likewife taken from *Levit.* x. 9, 10. And
the Reafon of the Prohibition is there given, that
they might *put a Difference between holy and
unholy, between clean and unclean,* i. e. that they
might be able exactly to determine the Cafes
relating to Legal Uncleannefs: Many of which
had a great deal of Nicenefs in them, by Reafon
of the Variety of Circumftances. Comp. Ver. 23.
of this Chapter.

Ver. 22.

Ver. 22. *Neither fhall they take for their Wives
a Widow, or her that is put away, &c.*] This Law
we find in *Levit.* xxi. 13, 14. But it is there fpoken of the High-Prieft only, here it is applied to
all the Priefts in general.

Ver. 23.

Ver. 23. *And in Controverfy they fhall ftand in
Judgment, &c.*] The Priefts were to determine all
Controverfies relating to the *Law,* as well the
Judicial as the Ceremonial Part of it, which were
brought before them: See *Deut.* xvii. 8, 9. and
the *People were to feek the Law at their Mouths,*
Mal. ii. 7. i. e. to enquire of them, what was
the Purport and meaning of it: and to ftand to
their Determination. And when the fupreme
judicial Power was placed in the *Sanhedrim,*
the Majority of that Court confifted chiefly of
fuch as had the chief Stations among the Priefts:
See *Acts* iv. 5, 6.

Ibid.

Ibid. *And they shall keep my Laws and my Statutes in all mine Assemblies,* &c.] As well upon the solemn Festivals, and the Assemblies proper to them (see *Exod.* xii. 16.) as on the ordinary Sabbaths.

Ibid. *And they shall hallow my Sabbaths.*] Whereas the Priests before the Captivity profaned them, and neglected to perform the Divine Worship prescribed upon them : See Chapt. xxii. 26.

Ver. 25. *They shall come at no dead Person to defile themselves.*] Whosoever touched a dead Body became legally unclean, *Num.* xix. 11. and thereby was unqualified to attend upon God's Worship in the Temple : See *Levit.* xxii. 3. upon which Account the Priests were forbidden to contract such a Defilement, unless for their nearest Relations, *Levit.* xxi. 1, 2, 3: which Prohibition is here renewed.

Ver. 26. *And after he is cleansed, they shall reckon unto him seven Days.*] His Uncleanness continued for seven Days by the fore-cited Law, *Num.* xix. 11. and the Priests were to reckon to him seven Days more, before he was to be admitted into the Sanctuary.

Ver. 27. *And in the Day that he goeth into the Sanctuary, unto the inner Court.*] See Ver. 17.

Ibid. *He shall offer his Sin-offering.*] He shall offer a young Bullock for a Sin-offering : See *Levit.* iv. 13.

Ver. 28. *And it shall be unto them for an Inheritance,* &c.] Their Ministry in my Sanctuary mentioned in the foregoing Verse, and the Perquisites thereto belonging, shall be to them instead of Lands and Cities, of which they shall not have

any

Chapter XLIV.

Ver. 29.

any Share as the other Tribes: See *Deut.* x. 9. *Joſh.* xiii. 14. excepting the Portion allotted to them in the beginning of the following Chapter.

Ver. 29. *They ſhall eat the Meat-offering, and the Sin-offering, and the Treſpaſs-Offering.*] They ſhall have their Share of it, after God's Part hath been conſumed upon the Altar : See *Levit.* vi. 18, 29. vii. 6.

Ibid. *And every dedicate Thing ſhall be theirs.*] Whatſoever Men dedicate to God, the Uſe of it ſhall accrue to the Prieſts : If it be a living Creature, it ſhall be killed, and the Prieſt ſhall have the Benefit of it : If it be a Piece of Land, it ſhall belong to the Prieſts: See *Levit.* xxvii. 27, 28. *Num.* xviii. 14.

Ver. 30.

Ver. 30. *And the firſt of all Firſt-fruits of all things, and every Oblation of every ſort of your Oblations ſhall be the Prieſts.*] The Words tranſlated *Firſt-fruits* and *Oblations,* are in the *Hebrew Biccurim* and *Trumah.* The former imports the Firſtripe, or beſt of the Fruits, while they were growing in the Field. Comp. *Exod.* xxiii. 19. with *Num.* xviii. 12. The latter denotes an Oblation out of the Product of the Ground, after it was made fit for Uſe : As out of the Corn after it was threſhed and laid in Heaps in the Floor or Granary : And ſo of Oyl and Wine, after they were preſſed and fitted for ſpending. Theſe Oblations are by ſome Authors, particularly by Mr. *Selden* in his Treatiſe of *Tithes,* Chap. 2. eſteemed to amount to the ſixtieth Part of the whole produce. *Schindler* rates the *Biccurim* at the loweſt Proportion to be the ſixtieth Part, and computes the *Trumah* at the fiftieth. Dr *Cumber* ſuppoſes the *Biccurim* to amount to an hundreth Part, and the *Trumah* at a Medium

to

to be the *Fiftieth*: See his Treatife of *Tithes,* Chapter
Part 1. Chapt. 2. and the Notes on Chapt. xlv. 13. XLIV.

Ibid. *Ye fhall alfo give unto the Prieft the firft of*
your Dough.] The firft Dough that you bake of the
new Corn every Year, fhall belong to the Priefts,
in the fame Proportion to be obferved here, as in
other Firft-fruits, *viz.* a fixtieth Part: See *Num.*
xv. 20.

Ibid. *That he may caufe a Bleffing to reft in thine*
Houfe.] That the Prieft, whofe Office it is to blefs
the People in God's Name (fee *Num.* vi. 23.
Deut. x. 8.) may procure a Bleffing upon thee from
him, according to the Promife he hath made of
Bleffing thofe with an extraordinary Degree of
Plenty, who confcientioufly pay their Tithes and Of-
ferings, as grateful Acknowledgments to God the
Giver of all good Things : See *Prov.* iii. 9, 10.
Mal. iii. 10. 2 *Chron.* xxxi. 10. Comp. *Deut.* xxvi.
13, 14, 15.

Ver. 31. *The Prieft fhall not eat of any Thing that* Ver. 31.
is dead of its felf or torn.] A Command given to
all the *Jews, Exod.* xxii. 31. and more particularly to the Priefts, *Levit.* xxii. 8.

C H A P.

Chapter
XLV.

CHAP. XLV.

The ARGUMENT.

The several Portions of Land appointed for the Sanctuary, the City, and the Prince; together with Ordinances concerning the Provisions for the ordinary and extraordinary Sacrifices.

Ver. 1.

Ver. 1. OREOVER *when ye shall divide the Land by lot for Inheritance,* ye shall offer an Oblation to the Lord.] The Land was divided by Lot in the first Division of it under *Joshua,* and is appointed to be divided so in the Partition of it, as it here follows: See Chap. xlvii. 14. 22. A particular Share of which was to be God's Portion, as an Acknowledgment of his Sovereign Dominion: See *Levit.* xxv. 23. 'tis therefore here called *Trumah* or *Oblation,* which Word properly signifies the Offering made to God out of the First-fruits, and other increase of the Ground; See Chapt. xliv. 30. *Num.* xviii. 24. *&c.*

because

becaufe this was a fort of Firft-fruits of the Land,
or Soil its felf, Chapt. xlviii. 14.

Ibid. *The Length fhall be five and twenty thou-*
fand Reeds, and the Breadth fhall be ten thoufand.]
The *Hebrew* doth not exprefs either *Reeds* or *Cu-*
bits : Our Tranflation fupplies the Word *Reeds*,
but many Interpreters expound the Place of *Cubits*,
which Senfe they think is plainly determined by
Ver. 3. where it is faid, *Of this Meafure*, (viz. the
Cubit Meafure mentioned Verfe 2.) *fhalt thou mea-*
fure the Length of five and twenty thoufand; &c.
According to this Meafure the Portion here fet a
part, will be almoft feven Miles fquare ; whereas
if we meafure by Reeds, it will arife to fix times
as much, and can only be underftood in a myftical
Senfe.

Ver. 2. *Of this there fhall be for the Sanctuary*
five hundred in length, with five hundred in breadth,
fquare round about.] If we underftand thefe Dimenfions of Cubits, it exactly agrees with the Opinion of the *Jews*, that the Temple ftood in an
Area of 500 Cubits fquare. See Dr. *Lightfoot of*
the Temple, Chap. 2. A fquare Figure is the Emblem of Solidity : See the Note on Chap. xlii. 20.

Ibid. *And fifty Cubits round about for the Suburbs*
thereof.] This likewife bears a fuitable Proportion
to the Content of a Square of 500 Cubits.

Ver. 3. *Of this Meafure fhalt thou meafure the*
length of five and twenty thoufand.] See the Note
upon Ver. 1.

Ibid. *And in it fhall be the Sanctuary, and the*
moft holy Place.] Both the outward Sanctuary and
the inward Oracle or Holieft of all, together with
.the

Chapter the Courts adjoining, ſhall be placed in the Cen-
XLV. ter or Middle of it: See Chapt. xlviii. 10.

Ver. 4. Ver. 4. *And it ſhall be a Place for their Houſes.*]
The Prieſts were divided into four and twenty
Courſes, 1 *Chron.* xxiv. who performed the Publick Worſhip by Turns : So the Houſes were for
them to live in, who were not in their Courſe of
waiting.

Ibid. *And an holy Place for the Sanctuary.*] See
Chap. xlviii. 10.

Ver. 5. Ver. 5. *And the five and twenty thouſand of
length, and ten thouſand of breadth, ſhall alſo the
Levites have for themſelves.*] The *French* Tranſlation renders the Senſe plainer thus, *There ſhall be
other five and twenty thouſand, &c.* See Chapt.
xlviii. 13. This appears to be the true Senſe of
the Place, becauſe elſe there will be wanting
10000 in breadth, to make an exact Square of
25000. See the following Verſe. The *Levites* being
very numerous (they were reckoned 38000 in *David*'s time, 1 *Chron.* xxiii. 3.) had as large a Piece
of Ground allotted to them, as belonged to the
Temple, and the whole Prieſtly Order. The
Word [*other*] is upon a like Occaſion ſupplied by
our Interpreters, Chapt. xlviii. 8.

Ibid. *For twenty Chambers.*] Moſt Commentators
underſtand this of ſeveral Rows of Chambers, or
Ranges of Building. The LXX read πλόεις κατοικεῖν,
Cities to inhabit : Such Cities as were allotted to
them by *Moſes, Num.* xxxv. 2. The Copies the
Septuagint followed, probably read, *Narim Laſhe-
beth,* inſtead of the preſent Reading, *Neſharim
Leſhacoth,* ב and כ being eaſily put one for another.

Ver. 6.

This Figure should have been placed at *Page* 425.

NORTH.

The Tribe of *Judah*'s Portion from **West** to **East**.

The Prince's Portion on the West Side.	The Priests Portion, 25000 long.	10000 broad.	The Prince's Portion on the East Side.
	The Levites Portion, 25000 long.	10000 broad.	
	10000 in length, Westward; Food for the City.	The City Portion, 5000 square.	10000 in length, Eastward; Food for the City.	5000 broad.

WEST.   EAST.

The Tribe of *Benjamin*'s Portion from **West** to **East**.

SOUTH.

Ver. 6. *And ye shall appoint the Possession of the* Chapter
City, five thousand broad, and five and twenty XLV.
thousand long, over against (or by the side of:
See Chapt. xlviii. 15.) *the oblation of the Holy por-* Ver. 6.
tion] This must run parallel in length with the holy
Portion, tho' but half its breadth.   By which means
these three Portions made an exact Square (See
Chapt. xlviii. 20.) as you may see in the following Draught.

Ibid. *It shall be for the whole House of Israel*]
The Capital City to which all the Tribes shall
resort upon the Solemn Festivals, and shall have
.twelve Gates according to the Number of the
Tribes of *Israel* : Chapt. xlviii. 31.

Ver. 7. *And a* Portion *shall be for the Prince on* Ver. 7.
the one side, and on the other Side of the oblation of
the Holy Portion *&c*] One half of the Prince's Portion was to lie on the West side of the three Portions laid out for the Priests and Sanctuary, the
Levites and the City : And the other half lay on the
East of it, and it lay parallel to them in breadth from
North to South.

Ibid. *And the length* shall be *over against one of*
these Portions from the West border to the East border]
I think the words may be Translated more plainly
thus, *and the length* shall be *answerable to every one*
of these Portions, both on the West border and the East :
i: e. It shall run parallel with them both on the
East and West side. The word *Leummath* translated *over against,* signifies likewise *parallel* or answerable, as it hath been observed upon Chapt. xl. 18.
the word *Echad, One,* signifies each one or every
one, and is understood so in this Text by *Noldius,*
p. 785. and the Phrase *from the West border to the*

Ι i i   *East,*

Eaft, is equivalent to that Expreffion which often occurs in the Sacred Text, *from fmall to great*, which is very properly rendred, both fmall and great.

Ver. 8. *In the Land fhall be his Poffeffion in Ifrael*] Or *this fhall be his Poffeffion of Land in Ifrael :* For the Particle *La*, in *Laaretz*, is fometimes the Note of the Genitive Cafe: Particularly in the 18*th* and 19*th* Verfes of this Chapter : Or, *As for Land, this fhall be his Poffeffion in Ifrael*

Ibid. *And my Princes fhall no more oppref my People*] As they formerly did : For which they are feverely reprov'd See Chapt. xxii. 27: Chapt. xix. 6, 7. and *Jerem.* xxii. 17.

Ver. 9.

Ver. 9. *Let it fuffice you, O ye Princes of Ifrael, &c.*] This is a Reproof of the Oppreffions of the former Kings, and their chief Officers : See the Note upon Chapt. xliv. 6.

Ver. 10.

Ver. 10. *Ye fhall have juft balances, &c.*] Ye fhall take care that there be no Deceit in Private Trade: Ye fhall provide juft Meafures, both for Buying and Selling both Dry things and Liquid: See the following Verfe.

Ver. 11.

Ver. 11. *The Ephah and the Bath fhall be of one Meafure.*] The Ephah was the Meafure of Dry things, as the Bath was of Liquid : The Homer was about ten Bufhells, which amounts to about eighty Gallons in Liquid things.

Ibid. *The Ephah the tenth part of an Homer*] We muft diftinguifh the word *Homer* or *Chomer* writ with a *Cheth* in the *Hebrew*, and *Omer* writ with an *Ain*. The Ephah is faid here to be the tenth part of an Homer, whereas the *Omer is but the tenth part of the Ephah, Exod.* xvi. 36.

Ver. 12.

Ver. 12. *And the Shekel fhall be twenty Gerahs*]
This

This is made the Standard of the Shekel, *Exod.* xxx. 13. which confutes the common Opinion that the Weights of the Sanctuary were double to those of common Use. Bishop *Cumberland* computes a Gerah to be Equivalent to an *Attic Obolus,* consisting of almost eleven Grains of Silver. The Shekel is usually Valued at 2*s* 6*d* of our Money : But the same Learned Author supposes it to be in Value but 2*s* 4*d* ¼. of our Money, and a little over. See his Treatise *of Script. Weights and Measures,* p. 104, &c.

Ibid. *Twenty Shekels, five and twenty Shekels, and fifteen Shekels shall be your Maneh*] Maneh is the same with the *Greek* μνᾶ, and the *Latin Mina,* being both deriv'd from it. A *Maneh* or *Mina,* consists of sixty Shekels, i. e. thirty Ounces of Silver. See Ibid. p. 1122. which, Reckoning every Shekel at 2 *s* 6*d.* Value, amounts to7*l* 10 *s.* The Dividing the *Maneh* into twenty, twenty-five, and fifteen Shekels, supposes there were Coins of these several Values, which taken all together are to be of the same Weight with the Mi*na.*

Ver. 13. *This is the oblation ye shall offer*] The Hebrew word translated *oblation* is *Trumah:* Which is always distinguish'd from the *Biccurim,* or *Fustfruits,* and signifies the Portion belonging to the Levites out of the Fruits of the Earth when they were gathered in : See Chapt. xliv. 30. For which Reason St. *Jerom* upon the Place supposes the following Words to express the Proportion the People ought to pay the Levites out of the increase of their ground : Which by their Rabbies was determined to amount to at least a sixtieth part, in which Determination they probably followed the

Rule

Chapter
XLV.

Rule laid down in this Verſe: Comp. Verſe 11. This Senſe is likewiſe favoured by the *Chaldee* Pharaphraſe: After which Separation a tenth part was to be paid out of the Remainder. The Portions allotted to the Prieſts and Levites were not intended only for their own Maintenance. But likewiſe to make a Conſtant Proviſion for thoſe Sacrifices both Ordinary and Extraordinary which were appointed by the Law: See *Malachi* iii. 10.

Ver: 14:

Ver. 14. *Concerning the Ordinance of Oyl, a Bath of Oyl, &c.*] Or, *Concerning the Ordinance of Oyl, even the Bath of Oyl.* The *Cor* and the *Homer* are mention'd as containing the ſame Quantity: So a Bath is the tenth part of a *Cor*, as an *Ephah* is the tenth part of an *Homer*: And the tenth part of a Bath of Oyl is the Hundredth part of a *Cor*, which amounts to about ſix Pints of our Meaſure, according to Biſhop *Cumberland*, p. 137.

Ver: 15:

Ver. 15. *And one Lamb out of the flock out of two hundred*] This offering is enjoyned, beſides the Setting apart the firſt-born for the Uſe of the Prieſts and Levites, *Numb.* xviii. 15. for making Proviſion for the daily Burnt Offering, *Numb.* xxviii. 3. and for Burnt offerings, and Peace offerings, or Sacrifices of Thankſgiving, that were to be made upon proper Occaſions: See Chapt. xliii. 27.

Ibid. *Out of the fat Paſtures of Iſrael*] This implies that theſe Lambs were to be of the beſt and fatteſt of their Kind: See *Malachi* i. 8, 14. as all other Tithes and things dedicated to God were to be: See *Numb.* xviii. 12.

Ibid. *For a Meat-Offering*] Theſe words relate to the 13*th* and 14*th* Verſes. *The Meat-Offering,* which

which might be more prope ly tranflated the
Bread-Offering, being made of fine Flower mingled with Oyl. *Levit.* ii. 5, 6.

Ibid. *To make Reconciliation for them*] This Effect
is afcribed to Burnt-Offerings as well as to thofe
which are properly Sacrific'd for Sin.: See *Levit.*
i. 4.

Ver. 16: *All the People of the Land fhall give
this Oblation for the Prince*] The Marginal Reading
is, *with the Prince,* which makes the plainer fenfe,
i. e. The Prince fhall join with the People in making thefe Oblations, whereas thofe that follow in
the next Verfe, are to be at the Sole Charge of
the Prince:

Ver. 17. *And it fhall be the Princes part to give
Burnt-Offerings, and Meat-Offering, and Drink-Offerings in the Feafts and in the New-Moons &c*] Or,
even *in the New-Moons,* as the particle *Vau* often
fignifies. Meat-Offerings and Drink-Offerings were
always joined with Burnt-Offerings : See *Numb.*
xxviii. 5, 7. The particular Sacrifices which the
Prince was to provide upon the Sabbaths and o-
ther Feftivals, are fpecified Chapt. xlvi. 4, 11.

Ibid. *He fhall prepare the Sin-Offering*] i e. Provide it : Concerning the Sin-Offering, See Chapt.
xl 39

Ibid. *To make Reconciliation for the Houfe of Ifrael*] See Verfe 15.

Ver. 18. *In the firft Month in the firft Day of the
Month, thou fhalt take a young bullock and cleanfe the
Sanctuary*] The words are directed to the Prince,
who is commanded on the firft Day of the new
Year, (which according to the Ecclefiaftical Com-
putation begun with the Month *Nifan,* and anfwers

to

to our tenth of *March* : See *Exod.* xii. 2.) to provide a Bullock for a Burnt-Offering, to cleanse the Temple from any Defilement it may have contracted, by the Peoples Offering their Sacrifices, or coming into any of the Courts belonging to it, while they were under any Legal Pollution. See *Levit.* xvi. 19.

Ibid. *A young Bullock without blemish*] Whatever was offered to God was to be perfect without blemish, and the very best in its Kind: See the Note upon Verse 15. and *Levit.* xxii. 20.

Ver. 19.

Ver. 19. *And the Priest shall take of the Blood of the Sin-Offering*] Of the Bullock which was offered for a Sin-Offering: See Chapt. xliii. 19. The Office of the Priest is here distinguished from that of the Prince : The Prince was to provide the Sacrifices, and the Priest was to offer them.

Ibid. *And put it upon the Posts of the House*] Upon the Lintels, or the Door Posts of the House: See Chapt. xli. 21.

Ibid. *And upon the four corners of the settle of the Altar*] See Chap. xliii. 14, 20.

Ibid. *And upon the Posts of the Gate of the inner Court*] See Chapt. xlvi. 1.

Ver. 20.

Ver. 20. *So shall ye do the seventh Day of the Month, for every one that erreth*) There were particular Sacrifices appointed for Sins of Ignorance, whether of private Persons or of the whole Congregation : See *Levit.* iv. 13, 27.

Ibid. *So shall ye reconcile the House*] Cleanse it from any Pollution it may have contracted, thro' the Ignorance of any of the common People : See Verse 18.

Ver. 22. *And upon that Day shall the Prince pre-* Chapter
pare for himself, &c.] See Ver. 17. XLV.

Ver. 23. *And seven Days of the Feast he shall*
prepare a Burnt-offering to the Lord] *Moses* in Ver. 22.
some Places speaks of the Feast of Unleavened Bread, Ver. 23.
which lasted seven Days, as distinct from the Day
wherein the Passover was to be eaten : See *Levit.*
xxiii. 5, 6. which is agreeable to the Injunction of
this and the foregoing Verse, and the Words may
be easily reconciled with those Texts, which include the whole Solemnity within the Compass of
seven Days, by supposing the Passover to be eaten
early in the Evening on the 14th Day, *between the*
two Evenings, as the *Hebrew* Text hath it, *Exod.*
xii. 6. immediately after which Ceremony was
over, they reckoned the 15th Day to begin, for
they reckoned their Days from one Evening to another : See *Levit.* xxiii. 32.

Ibid. *Seven Bullocks, and seven Rams.*] Seven
was a Number often used in Religious Rites : Most
of the Feasts under the Law continued seven Days;
and this Number of Sacrifices seems to be derived from Patriarchal Institution, because such a
Custom prevailed where *Moses's* Law was not
known : See *Numb.* xxiii. 1, 2. *Job* xlii. 8.

Ibid. *And a Kid of the Goats daily for a Sin-offer-*
ing.] This was the Sin-offering most commonly prescribed : See *Numb.* xxviii. 15, 22, 30. xxix. 5, 11,
16, 19, &c.

Ver. 24. *And he shall prepare a Meat Offering of* Ver. 24.
an Ephah, &c.] See Ver. 11 and 15.

Ibid.

Ibid. *And an Hin of Oil for an Ephah.*] For each Ephah of fine Flour : an *Hin* was the sixth Part of an Ephah or Bath : Which contains one Gallon and two Pints, according to Bishop *Cumberland* in the forecited Place.

Ver. 25.   Ver. 25. *In the seventh Month, in the fifteenth Day of the Month.*] When the Feast of Tabernacles was kept : See *Levit.* xxiii. 34.

C H A P.

CHAP. XLVI.

The ARGUMENT.

*A Continuation of the Ordinances relating to the
Worſhip of the Prince and People: And concerning
the Gifts he ſhall beſtow on his Sons and Servants.
Then follows a Deſcription of the Courts appointed
for boiling and baking any Part of the Holy
Oblations.*

Ver. 1. HE Gate of the inner Court
that looketh towards the Eaſt,
ſhall be ſhut the ſix working
Days.] See the Notes upon
Chap. xliv. 1, 2.
Ibid. *But on the Sabbath it
ſhall be opened, and in the Day of the New-Moon.*]
Under the Sabbath and New-Moon, all the other
Feaſts may probably be comprehended: See Chap.
xlv. 17.

Ver. 2. *And the Prince ſhall enter in by the Porch
of that Gate, without.*] He ſhall go through the
outer Gate of that Court, and ſo paſs to the inner

Ver. 1.

Ver. 2.

K k k   Gate,

Gate, where he may see the whole Service performed at the Altar. Or *the Porch of the Gate without* may signify, the further-most Porch of the Gate, with respect to those that are coming towards the Temple, which is the same with the innermost, in respect of the Temple it self. In this Sense the Word is taken Chapt. xl. 44. The Word *Michuts*, or *Michutsah*, signifies both the hither, and the further Side, both being Relative Terms, and applicable to the same Place, as Persons are going out, or coming into the Temple. It signifies the hither Side, Chapt. xl. 19. and the further Side, *ibid.* ver. 44. and in this Verse. So the Word *Neber* signifies both the further and hither Side of a River. See *Noldius*, p. 660.

Ibid. *Shall stand by the Post of the Gate.*] i. e. by the Entrance of the Gate, where there was a Seat prepared for him : See the Note upon Chapt. xliv. 3.

Ibid. *And the Priest shall prepare his Burnt-offering.*] Or, *offer his Burnt-offering* : For so the Verb *Nasah* often signifies, as *Facio* does in *Latin.*

Ibid. *And he shall worship at the threshold of the Gate.*] By bowing his Head, and bowing down his Face to the Earth, or falling down upon the Ground, as the Posture of Divine Worship is elsewhere described: See *Gen.* xxiv. 26, 52. *Exod.* xii. 27. 1 *Chron.* xxix. 20. 2 *Chron.* xxix. 29. *Job* 1. 20.

Ibid. *But the Gate shall not be shut until the Evening.*] Because the People were to pay their solemn Worship in the same Place, as it is prescribed in the following Verse.

Ver. 3. *Likewise the People of the Land shall worship at the Door of this Gate,* &c.] During the
Con-

Continuance of the Tabernacle, they that would offer any Sacrifice, were required to bring it to the *Door of the Tabernacle of the Congregation:* and there lay their Hands upon the Head of it. *Levit.* i. 3, 4. and under the Temple they came to the North, or South-gate of the inner Court, according as the Sacrifice was to be flain on the North or South-fide of the Altar, and there prefented their Sacrifice: See Dr. *Lightfoot's* Temple, Chap. 34. Here the inner Porch of the Eaft-gate is affign'd for their Station, who came to prefent themfelves before the Lord upon the folemn Feftivals, and they were to come no further into the inner Court.

Ver. 4. *And the Burnt-offering that the Prince fhall offer-in the Sabbath-day, &c.*] It was the Prince's Part to provide Sacrifices for the Sabbaths and other Feftivals: See Chapt. xlv. 17. This was a new Ordinance, whereupon the Number of the Beafts that were to be offered, and the Proportions of the Meat and Drink-offerings, are different here from thofe prefcribed in the Law: As will appear by comparing the 4th, 6th, 7th, and 14th Verfes of this Chapter, with *Numb.* xxviii. 9, 11, 12, and 5.

Ver. 5. *And the Meat-offering fhall be an Ephah for a Ram, and an Hin of Oil to an Ephah.*] See Chapt. xlv. 24.

Ibid. *And the Meat-offerings for the Lambs, as he fhall be able to give.*] The Margin reads from the *Hebrew, according to the Gift of his Hand,* i. e. As much as he fhall think fufficient: See the fame Expreffion *Deut.* xvi. 17.

Ver. 8. *He fhall go in by the way of the Porch of that Gate.*] See Ver. 2. To go in at the Eaftern Gate, was the Privilege of the Prince and the Priefts

only

only : The People were to enter in by the North or South-gates, as it is said in the following Verse:

Ver. 9. *He that entreth in by the North gate to worship, shall go out by the way of the South-gate.*] The Words imply the Reason why the People were not to come in at the East-gate, because there being no Passage or Thorow-fare out of the Temple westward; if they had entred in at the East-gate, they must have returned back the same way they came in, which would have been turning their Back upon God, and the Place of his Residence: See Note upon Chapt. VIII. 16.

Ver. 10. *And the Prince in the midst of them when they go in, shall go in.*] He shall pay the same Attendance upon God's Worship with the People, since all Men are equal in the Sight of God.

Ver. 12. *When the Prince shall prepare a voluntary Burnt-offering.*] The foregoing Verses gave orders about the Sacrifices, the Prince was enjoined to offer upon solemn Days: This gives Directions concerning Free-will-Offerings: Concerning which see *Levit.* xxii. 18, 21.

Ibid. *One shall then open him the Gate, &c.*] when the Service is performed, he shall go back the same Way : See Ver. 8. and the Porter shall shut the Gate after him, because it may not stand open upon ordinary Days, Ver. 1.

Ver. 13. *Thou shalt daily prepare a Burnt-offering unto the* LORD.——*Thou shalt prepare it every Morning.*] The daily Evening Sacrifice is generally supposed to be here implied, according to Prescription of the Law, *Numb.* xxviii. 3, 4. And both together called by the Name of the *daily Sacrifice, Dan.* viii. 11, 12. The daily Oblation seems to
have

have been provided at the joint charge of Prince and People. See Chapt. xlv. 16, 17.

Ver. 14. *The sixth part of an Ephah, and the third part of an Hin of Oyl.*] In *Numb.* xxviii. 5. the Proportion required is the *tenth part of an Ephah,* and *the fourth part of an Hin of Oyl.*

Ibid. *By a perpetual Ordinance unto the LORD*] So the Law of the Passover is call'd a *perpetual Ordinance, Exod.* xii. 17. and likewise Ordinances about the First-fruits, *Levit.* xxiii. 14. the Hebrew word *Olam* is used in each of these places : But that does not always denote Perpetuity in a strict Sense, but only a remarkable Period or Succession of time ; accordingly the *Jews* themselves divide the Duration of the World into three *Olams,* or Ages, that before the Law, that under the Law, and the times of the Messias.

Ver. 17. *It shall be his to the Year of Liberty*] So the Year of *Jubilee* is called by the name of Liberty, *Levit.* xxvi. 10. because it freed both Mens Persons from the Service of their Masters, and their Estates from any Engagements, by which the Right of them was transferred from their proper Owners.

Ibid. *After, it shall return to the Prince*] Or to his Heirs, if he be Dead.

Ibid. *But his Inheritance shall be his Sons for them*] Or, his Inheritance shall belong to his Sons, it shall be theirs : So as not to be alienated.

Ver. 18. *Moreover the Prince shall not take of the Peoples Inheritance by Oppression*] As *Ahab* did, 1 *Kings* xxi. 16. Comp. Chapt. xlv. 8.

Ibid. *That my People be not scattered every Man from his Possession*] Lest being turned out of their own

Chapter
XVLI.

Ver. 19.

own, they be forced to wander up and down the Country for a Lively-hood:

Ver. 19. *Afterwards he brought me through the entry which was at the side of the Gate, into the Holy Chambers of the Priests, which looked towards the North.*] This entry or private passage (See Chapt. xlii. 9.) led to the Priests Chambers which were on the North side of the Inner Court, and are described Chapt. xl. 44, 46.

Ibid. *Behold there was a Place on the two sides Westward.*] Or, *on their sides Westward :* i. e. There was an inclosure on the West sides of these Chambers : If we follow the Sense of the *English* Translation, we may suppose a walk or way between these Western Buildings, which divided them into two Rows or equal Parts. See Chapt. xlii. 4.

Ver. 20.

Ver. 20. *This is the Place where the Priests shall boil the Trespass-Offering and the Sin-Offering.*] See Chapt. xlii. 13. xliv. 29. The Flesh of the Sacrifices which were to be eaten was to be boiled, except the Flesh of the Passover : See 2 *Chron.* xxxv. 13. So it is taken notice of as a piece of Daintiness and an over nice Palate in the Sons of *Eli,* that they would not have the Flesh which came to their Share *Sodden,* but *Roasted,* 1 *Sam.* ii. 15.

Ibid. *Where they shall bake the Meat-Offering*] According to the Directions given *Levit.* ii. 4, 5, 7.

Ibid. *That they bear them not into the utter Court, to sanctifie the People.*] The Flesh of those Sacrifices and the Remainder of the Meat-Offering was accounted most Holy : See *Levit.* vi. 17, 29. vii. 6. and consequently did convey some Holiness to those that touched it : See the Note on Chapt. xliv. 19.

Ver. 21.

Ver. 21. *Then he brought me forth to the utter*
Court] The Court of the People, mentioned in the
foregoing Verse.

Ibid. *And behold in every corner of the Court there*
was a court.] At every corner where the side walls
met in right Angles, there was another little Court.

Ver. 22. *In the four corners of the Court there were*
Courts joined, of forty Cubits *long, and thirty broad*]
These little Courts were in the shape of an Oblong
Square, joined with inner Walls to the outside Walls
of the Greater Court. The Hebrew word *Keturoh*,
translated *joined*, is rendered in the Margin, *made*
with Chimneys, which Sense very well agrees with
the Description that follows of the uses for which
these Courts were designed.

Ver. 23. *And there was a Row* of Buildings
round about in them.] On the inside of these Courts.

Ver. 24. *These are the Places where the Mini-*
sters of the House shall boil the Sacrifice of the People.]
As there was a place in the inner Court for boiling the Trespass and Sin-Offering, Verse 19, 20.
So these Boiling places might be appointed for the
Boiling the Peace-Offerings, which were esteemed inferior in Holiness to those above-mentioned, (see the
Note upon Chapt. xlii. 13.) and therefore perhaps
were dressed by the Levites, or inferior Ministers: Whereas the Former were boiled by the Priests
in the Court properly belonging to them. Altho'
it must be granted, the Priests and Levites are often
taken promiscuously in this Prophecy: See the
Note upon Chap. xl. 45.

CHAP.

CHAP. XLVII.

The ARGUMENT.

The Vision of the Holy Waters Issuing out of the Temple, and the Virtue of them: together with a Description of the several bounds of the Holy Land, which is to be indifferently shared between the Israelites and the Proselytes that sojourned among them.

Ver. 1.   Ver. 1.  FTER WARD he brought me again unto the Door of the House.] The Door of the Temple, which is described Chapt. xli. 2.

Ibid. *And behold Waters issued out from under the Threshold Eastward.*] There was a great Quantity of Water necessary for the Uses of the Temple, for washing the Bodies of those that officiated, as well as the Sacrifices which they offered. This was conveyed in Pipes under ground from the Fountain *Etam*, as Dr. *Lightfoot* observes from the Rabbins, and from *Aristeas*, an Eye Witness: See his *Temple*, Chapt. 23. These Waters gave Occasion to the Vision here related.

Ibid.

Ibid. *For the Forefront of the House* stood *toward the East.*] The inward Sanctuary being placed to- wards the West : See the Note upon Chapt. viii. 16.

Ibid. *And the Waters came down from under the right-side of the House, at the South-side of the Altar.*] This is spoke with respect to those that come out of the Temple, and direct their Faces Eastward; for then the South-side is on a Man's Right-hand. These Waters were conveyed by the right-side of the Altar, into a Room they called the Well-room : See Dr. *Lightfoot*, in the fore-cited Place.

Ver. 2. *Then brought he me out of* [or by] *the Way of the Gate, North-ward.*] The East-gate being shut : See Chapt. xlvi. 1. The Prophet in this Vision is led to the North-gate of the inner Court.

Ibid. *And led me about the way without, unto the utter Gate.*] He led me into the outward Court, and so on till he came to the outmost North-Wall, that encompassed the whole Mountain of the Lord's-House : See Chapt. xlii. 20.

Ibid. *By the way that looketh Eastward.*] when the Prophet was come quite through all the Courts, and is on the outside of the outermost, he is dire-ted to come from the North-gate toward the East-gate.

Ibid. *And behold there ran Waters out on the right-side.*] On the South-side : See Ver. 1. These were the spare Waters not used in the Service of the Temple, which were conveyed away by the East-part of the Mountain, and by Degrees en-creased its Stream, till it became a River, and fell at last into the *Dead-Sea* : See Ver. 8, 10. and Comp. *Joel* iii. 18.

Chapter
XLVII.
~~~
Ver. 3.

Ver. 3. *And the Man that had the Line in his Hand went forth Eastward.*] The Angel described with a Line in his Hand, Chapt. xl. 3. went on directly from the East-gate before the Holy Mountain.

Ver. 4, 5.
Ibid. and Ver. 4, 5. *He measured a thousand Cubits, and he brought me through the Waters, and the Waters were to the Ancles, &c.*] The gradual Rise of the Waters represented in this Vision, denotes the large Effusion of the Spirit, which was very remarkable at the first Publication of the Gospel, and its wonderful Increase from small Beginnings ; and will be so again, when God shall *pour the Spirit of Grace* upon the *Jews*, in order to their Conversion : *Zech.* xii. 10. See the Note upon *Isa.* liv. 13. The Supplies of Grace are often represented in the Holy Writers under the Metaphor of a River, and Streams watering the dry and thirsty Earth, both cleansing and making fruitful the Ground where they pass. The Metaphor is probably taken from the River that watered Paradise : See *Revel.* xxii. 1: and Compare *Zech.* xiii. 1. xiv. 8. *Isa.* xliv. 3. and see the Notes upon *Isa.* xxx. 25.

Ver. 6.
Ver. 6. *And he said unto me, Son of Man, hast thou seen this?*] Hast thou considered or taken Notice of this Vision now shewed unto thee ? Comp. Chapt. xl. 4. To *see*, often signifies to take Notice of what we see ; on the contrary, they are said to *have Eyes, and see not*, who do not observe what is placed before their Eyes.

Ibid. *Then he caused me to return to the Brink of the River.*] He made me go along by the River side.

Ver. 7.

··Ver. 7. *Behold, on the Bank of the River were very many Trees, on the one Side, and on the othe*.] The Words allude to the Trees planted in Paradife, and defigned for Man's Food in the State of Innocence, and efpecially to the Tree of Life which grew there : See Ver. 12. and Comp. Revel. xxii. 2.

Ver. 8. *Thefe Waters iffue out towards the Eaft-Country, and go down into the Defart, and go into the Sea.*] Thefe Waters are defcribed as taking their Courfe along the Plain or Champagne Country (for that is the Senfe of the Word *Araba*, here rendred *Defart*) toward the Lake where *Sodom* formerly ftood, called the *Dead-Sea*, and by *Mofes*, the *Salt-Sea* : Comp. *Deut*. iii. 17. with this Verfe.

··*Ibid.* Which being *brought forth into the Sea, the Waters fhall be healed.*] This is the Obfervation of all Writers who defcribe this Lake, that nothing can live in it: And the Text here tells us, that thefe living Streams fhall by mixing with thefe Salt and brackifh Waters, make them wholefome and fit for Ufe : Myftically denoting the healing Vertue of God's Grace to cure the Vices and Corruptions of wicked Men.

Ver. 9. *And it fhall come to pafs, that every Thing that liveth, which moveth whither foever the Rivers fhall come, fhall live, &c.*] The Metaphor is ftill continued, to this Senfe : That as the Fifh which move or fwim, (Comp. *Gen.* i. 20.) in Waters cured or made wholefome, have Life and Nourifhment from thence, whereas no Fifh can live in the *Dead-Sea* : So the Waters which flow from the *Wells of Salvation,* as the Prophet *Ifaiah* expreffes it, *Ifa.* xii. 3. fhall make all thofe thrive and multiply

who

who enjoy the Benefit of them, though their Condition before were never so desperate. The Word *Rivers* and *River* are promiscuously used in this Verse, tho' some of the *Jewish* Writers are of Opinion that these Waters divide themselves, and some flow Eastward, and others Westward: Which Opinion they ground partly upon the Plural Number used in this Verse, but chiefly upon the Words of *Zechariah*, Chapt. xiv. 8.

Ver. 10.

Ver. 10. *And it shall come to pass, that the Fishers shall stand upon it, from En-gaddi to En-eglaim.*] *Engaddi* was a Town that lay on the South-west of of the Lake of *Sodom*, or the *Dead-Sea*, called *Hazezon-tamar*, *Gen.* xiv. 7. compared with 2 *Chron.* xx. 2. *En-eglaim*, or *En-gallim* as St. *Jerom* reads the Word, is another on the East-side of the same Lake, where *Jordan* falls into it; upon the Confines of *Moab*, as may be conjectured from *Isa.* xv. 8. which is confirmed by the Parallel Text in *Joel* iii. 18. where it is said that *a Fountain shall come forth of the House of the* LORD, *and shall water the Valley of Shittim:* Which we know was in the Country of *Moab*: See *Num.* xxv. 1. So these two Places denote the whole extent of that Lake, which the Prophet saith, shall be full of Fish, still prosecuting the Allegory begun in the foregoing Verses.

Ibid. *They shall be a Place to spread forth their Nets.*] These two Towns shall afford Convenience for the Fishers to hang out their Nets a drying: See Chapt. xxvi. 5.

Ibid. *Their Fish shall be according to their Kinds, as the Fish of the great Sea.*] This Lake for plenty of Fish may compare with the *Mediterranean-Sea*, called

called the *Great Sea* here, and ver. 15, 19. and Chapter
Chapt. xlviii. 28. and more diſtinctly deſcribed in XLVII.
Joſhua, by *the Great Sea weſtward*, *Joſh.* xxiii. 4.
Perhaps Chriſt may allude to this Place, when he
tells his Diſciples, he *will make them Fiſhers of Men*,
Matth. iv. 19.

V. 11. *But the miry-places ſhall not be healed, they* Ver. 11.
ſhall be given to Salt.] By thoſe unſound, rotten
Places may be underſtood Hypocrites; who ſhall
receive no Benefit by theſe healing Waters, no
more than ſome ſort of Marſhland can be made
fruitful: But after all the Care or Culture that can
be beſtowed upon it, continues barren and unpro-
fitable, which the *Hebrew* Language expreſſeth by
being *given to Salt*: Saltneſs is equivalent to Bar-
renneſs in that Language: See *Pſal.* cvii. 34. *Deut.*
xxix. 23. *Jerem.* xvii. 6. ſo we read *Judg.* ix. 45.
when *Abimelech* deſtroyed *Sichem*, he *ſowed* the
Ground whereon it ſtood *with Salt*, to denote
that it ſhould never be cultivated or inhabited
again.

V. 12. *And by the River upon the Bank thereof,* Ver. 12.
ſhall grow all Trees for Meat.] See the Note on
ver. 7.

Ibid. *Whoſe Leaf ſhall not fade, neither ſhall the
Fruit thereof be conſumed.*] They ſhall be perpetually in a thriving Condition, like the Trees of Pa-
radiſe, never barren or withering: A proper Emblem of the Flouriſhing State of the Righteous
ſtill bringing forth *Fruit unto Holineſs*, and whoſe
End is everlaſting Life: See *Pſal.* i. 3. *Jerem.* xvii. 8.

Ibid. *It ſhall bring forth new Fruit according to its
Months.*] It ſhall be conſtantly fruitful, not only
once a Year, as Fruit-trees commonly are, Comp.
Rev. xxii. 2. Ibid.

Ibid. *The Fruit thereof shall be for* Meat, *and the Leaf thereof for Medicine.*] As the Waters issuing from the Sanctuary have an healing Vertue: See ver. 8. so the Leaves of the Trees shall have the same Quality. The Expression alludes to the Opinion commonly received among Naturalists and Physicians, that the Leaves of several Trees are Medicinal.

Ver. 13. Ver. 13. *This* shall be *the Border,* &c.] The Borders described in the following Part of this Chapter, shall be the Limits or Boundaries of your Country. By the several Captivities both of *Israel* and *Judah,* the several Limits or Borders belonging to the Inheritance of each Tribe were obliterated and forgotten: Whereupon here is a new Boundary and Division made of the Holy Land, a full Possession of which they might have expected to enjoy, if their Sins had not prevented such a Blessing. This may perhaps be the literal Sense of the following Part of the Prophecy; though there is without Question a mystical Sense implied under this literal Description: See the Note on Chapt. xlviii. 7, 20.

Ibid. *Joseph shall have* two *Portions.*]Upon *Reuben's* forfeiting his Birth-right, the double Portion belonging to the First-born, accrued to *Joseph's* two Sons, *Manasseh* and *Ephraim,* according to *Jacob's* own Appointment: See *Gen.* xlviii. 5. 1 *Chron.* v. 1.

Ver. 14. Ver. 14. *And ye shall inherit it, one as well as another*] The *Ten Tribes* which are scattered abroad, as well as *Judah* and *Benjamin*: (See Chapt. xlviii. 1, 7, 23, 27.) who together with some of the Families of the Tribe of *Levi,* made up the principal part of those who returned from the *Babylonish*

lonish Captivity ; from hence we may conclude that this Prophecy relates to the general Restoration of the Jews, an Event often foretold in the Prophecies of the old Testament: See the Note upon Chapt. xxviii. 25.

Ibid. Concerning the *which I lifted up my Hand to give it to your Fathers.*] See Chapt. xx. 5, 6.

Ibid. *And this Land shall fall unto you for Inheritance.*] The Word *Fall*, is taken from the manner of their first acquiring the Possession of the Land, which was by Lot, as it had formerly been, when they first took Possession of it : See Verse 22. Chapt. xlviii. 29. By which means all Controversies will be prevented, the Lot referring all Things to the Divine Designation and Appointment. *Prov.* xvi. 33.

Ver. 15. *From the great Sea, the way of Hethlon as Men go to Zedad.*] The Northern border of the Land was to begin from the West-point, on which side lay the *Mediterranean Sea* (See Verse 10.) and go on North-ward toward *Hethlon*, a place near *Damascus:* See Chapt. xlviii. 1. and so on forward, to *Zedad*, mentioned *Nehem.* xxxiv. 8.

Ver. 16. *Hamath, Berothah, Sibraim, which is* *between the border of Damascus, and the border of Hamath,*] The Places here mentioned were within this tract of Ground. *Hamath* was the utmost point of the Land North-ward, therefore called the *Entrance of Hamath,* and described as the opposite point to the River of *Egypt,* See 1 *Kings* viii. 65. *Amos* vi. 14. The other two Towns were Situate between *Hamath* and *Damascus.*

Ibid. *Hazar-hatticon, which is by the Coast of Hauran.*] Or, as our Margin reads, *the middle Villages*

Chapter
XLVII.
⌐⌐⌐
Villages between *Hamath* and *Hauran*, a place lying Eaftward from *Hamath*, from whence that Country was called *Auranitis.*

Ver. 17.
Ver. 17. *And the border from the Sea, fhall be Hazar-enan, &c.*] Or, *fhall be to Hazar-enan*, even *the border of Damafcus, and all the Northern frontier, and the border of Hamath*: i. e. That tract of Land which is called the *Entrance of Hamath*, as was obferved before. Your North border fhall be, as if a Line were drawn from the *Mediterranean Sea* along by *Hamath*, and fo to *Hazarenan*: (See *Numb.* xxxiv. 9.) Keeping along by the frontier of that part of *Syria*, called *Syria* of *Damafcus*: So as to diftinguifh the Northern Boundaries of *Ifrael*, from the Southern Limits of *Syria*.

Ver. 18.
Ver. 18. *And the Eaft fide ye fhall Meafure from Hauran and from Damafcus, and from Gilead.*] *Damafcus* lay moreNortherly than *Hauran*, but the Country called *Auranitis* might reach near it. *Gilead* was a long tract of Ground that joined to Mount *Libanus*, and was extended to the Land of *Sihon* King of the *Amorites*, as St. *Jerom* tells us in his Book *de Locis Hebraicis*: it is called the Land of *Gilead*, and reached unto *Dan. Deut.* xxxiv. 1.

Ibid. *From the Land of Ifrael by Jordan, from the border unto the Eaft Sea.*] From the Northern Limits of the Land of *Ifrael* Verfe 17. near *Cæfarea* or *Dan*, where the River *Jordan* takes its rife, unto the *Dead Sea* or the lake of *Sodom*: See Verfe 8.

Ver. 19.
Ver. 19. *And the fouth fide Southward, from Tamar even to the Waters of ftrife in Kadefh,* [to] *the River,*

River, to the great Sea.] Comp. Chapt. xlviii. 28. Chapter The Southern Frontiers shall be from *Engeddi*, XLVII. called *Hazazon-tamar*, 2 *Chron.* xx. 2. (See Dr. Lightfoot's *Descript. of the Land of Israel.* Chapt. 6.) to the Waters of *Meribah* or strife, in *Kadesh*, *Deut.* xxxii. 52. and from thence to the River of *Egypt.* The River of *Egypt* riseth out of Mount *Paran*, taketh his Course westward to *Rhinocorura*, and from thence falls into the *Mediterranean* called *the great Sea*, Verse 10. See 1 *Kings* viii. 65. *Gen.* xv. 18. *Josh.* xv. 47. *Isa.* xxvii. 12. where the lxx. translate it, Εὼς ῥινοκορϩϛης , *to Rhinocorura*, into which it falls. This River seems to be the same with *Sihor*, mentioned *Josh.* xiii. 3. tho' that Name be commonly understood to signifie the *Nile* : See the Notes upon *Jer.* ii. 18.

Ver. 20. *The west-side also* shall be *the great Sea* Ver. 20. *from the border.*] i. e. From the south border mentioned in the foregoing Verse : So Verse 18, *from the border*, means the Northern border, mentioned Verse 17.

Ibid. *Till a Man come over against Hamath.*] Or rather, *till a Man come to Hamath* : For so the Particle *Nad-Nocah* signifies : See *Noldius*, p. 657. Till you come to *Hamath* the Northern Point toward the west Frontier.

Ver. 22. *Ye shall divide it by Lot for an Inheri-* Ver. *tance unto you.*] See the Note upon Verse 14.

Ibid. *And to the Strangers that sojourn among you.*] Foreigners never before had the Privilege of purchasing or possessing any Inheritance among the Jews : So this Mystically denotes the Incorpora-

M m m ting

Chapter ting the *Gentiles* into the same Church with the
XLVII. Jews: Making them *Fellow-heirs and of the same*
Body with them by the Gospel: *Ephes.* iii. 6.

Ibid. *They shall have Inheritance with you*
among the Tribes of Israel.] In whatsoever
Tribe they sojourn, as it is exprest in the next
Verse.

CHAP.

CHAP. XLVIII.

The ARGUMENT.

This last Chapter contains a Description of the several Portions of Land belonging to each Tribe: Together with the Portions allotted to the Sanctuary, City, Suburbs, and Prince: As also the Measure and Gates of the New City.

Ver. 1. ROM the North-end to the Ver. 1.
Coast of the Way of Hethlon.]
As the Description of the
Limits or Boundaries of the
Land began on the North-
side, Chapt. xlvii. 15, &c. so
the Portion of that Tribe to whom the most
Northern Lot fell is first named, which is
Dan.

Ibid. *For these are his sides, East and West.*]
These are the Boundaries belonging to that Tribe,
from the East Point near Mount *Libanus* and
Gilead, to the West Point which is bounded by the
Mediterranean Sea. See Chapt. xlvii. 15, &c.

Ver. 2. *And by the border of Dan, from the East
side to the West side,* a Portion for Asher.] All
along from the South side of *Dan* Measuring·
from East to West, shall the share of *Asher* be.

Ver. 7. *And by the border of Reuben — a Portion
for Judah.*] From the *first* Verse to the *seventh,*
the Situation of seven of the twelve Tribes is
described, which were placed on the North side
of the Holy Portion, the length of *Judea* from
North to South being divided into twelve E-
qual Parts, See Chapt. xlvii. 14. beside the Allotment for the Holy Portion and for the Prince;
and the City and Temple being placed where
they stood formerly, there must be *seven* shares
on the North side of that Allotment, and but
five on the South side. For *Jerusalem* did not
stand in the middle of the Holy Land, but more
toward the South, as may appear to any one that
consults the Map of *Judea.*

But for the fuller Explaining this Difficulty,
we may reasonably conclude, that *Judah's* Portion lay nearest to that which was allotted for
the Priests and Sanctuary.

It is the Opinion of some Learned Men, that
so particular a Description of the several Portions
allotted to each Tribe relates to the Jews Settlement in their own Country after their Conversion. Several Passages in the Prophets looking that way: See the xxxvi. and xxxvii. Chapters of this Prophecy. But without laying too
great a stress upon this Opinion, we may fairly suppose some Mystical Sense contained under this
Description. The twelve Tribes denote the Pure
Christian Church in the New Testament: See *Luke*
xxii.

xxii. 30. *Rev.* vii, 4, *&c. Twelve* is an Hieroglyphical Number in the same Book, denoting the
true Church, built upon the Doctrine of the twelve
Apostles. See *Rev.* xii. 1. xxi. 14. By the same
Analogy the Number of an *Hundred and forty and
four Thousand, Revel.* vii. 4. xiv. 1. signifies the
Church of Pure Christians, who continue stedfast
in the Apostolical Doctrine, twelve being the
Square Root out of which that Number ariseth : So
this Division of the Land among the twelve
Tribes may imply, that all true Christians shall
be equally Sharers in the Privileges of the Gos-
ple.

Ver. 8. *And by the border of Judah, from the*
*East-side unto the West side, shall be the Offering
which ye shall offer of five and twenty thousand* Reeds
in breadth.] Next to the border of *Judah* which
runs in length from East to West, shall be the
Offering ye shall set apart for the Service of God,
Chapt. xlv. 1. The word *Reeds* is not in the Original either here, or in that Text : And we may
more probably understand the Measure in both
places of Cubits : See the Note there.

Ibid. *And in length as one of the* other *Parts*
[are,] *from the East side to the West side.*] Which
was likewise five and twenty thousand, according
to the Dimensions of the Holy Portion set down
Chapt. xlv. 1 —— 6. For the Oblation was to be
four-square, consisting of five and twenty thous-
and multiplied by five and twenty thousand : See
Verse 20. of this Chapter.

Ver. 9. *The Oblation that ye shall offer unto the*
*LORD shall be of five and twenty thousand in
length, and ten thousand in breadth.*] This shall be

set apart for the Sanctuary, and the most Holy
Place, and the Priests Houses: See Chapt. xlv. 3,
4.

Ver. 10. *Toward the North five and twenty thouf-
fand* in length, *and toward the West, ten thousand
in breadth,* &c.] The Dimensions from East to West
are called by the Name of Breadth here, but of
length Verse 8. And so they truly are, as may appear from the Plan of the whole described in the
Notes upon the xlv*th* Chapter. But if we suppose that
space of Ground which is expressed by the Breadth
in one Place, to be called by the Name of length
in another, there will be no impropriety in the
Expression, because in an exact square, as the
whole Compass of Ground is here supposed to
be, all sides are equal.

Ver. 11.

Ver. 11. It shall be *for the Priests that* are
sanctified, of the Sons of Zadok.] See Chapt. xliv.
10, 15.

Ibid. *As the Levites went astray.*] Or, *as the
other Levites went astray:* So the word [*Other*]
is supplied Verse 8. The Levites denote in general
the Sons of *Levi,* so as to comprehend the Priests
too : See Verse 22. Many of these had defiled
themselves with Idolatry, for which Crime they
were to be degraded from the Honours and Privileges due to those Priests who had continued
faithful in their Office. See the Notes upon Chapter xliv. 10, 11.

Ver. 12

Ver. 12. *And* this *Oblation* —— *shall be unto
them a thing most holy.*] As all things dedicated
to God were ; See *Levit.* xxvii. 28.

Ibid. *By the Border of the Levites.*] It shall
lie next to the Portion of the *Levites,* which lay
South-

South-ward between the Priefts and the Cities
Portion. See the Scheme placed at the xlvth Chapter.

Ver. 13. *And over againſt the Border of the
Priefts, the Levites* ſhall have *five and twenty thouſand in Length,* &c.] It might be better tranſlated,
juſt by the Border of the Prieſts, or, *beſide the Border
of the Prieſts,* as the Word *Leummath* is tranſlated
in our *Engliſh* Bible, Chapt. x. 19. xi. 22. The
Words import that the Border of the Levites ran
parallel to that of the Prieſts. And to the ſame
Senſe the Word ſhould be tranſlated in the 15th,
18th, and 21ſt Verſes of this Chapter. See the
Note upon Chapt. xl. 18.

Ver. 13.

Ver. 14. *They ſhall not ſell of it, neither exchange,
nor alienate the Firſt-Fruits of the Land,* &c.] It being God's Portion, they were not to ſell nor part
with it upon any Pretence of Advantage or greater
Convenience. This Portion of Land is called the
Firſt-fruits, as it is ſtyled an *Oblation,* ver. 8. and
12. to denote that the whole Land was God's
Property. See the Note upon Chapt. xlv. 1.

Ver. 14.

Ver. 15. *And the five thouſand that are left in
the Breadth, over againſt* [or beſide, See ver. 13.]
the five and twenty thouſand.] which was the Portion aſſigned to the Levites, Ibid. This five thouſand added to the five and twenty thouſand in
Length, and two ten thouſands in Breadth, mentioned ver. 10. makes up a Square of five and
twenty thouſand every Way. See ver. 20.

Ver. 15.

Ibid. *Shall be for a profane Place for the City,* &c.]
See Chapt. xlv. 6. It is called a profane Place com-
paratively, becauſe it was not ſo Holy as the
Temple and the Sanctuary. See the Note upon
Chapt. xlii. 20:

Ibid.

Chapter
XLVIII.

Ibid. *And the City shall be in the midst thereof.*]
A square Piece of Ground of four thousand and
five hundred Cubits on every Side, shall be taken
out of the middle of the five and twenty thousand
Cubits in Length, for the Area of the City. ver.
16.

Ver. 16.

Ver. 16. *And these shall be the Measures thereof: the North-side four thousand and five hundred,
&c.*] It shall be an *Equi-lateral Square*, every side
being exactly of the same Measure, consisting in
all of eighteen thousand Measures. See ver. 35.

Ver. 17.

Ver. 17. *And the Suburbs of the City shall be toward the North two hundred and fifty, and toward
the South two hundred and fifty, &c.*] these Dimensions of the Suburbs, added to those of the City,
make the whole Area or *Equi-lateral Square* of five
thousand Cubits on every Side: Adding five hundred in Breadth, and five hundred in Length, to
the 4500 Cubits, which was the Compass of the
City.

Ver. 18.

Ver. 18. *And the residue in Length over against,*
[or beside, See ver. 13.] *the Oblation of the holy
Portion, shall be ten thousand East-ward, and ten
thousand West-ward.*] these two Dimensions of ten
thousand in Length, both Eastward and Westward, remain on each side of the Area, which is
five thousand Cubits Square, and set apart for the
site of the City.

Ibid. *It shall be over against,* [or beside] *the Oblation of the holy Portion.*] It shall join to the Levites Portion, both on the East and West Side:
And it shall lie Parallel with the two Portions belonging to the Priests and Leyites. Consult the
Scheme placed above.

Ibid.

Ibid. *And the increase thereof shall be for Food to* Chapter
them that serve in the City.] That perform inferior XLVIII.
Offices in the City. The Priests and Levites having a large Portion already assigned for their
Suftenance.

Ver. 19. *And they that serve the City, shall serve* Ver. 19
it out of all the Tribes of Israel.] This Service being a Burden, it is fit that all the Tribes should
bear their part in it.

Ver. 20. *All the Oblation* shall be *five and twenty* Ver. 20.
thousand, by five and twenty thousand.] Five and
twenty thousand in length, multiplied by five
and twenty thousand in breadth. See Verfe 10.

Ibid. *Ye shall offer the Oblation foure-fquare.*] So
the *Heavenly Jerusalem* is described as lying *four-
fquare, Revel.* xxi. 16. A square Figure being the
Emblem of Perpetuity, strength and Solidity.
Comp. Chapt. xlii. 16 —— 20.

A great Part of the Wisdom of the *Eastern* Nations was wrapped up in *Hieroglyphical* Emblems
and Numbers. The *Symbols* of *Phythagoras* are a
remarkable Instance of this fort of Ancient Learning. This Method God hath thought fit to make
use of to difcover fome Mysterious Truths in his
Word: Such as perhaps he thinks not convenient
to be more clearly revealed till its proper Time
and Seafon : Intending by fuch obfcure Hints to
encourage Men's Searching into the more abftrufe
Parts of the Scriptures, and to fhew that all Human
Knowledge may be made Subfervient to Divine.

The Text before us compared with its Parallel in the xlii Chapter of this Prophecy, and in
the *Revelation,* plainly fhews that a fquare is an

Em-

Emblematical Figure. In like manner the Number *Twelve* is a Sacred Number, as I observed upon Verse 7 : and the learned Mr. *Potter* in his Book of *the Number 666*, hath with great Acuteness reconciled the 12000 Furlongs, the Measure of the *New Jerusalem* in the *Revelation*, with the Measures of *Ezekiel* here, by interpreting them of Solid Measures, and extracting the Root of each of them.

Ibid. *With the Possession of the City.*] Or the land assigned for the site of the City : Which was a square of five thousand Cubits ; and being added to the Portion of the Priests and Levites, made their twice ten thousand, to be five and twenty thousand in breadth. See Verse 10, 15.

Ver. 21. Ver. 21. *And the residue* shall be *for the Prince, on the one side and on the other of the holy Oblation, and of the Possession of the City.*] The Princes part shall be extended both on the East and West side of the several Allotments belonging to the Priests, the Levites and the City. The particular Extent of the Princes Portion is not here specified, but it is computed by some to contain above four times as much as those Allotments. See the Note upon Verse 22.

Ibid. *Overagainst the five and twenty thousand of the Oblation toward the East border, and West-ward overagainst the five and twenty thousand toward the West border.*] The particle *Elpene* translated *overagainst* is rendered *Before*, in the parallel Text, Chapt. xlv. 7. and thus interpreted makes the Sense clearer ; the Words then importing, that the Prince's Portion ran along Eastward and Westward, like a Frontier before the Holy Portions. See the forementioned *Scheme.* Ibid.

Ibid. *Overagainſt the Portions for the Prince, and it ſhall be the Holy Oblation,* &c.] Our Tranſlation hath rendered the latter part of this Verſe very imperfectly: Which ſhould be thus tranſlated : *Beſide theſe* [or joining to theſe] *Portions,* (ſo *Lemmmath* ſignifies, ſee Verſe 13.) *ſhall be that belonging to the Prince : And this ſhall be the Holy Oblation, and the Sanctuary of the Houſe ſhall be in the midſt thereof.* The laſt Part of the Sentence is only a Recapitulation of what is ſaid more at large, Verſe 8.

Ver. 22. *Moreover, from the Poſſeſſion of the Levites, and from the Poſſeſſion of the City, being in the midſt of that which is the Princes.*] The words might be more plainly tranſlated thus, *Moreover, beyond the Poſſeſſion of the Levites, and beyond the Poſſeſſion of the City*—— to this Senſe: That the Poſſeſſions belonging to the Prieſts and Levites, (See Verſe 11.) and the City, were bounded on the Eaſt and Weſt ſide with the Prince's Portion : So thoſe lay in the middle, and this beyond them. The Hebrew Particle *Min* ſignifies *Beyond,* in ſeveral places : Examples of which may be ſeen in *Noldius,* p. 564.

Ibid. *Between the border of Judah, and the border of Benjamin ſhall be for the Prince.*] The border of *Judah* was extended from Eaſt to Weſt next to the Holy Portion on the North-ſide, See Verſe 15——8. The Portion of *Benjamin* lay from Eaſt to Weſt next the Allotment ſet apart for the City, on the South-ſide, Verſe 23,—— 28. The ſeveral Portions allotted for the Prieſts, the Levites and the City, extended only to the length of five and twenty thouſand Cubits from Eaſt to Weſt : So that what ever ground ran in a Parallel Line Eaſt-ward

and

Chapter and West-ward beyond that Boundary, even to the
XLVIII. Lands end, belonged to the Prince: And supposing
the whole Country to be sixty Miles in b eadth,
(as St. *Jerom* reckons it from *Joppa* to *Jordan*,
Epist. ad Dardanum) and the Holy Portion about
seven Miles Square.: (See the Note upon Chapt.
xlv. 1.) there will remain above six and twenty
Miles both on the East and West Side for the Prince's
Share. See the *Scheme* placed at the xlvth Chapter.

Ver. 23.   Ver. 23. *As for the rest of the Tribes, from East
to West, Benjamin* shall have a Portion.] The Portion assigned to Judah was situate next to the Holy Portion on the North-side: See Verse 1, —— 8.
The Portion assigned to Benjamin lay next to the
Ground allotted for the City on the South-side:
See Verse 28. All these Allotments run from East
to West in length, and from North to South in
breadth.

V. 24, 27.   Ver. 24 —— 27. *And by the border of Benjamin*,
&c.] In these Verses the four remaining Tribes have
their Allotments assigned them, lying on the South
side of the Holy Portion. These Appointments
are not laid out with any Regard to the Division
of the Land made in *Joshua's* time; for here a Platform of a New Church and State is set forth.

Ver. 28.   Ver. 28. *And by the border of Gad, at the South-
side —— the border shall be toward the Great Sea.*]
This is a Description of the Southermost borders
of the Land, extending by the South and West
to the *Mediterranean* Sea. See Chapt. xlvii. 19.

Ver. 29.   Ver. 29. *This is the land which ye shall divide by
lot &c.*] See Chapt. xlvii. 14; 22.

Ver. 30.   Ver. 30. *And these are the goings out of the City,
on the North-side, &c.*] The same Measures of the
City

City are already set forth, Verse 16. beginning
with those on the North-side, as the general Division of the Land doth : See Verse 1.

Ver. 31. *And the Gates of the City* shall be *after*
the Names of the Tribes of Israel.] The same Description is given of the Gates of the *New Jerusalem,*
Revel. xxi. 12, 13. to signify that all true Israelites
have their Share in this Heavenly City, and a right
to enter into it, *Revel.* xxii. 14.

Ver. 35. *And it was round about eighteen thou-*
sand Measures] See Verse 16.

Ibid. *And the Name of the City from that Day*
shall be, *the LORD is there.*] *Jerusalem* was formerly called the *City of God, Psal.* lxxxvii. 3. and
the *City of the great King, Psal.* xlviii. 2. But in
this *New Jerusalem* God shall dwell in a more
glorious manner, and make it the Place of his
perpetual Residence. So that every Part of that
City, and every Member of it, shall be as
Holy as the Temple it self, where God *had*
placed his Name, 1 *Kings* viii. 29. Comp. with
Revel. xxi. 22. this is in a lower Degree fulfilled in all good Christians, who are called the *Tem-*
ples of the living God, 2 *Cor.* vi. 16. 1 *Pet.* ii. 5.
and *an Habitation of God through the Spirit. Eph.*
ii. 22.

TEXTS

ERRATA.

ADDENDA & CORRIGENDA.

PAGE 6. Line 19. after *Rev.* iv. 6. add ; And in that Text the *four living Creatures* denote fome Part of the Chriftian Church, as appears by comparing that Place with *Rev.* v. 8, 9.

Page 91. l. 9. The learned *Gataker,* in his *Cinnus, p.* 200. thinks the Words may more properly be rendered, *That put* (or faften) *Pillows to all Armholes ;* fo he underftands the fame Word, *Job* xvi. 15. *I have put Sackcloth upon my Skin.*

Page 115. l. 3. Great and crying Sins are compared to thofe of *Sodom ;* fee *Ifa.* i. 9. iii. 9. *Matt.* xi. 23. *Rev.* xi. 8.

Page 174. l. 4. add, And fee the Note upon Chap. xx. 8.

Page 239. l. 22. This Captivity of the *Egyptians,* though not taken Notice of by *Herodotus,* is mentioned by *Berofus*

in

ADDENDA & CORRIGENDA.

in one of the Fragments of his History, quoted by *Josephus*, *Antiq. l.* 10. *c.* 11. and publiſhed with Notes by *Scaliger*, at the End of his Books *de Emendatione Temporum*, whoſe Remark upon the Place is very obſervable, *viz.* " The Ca- " lamities that befel the *Egyptians* are paſſed over by *Hero-* " *dotus*, becauſe the *Egyptian* Prieſts would not inform him " of any Thing that tended to the Diſgrace of their Nation."

Ibid. l. 25. All the following Note is to be expunged, Archbiſhop *Uſher* being cited there by a Miſtake. The Story is told by *Herodotus*, at the Beginning of his 3d Book, to this Purpoſe : That this Daughter of *Apries*, whoſe Name was *Nitetis*, paſſed for ſome Time for the Daughter of *Amaſis* ; but after having had ſeveral Children by *Cyrus*, ſhe diſcovered the Truth of the whole Matter ; and excited him to revenge the Wrongs done to her Father by *Amaſis* ; which might occaſion *Amaſis's* Revolt.

But Dr. *Prideaux* conjectures, that *Cyrus's* Death, which happened the following Year, might be the true Reaſon of it. See his *Connect. of Script. Hiſt. p.* 167. *Edit.* 8*vo.*

Page 266. l. 6. It is uſual in the Prophets to ſpeak of what is to come, as if it were already paſt, as hath been obſerved elſewhere.

Page 395. l. 5. Blot out the three following Lines, and inſtead thereof *read*, The Wall was 500 Cubits every way, See ver. 16. as it compoſed the Length and Breadth of the Temple, and its Courts. See the ſame Expreſſion, Chap. xl. 47.

Page 461. l. 18. Every Part of that City ſhall be honoured with evident Tokens of the Divine Preſence ; and every Member of it being dedicated to God's Service, and becoming *an Habitation of God through his Spirit*, ſhall have ſome Degree of the Holineſs of the Temple.

The Dying Speechs and Behaviour of the several State-Prisoners that have been Executed the last 300 Years, with their several Characters from the best Historians, as *Cambden*, *Spotswood*, *Clarendon*, *Sprat*, *Burnet*, &c. And a Table, shewing how the respective Sentences were Executed; and which of them were mitigated, or pardoned. Being a proper Supplement to the above State-Tryals.

Sir *V. William Petty*'s Political Survey of *Ireland*, with the Establishment of that Kingdom when the late Duke of *Ormond* was Lord Lieutenant: Also an exact List of the Peers, present Members of Parliament, and principal Officers of State. To which is added, an Account of the Wealth and Expences of *England*, and the Method of raising Taxes in the most equal Manner, shewing likewise that *England* can bear the Charge of four Millions *per Annum*, when the Occasions of the Government require it. The Second Edition carefully corrected with Additions. By a Fellow of the *Royal Society*.

A Journal, or full Account of the late Expedition of *Canada*, with an Appendix, containing Commissions, Orders, Instructions, Letters, Memorials, Court-Martial, Councils of War, relating thereto. By Sir *Hovenden Walker*, Kt.

Memoirs of the Life of the Reverend Mr. *John Kettlewell* sometime Fellow of *Lincoln* College in *Oxford*, and Vicar of *Coles-Hall* in *Warwickshire*, in the Diocess of *Litchfield*, wherein is contained some Accounts of the Transactions of his Time, compiled from the Collections of Dr. *George Hicks*, and *Robert Nelson*, Esq; with several Original Papers.

Memoirs of the Life and Times of Dr. *Thomas Tennison*, late Arch-bishop of *Canterbury*, wherein are contained, the Publick Benefactions of that Great Man, from his first Entrance into Holy Orders, 'till his departure from this Life, in the highest Station in the Church of *England*, as by Law Established at the Archiepiscopal Pallace of *Lambeth*: With an Account of his Examplary Piety, his diffusive Charity, and Irreprochable Probity, from his Birth to his much Lamented Death; together with his last Will and Testament; collated with the Original.

The Civil Law in its Natural Order, together with the Publick Law, Written in French by Monsieur *Domat*, and Translated into English by *William Strahan*, L. L. D. 2 Vols.

Archælogia Græca, or the Antiquities of *Greece*, the fourth Edition. By *John Potter*, D. D. Now Lord Bishop of *Oxford*, 2 Vols.

Original Letters Familiar, Moral and Critical, by Mr. *Dennis* in 2 Vols.

The History of *Dion-Cassius* abridg'd by *Xiphilin*, containing the most considerable Passages under the *Roman* Emperours, from the Time of *Pompey* the Great, to the Reign of *Alexander Severus*, in 2 Vols. Done from the G reek by Mr. *Manning*.

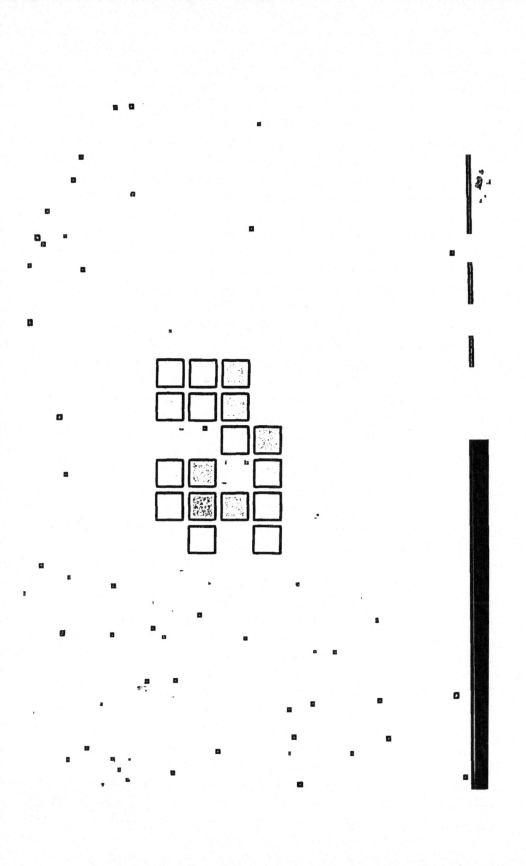

CPSIA information can be obtained
at www.ICGtesting.com
Printed in the USA
LVOW13*0922291017

554198LV00009B/91/P